Dengeki Daisy

Vol. 16

Kyousuke Motomi

Dengeki Daisy

Volume 16 CONTENTS

DAISY

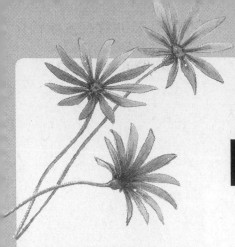

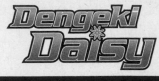

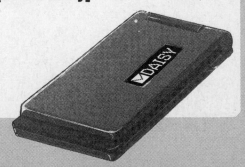

Dengeki Daisy Vol. 16

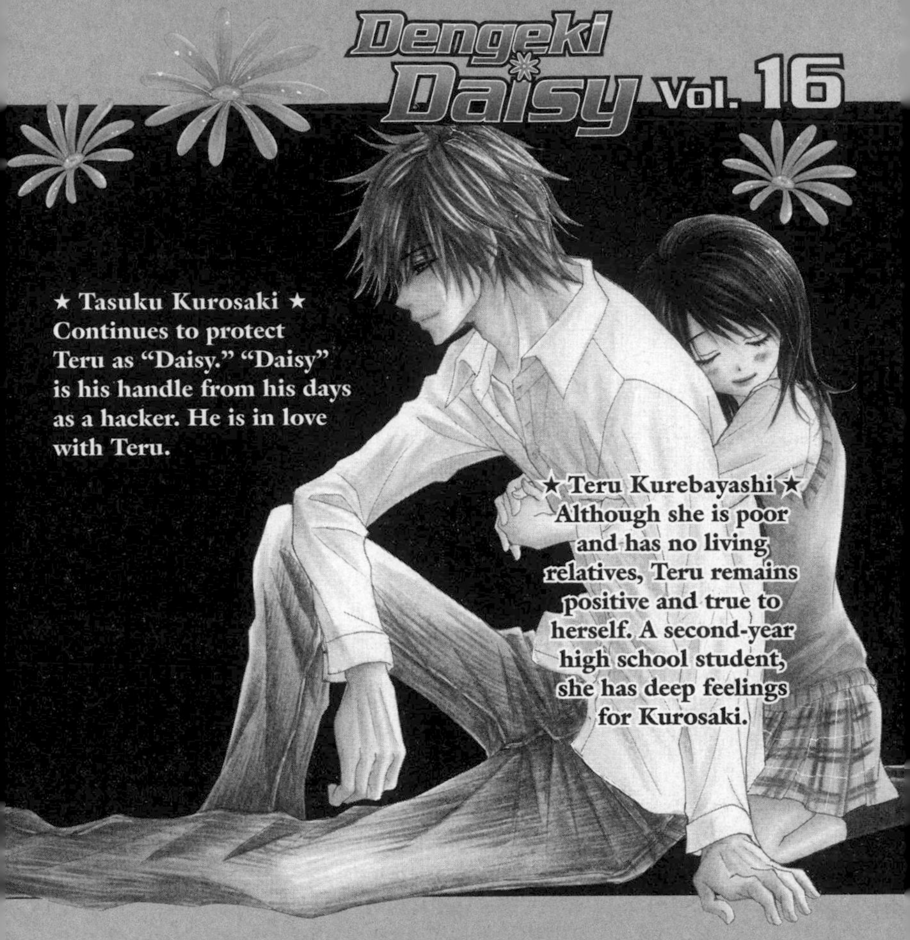

★ Tasuku Kurosaki ★
Continues to protect Teru as "Daisy." "Daisy" is his handle from his days as a hacker. He is in love with Teru.

★ Teru Kurebayashi ★
Although she is poor and has no living relatives, Teru remains positive and true to herself. A second-year high school student, she has deep feelings for Kurosaki.

★ Teru discovers that Kurosaki is Daisy, the mysterious person who supported and encouraged her after her brother Soichiro's death. Thinking that there must be a reason why Kurosaki has chosen to hide his identity, Teru decides to keep this knowledge to herself.

★ During this time, Teru's life is threatened, and strange incidents involving Teru and Kurosaki occur. Kurosaki decides to disclose the truth to Teru, but Akira beats him to it and tells her about Kurosaki's past "sin." Learning what Akira has done, Kurosaki disappears from sight. Seeing Teru so despondent, the Director and Riko tell her about Kurosaki's past.

★ Teru learns that Kurosaki's father was involved with the development of a top-secret government code, and his death was shrouded in mystery. Kurosaki became a hacker to clear his father's

CHARACTERS...

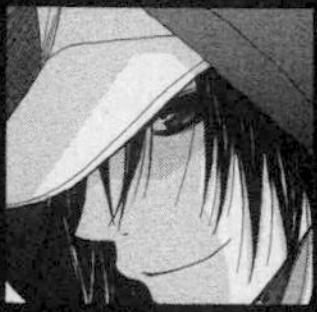

★ Akira ★
A mathematical genius who's obsessed with "M's Last Testament." Was Chiharu Mori's partner-in-crime.

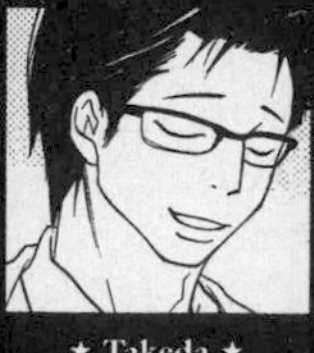

★ Takeda ★
Soichiro's former coworker. He is the owner of Kaoruko, a Shiba dog.

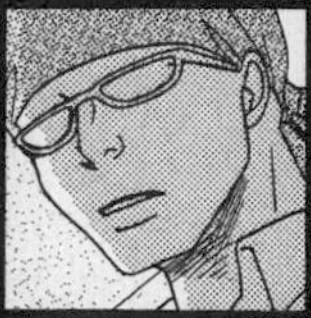

★ Boss (Masuda) ★
Currently runs the snack shop "Flower Garden" but has connections to the Ministry of Internal Affairs.

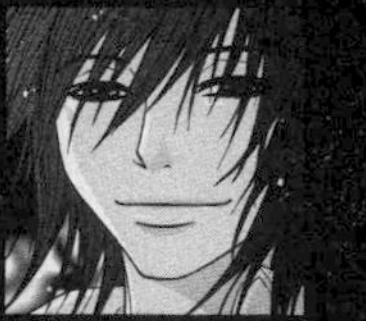

★ Soichiro Kurebayashi ★
Teru's older brother and a genius systems engineer. He died after leaving Teru in Kurosaki's care.

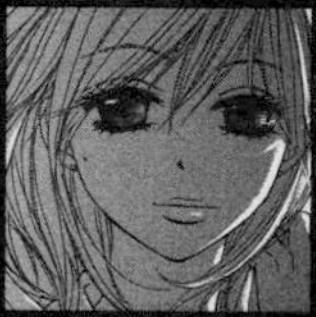

★ Chiharu Mori ★
She used to work at Teru's school and later teamed up with Akira. She continues to target Teru and Kurosaki.

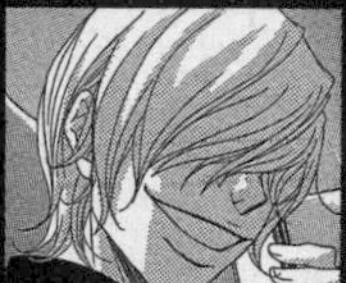

★ Antler ★
He tricked Kurosaki into creating the "Jack Frost" virus.

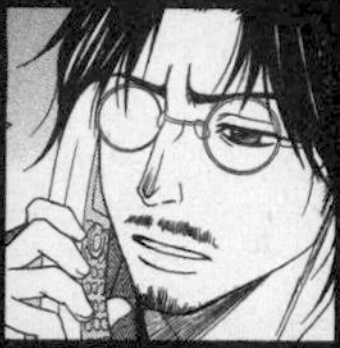

★ Director (Kazumasa Ando) ★
He used to work with Soichiro and is currently the director of Teru's school.

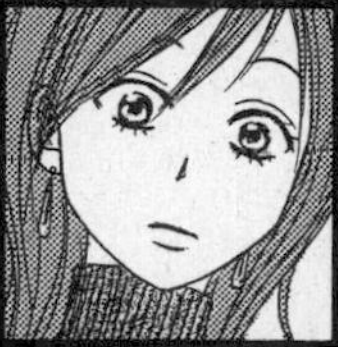

★ Riko Onizuka ★
She was Soichiro's girlfriend and is now a counselor at Teru's school.

STORY...

name and created the code virus known as "Jack Frost." In order to save Kurosaki from being charged with a "Jack Frost"-related murder, Soichiro worked nonstop to decipher the code and died in the process. Teru accepts this newfound knowledge about Kurosaki. She thanks him for all that he has done for her and asks him to stay by her side.

★ Kurosaki and friends learn that M's Last Testament isn't Professor Midorikawa's will—it's actually a trap to lure out and kill Akira, who poses a threat to national security. Around that time, Teru is abducted and taken to an uninhabited island where the trap has been set. Akira unknowingly tries to activate a detonation system but is stopped by a desperate Teru.

★ Kurosaki meets up with Teru and Akira, and they rush to get off the island, but the detonator is activated and sets off a huge explosion...?!

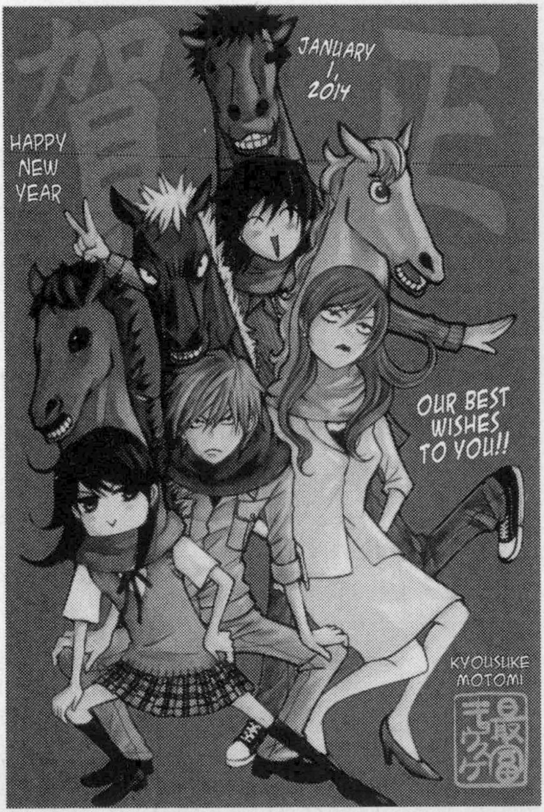
JANUARY 1, 2014
HAPPY NEW YEAR
OUR BEST WISHES TO YOU!!
KYOUSUKE MOTOMI

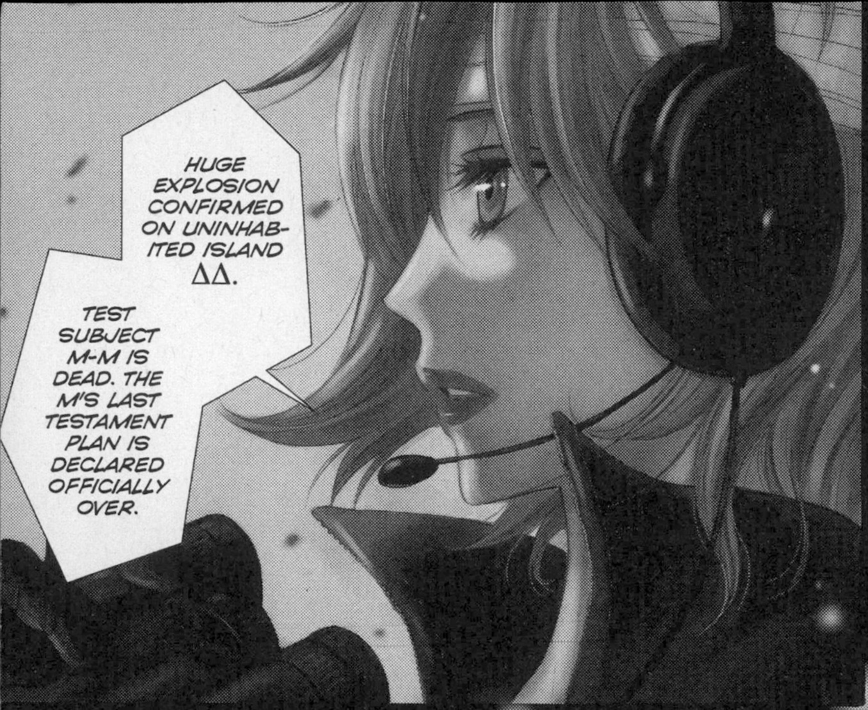
HUGE EXPLOSION CONFIRMED ON UNINHAB-ITED ISLAND ΔΔ.
TEST SUBJECT M-M IS DEAD. THE M'S LAST TESTAMENT PLAN IS DECLARED OFFICIALLY OVER.
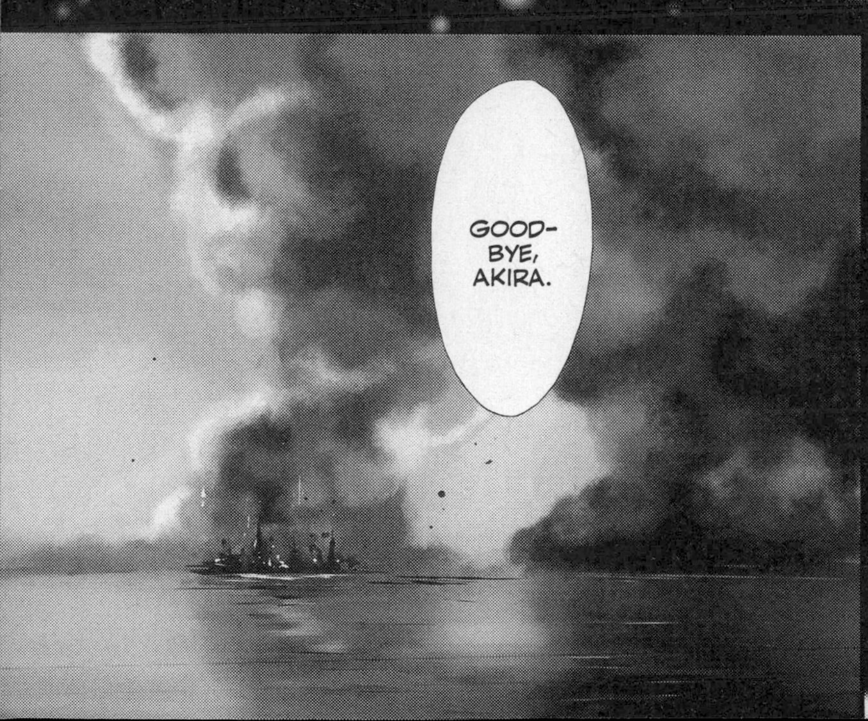
GOOD-BYE, AKIRA.

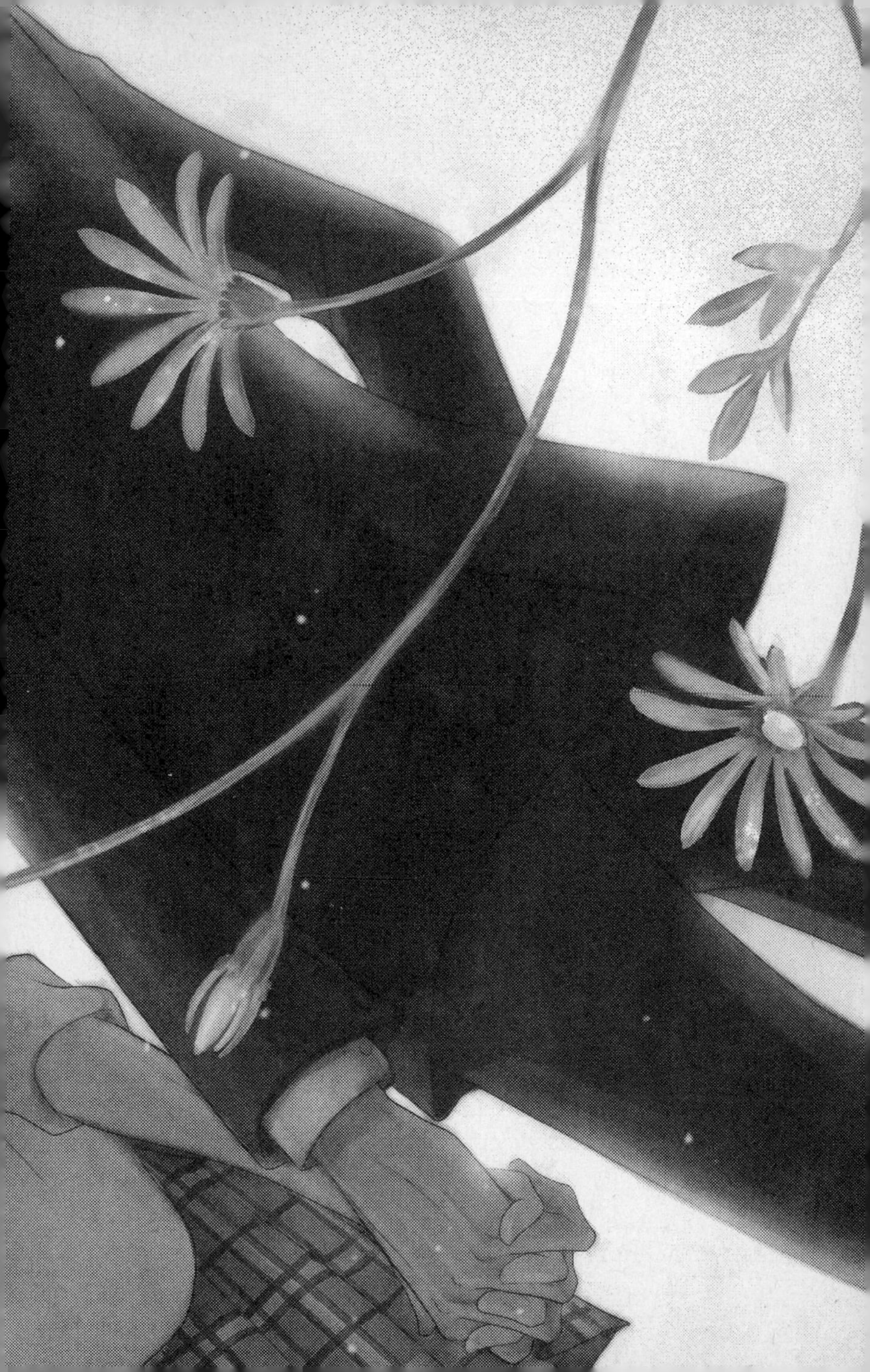

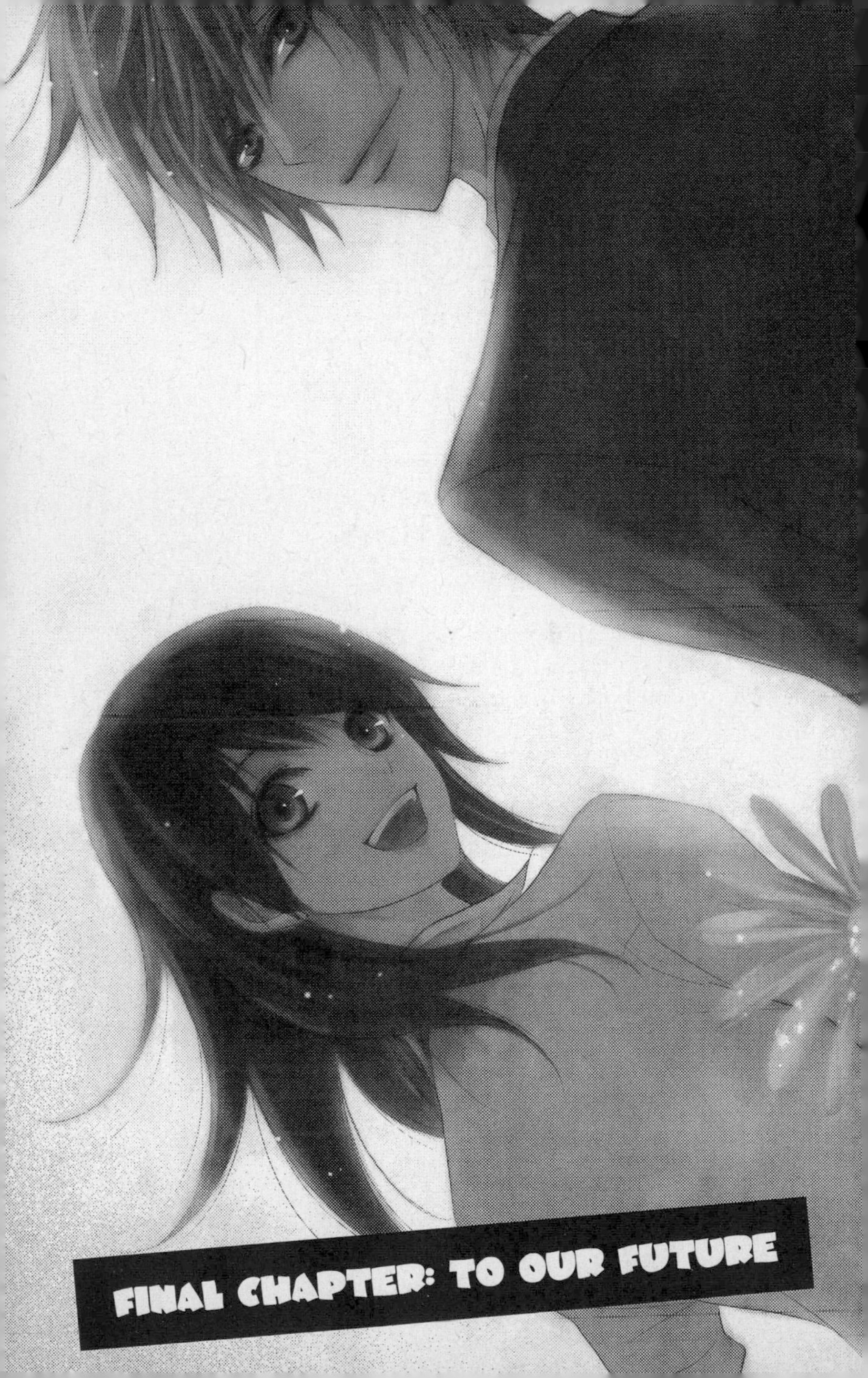
FINAL CHAPTER: TO OUR FUTURE

AT LAST! THE FINAL VOLUME!

THE BEST ☆ OF ☆ THE SECRET SCHOOL CUSTODIAN OFFICE

THE "BEST OF" FOR VOLUME 16 IS... "THE DAISY CHRONOLOGY"

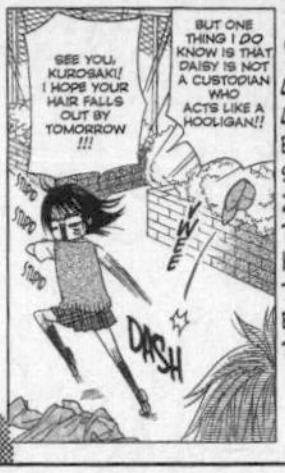

BUT ONE THING I DO KNOW IS THAT DAISY IS NOT A CUSTODIAN WHO ACTS LIKE A HOOLIGAN!!
SEE YOU, KUROSAKI! I HOPE YOUR HAIR FALLS OUT BY TOMORROW !!!
DASH

2007

JUNE ISSUE DENGEKI DAISY BEGINS SERIALIZATION! TERU TELLS KUROSAKI TO GO BALD FROM THE START!

JULY "BILLY'S BOOT CAMP" TOPS ONE MILLION SETS IN SALES!

AUG ISSUE BOSS MAKES HIS DEBUT!

OCTOBER PRIVATIZATION OF POSTAL SERVICE

OCT ISSUE LIVE-IN SLAVE TERU BEGINS LIVING WITH KUROSAKI.

NOV ISSUE RIKO MAKES HER DEBUT!

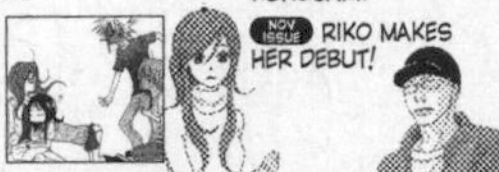

2008

JAN ISSUE TERU'S PANTY INCIDENT TERU APPEARS WEARING WHITE PANTIES.

FEBRUARY BLACK ENKA SINGER JERO DEBUTS.

FEB ISSUE KUROSAKI APPEARS WEARING SUNGLASSES. BUT TERU CALLS THEM "OLD MAN SHADES." KIYOSHI BECOMES A SLAVE.

JULY IPHONE 3G DEBUTS IN JAPAN.

JULY ISSUE TERU DISCOVERS THAT KUROSAKI IS DAISY.

AUGUST OPENING OF THE BEIJING OLYMPICS

SEPT ISSUE TERU ATTENDS HER FIRST MIXER. (A FAILURE) KUROSAKI IS SO ANXIOUS, HE REVEALS HIS FEELINGS.

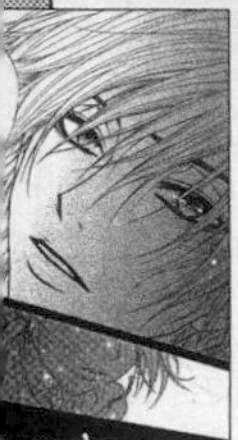

NOV ISSUE ANDY DEBUTS!

2009

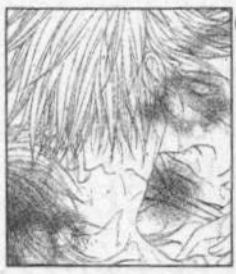

JANUARY BARACK OBAMA IS ELECTED PRESIDENT OF THE U.S.

JULY ISSUE TERU IS KIDNAPPED. ①

TERU GETS INTO A STRUGGLE WITH CHIHARU AND FALLS INTO THE OCEAN. KUROSAKI REVIVES TERU WITH CPR AND A FIRST KISS. ♥ (DOES NOT COUNT)

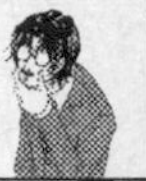

OCT ISSUE TERU AND AKIRA'S FIRST ENCOUNTER

NOVEMBER BUDGET SCREENING ENFORCEMENT BEGINS.

NOV ISSUE EVERYONE'S PRINCESS, KAORUKO, DEBUTS. ♥

DECEMBER 3D MOVIE "AVATAR" OPENS IN JAPAN.

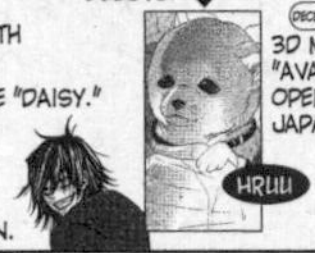

HRUU

2010

JAN ISSUE TERU AND AKIRA'S SECOND ENCOUNTER AKIRA FORCES A KISS ON TERU.

DECEMBER AUTOGRAPH SESSION WITH MOTOMI SENSEI

MAR ISSUE KUROSAKI AND TERU'S FIRST DATE

APR ISSUE KUROSAKI DISAPPEARS. AFTER TERU LEARNS THAT KUROSAKI WAS THE CAUSE OF SOICHIRO'S DEATH, KUROSAKI LEAVES TOWN.

JUNE JAPAN'S SOCCER TEAM MAKES ROUND 16 IN THE SOUTH AFRICA WORLD CUP.

JUNE ISSUE TERU LEARNS WHY KUROSAKI BECAME "DAISY."

JULY ISSUE START OF THE ARC ABOUT KUROSAKI AND SOICHIRO'S PAST.

NOV ISSUE START OF "PLAN DG" TERU AND KUROSAKI HAVE A REUNION.

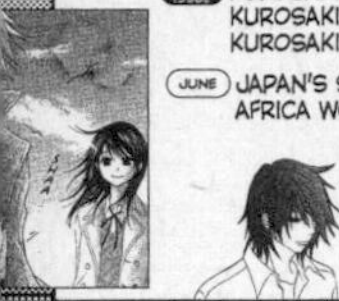

2011

JAN ISSUE TERU AND KUROSAKI SPEND A NIGHT ALONE IN A HOTEL. AFTER RIKO WARNS HIM, KUROSAKI FEELS THE PRESSURE AND STAYS UP ALL NIGHT CHANTING SUTRAS.

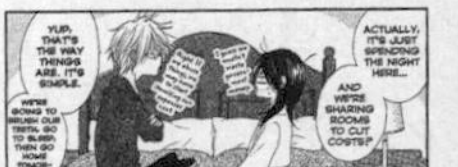

YUP, THAT'S THE WAY THINGS ARE. IT'S SIMPLE.
ACTUALLY, IT'S JUST SPENDING THE NIGHT HERE...
AND WE'RE SHARING ROOMS TO CUT COSTS?

FEBRUARY THE UENO ZOO ACQUIRES PANDAS.

JULY NADESHIKO JAPAN WINS THE GOLD IN WOMEN'S SOCCER.

SEPT ISSUE AKIRA APPEARS BEFORE TERU AGAIN.

FEB ISSUE MORIZONO, WHO IS AFTER "JACK FROST," APPEARS BEFORE TERU.

MAY THE EXISTENCE OF M'S LAST TESTAMENT IS REVEALED.

2012

FEB ISSUE RENA'S RESCUE PLAN BEGINS.

MAY TOKYO SKYTREE OPENS.

MAY ISSUE THE TEAM OBTAINS THE KEY TO "M'S LAST TESTAMENT" FROM ANTLER.

JULY AT THE JAPAN EXPO IN PARIS, "DENGEKI DAISY" WINS THE GRAND PRIX PRIZE FOR MANGA.

SEPT ISSUE AKIRA INVADES TAKEDA'S HOUSE. HE TAKES THE KEY TO "M'S LAST TESTAMENT."

DECEMBER SHINYA YAMANAKA WINS THE NOBEL PRIZE FOR HIS IPS CELL RESEARCH.

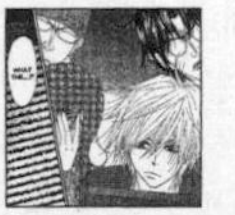

DEC ISSUE THE TEAM FINDS PROFESSOR MIDORIKAWA'S DATA IN A DISK THAT WAS LEFT TO THEM BY SOICHIRO.

2013

MAR ISSUE THE TEAM BEGINS IN EARNEST TO DECIPHER "M'S LAST TESTAMENT."

APR ISSUE THE TASK IS FINALLY ACCOMPLISHED! KUROSAKI AND TERU SHARE THEIR FIRST KISS ON A FERRIS WHEEL.♥

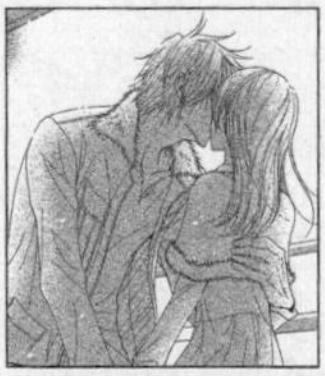

MAY ISSUE TERU IS KIDNAPPED. ② TERU IS TAKEN TO THE SITE WHERE "M'S LAST TESTAMENT" WILL BE CARRIED OUT.

JUNE AUTOGRAPH SESSION WITH MOTOMI SENSEI

AUG ISSUE THE PLAN TO RESCUE TERU AND AKIRA; KUROSAKI AND BOSS INFILTRATE THE SITE OF "M'S LAST TESTAMENT."

SEPTEMBER TOKYO IS CHOSEN AS THE SITE FOR THE OLYMPICS.

BETSUCOMI NOV ISSUE SERIALIZATION COMPLETE!

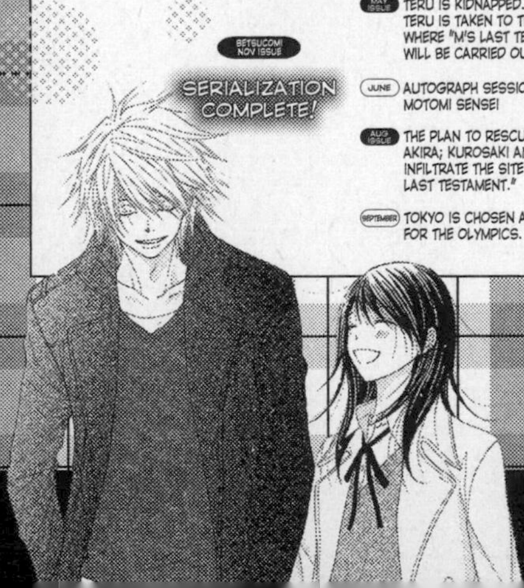

Thank you for your support!

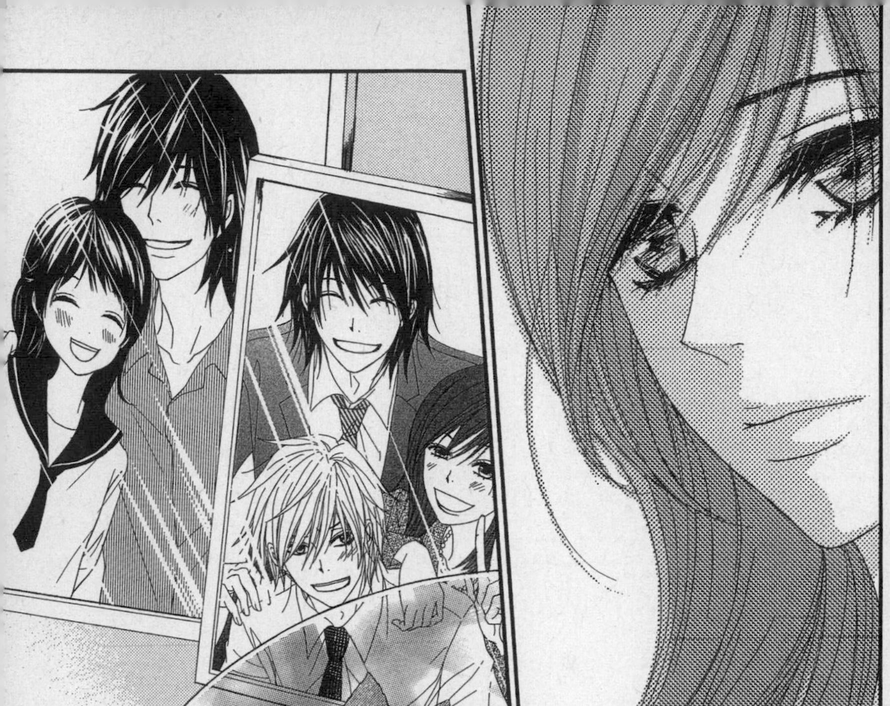

HELLO, EVERYONE! IT'S KYOUSUKE MOTOMI.

THIS IS VOLUME 16 OF *DENGEKI DAISY*.

IT'S THE FINAL VOLUME. MY WISH IS ALWAYS THE SAME—THAT YOU ENJOY THIS VOLUME TOO, TO THE VERY LAST PAGE. NOW THEN, READ ON!!

IT'S JANUARY (THE MIDDLE OF WINTER), BUT SO MANY BLUE DAISIES ARE ABLOOM IN MY GARDEN! THEY ARE HARDY FLOWERS OF HAPPINESS. THANK YOU FOR EVERYTHING!!

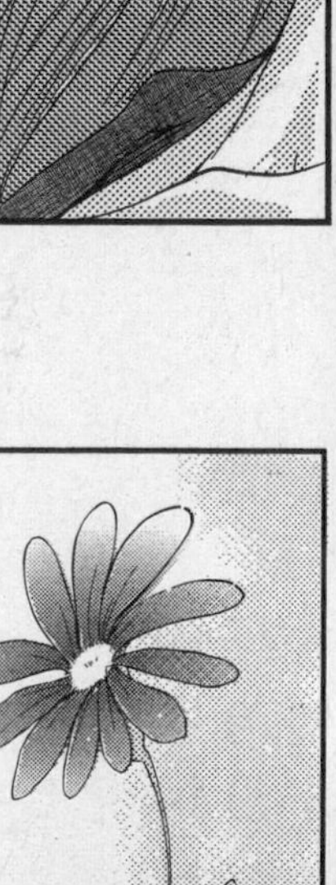

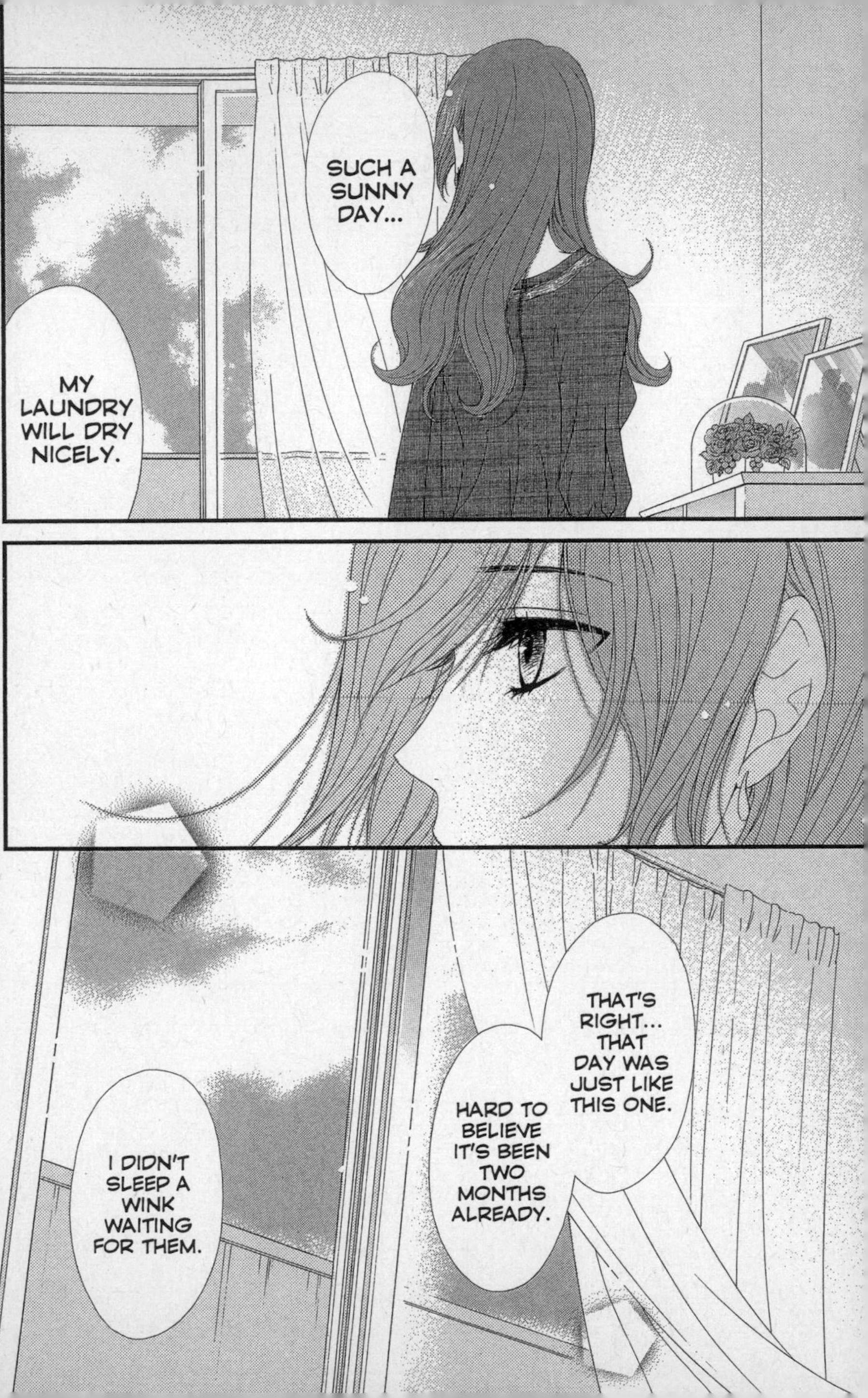
SUCH A SUNNY DAY...
MY LAUNDRY WILL DRY NICELY.
THAT'S RIGHT... THAT DAY WAS JUST LIKE THIS ONE.
HARD TO BELIEVE IT'S BEEN TWO MONTHS ALREADY.
I DIDN'T SLEEP A WINK WAITING FOR THEM.

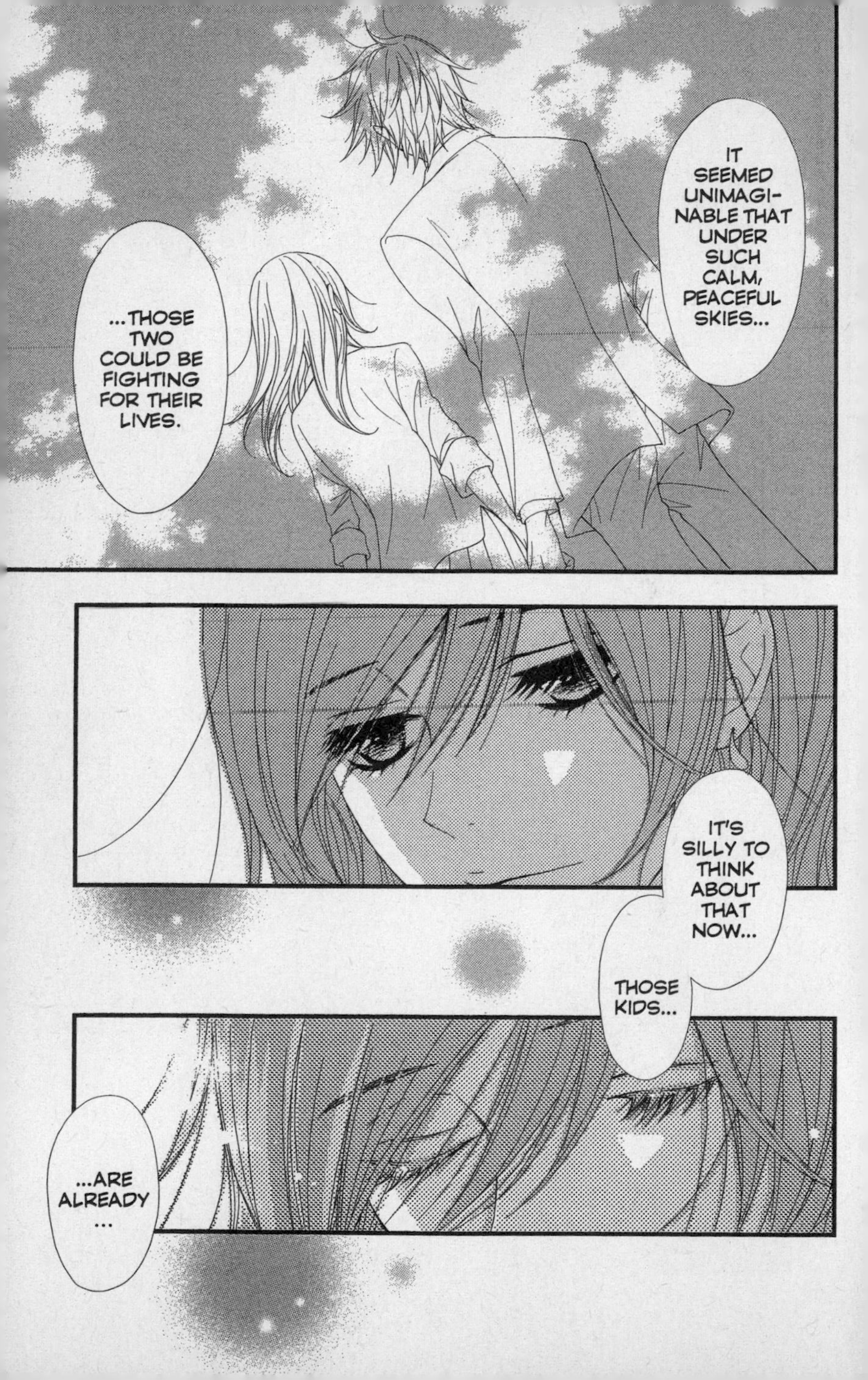
IT SEEMED UNIMAGINABLE THAT UNDER SUCH CALM, PEACEFUL SKIES...
...THOSE TWO COULD BE FIGHTING FOR THEIR LIVES.
IT'S SILLY TO THINK ABOUT THAT NOW...
THOSE KIDS...
...ARE ALREADY ...

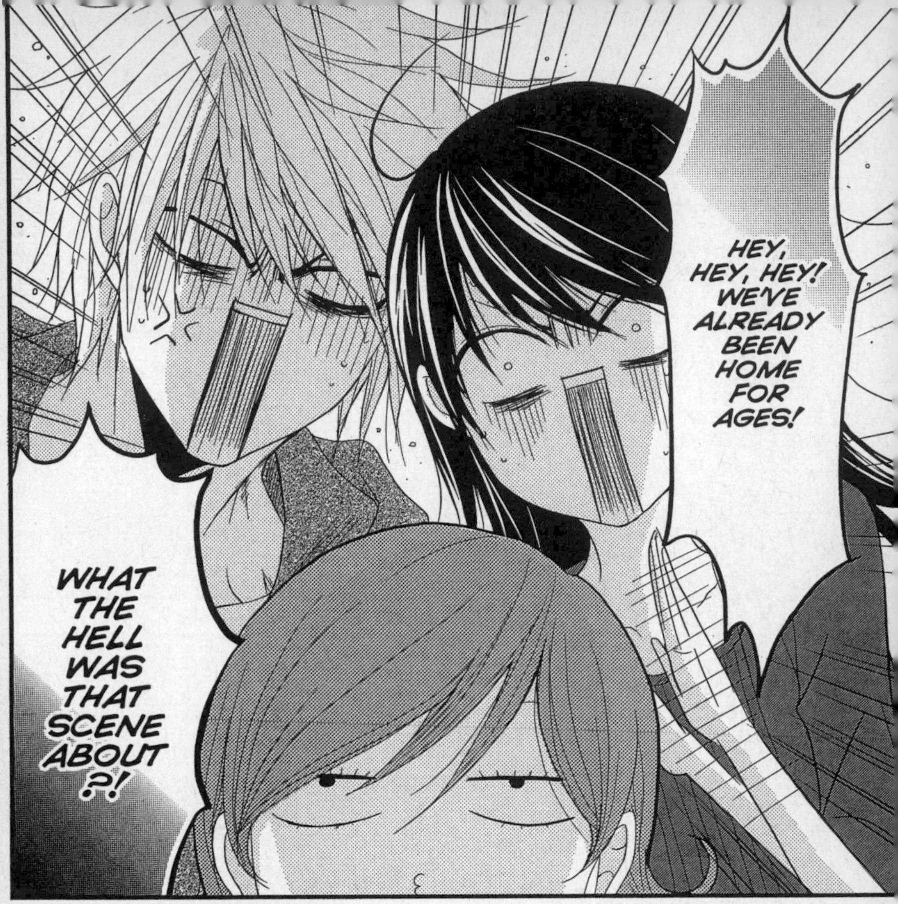
HEY, HEY, HEY! WE'VE ALREADY BEEN HOME FOR AGES!
WHAT THE HELL WAS THAT SCENE ABOUT?!

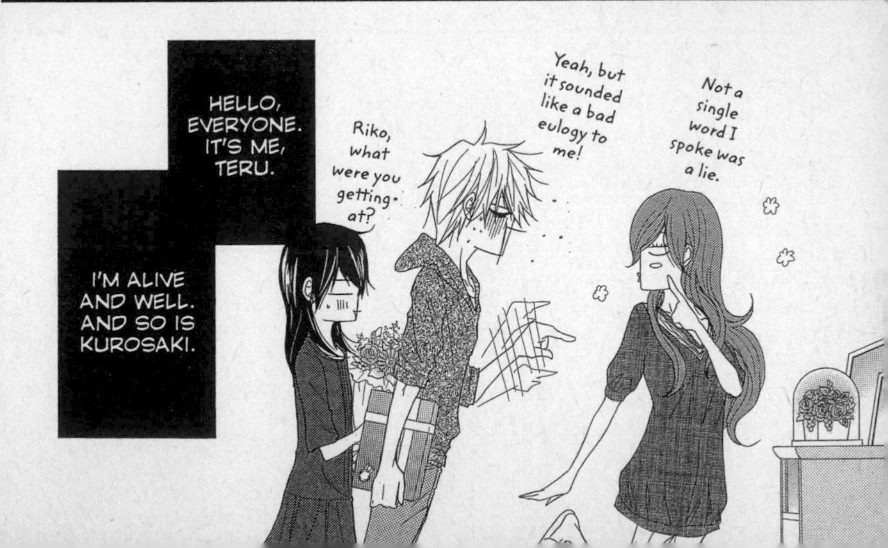
HELLO, EVERYONE. IT'S ME, TERU.
I'M ALIVE AND WELL. AND SO IS KUROSAKI.
Riko, what were you getting at?
Not a single word I spoke was a lie.
Yeah, but it sounded like a bad eulogy to me!

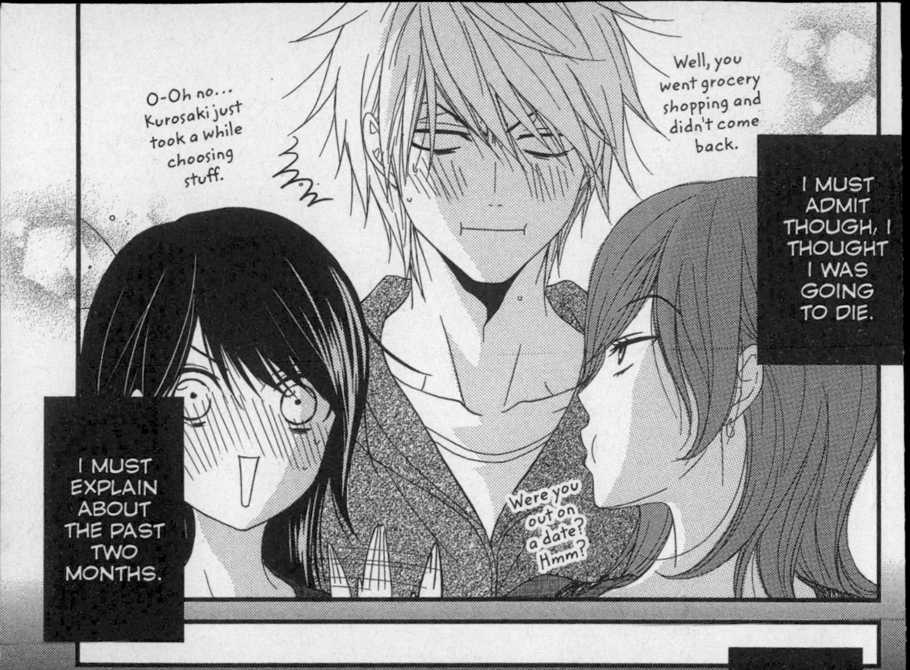
Well, you went grocery shopping and didn't come back.
I MUST ADMIT THOUGH, I THOUGHT I WAS GOING TO DIE.
O-Oh no... Kurosaki just took a while choosing stuff.
Were you out on a date? Hmm?
I MUST EXPLAIN ABOUT THE PAST TWO MONTHS.
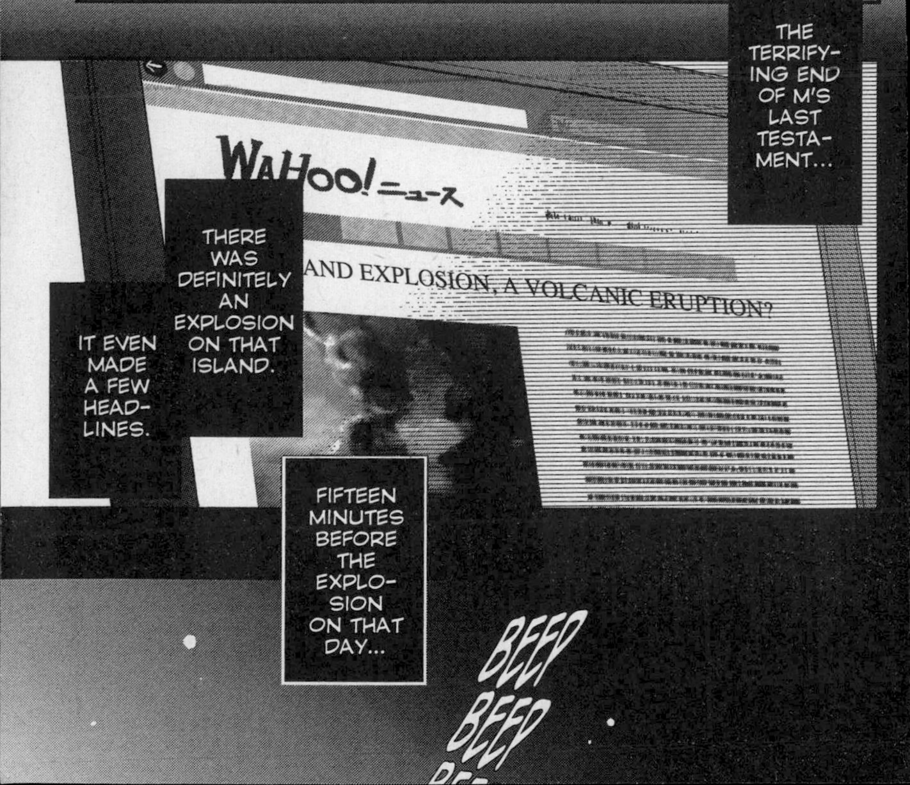
THE TERRIFYING END OF M'S LAST TESTAMENT...
WAHOO! ニュース
AND EXPLOSION, A VOLCANIC ERUPTION?
THERE WAS DEFINITELY AN EXPLOSION ON THAT ISLAND.
IT EVEN MADE A FEW HEADLINES.
FIFTEEN MINUTES BEFORE THE EXPLOSION ON THAT DAY...
BEEP
BEEP

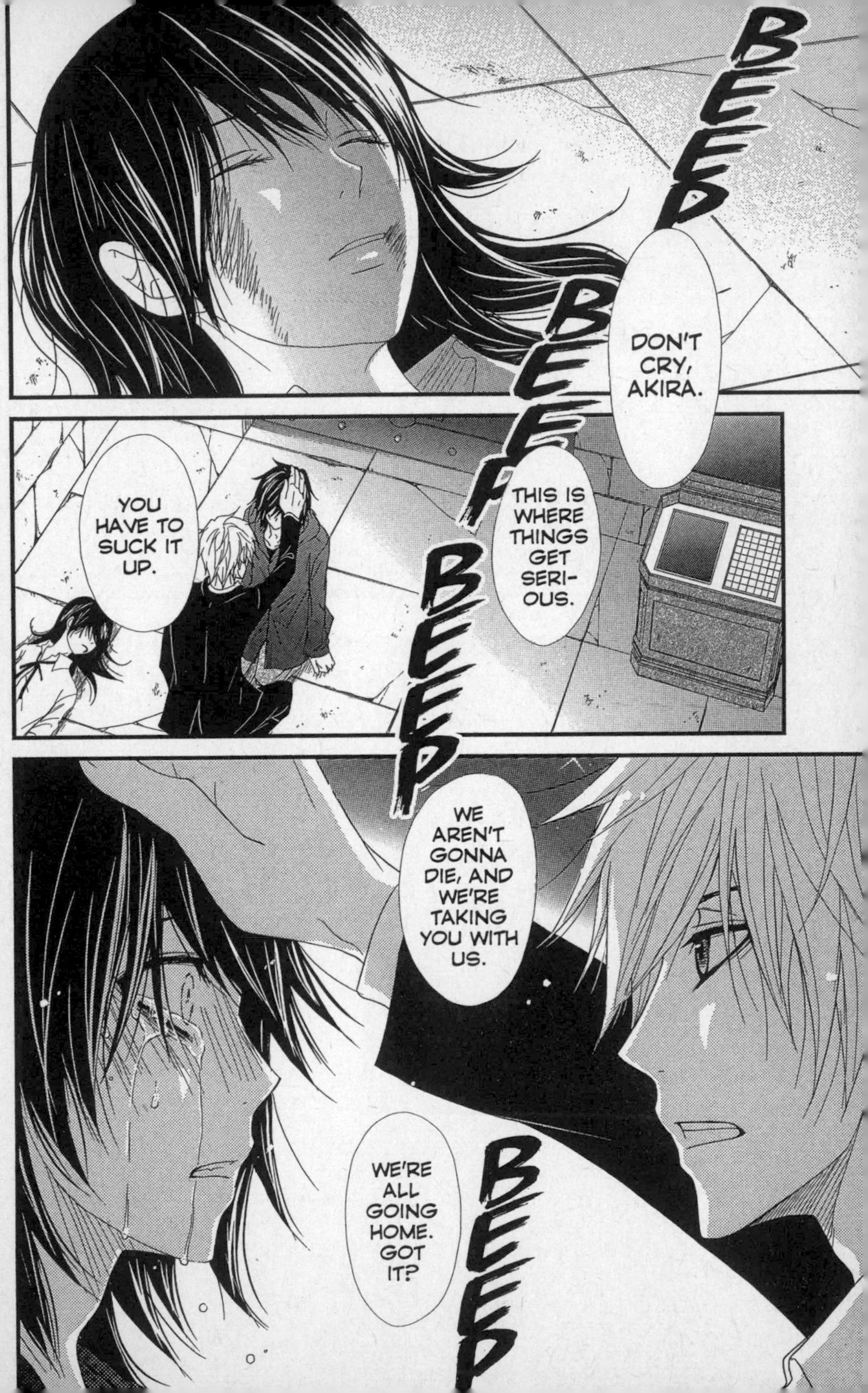
BEEP
DON'T CRY, AKIRA.
BEEP
BEEP
THIS IS WHERE THINGS GET SERIOUS.
YOU HAVE TO SUCK IT UP.
WE AREN'T GONNA DIE, AND WE'RE TAKING YOU WITH US.
BEEP
WE'RE ALL GOING HOME. GOT IT?

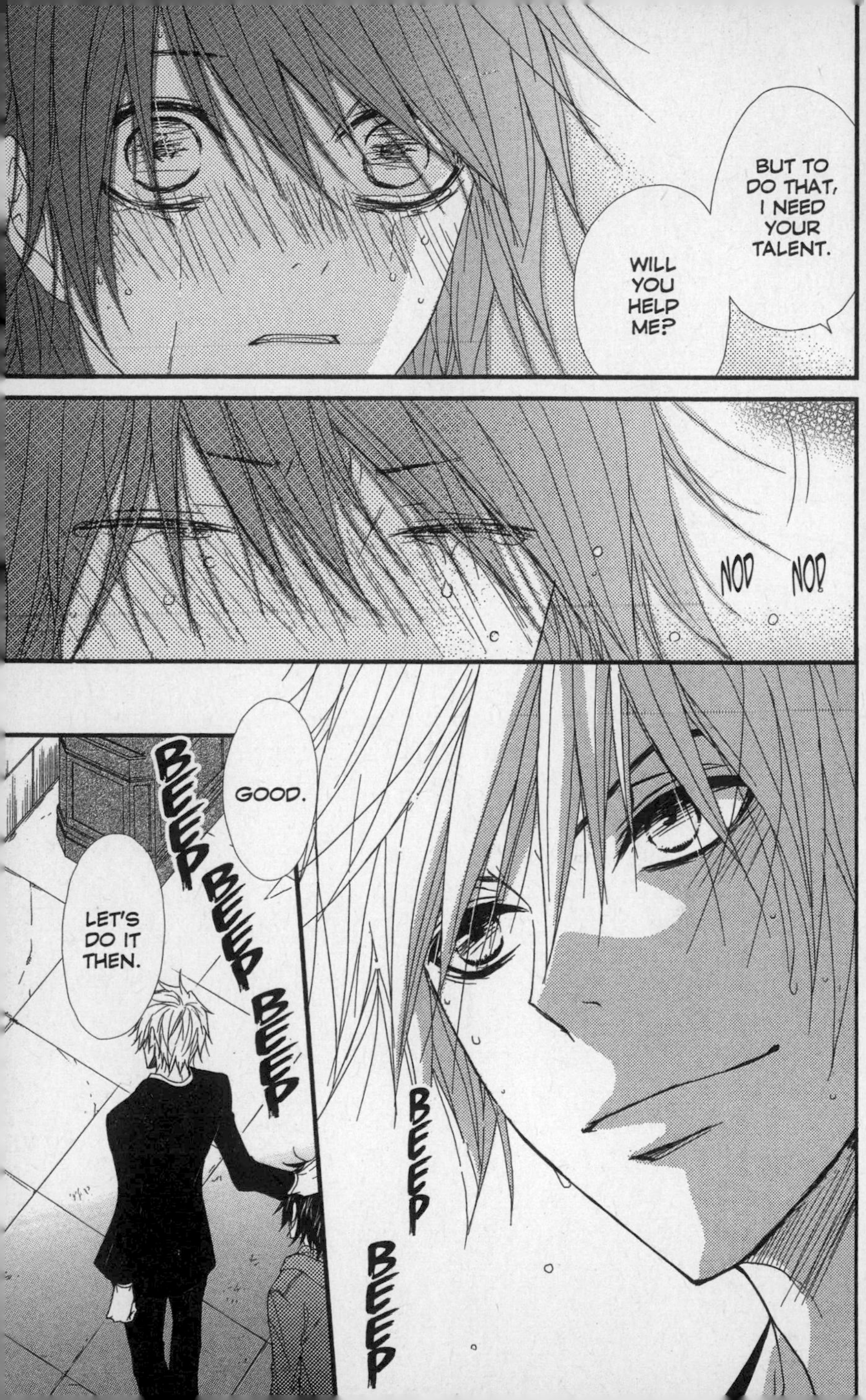
BUT TO DO THAT, I NEED YOUR TALENT.
WILL YOU HELP ME?
NOD NOD
GOOD.
LET'S DO IT THEN.
BEEP BEEP BEEP
BEEP BEEP

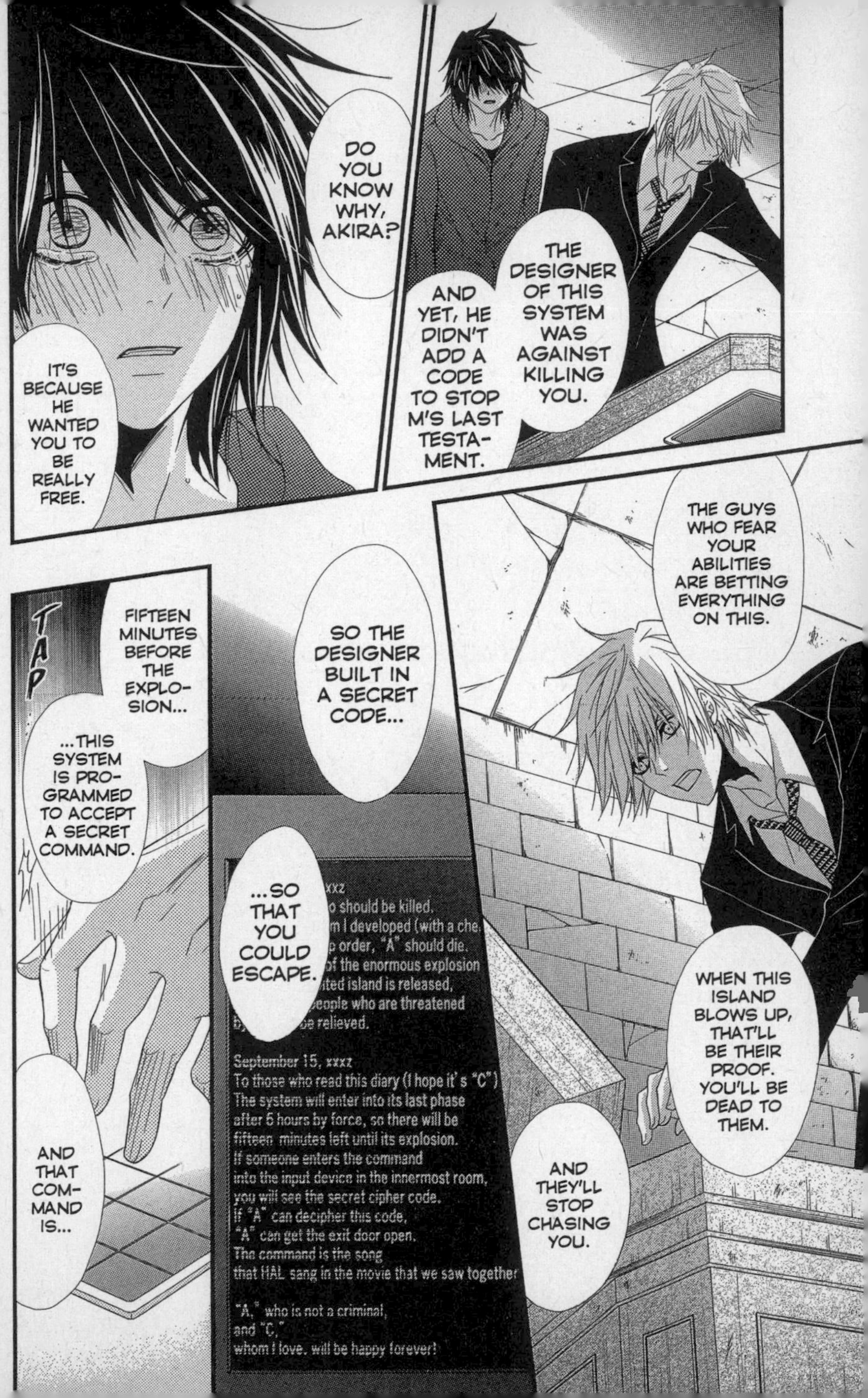
THE DESIGNER OF THIS SYSTEM WAS AGAINST KILLING YOU.
AND YET, HE DIDN'T ADD A CODE TO STOP M'S LAST TESTAMENT.
DO YOU KNOW WHY, AKIRA?
IT'S BECAUSE HE WANTED YOU TO BE REALLY FREE.
THE GUYS WHO FEAR YOUR ABILITIES ARE BETTING EVERYTHING ON THIS.
WHEN THIS ISLAND BLOWS UP, THAT'LL BE THEIR PROOF. YOU'LL BE DEAD TO THEM.
AND THEY'LL STOP CHASING YOU.
SO THE DESIGNER BUILT IN A SECRET CODE...
...SO THAT YOU COULD ESCAPE.
should be killed.
I developed (with a
order, "A" should die.
of the enormous explosion
island is released,
people who are threatened
be relieved.
September 15, xxxz
To those who read this diary (I hope it's "C")
The system will enter into its last phase
after 6 hours by force, so there will be
fifteen minutes left until its explosion.
If someone enters the command
into the input device in the innermost room,
you will see the secret cipher code.
If "A" can decipher this code,
"A" can get the exit door open.
The command is the song
that HAL sang in the movie that we saw together
"A," who is not a criminal,
and "C,"
whom I love, will be happy forever!
TAP
FIFTEEN MINUTES BEFORE THE EXPLOSION...
...THIS SYSTEM IS PROGRAMMED TO ACCEPT A SECRET COMMAND.
AND THAT COMMAND IS...

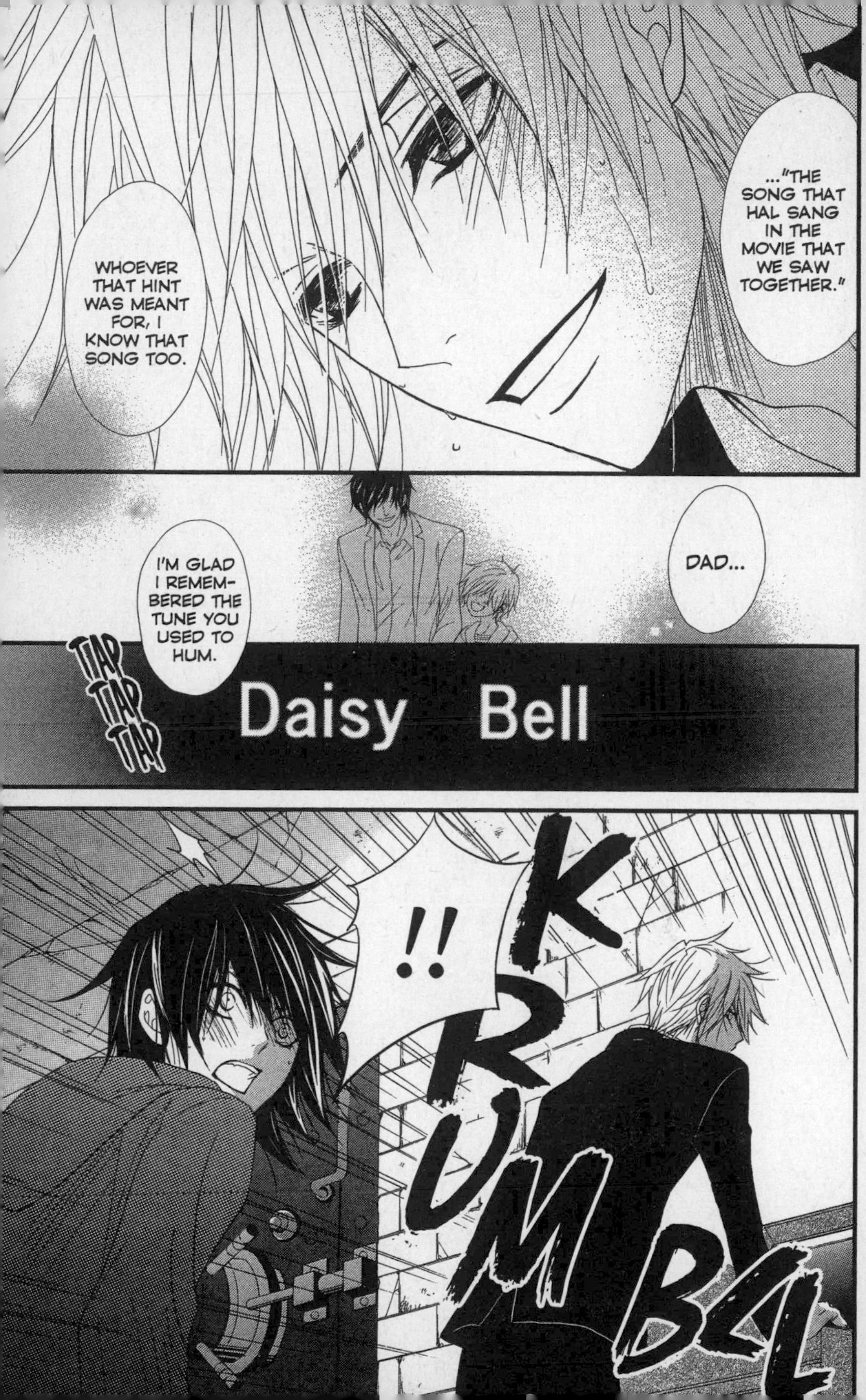
..."THE SONG THAT HAL SANG IN THE MOVIE THAT WE SAW TOGETHER."
WHOEVER THAT HINT WAS MEANT FOR, I KNOW THAT SONG TOO.
DAD...
I'M GLAD I REMEMBERED THE TUNE YOU USED TO HUM.
TAP TAP TAP
Daisy Bell
!!
KRUMBAL

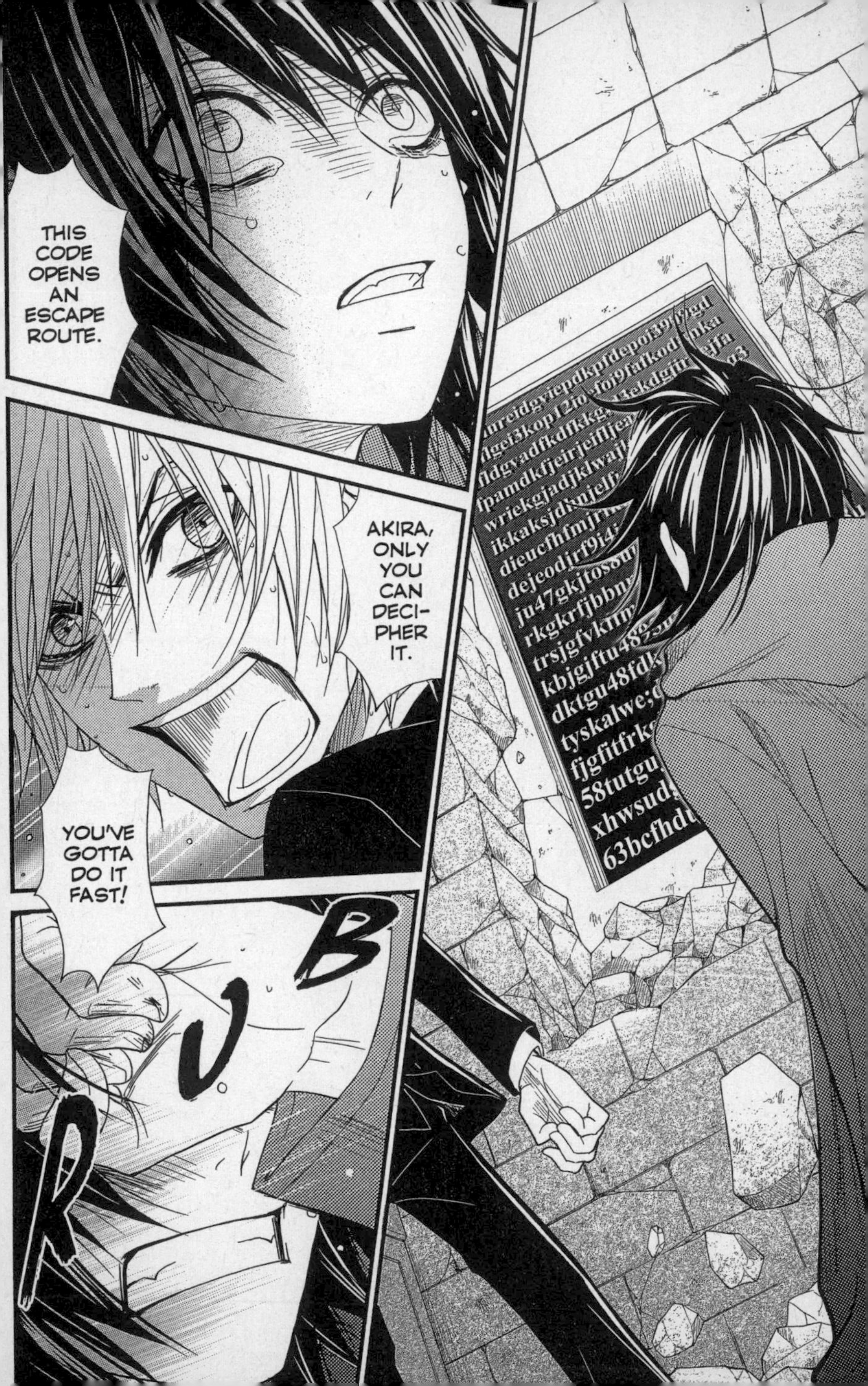
THIS CODE OPENS AN ESCAPE ROUTE.
AKIRA, ONLY YOU CAN DECIPHER IT.
YOU'VE GOTTA DO IT FAST!
RUB

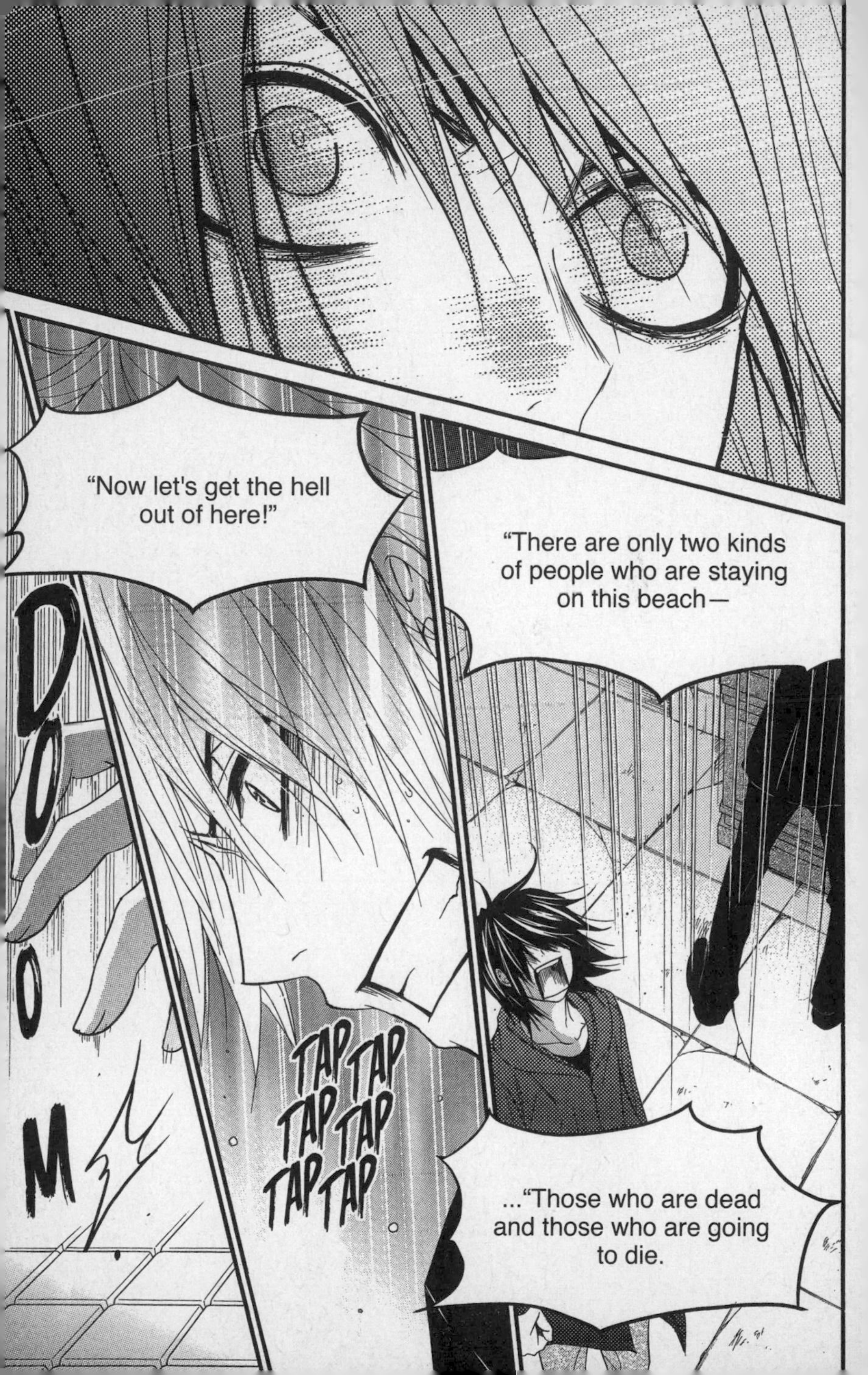
"There are only two kinds of people who are staying on this beach—
..."Those who are dead and those who are going to die.
"Now let's get the hell out of here!"
TAP TAP TAP TAP TAP TAP
DOOM

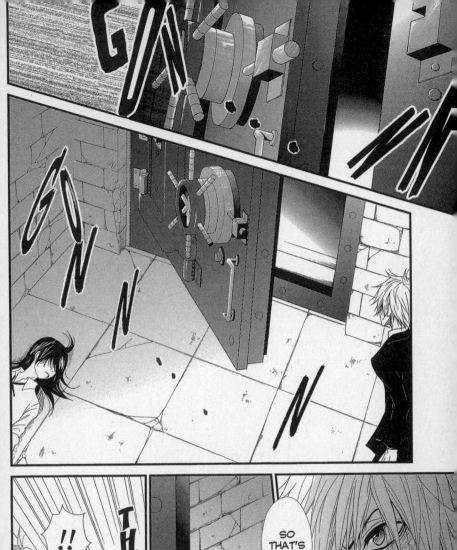

GUNN

GONNN

GONNN

N

N

!!

THUD

THIS OPENS TO OUR ESCAPE ROUTE.

SO THAT'S IT.

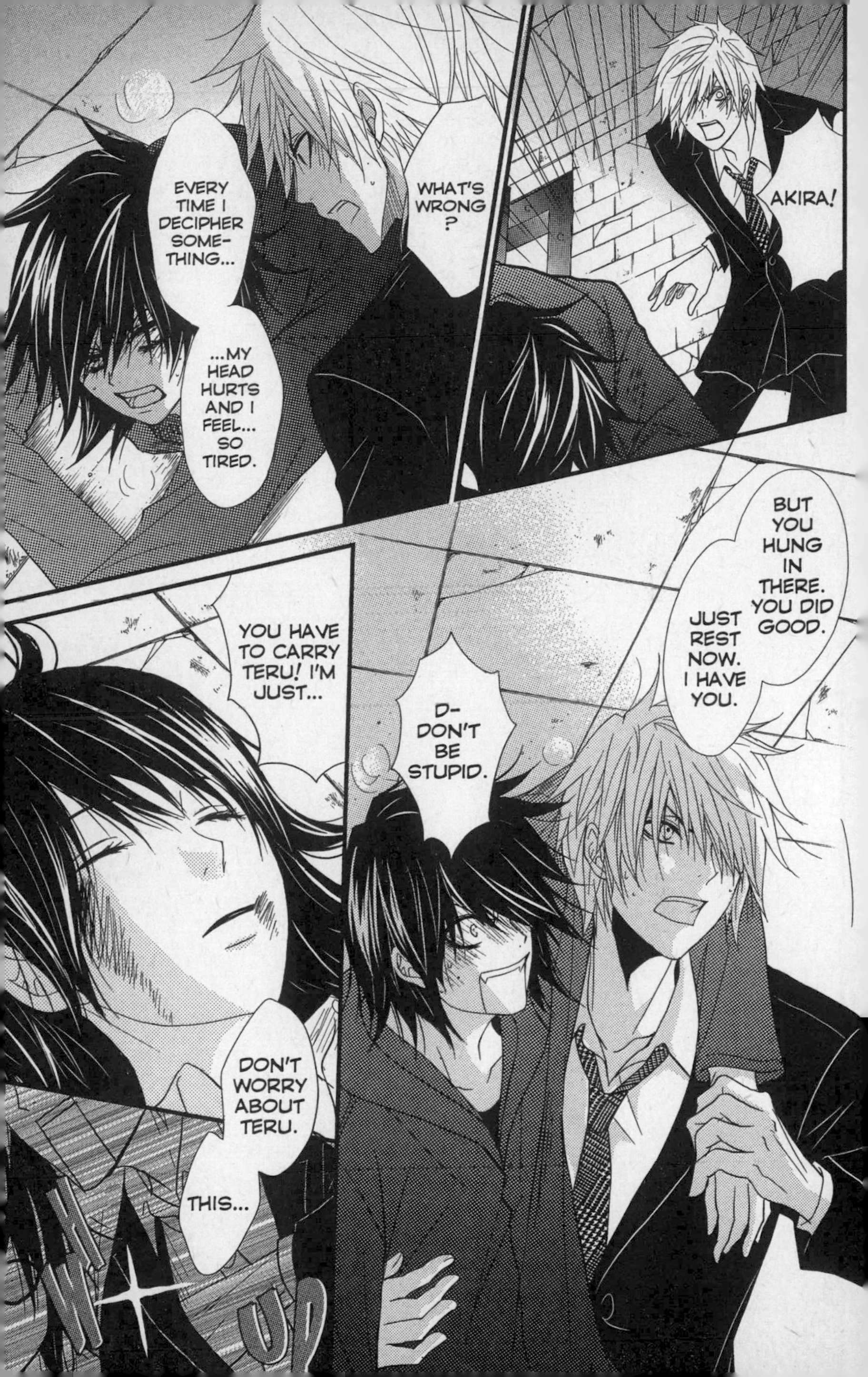
AKIRA!
WHAT'S WRONG?
EVERY TIME I DECIPHER SOME-THING...
...MY HEAD HURTS AND I FEEL... SO TIRED.
BUT YOU HUNG IN THERE. YOU DID GOOD.
JUST REST NOW. I HAVE YOU.
D-DON'T BE STUPID.
YOU HAVE TO CARRY TERU! I'M JUST...
DON'T WORRY ABOUT TERU.
THIS...

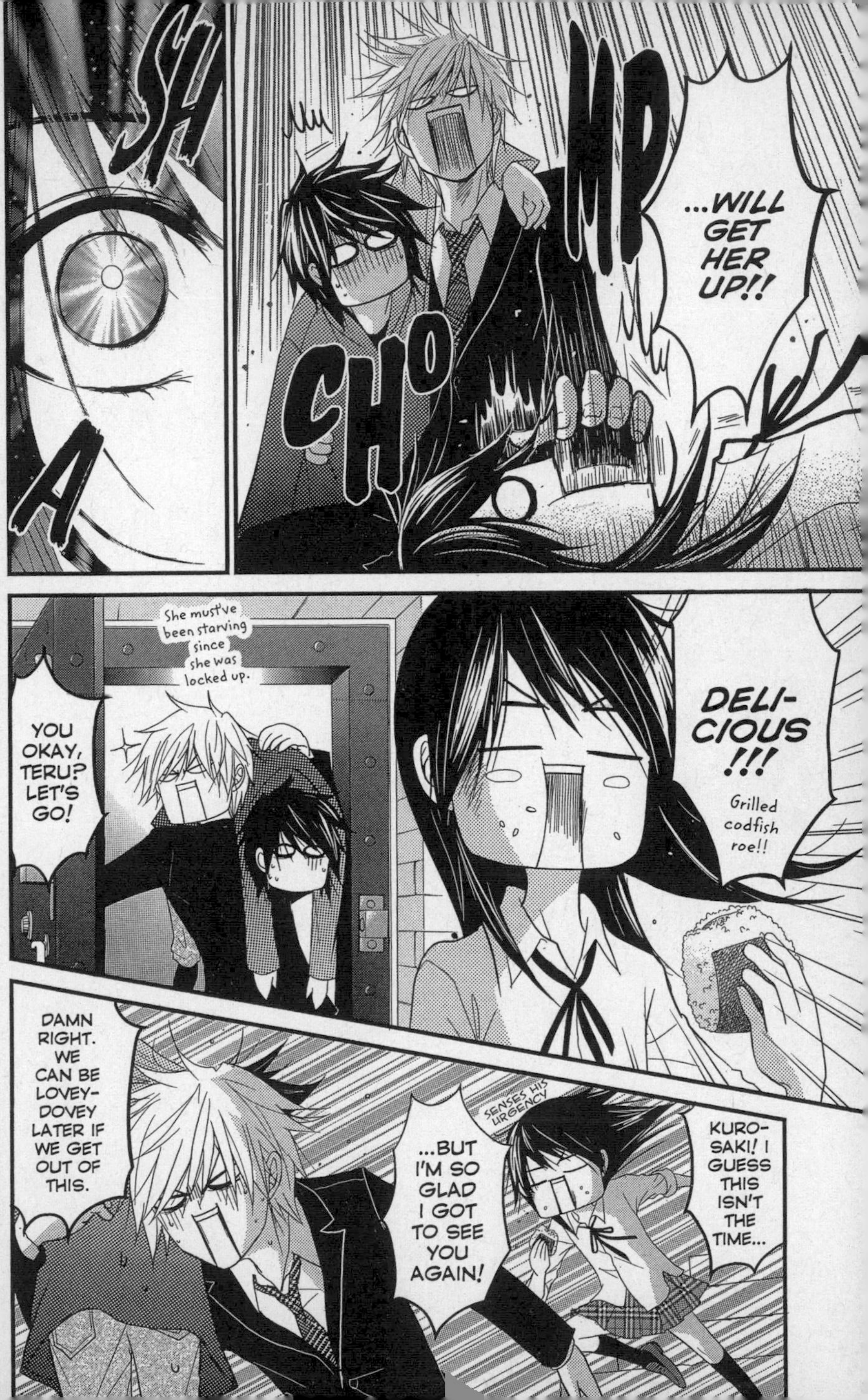
...WILL GET HER UP!!
MU
CHO
MP
SH
A
DELICIOUS!!!
Grilled codfish roe!!
She must've been starving since she was locked up.
YOU OKAY, TERU? LET'S GO!
KUROSAKI! I GUESS THIS ISN'T THE TIME...
SENSES HIS URGENCY
...BUT I'M SO GLAD I GOT TO SEE YOU AGAIN!
DAMN RIGHT. WE CAN BE LOVEY-DOVEY LATER IF WE GET OUT OF THIS.

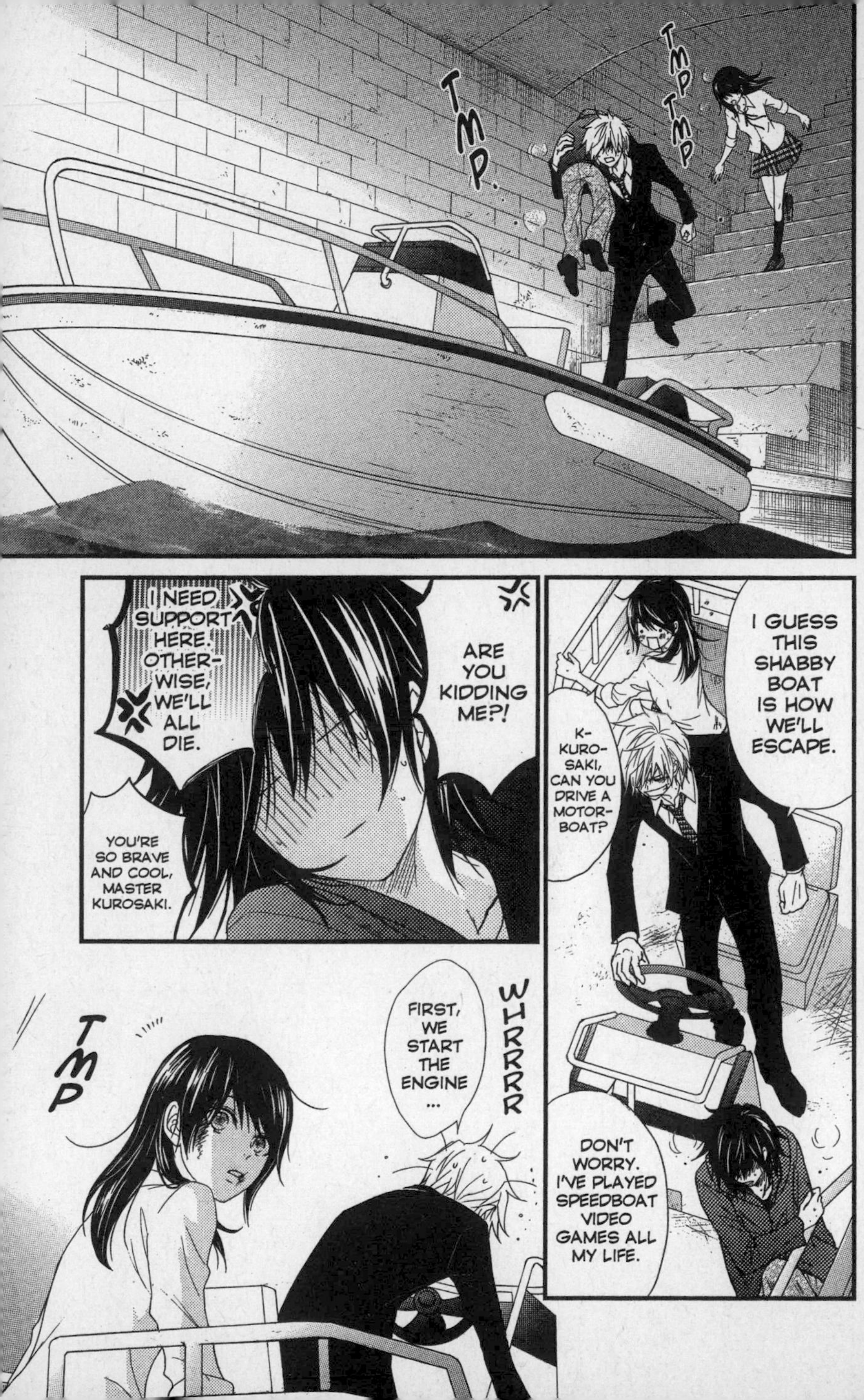
TMP TMP
TMP.
I GUESS THIS SHABBY BOAT IS HOW WE'LL ESCAPE.
K-KUROSAKI, CAN YOU DRIVE A MOTORBOAT?
DON'T WORRY. I'VE PLAYED SPEEDBOAT VIDEO GAMES ALL MY LIFE.
ARE YOU KIDDING ME?!
I NEED SUPPORT HERE. OTHERWISE, WE'LL ALL DIE.
YOU'RE SO BRAVE AND COOL, MASTER KUROSAKI.
WHRRRR
FIRST, WE START THE ENGINE...
TMP

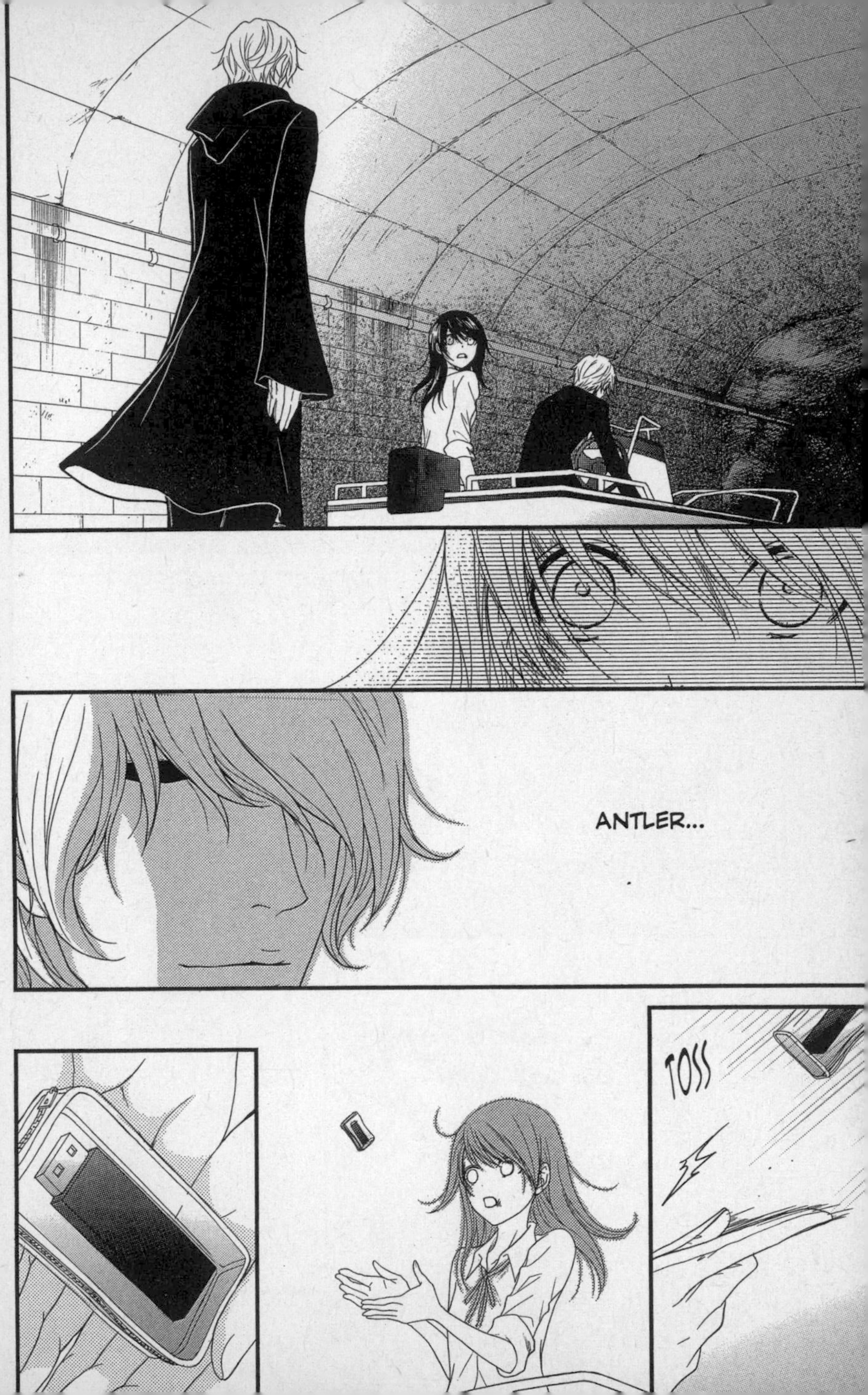
ANTLER...
TOSS

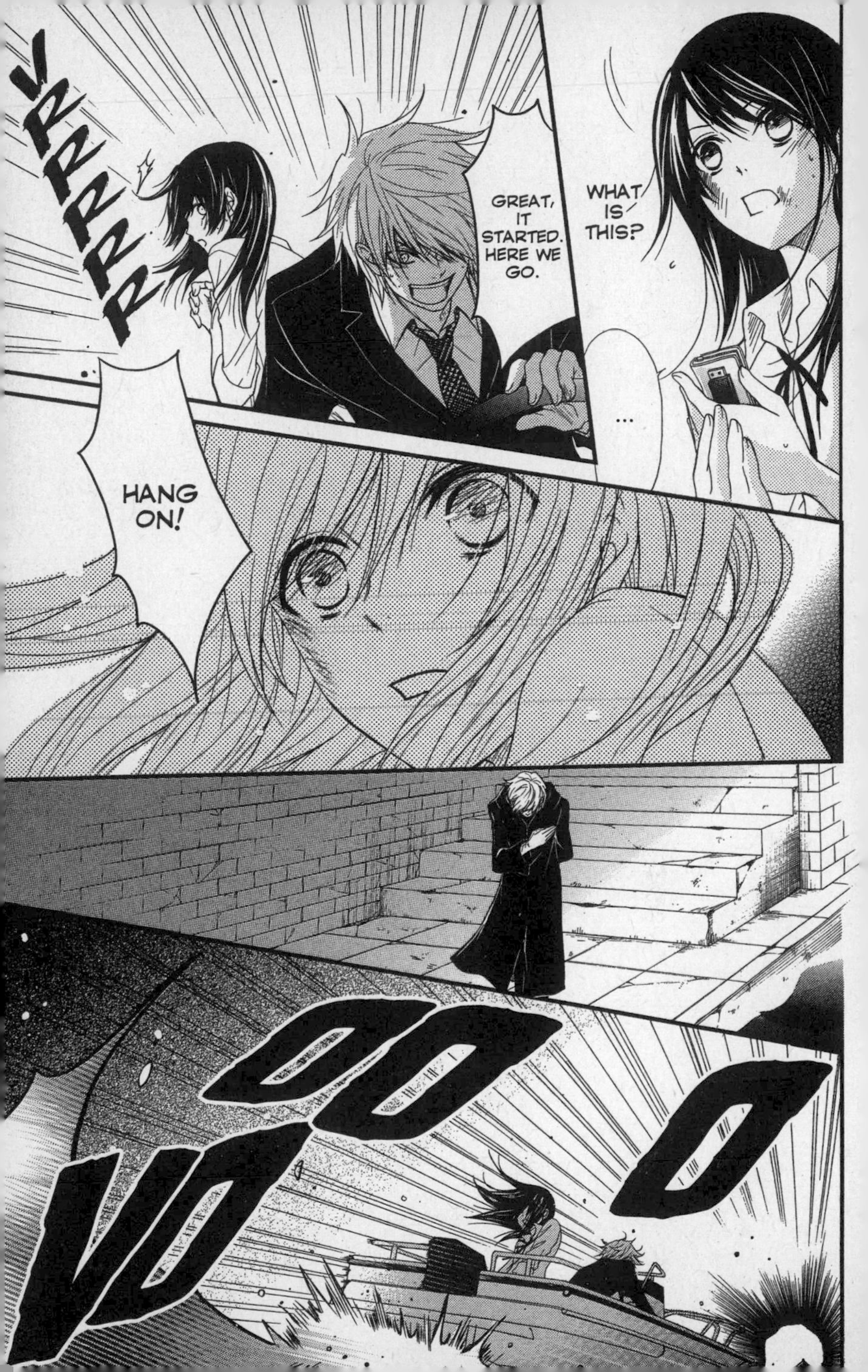
WHAT IS THIS?
...
GREAT, IT STARTED. HERE WE GO.
VRRRRR
HANG ON!

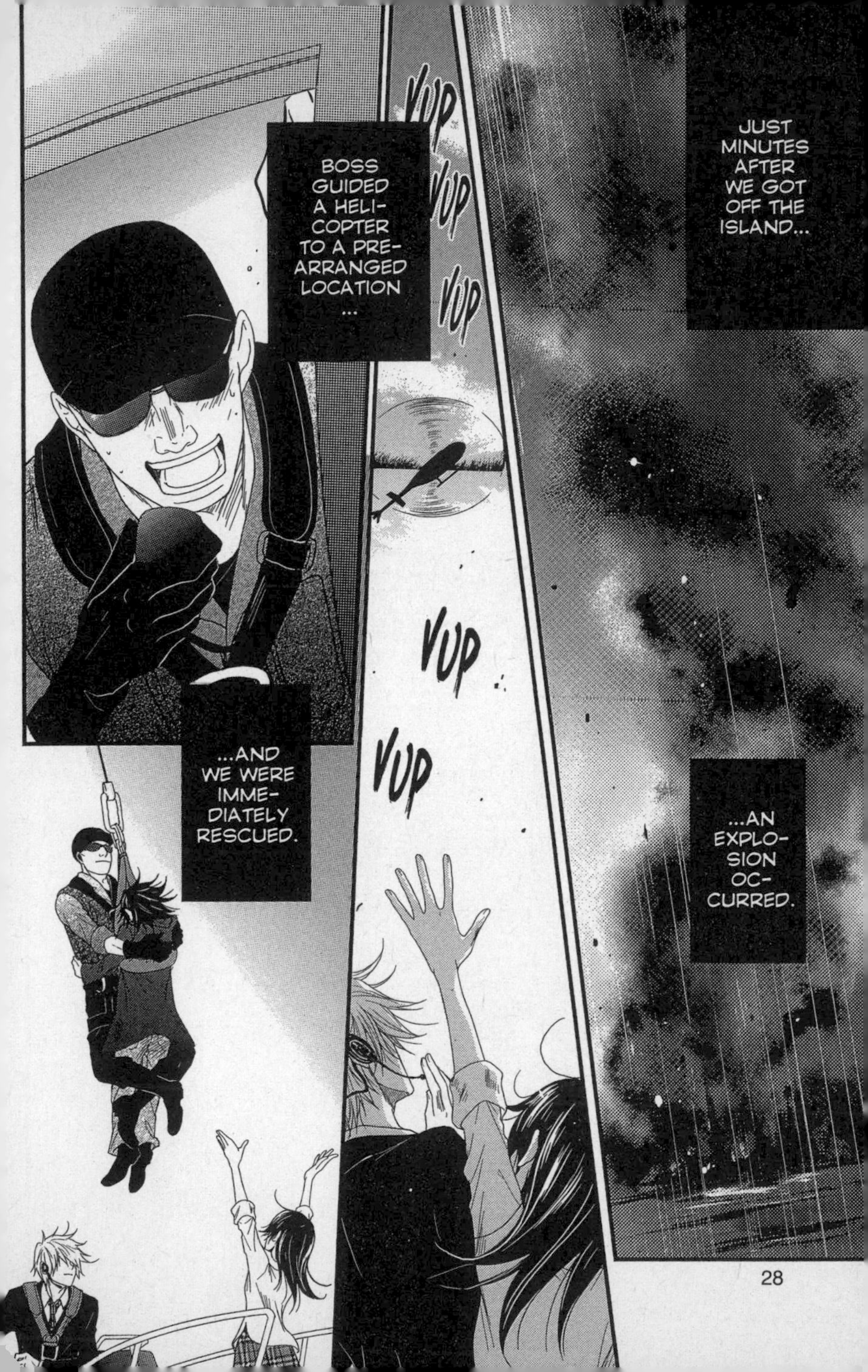
JUST MINUTES AFTER WE GOT OFF THE ISLAND...
...AN EXPLOSION OCCURRED.
VUP
VUP
VUP
VUP
VUP
BOSS GUIDED A HELICOPTER TO A PREARRANGED LOCATION...
...AND WE WERE IMMEDIATELY RESCUED.

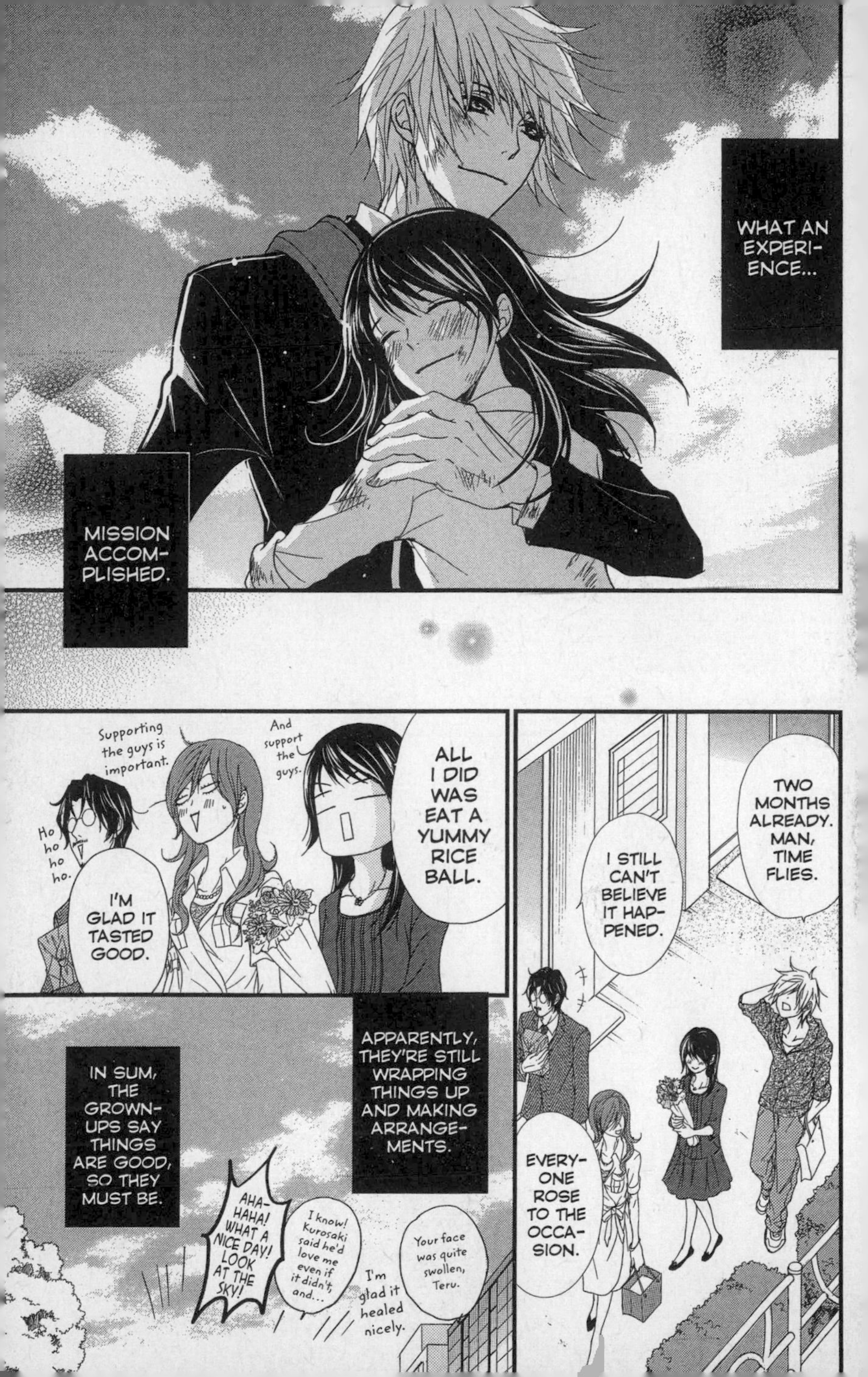
WHAT AN EXPERIENCE...
MISSION ACCOMPLISHED.
TWO MONTHS ALREADY. MAN, TIME FLIES.
I STILL CAN'T BELIEVE IT HAPPENED.
EVERYONE ROSE TO THE OCCASION.
ALL I DID WAS EAT A YUMMY RICE BALL.
And support the guys.
Supporting the guys is important.
Ho ho ho ho.
I'M GLAD IT TASTED GOOD.
APPARENTLY, THEY'RE STILL WRAPPING THINGS UP AND MAKING ARRANGEMENTS.
IN SUM, THE GROWN-UPS SAY THINGS ARE GOOD, SO THEY MUST BE.
Your face was quite swollen, Teru.
I'm glad it healed nicely.
I know! Kurosaki said he'd love me even if it didn't, and...
AHAHAHA! WHAT A NICE DAY! LOOK AT THE SKY!

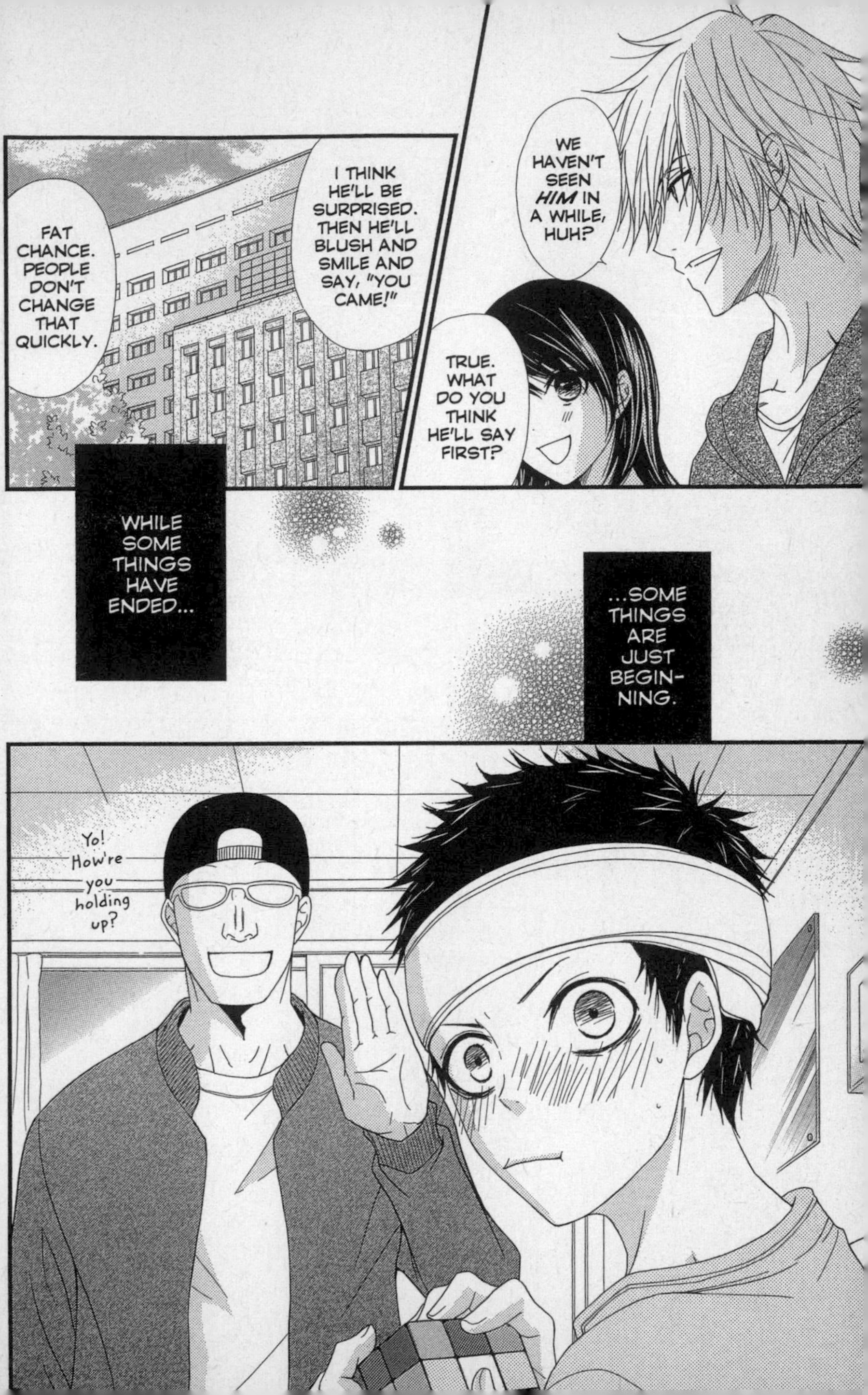
WE HAVEN'T SEEN *HIM* IN A WHILE, HUH?
TRUE. WHAT DO YOU THINK HE'LL SAY FIRST?
I THINK HE'LL BE SURPRISED. THEN HE'LL BLUSH AND SMILE AND SAY, "YOU CAME!"
FAT CHANCE. PEOPLE DON'T CHANGE THAT QUICKLY.
WHILE SOME THINGS HAVE ENDED...
...SOME THINGS ARE JUST BEGINNING.
Yo! How're you holding up?

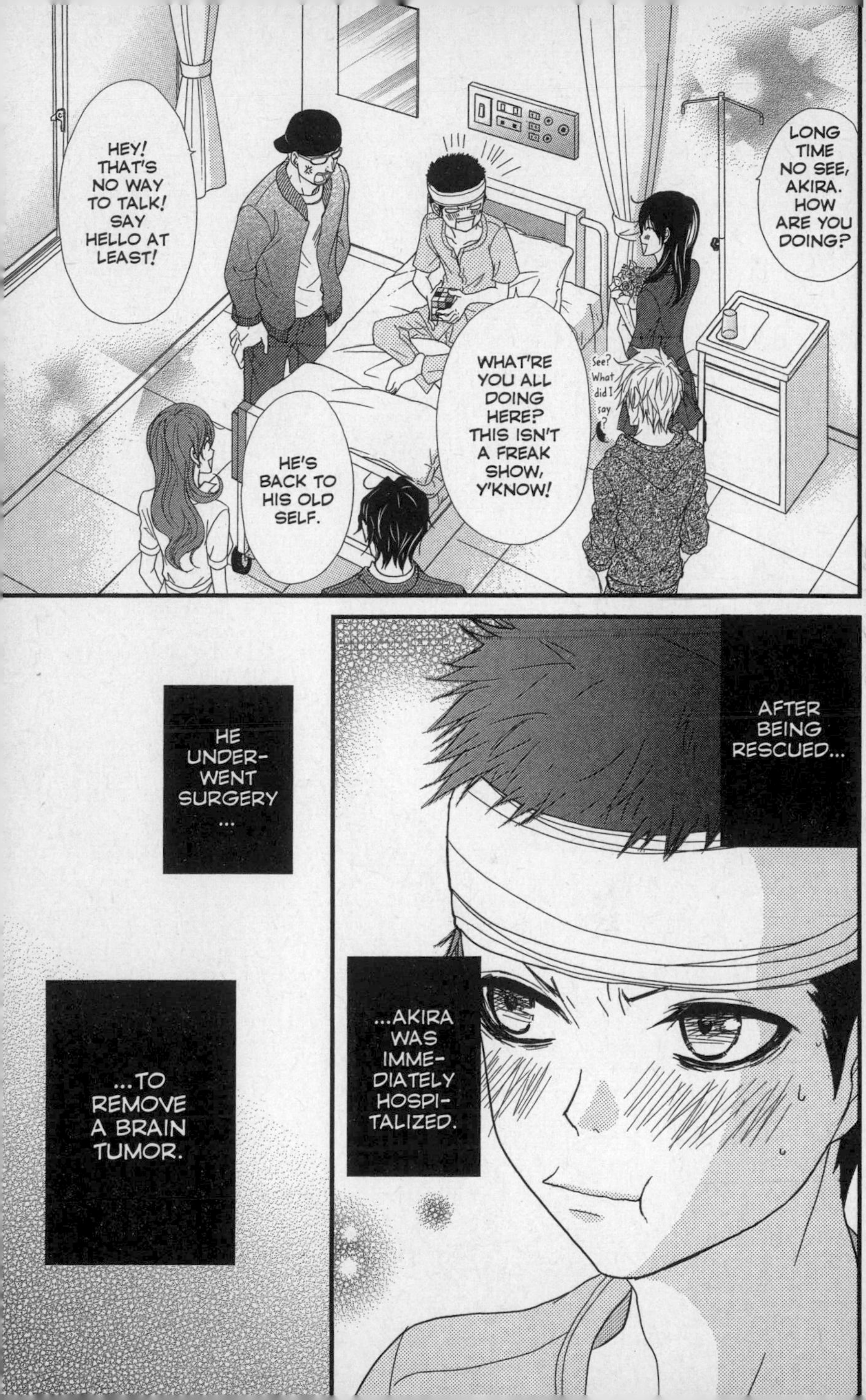
LONG TIME NO SEE, AKIRA. HOW ARE YOU DOING?
WHAT'RE YOU ALL DOING HERE? THIS ISN'T A FREAK SHOW, Y'KNOW!
See? What did I say?
HEY! THAT'S NO WAY TO TALK! SAY HELLO AT LEAST!
HE'S BACK TO HIS OLD SELF.
AFTER BEING RESCUED...
...AKIRA WAS IMMEDIATELY HOSPITALIZED.
HE UNDERWENT SURGERY...
...TO REMOVE A BRAIN TUMOR.

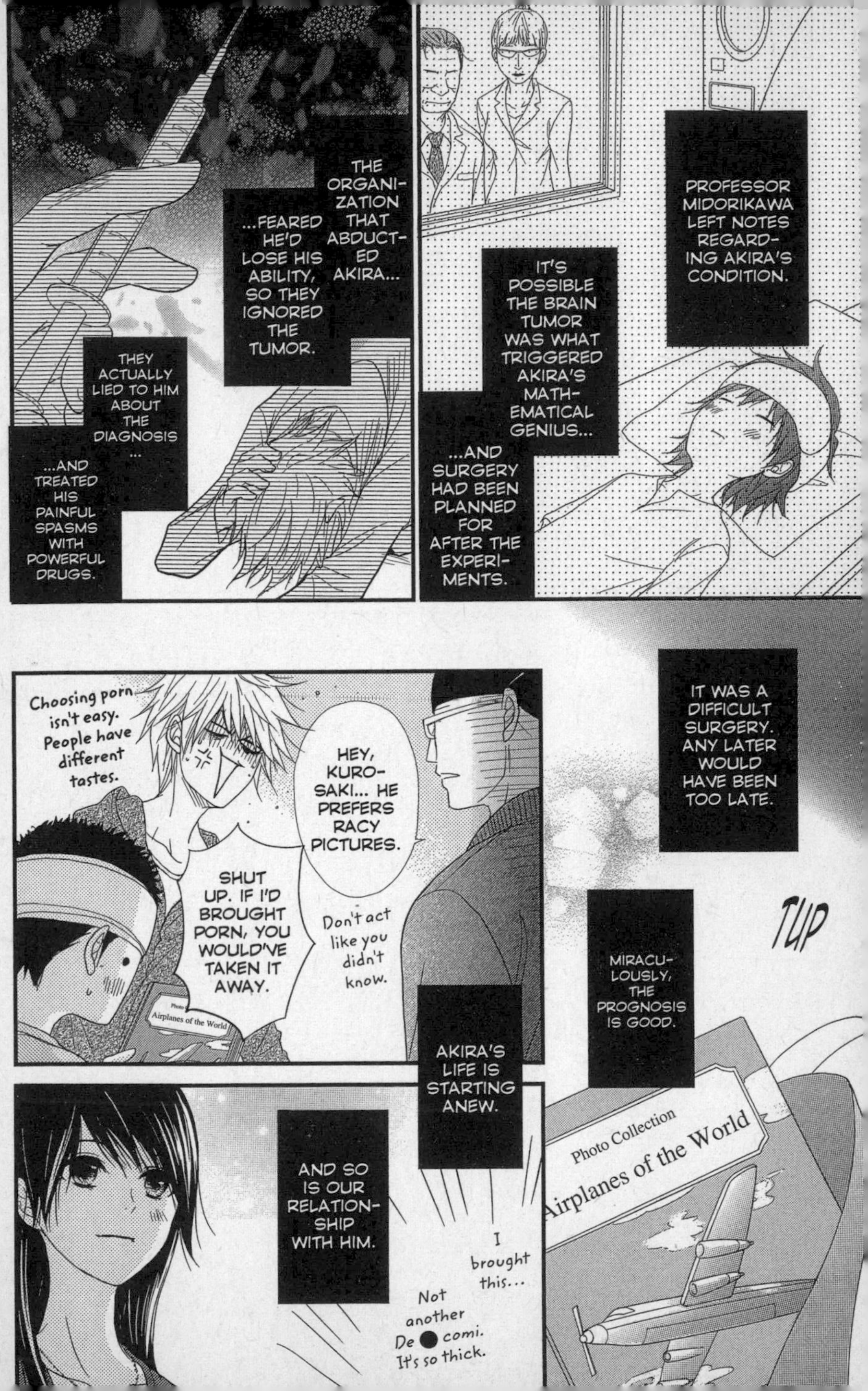
PROFESSOR MIDORIKAWA LEFT NOTES REGARDING AKIRA'S CONDITION.
IT'S POSSIBLE THE BRAIN TUMOR WAS WHAT TRIGGERED AKIRA'S MATHEMATICAL GENIUS...
...AND SURGERY HAD BEEN PLANNED FOR AFTER THE EXPERIMENTS.
THE ORGANIZATION THAT ABDUCTED AKIRA...
...FEARED HE'D LOSE HIS ABILITY, SO THEY IGNORED THE TUMOR.
THEY ACTUALLY LIED TO HIM ABOUT THE DIAGNOSIS...
...AND TREATED HIS PAINFUL SPASMS WITH POWERFUL DRUGS.
IT WAS A DIFFICULT SURGERY. ANY LATER WOULD HAVE BEEN TOO LATE.
TUP
MIRACULOUSLY, THE PROGNOSIS IS GOOD.
AKIRA'S LIFE IS STARTING ANEW.
Photo Collection
Airplanes of the World
HEY, KUROSAKI... HE PREFERS RACY PICTURES.
Choosing porn isn't easy. People have different tastes.
SHUT UP. IF I'D BROUGHT PORN, YOU WOULD'VE TAKEN IT AWAY.
Don't act like you didn't know.
Photo
Airplanes of the World
AND SO IS OUR RELATIONSHIP WITH HIM.
I brought this...
Not another De●comi. It's so thick.

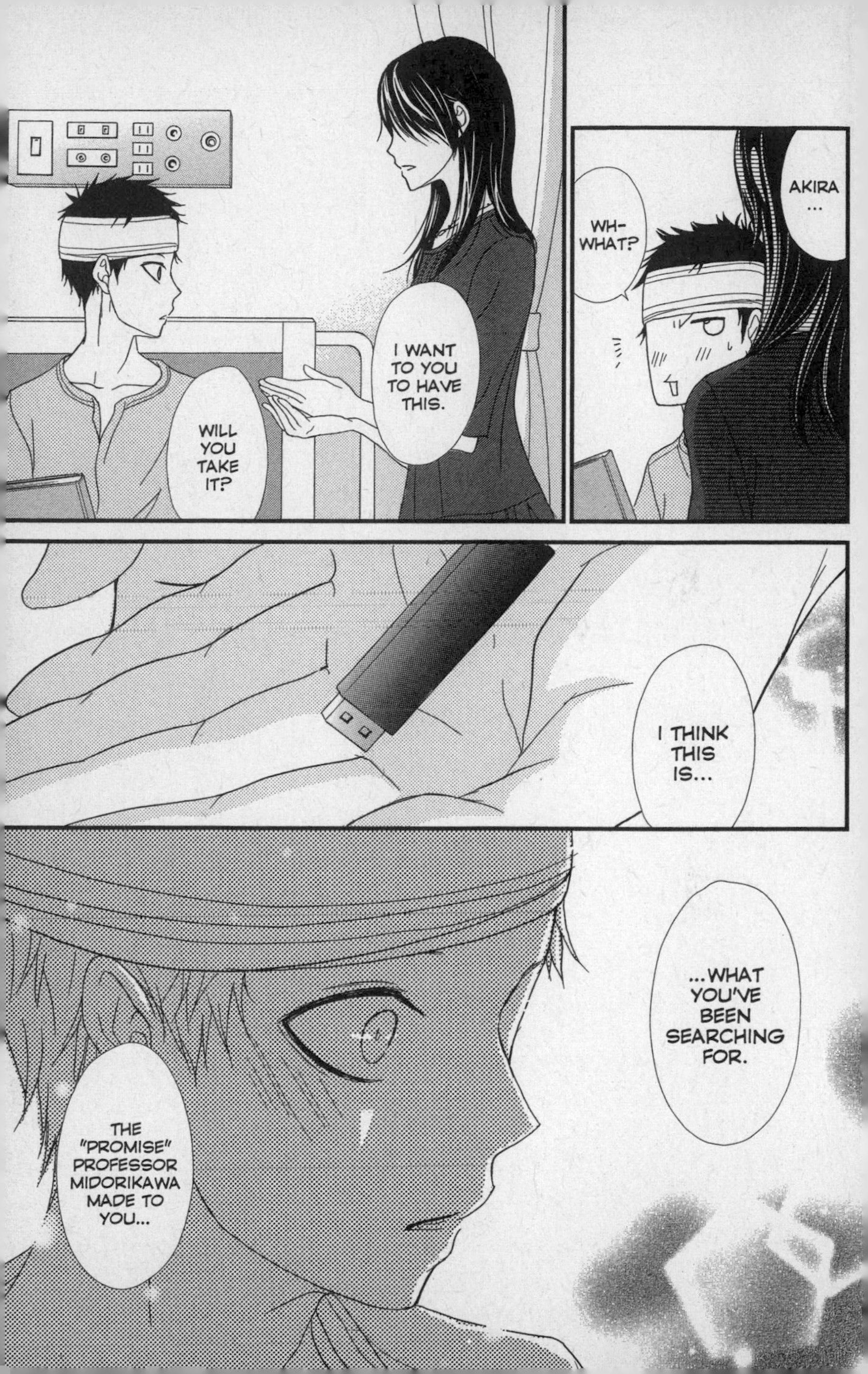
AKIRA...
WH-WHAT?
I WANT TO YOU TO HAVE THIS.
WILL YOU TAKE IT?
I THINK THIS IS...
...WHAT YOU'VE BEEN SEARCHING FOR.
THE "PROMISE" PROFESSOR MIDORIKAWA MADE TO YOU...

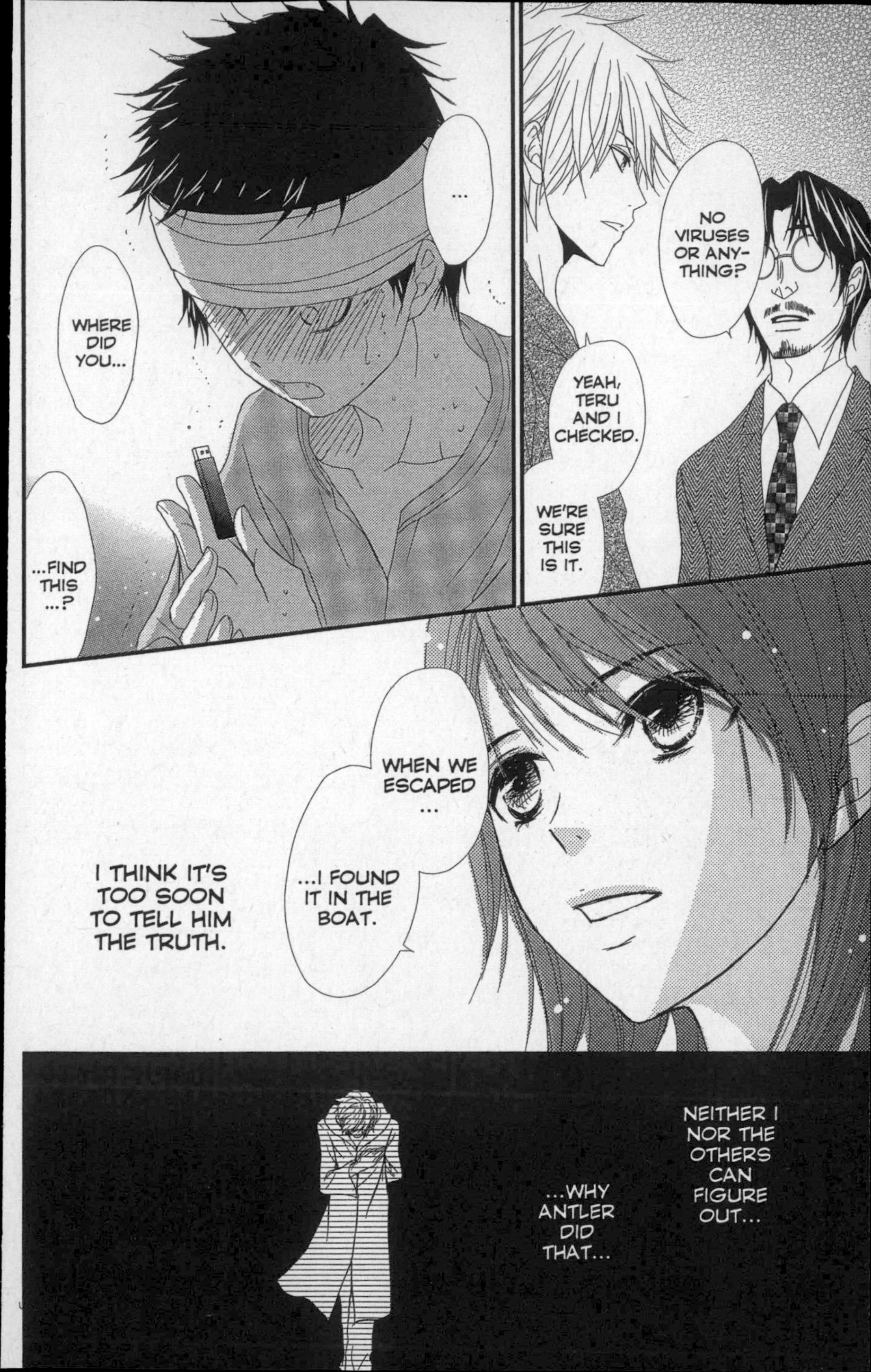
NO VIRUSES OR ANY-THING?
YEAH, TERU AND I CHECKED.
WE'RE SURE THIS IS IT.
...
WHERE DID YOU...
...FIND THIS ...?
WHEN WE ESCAPED ...
...I FOUND IT IN THE BOAT.
I THINK IT'S TOO SOON TO TELL HIM THE TRUTH.
NEITHER I NOR THE OTHERS CAN FIGURE OUT...
...WHY ANTLER DID THAT...

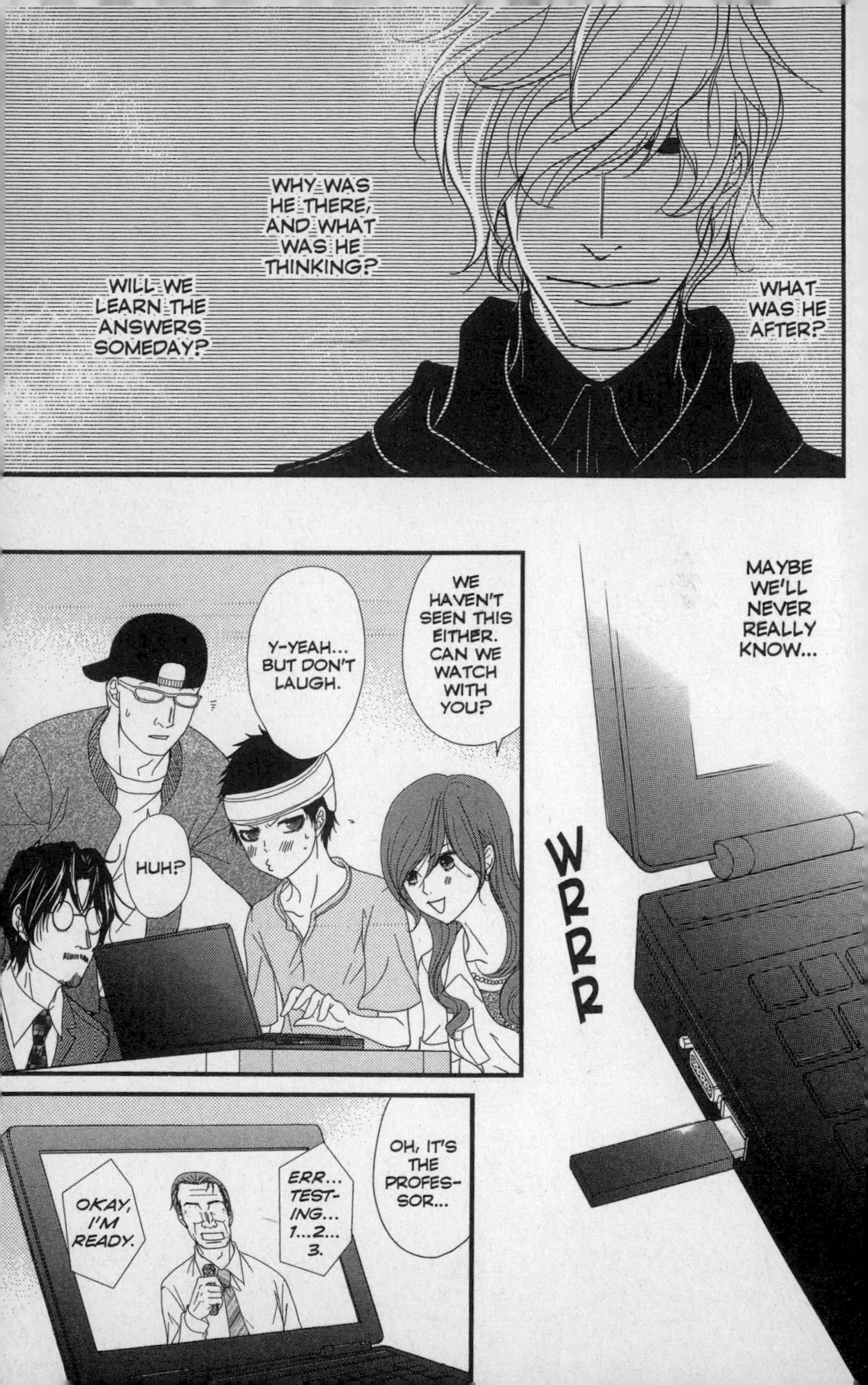
WHAT WAS HE AFTER?
WHY WAS HE THERE, AND WHAT WAS HE THINKING?
WILL WE LEARN THE ANSWERS SOMEDAY?
MAYBE WE'LL NEVER REALLY KNOW...
WRRR
WE HAVEN'T SEEN THIS EITHER. CAN WE WATCH WITH YOU?
Y-YEAH... BUT DON'T LAUGH.
HUH?
OH, IT'S THE PROFES-SOR...
ERR... TEST-ING... 1...2... 3.
OKAY, I'M READY.

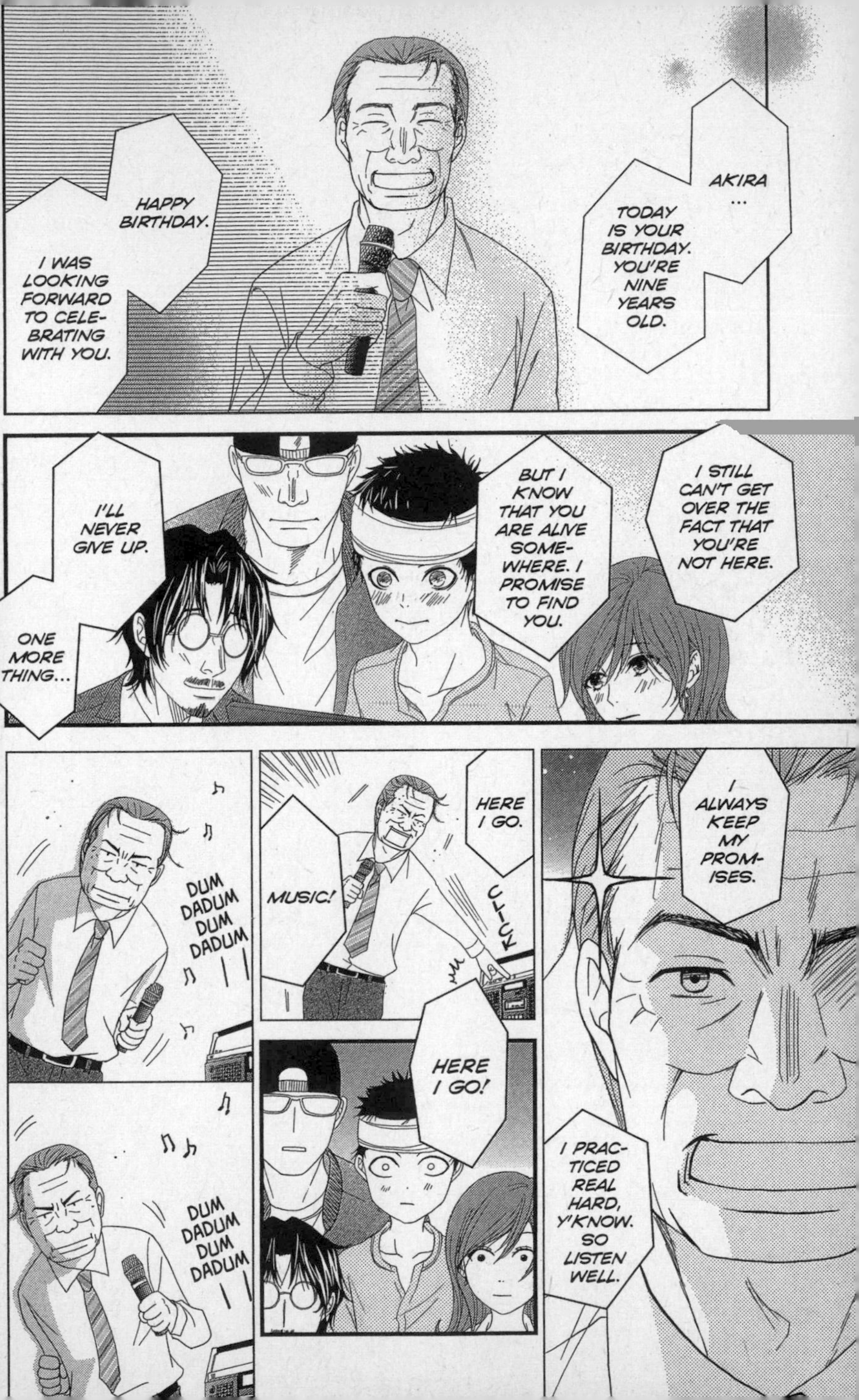
AKIRA ...
TODAY IS YOUR BIRTHDAY. YOU'RE NINE YEARS OLD.
HAPPY BIRTHDAY.
I WAS LOOKING FORWARD TO CELEBRATING WITH YOU.
I STILL CAN'T GET OVER THE FACT THAT YOU'RE NOT HERE.
BUT I KNOW THAT YOU ARE ALIVE SOMEWHERE. I PROMISE TO FIND YOU.
I'LL NEVER GIVE UP.
ONE MORE THING...
I ALWAYS KEEP MY PROMISES.
I PRACTICED REAL HARD, Y'KNOW. SO LISTEN WELL.
HERE I GO.
MUSIC!
CLICK
DUM DADUM DUM DADUM
HERE I GO!
DUM DADUM DUM DADUM

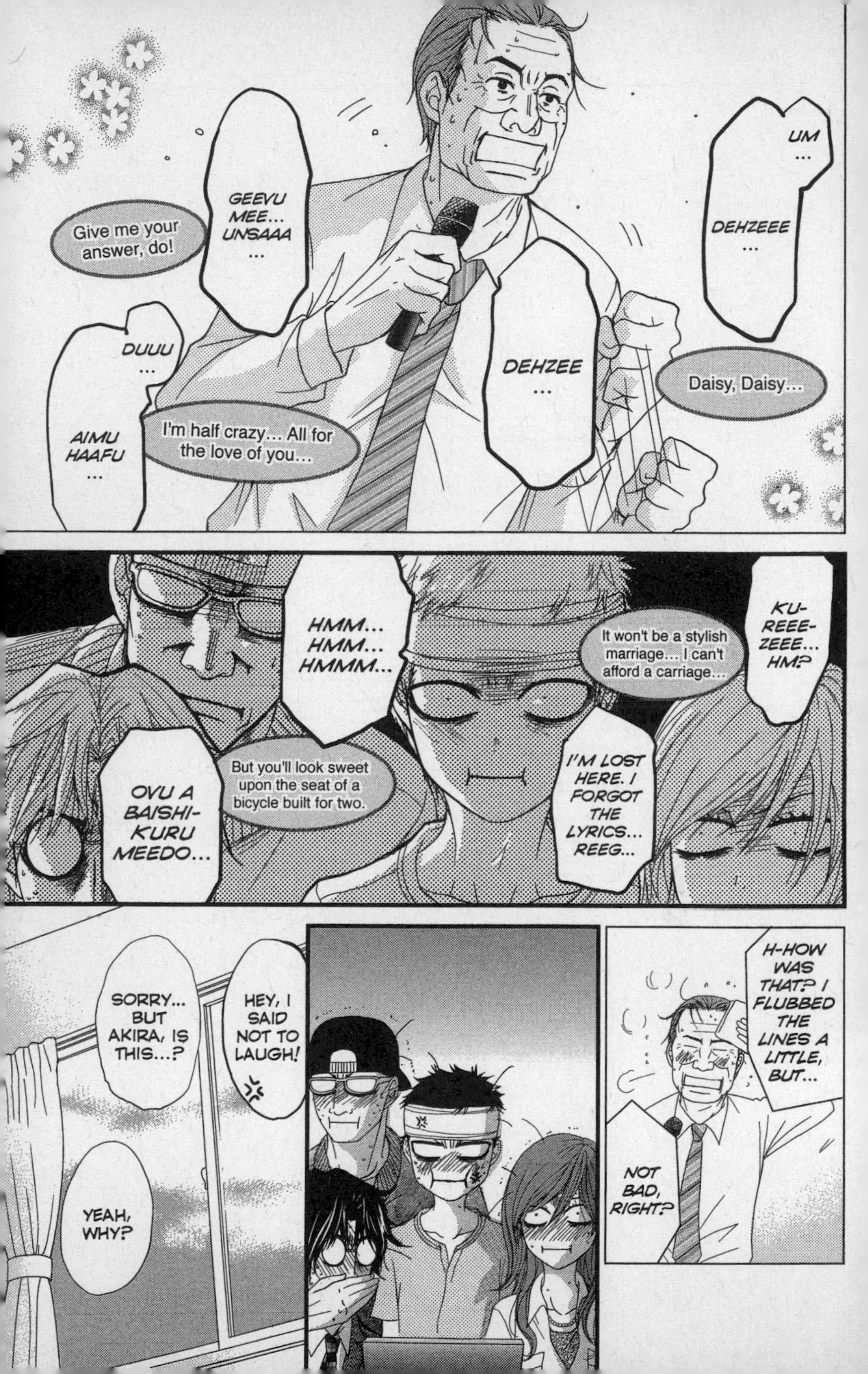

UM... DEHZEEE...
Daisy, Daisy...
DEHZEE...
GEEVU MEE... UNSAAA...
Give me your answer, do!
DUUU... AIMU HAAFU...
I'm half crazy... All for the love of you...
KU-REEE-ZEEE... HM?
It won't be a stylish marriage... I can't afford a carriage...
HMM... HMM... HMMM...
I'M LOST HERE. I FORGOT THE LYRICS... REEG...
But you'll look sweet upon the seat of a bicycle built for two.
OVU A BAISHI-KURU MEEDO...
H-HOW WAS THAT? I FLUBBED THE LINES A LITTLE, BUT...
NOT BAD, RIGHT?
HEY, I SAID NOT TO LAUGH!
SORRY... BUT AKIRA, IS THIS...?
YEAH, WHY?

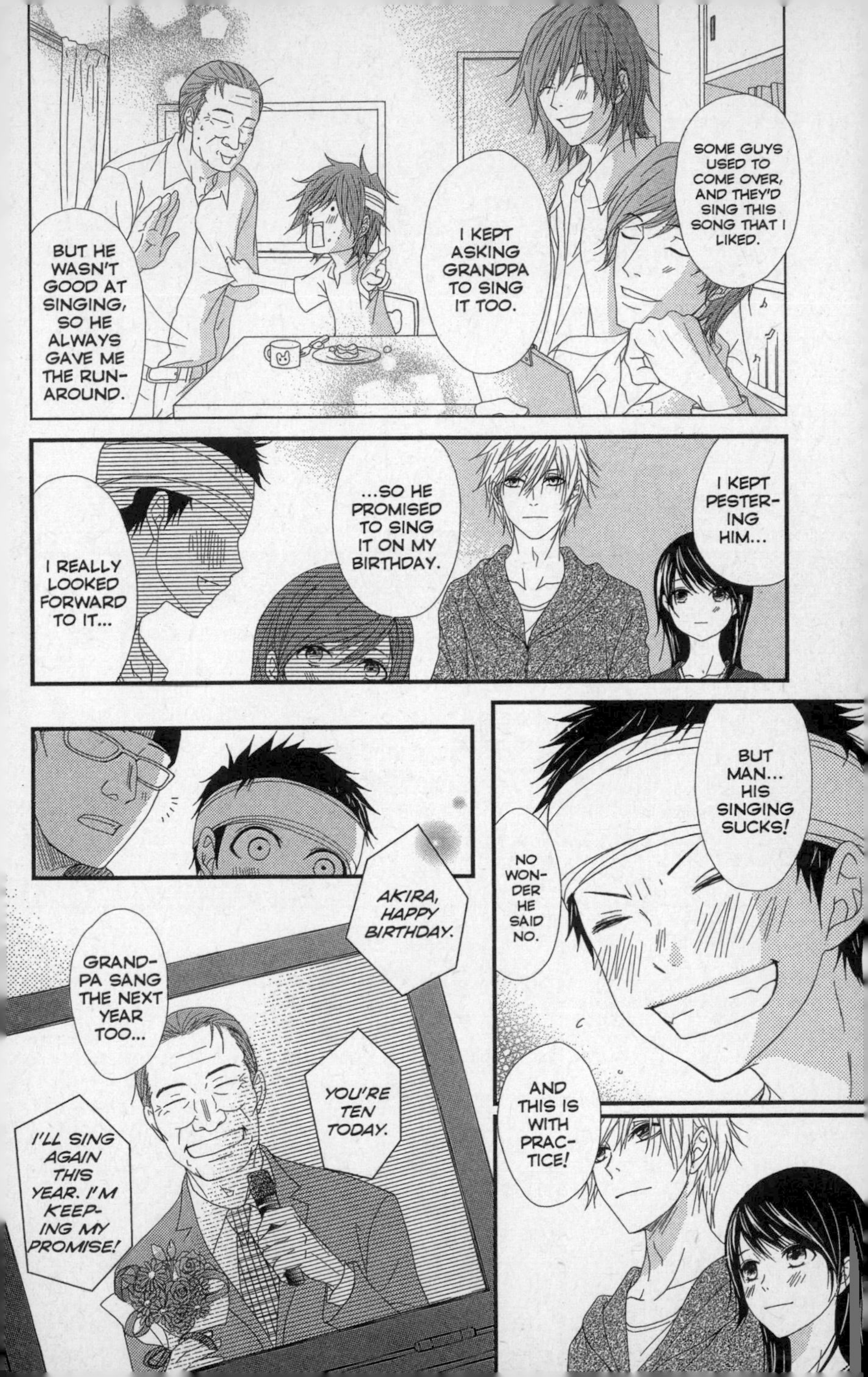
SOME GUYS USED TO COME OVER, AND THEY'D SING THIS SONG THAT I LIKED.
I KEPT ASKING GRANDPA TO SING IT TOO.
BUT HE WASN'T GOOD AT SINGING, SO HE ALWAYS GAVE ME THE RUN-AROUND.
I KEPT PESTER-ING HIM...
...SO HE PROMISED TO SING IT ON MY BIRTHDAY.
I REALLY LOOKED FORWARD TO IT...
AKIRA, HAPPY BIRTHDAY.
YOU'RE TEN TODAY.
GRAND-PA SANG THE NEXT YEAR TOO...
I'LL SING AGAIN THIS YEAR. I'M KEEP-ING MY PROMISE!
BUT MAN... HIS SINGING SUCKS!
NO WON-DER HE SAID NO.
AND THIS IS WITH PRAC-TICE!

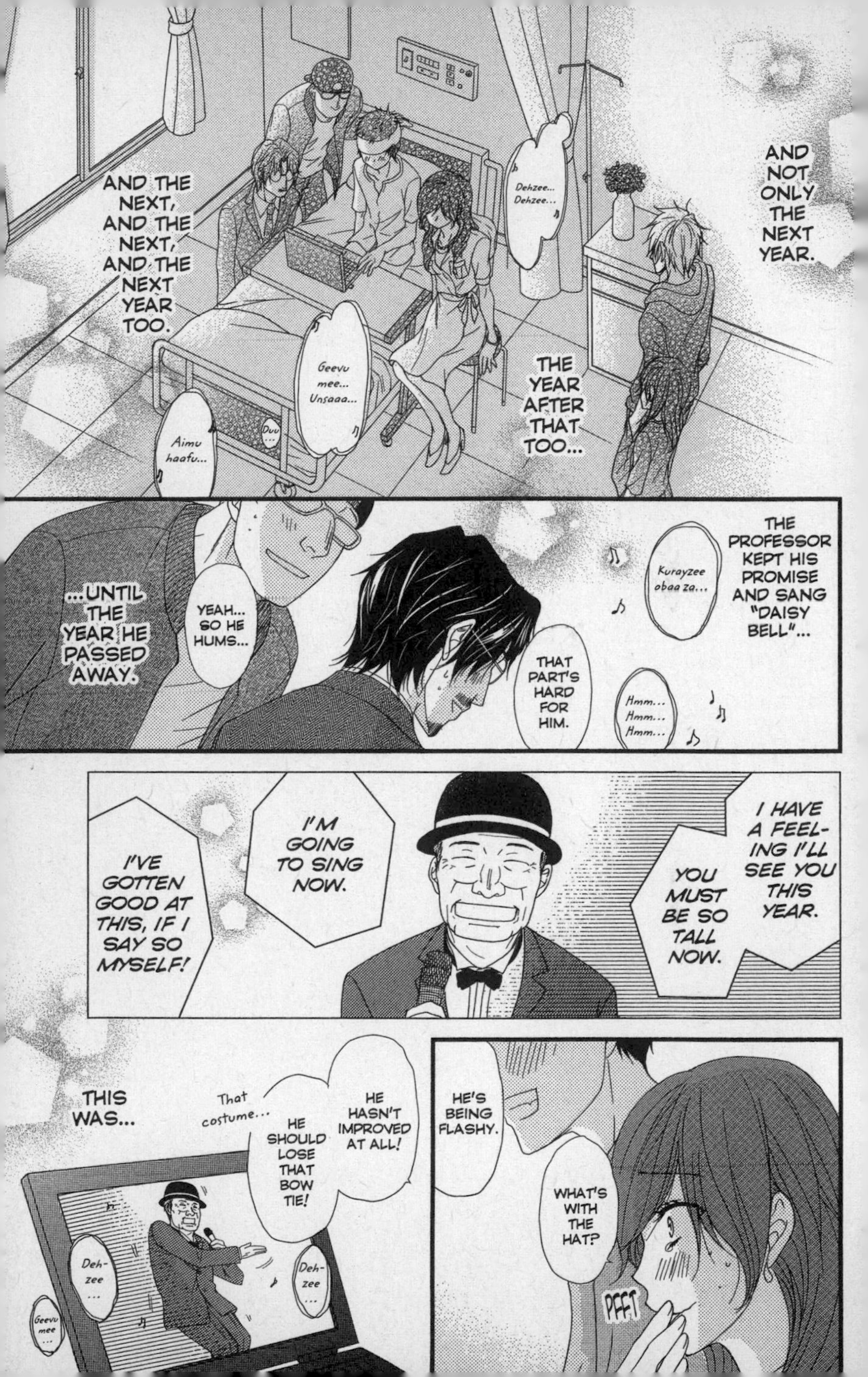
AND NOT ONLY THE NEXT YEAR.
THE YEAR AFTER THAT TOO...
Dehzee... Dehzee...
AND THE NEXT, AND THE NEXT, AND THE NEXT YEAR TOO.
Geevu mee... Unsaaa...
Duu...
Aimu haafu...
THE PROFESSOR KEPT HIS PROMISE AND SANG "DAISY BELL"...
Kurayzee obaa za...
Hmm... Hmm... Hmm...
THAT PART'S HARD FOR HIM.
YEAH... SO HE HUMS...
...UNTIL THE YEAR HE PASSED AWAY.
I HAVE A FEELING I'LL SEE YOU THIS YEAR.
YOU MUST BE SO TALL NOW.
I'M GOING TO SING NOW.
I'VE GOTTEN GOOD AT THIS, IF I SAY SO MYSELF!
HE'S BEING FLASHY.
WHAT'S WITH THE HAT?
PFFT
HE HASN'T IMPROVED AT ALL!
HE SHOULD LOSE THAT BOW TIE!
That costume...
THIS WAS...
Deh-zee...
Deh-zee...
Geevu mee...

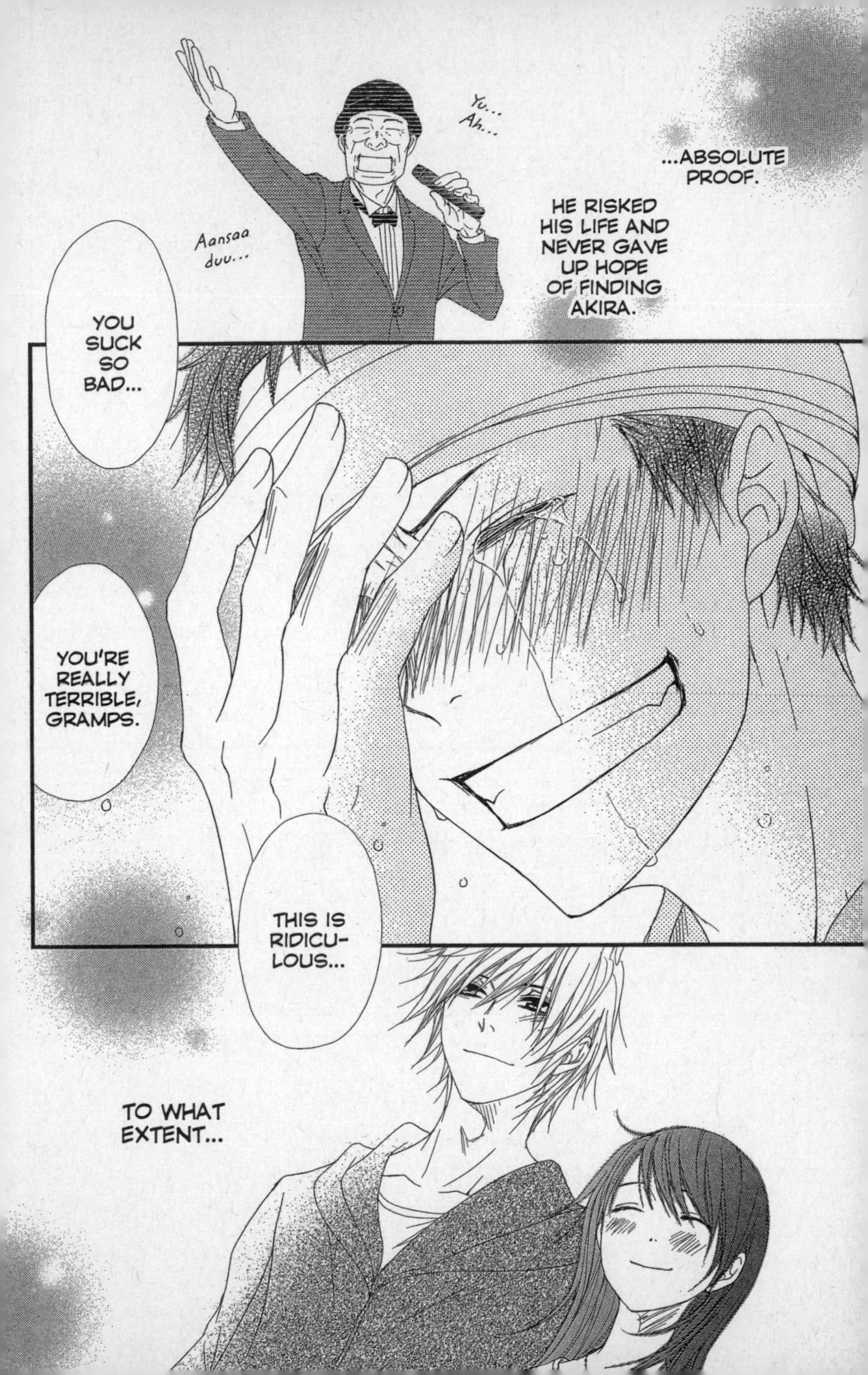
...ABSOLUTE PROOF.
HE RISKED HIS LIFE AND NEVER GAVE UP HOPE OF FINDING AKIRA.
Yu... Ah...
Aansaa duu...
YOU SUCK SO BAD...
YOU'RE REALLY TERRIBLE, GRAMPS.
THIS IS RIDICULOUS...
TO WHAT EXTENT...

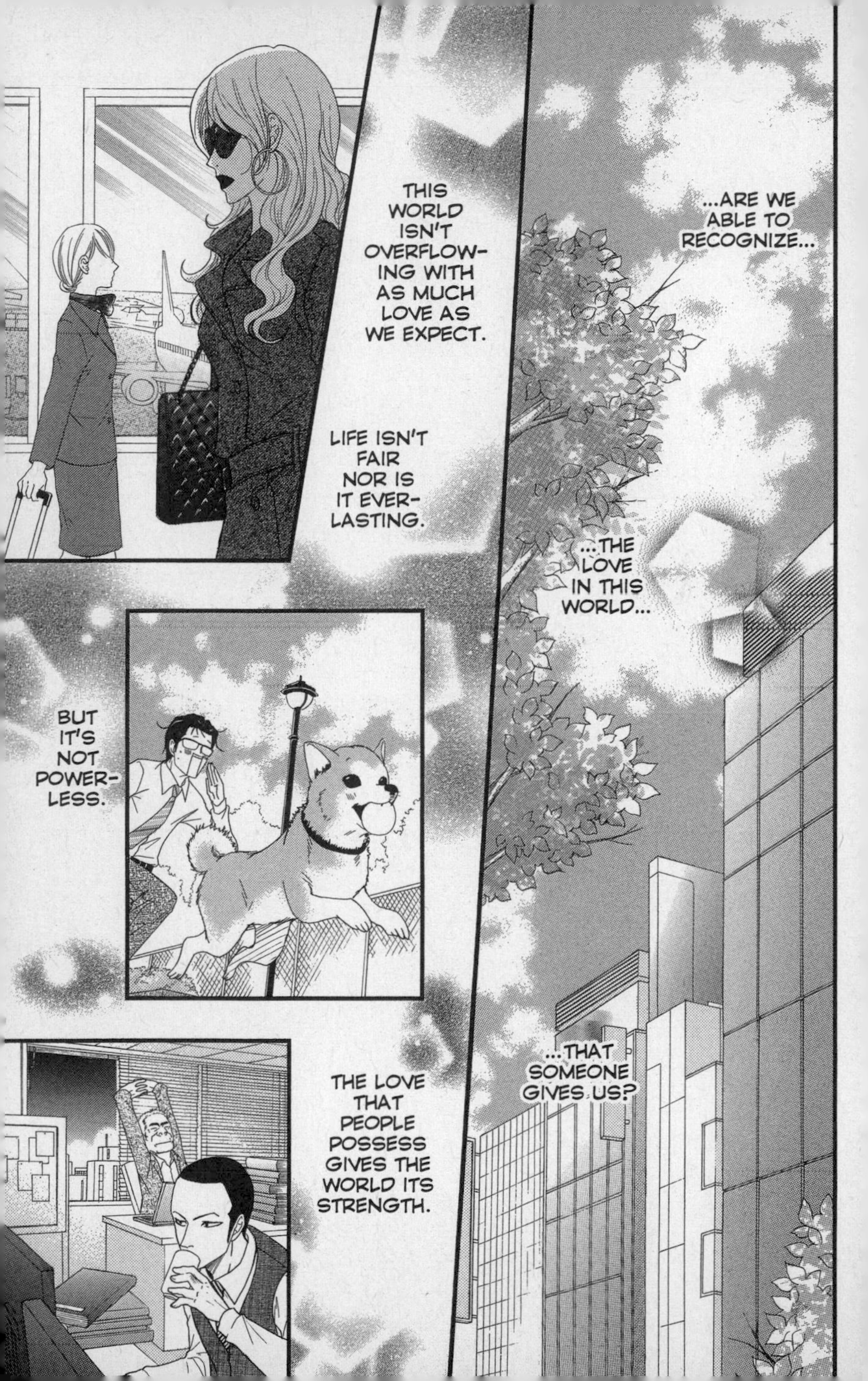
THIS WORLD ISN'T OVERFLOWING WITH AS MUCH LOVE AS WE EXPECT.
LIFE ISN'T FAIR NOR IS IT EVERLASTING.
BUT IT'S NOT POWERLESS.
THE LOVE THAT PEOPLE POSSESS GIVES THE WORLD ITS STRENGTH.
...ARE WE ABLE TO RECOGNIZE...
...THE LOVE IN THIS WORLD...
...THAT SOMEONE GIVES US?

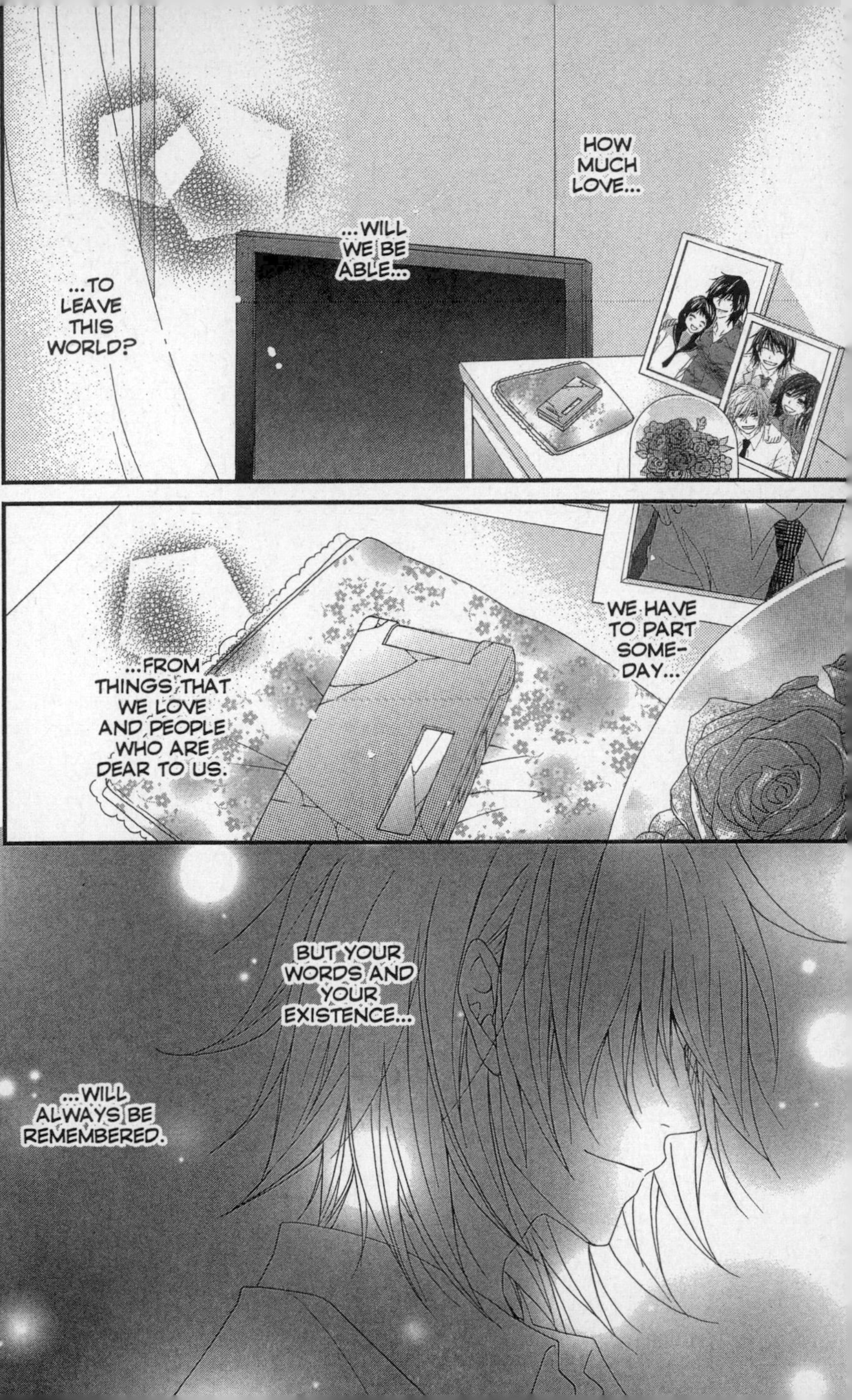
HOW MUCH LOVE...
...WILL WE BE ABLE...
...TO LEAVE THIS WORLD?
WE HAVE TO PART SOME-DAY...
...FROM THINGS THAT WE LOVE AND PEOPLE WHO ARE DEAR TO US.
BUT YOUR WORDS AND YOUR EXISTENCE...
...WILL ALWAYS BE REMEMBERED.

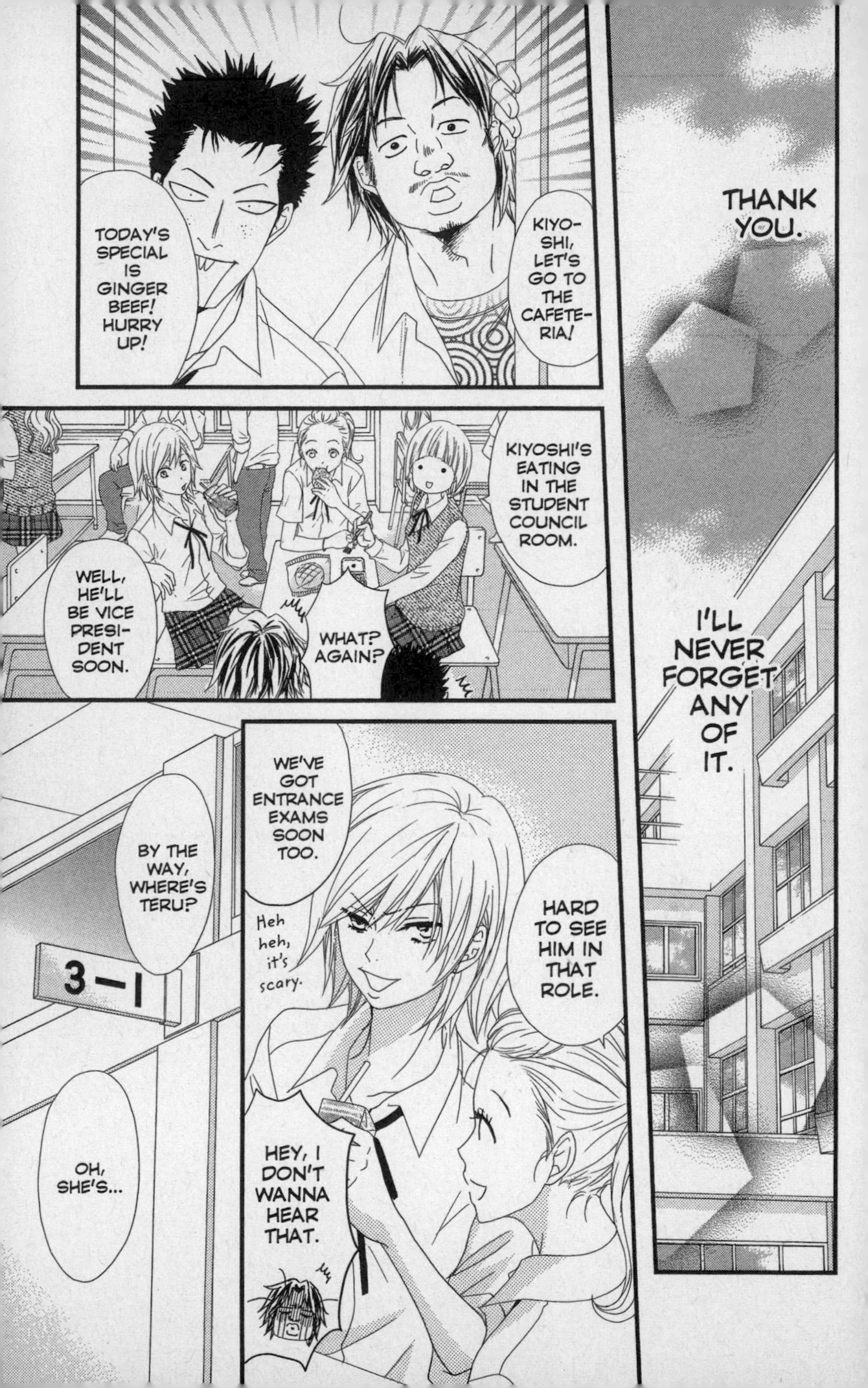
THANK YOU.
I'LL NEVER FORGET ANY OF IT.
KIYO-SHI, LET'S GO TO THE CAFETE-RIA!
TODAY'S SPECIAL IS GINGER BEEF! HURRY UP!
KIYOSHI'S EATING IN THE STUDENT COUNCIL ROOM.
WHAT? AGAIN?
WELL, HE'LL BE VICE PRESI-DENT SOON.
HARD TO SEE HIM IN THAT ROLE.
WE'VE GOT ENTRANCE EXAMS SOON TOO.
Heh heh, it's scary.
HEY, I DON'T WANNA HEAR THAT.
3-1
BY THE WAY, WHERE'S TERU?
OH, SHE'S...

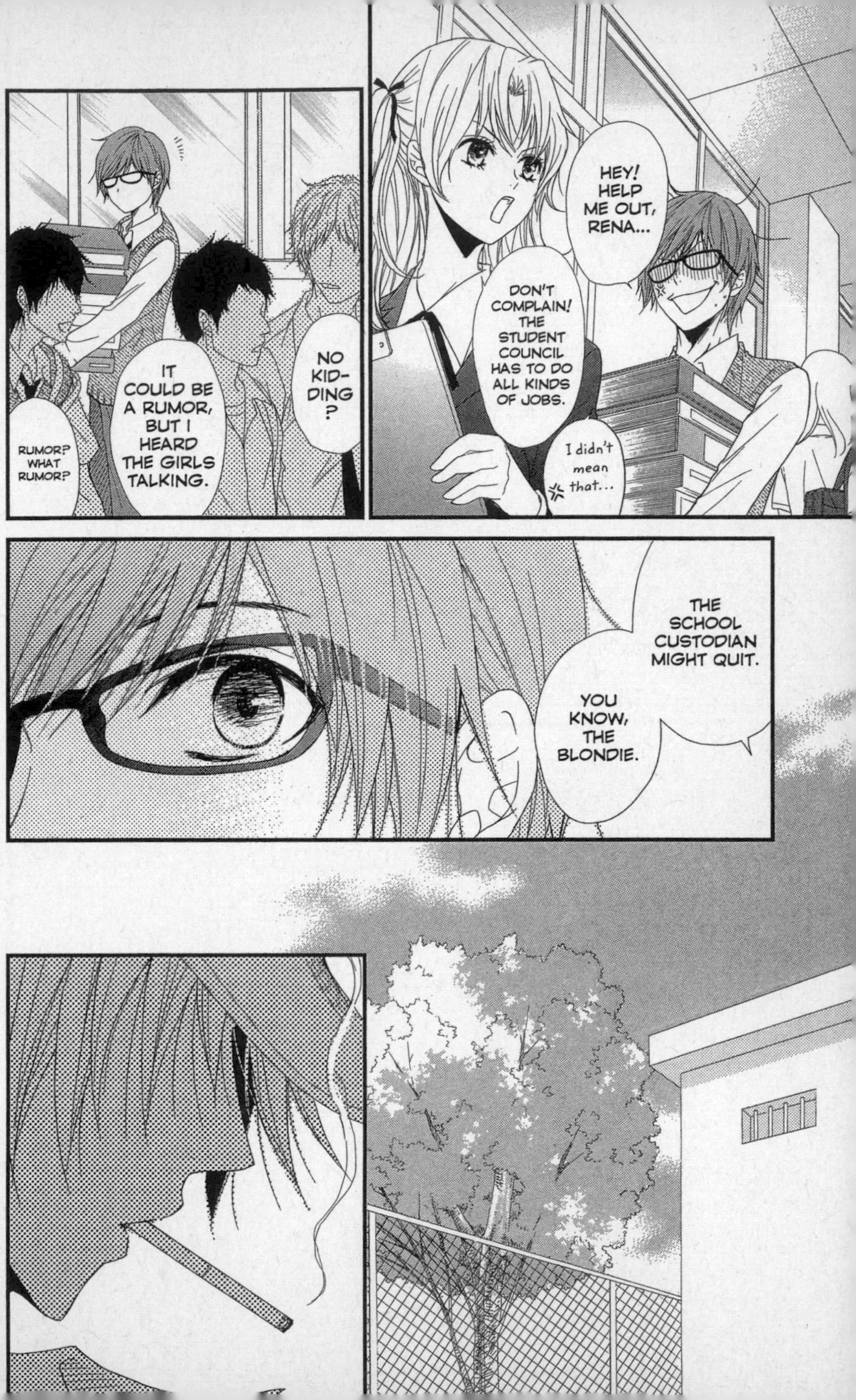
HEY! HELP ME OUT, RENA...
DON'T COMPLAIN! THE STUDENT COUNCIL HAS TO DO ALL KINDS OF JOBS.
I didn't mean that...
NO KID-DING?
IT COULD BE A RUMOR, BUT I HEARD THE GIRLS TALKING.
RUMOR? WHAT RUMOR?
THE SCHOOL CUSTODIAN MIGHT QUIT.
YOU KNOW, THE BLONDIE.

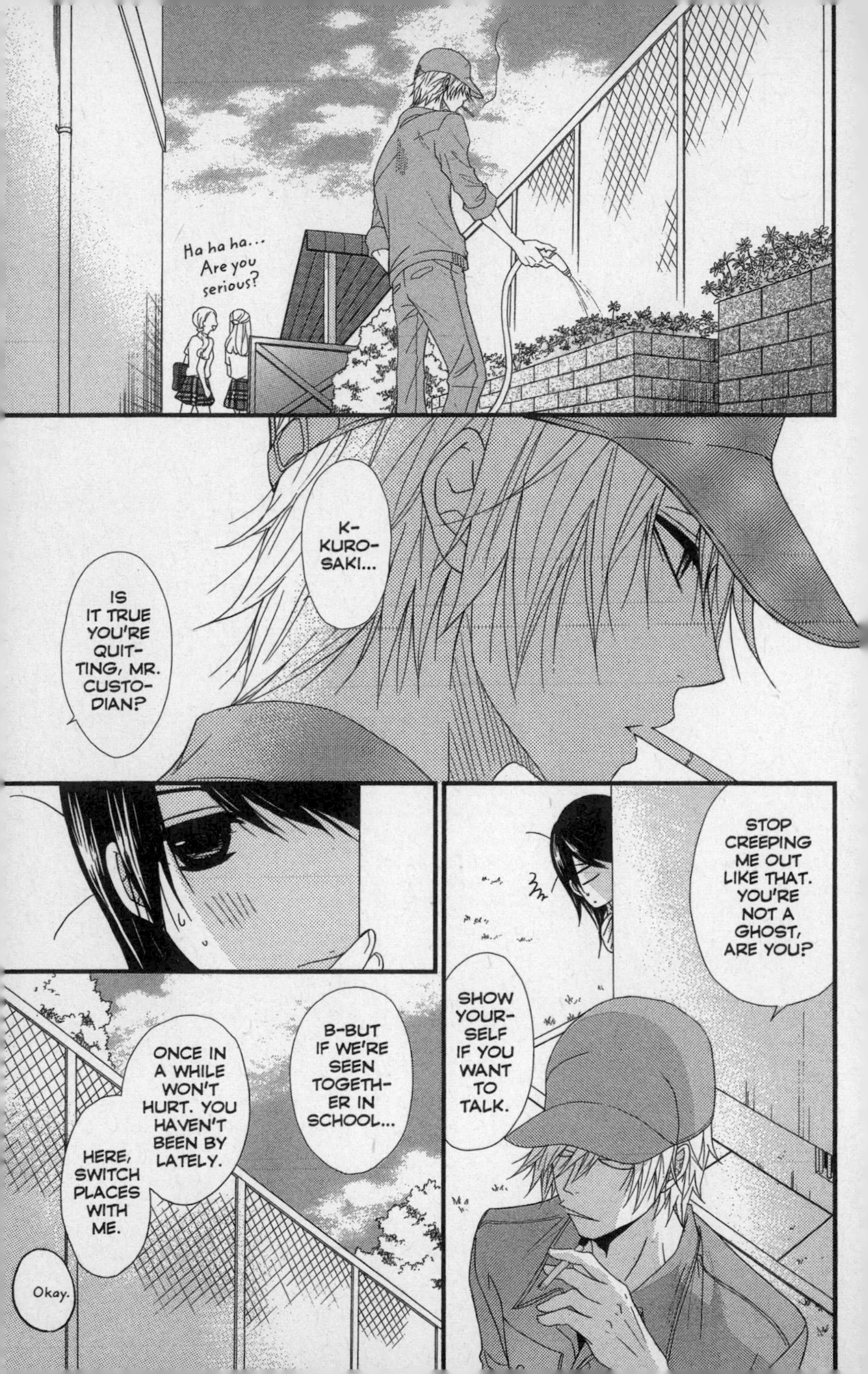
Ha ha ha... Are you serious?
K-KURO-SAKI...
IS IT TRUE YOU'RE QUIT-TING, MR. CUSTO-DIAN?
STOP CREEPING ME OUT LIKE THAT. YOU'RE NOT A GHOST, ARE YOU?
SHOW YOUR-SELF IF YOU WANT TO TALK.
B-BUT IF WE'RE SEEN TOGETH-ER IN SCHOOL...
ONCE IN A WHILE WON'T HURT. YOU HAVEN'T BEEN BY LATELY.
HERE, SWITCH PLACES WITH ME.
Okay.

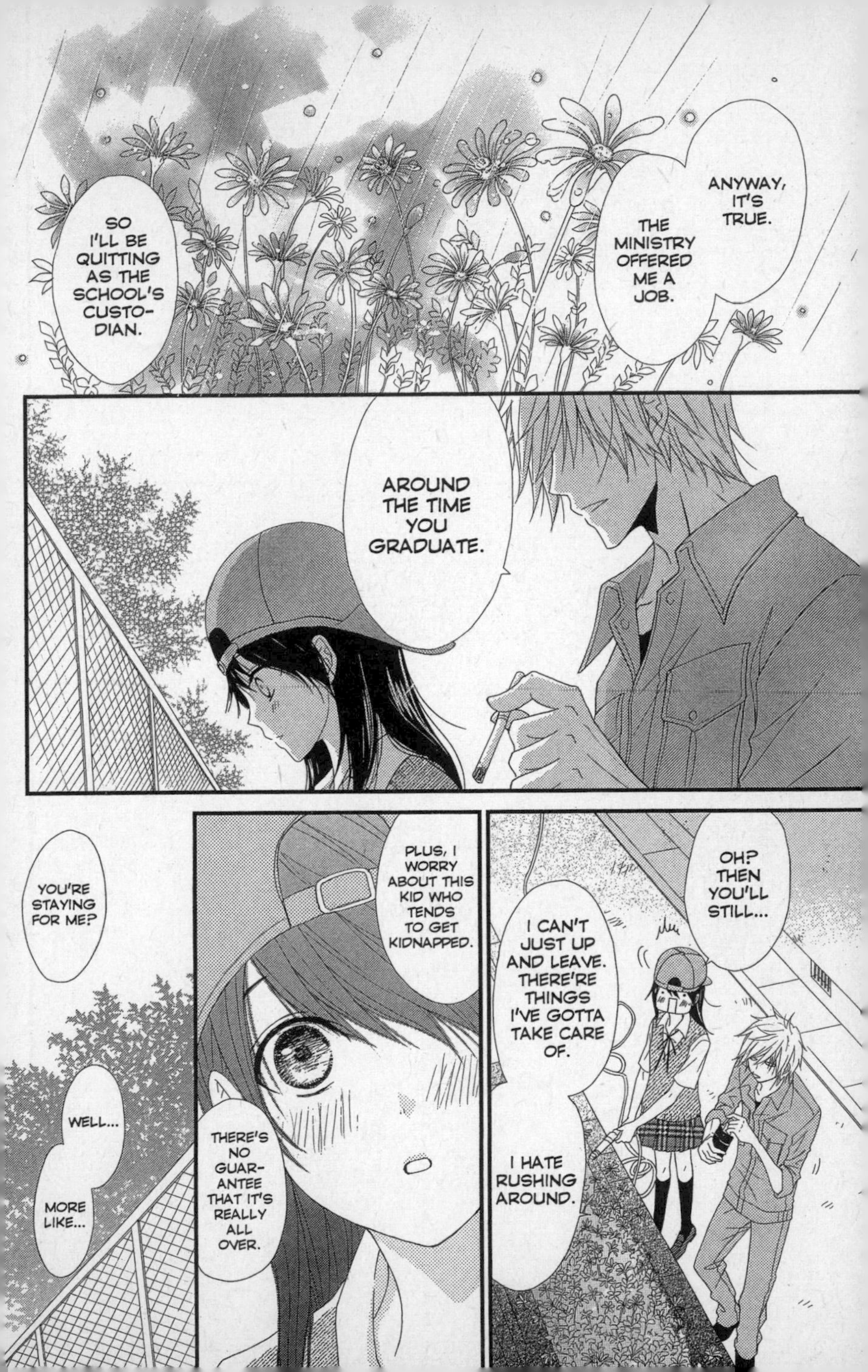
ANYWAY, IT'S TRUE.
THE MINISTRY OFFERED ME A JOB.
SO I'LL BE QUITTING AS THE SCHOOL'S CUSTO-DIAN.
AROUND THE TIME YOU GRADUATE.
OH? THEN YOU'LL STILL...
I CAN'T JUST UP AND LEAVE. THERE'RE THINGS I'VE GOTTA TAKE CARE OF.
I HATE RUSHING AROUND.
PLUS, I WORRY ABOUT THIS KID WHO TENDS TO GET KIDNAPPED.
THERE'S NO GUAR-ANTEE THAT IT'S REALLY ALL OVER.
YOU'RE STAYING FOR ME?
WELL...
MORE LIKE...

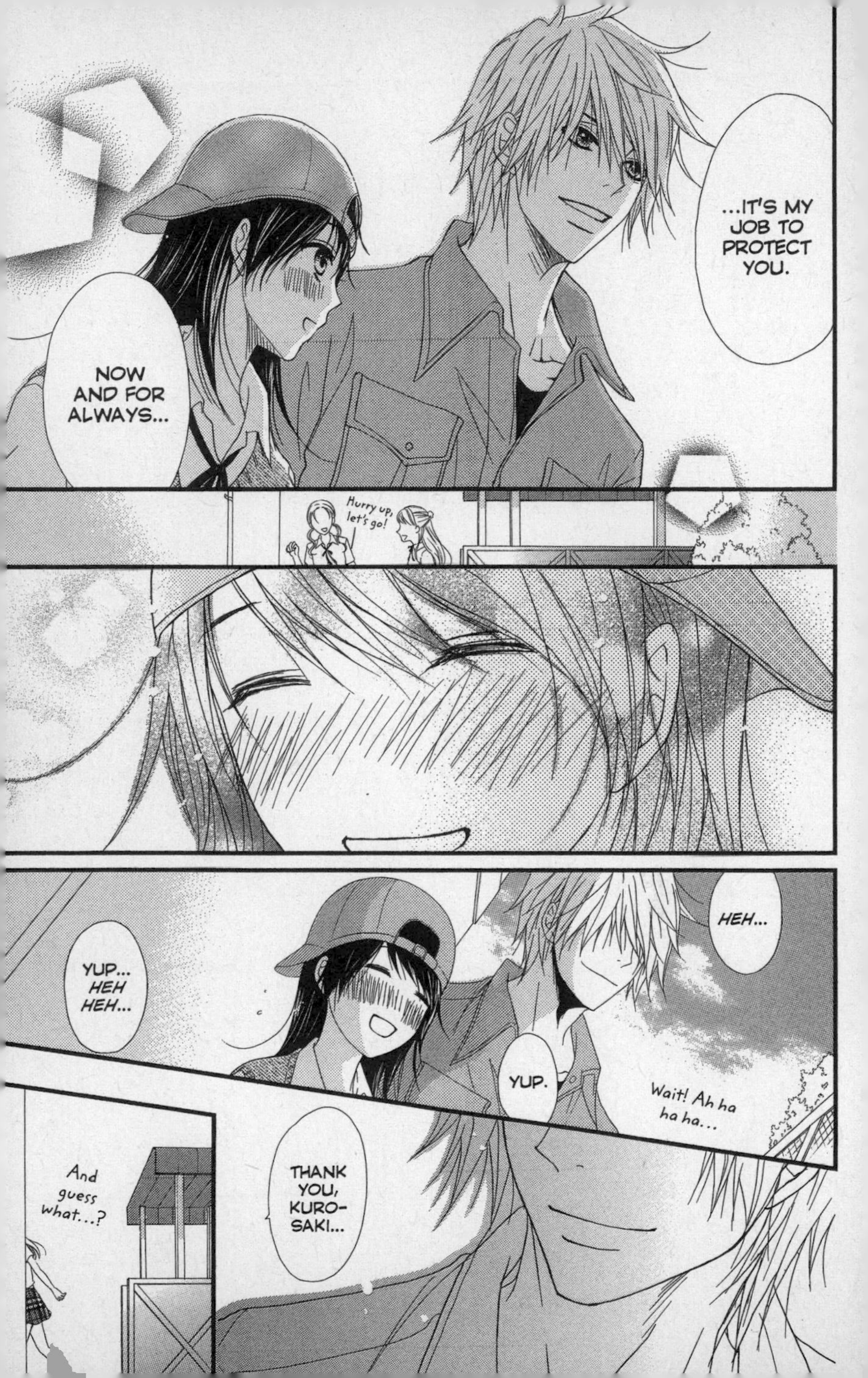
...IT'S MY JOB TO PROTECT YOU.
NOW AND FOR ALWAYS...
Hurry up, let's go!
HEH...
YUP... HEH HEH...
YUP.
Wait! Ah ha ha ha...
THANK YOU, KURO-SAKI...
And guess what...?

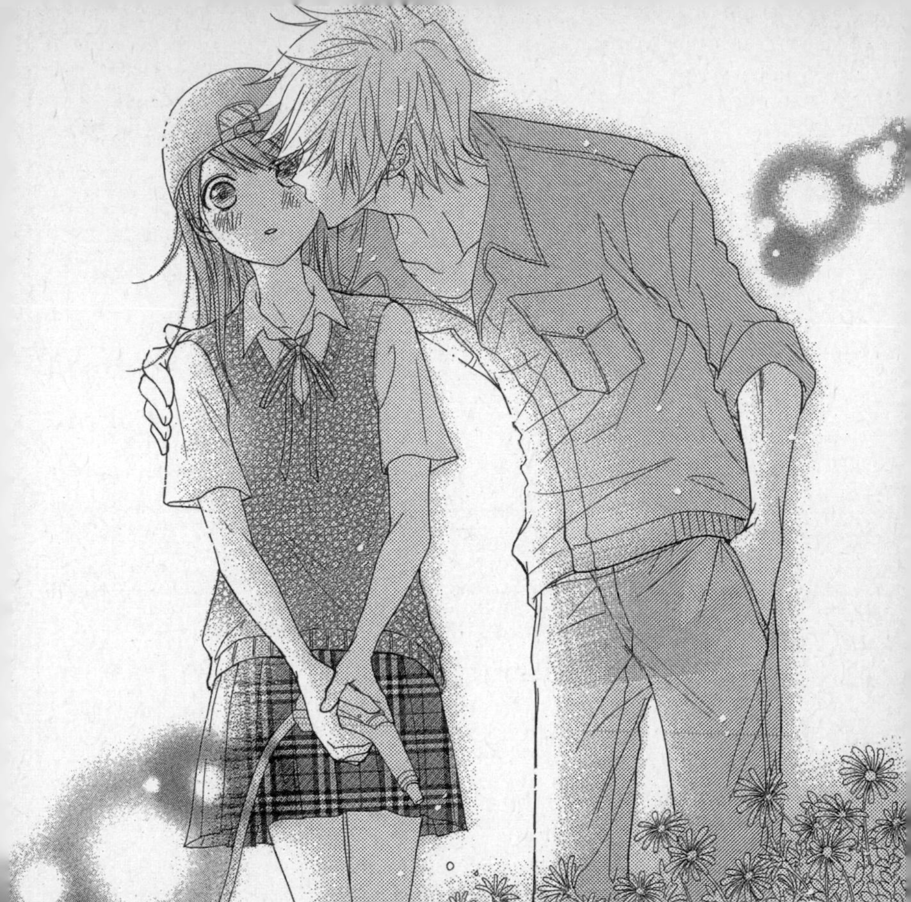

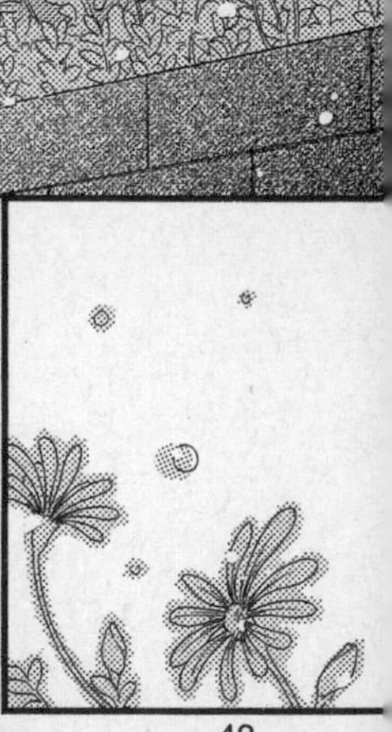

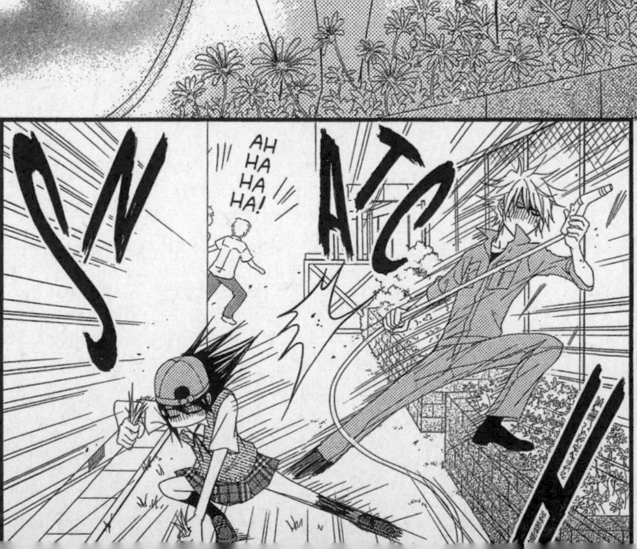
AH HA HA HA!
SNATCH

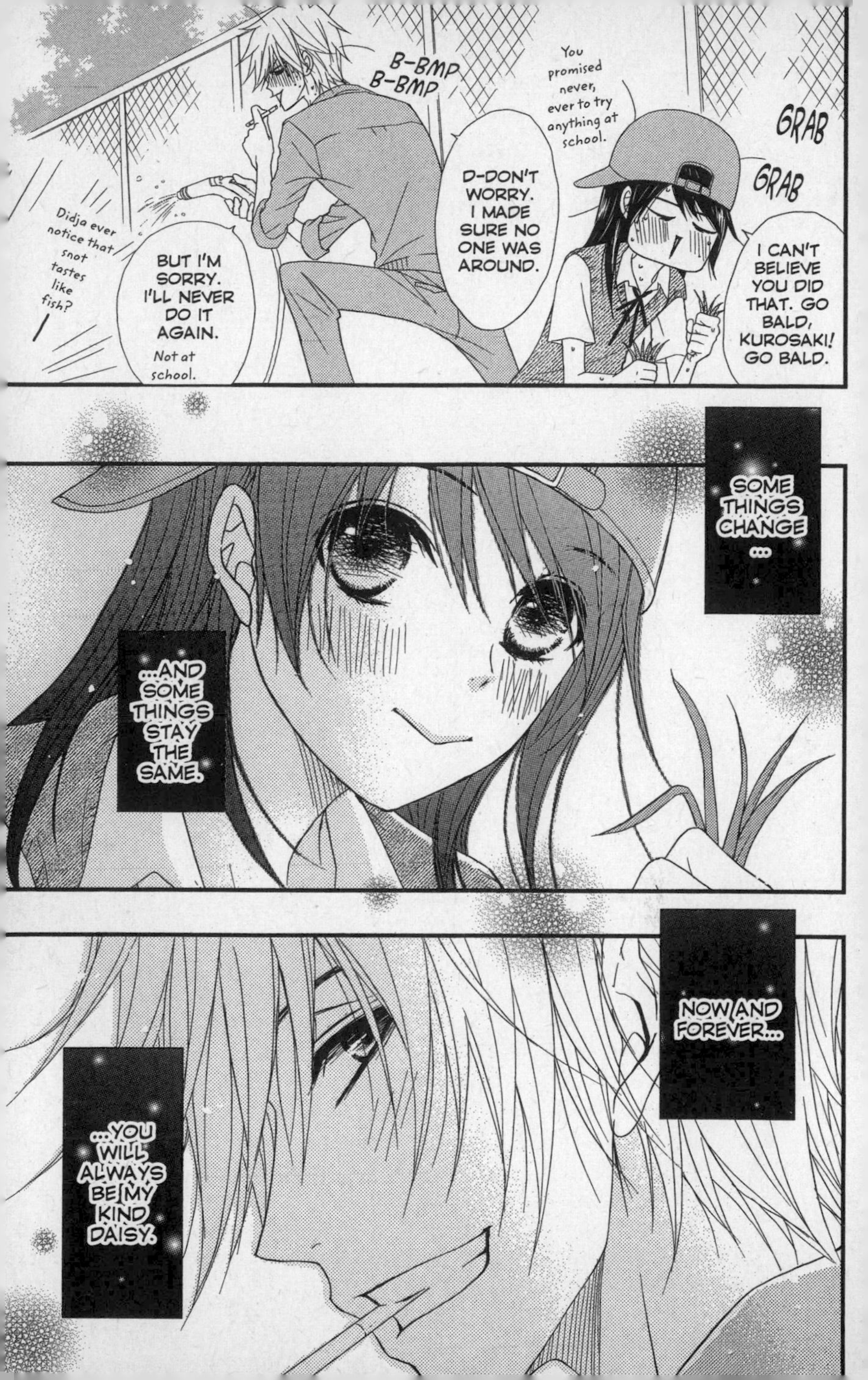
GRAB
GRAB
I CAN'T BELIEVE YOU DID THAT. GO BALD, KUROSAKI! GO BALD.
You promised never, ever to try anything at school.
D-DON'T WORRY. I MADE SURE NO ONE WAS AROUND.
B-BMP B-BMP
BUT I'M SORRY. I'LL NEVER DO IT AGAIN.
Not at school.
Didja ever notice that snot tastes like fish?
SOME THINGS CHANGE...
...AND SOME THINGS STAY THE SAME.
NOW AND FOREVER...
...YOU WILL ALWAYS BE MY KIND DAISY.

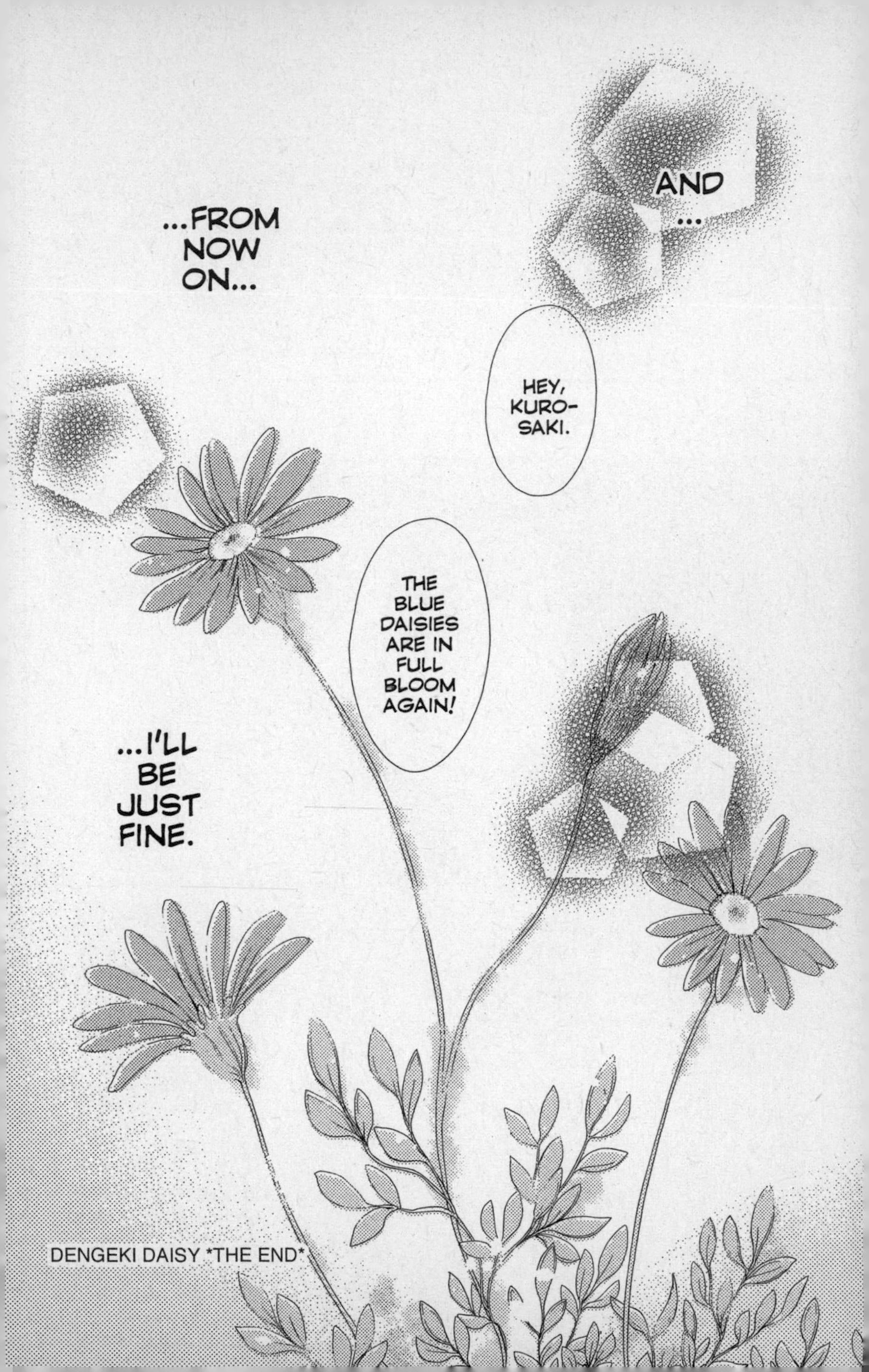
AND ...
...FROM NOW ON...
HEY, KURO-SAKI.
THE BLUE DAISIES ARE IN FULL BLOOM AGAIN!
...I'LL BE JUST FINE.
DENGEKI DAISY *THE END*

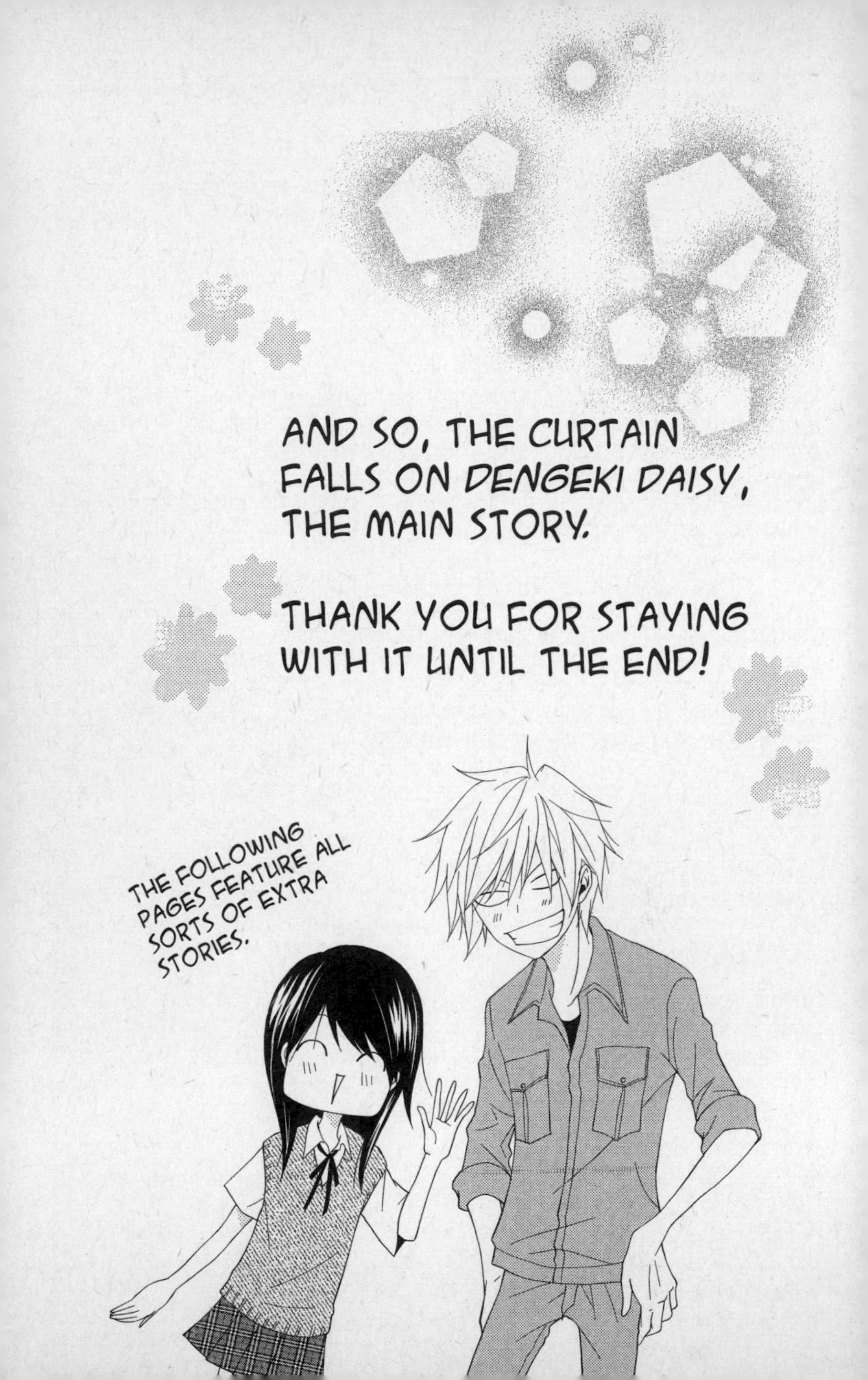
AND SO, THE CURTAIN FALLS ON *DENGEKI DAISY*, THE MAIN STORY.
THANK YOU FOR STAYING WITH IT UNTIL THE END!
THE FOLLOWING PAGES FEATURE ALL SORTS OF EXTRA STORIES.

OKAY... WHAT FOLLOWS ARE EXTRA FEATURES FOR *DENGEKI DAISY*.

THESE TWO TWO-PARTERS WERE WRITTEN QUITE SOME TIME AGO, AND I'VE BEEN WAITING TO INCLUDE THEM IN A GRAPHIC NOVEL.

THE FIRST 8-PAGE EXTRA CASTS A LIGHT ON THE DELICATE RELATIONSHIP BETWEEN KUROSAKI AND TERU AFTER KUROSAKI RETURNS FROM HIS SELF-IMPOSED ABSENCE, BEFORE HE CON-FESSES HIS LOVE TO HER. I HAD FEEDBACK (FROM MY ASSIS-TANT AND EDITOR) THAT PERHAPS THE SCREENTONE ON THE CHARACTERS IN A CERTAIN PANEL WAS TOO DARK. OH WELL, IT CAN'T BE HELPED. AFTER ALL, *DENGEKI DAISY* IS A TAME SHOJO MANGA.

THE TWO-PAGE NEW YEAR EXTRA IS ABOUT TERU'S NEW YEAR DURING HER SECOND YEAR IN HIGH SCHOOL. I GUESS THE TIMELINE WOULD BE AROUND THE DAY AFTER THE NEW YEAR EXTRA FEATURED IN VOLUME 6. IT'S ONLY TWO PAGES LONG, BUT I SEEM TO RECALL HAVING A HARD TIME WITH THE LINES. I THINK IT TURNED OUT NICELY THOUGH.

THE TWO OTHER EXTRAS THAT FOLLOW WERE DONE AFTER THE SERIES ENDED.

THESE ARE LITTLE EPISODES ABOUT SOICHIRO'S LIFE THAT I HAD KEPT WARM INSIDE OF ME. I'M GLAD I WAS ABLE TO DRAW IT TO MY LIKING. I THINK THIS WILL SHED LIGHT ON SOME PARTS OF THE STORY THAT MAY HAVE BEEN VAGUE.

AND FINALLY, THE 60-PAGE SPECIAL FEATURE. THIS STORY IS ABOUT TERU, KUROSAKI AND THE OTHERS AFTER THE END OF *DENGEKI DAISY*. THE MAIN STORY WAS ALWAYS FULL OF SERIOUS INCIDENTS, SO I WANTED TO MAKE THIS LAST ONE A HAPPY STORY. (ALTHOUGH EVEN HERE, THERE ARE INCIDENTS...) IN A SENSE, THIS IS TRULY THE END OF *DAISY*.

I HOPE YOU ENJOY ALL THE STORIES. PLEASE DO!!

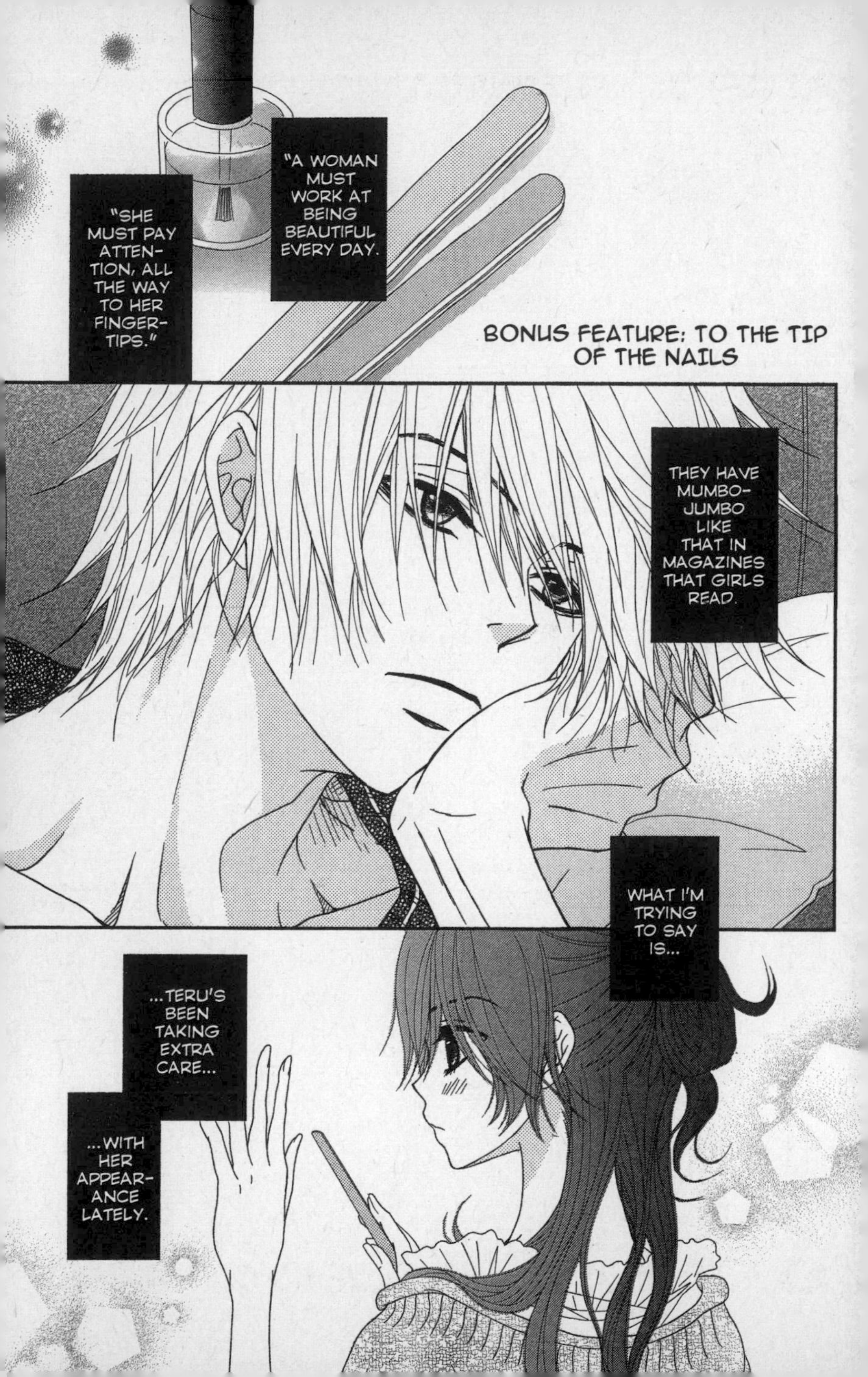
"A WOMAN MUST WORK AT BEING BEAUTIFUL EVERY DAY.
"SHE MUST PAY ATTEN-TION, ALL THE WAY TO HER FINGER-TIPS."
BONUS FEATURE: TO THE TIP OF THE NAILS
THEY HAVE MUMBO-JUMBO LIKE THAT IN MAGAZINES THAT GIRLS READ.
WHAT I'M TRYING TO SAY IS...
...TERU'S BEEN TAKING EXTRA CARE...
...WITH HER APPEAR-ANCE LATELY.

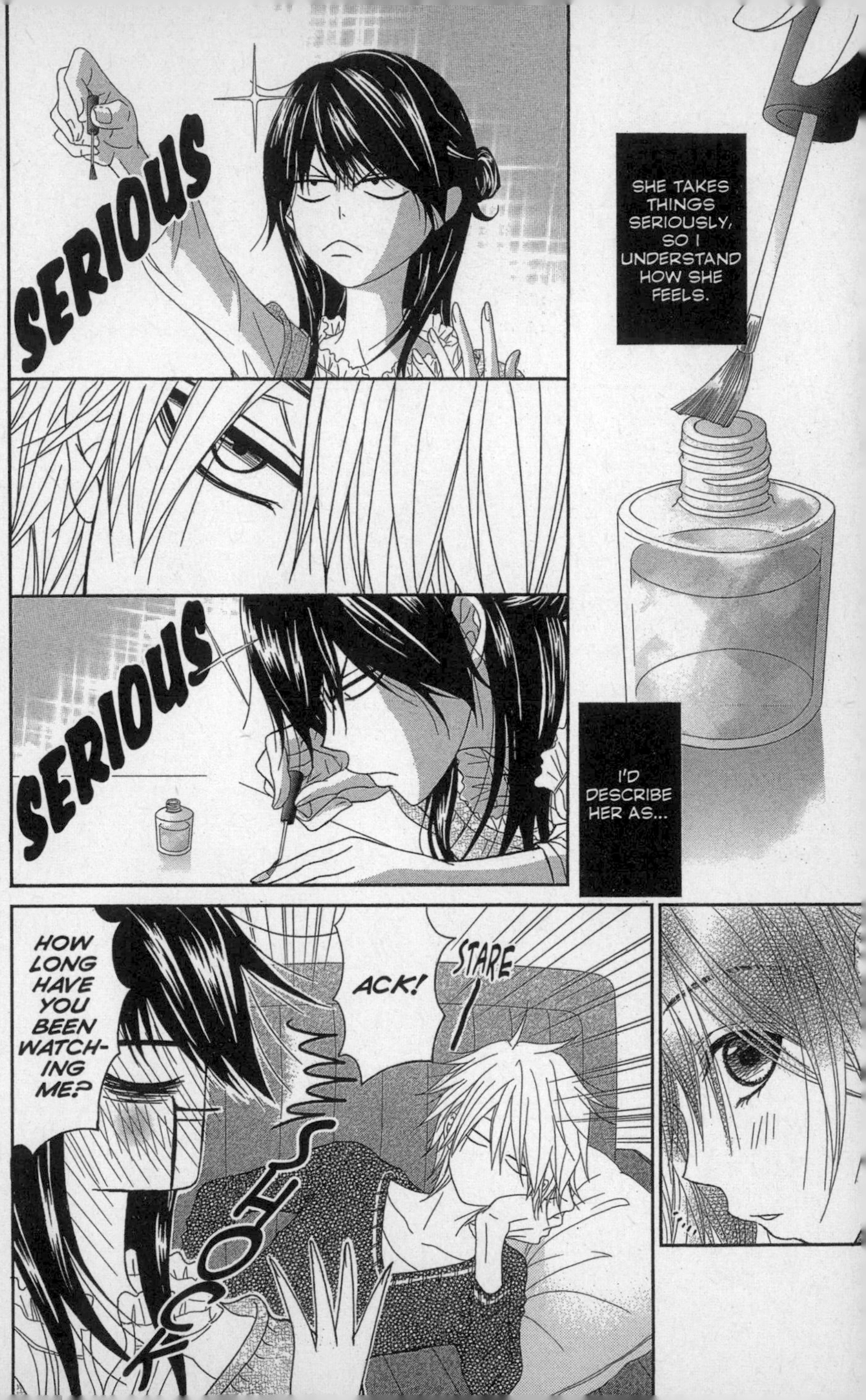
SHE TAKES THINGS SERIOUSLY, SO I UNDERSTAND HOW SHE FEELS.
I'D DESCRIBE HER AS...
SERIOUS
SERIOUS
STARE
ACK!
HOW LONG HAVE YOU BEEN WATCHING ME?
SHOCK

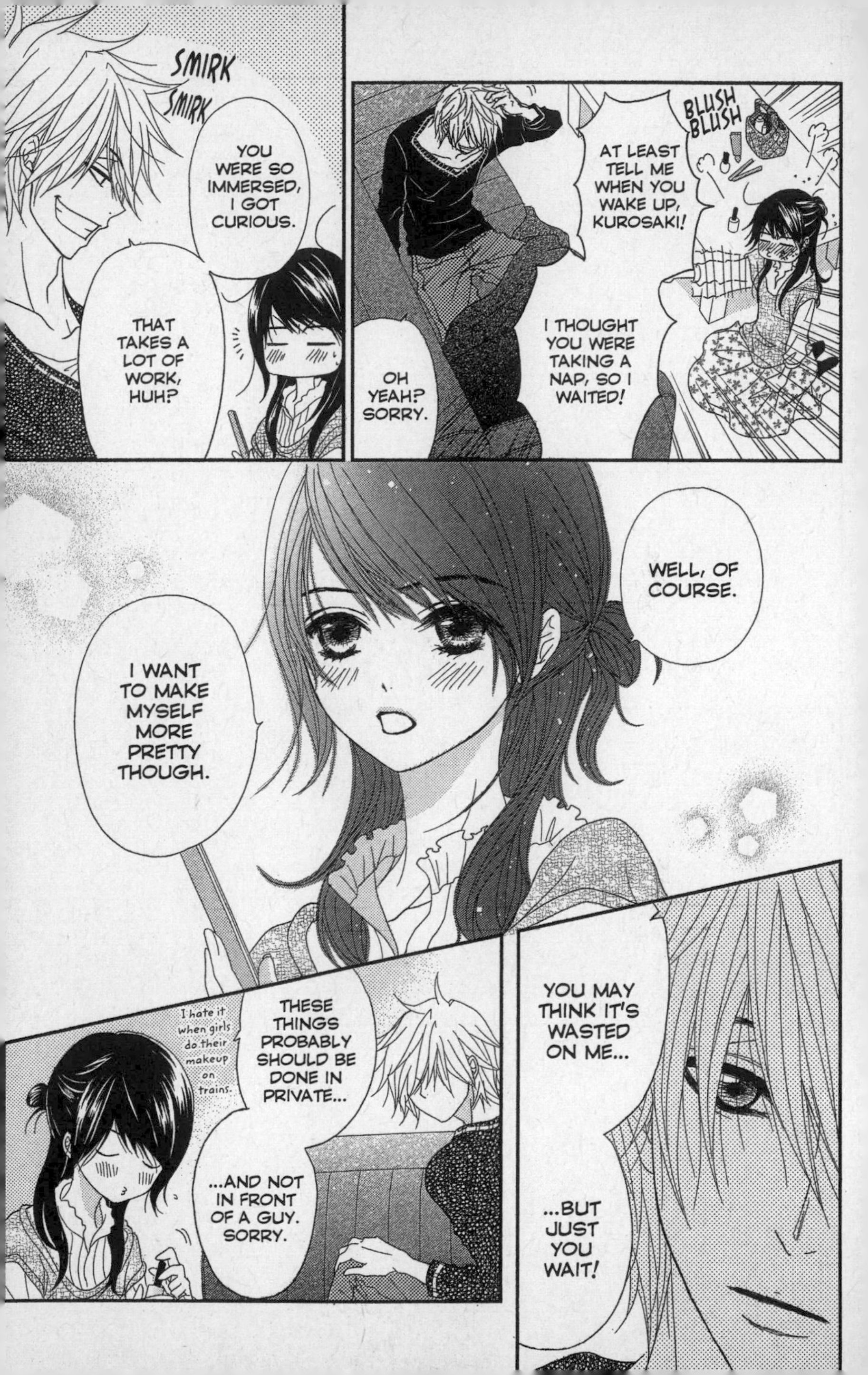
BLUSH BLUSH
AT LEAST TELL ME WHEN YOU WAKE UP, KUROSAKI!
I THOUGHT YOU WERE TAKING A NAP, SO I WAITED!
OH YEAH? SORRY.
SMIRK SMIRK
YOU WERE SO IMMERSED, I GOT CURIOUS.
THAT TAKES A LOT OF WORK, HUH?
WELL, OF COURSE.
I WANT TO MAKE MYSELF MORE PRETTY THOUGH.
YOU MAY THINK IT'S WASTED ON ME...
...BUT JUST YOU WAIT!
THESE THINGS PROBABLY SHOULD BE DONE IN PRIVATE...
I hate it when girls do their makeup on trains.
...AND NOT IN FRONT OF A GUY. SORRY.

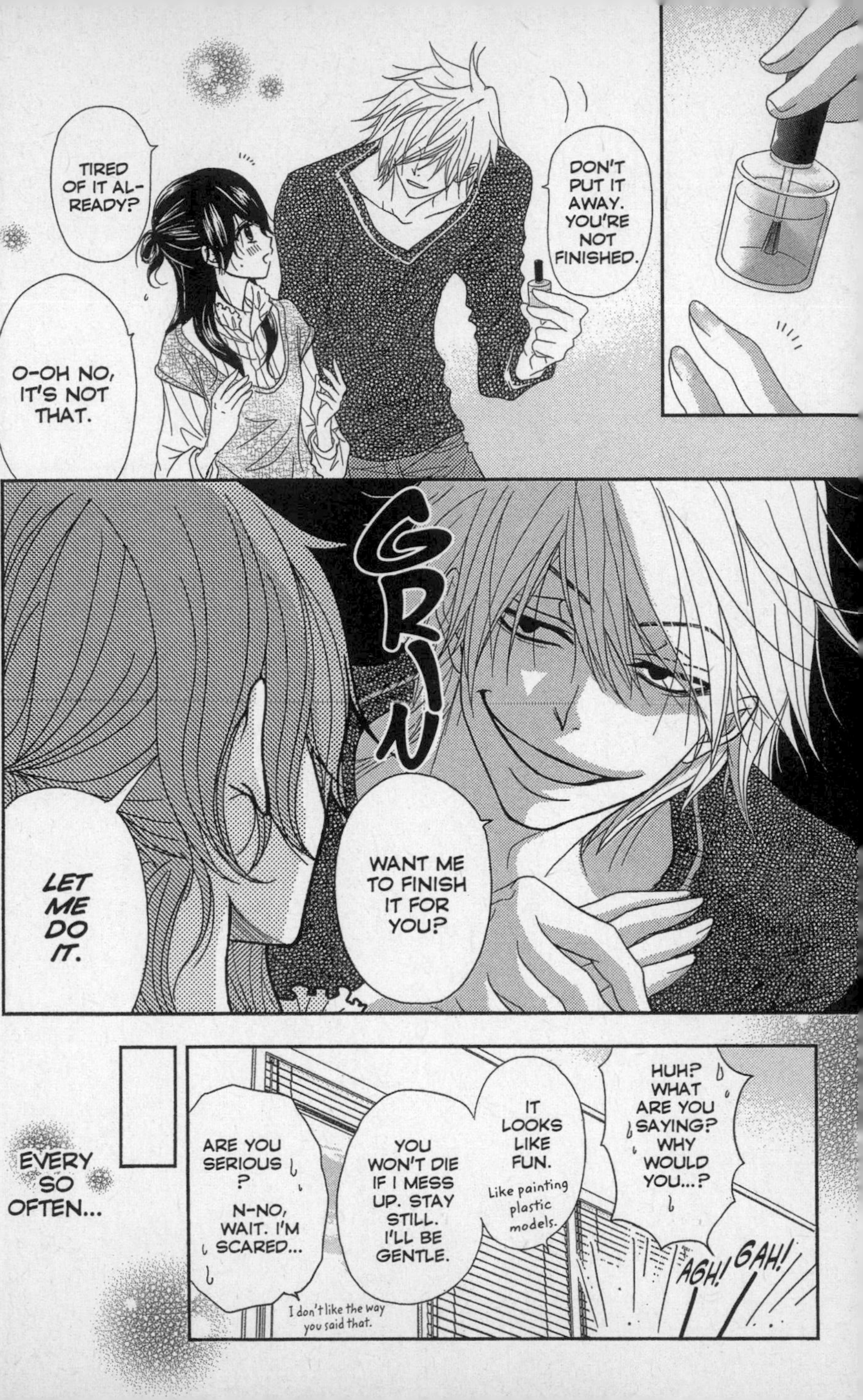
DON'T PUT IT AWAY. YOU'RE NOT FINISHED.
TIRED OF IT AL-READY?
O-OH NO, IT'S NOT THAT.
GRIN
WANT ME TO FINISH IT FOR YOU?
LET ME DO IT.
HUH? WHAT ARE YOU SAYING? WHY WOULD YOU...?
GAH!
AGH!
IT LOOKS LIKE FUN.
Like painting plastic models.
YOU WON'T DIE IF I MESS UP. STAY STILL. I'LL BE GENTLE.
I don't like the way you said that.
ARE YOU SERIOUS?
N-NO, WAIT. I'M SCARED...
EVERY SO OFTEN...

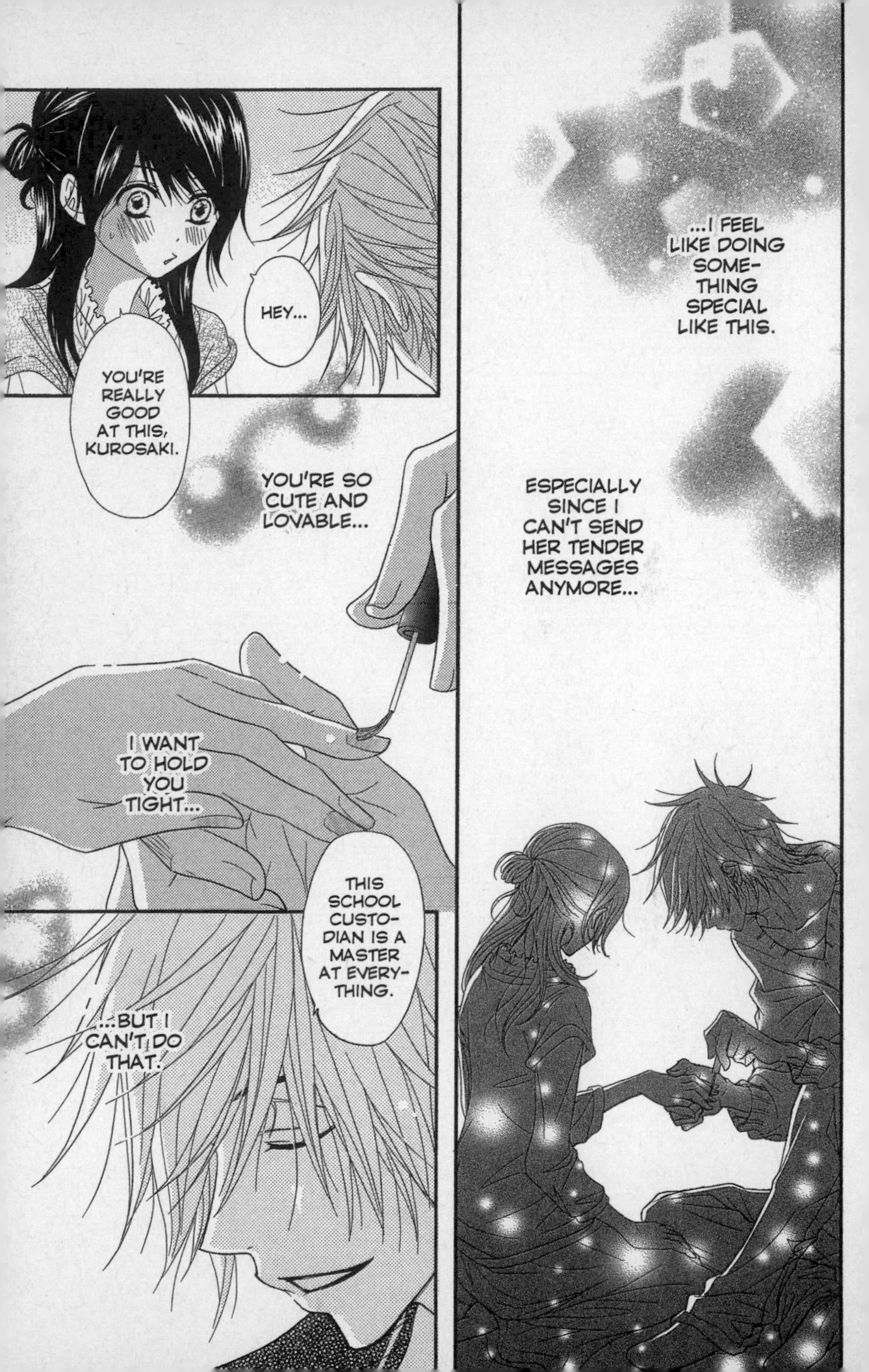
HEY...
YOU'RE REALLY GOOD AT THIS, KUROSAKI.
YOU'RE SO CUTE AND LOVABLE...
I WANT TO HOLD YOU TIGHT...
THIS SCHOOL CUSTODIAN IS A MASTER AT EVERYTHING.
...BUT I CAN'T DO THAT.
...I FEEL LIKE DOING SOMETHING SPECIAL LIKE THIS.
ESPECIALLY SINCE I CAN'T SEND HER TENDER MESSAGES ANYMORE...

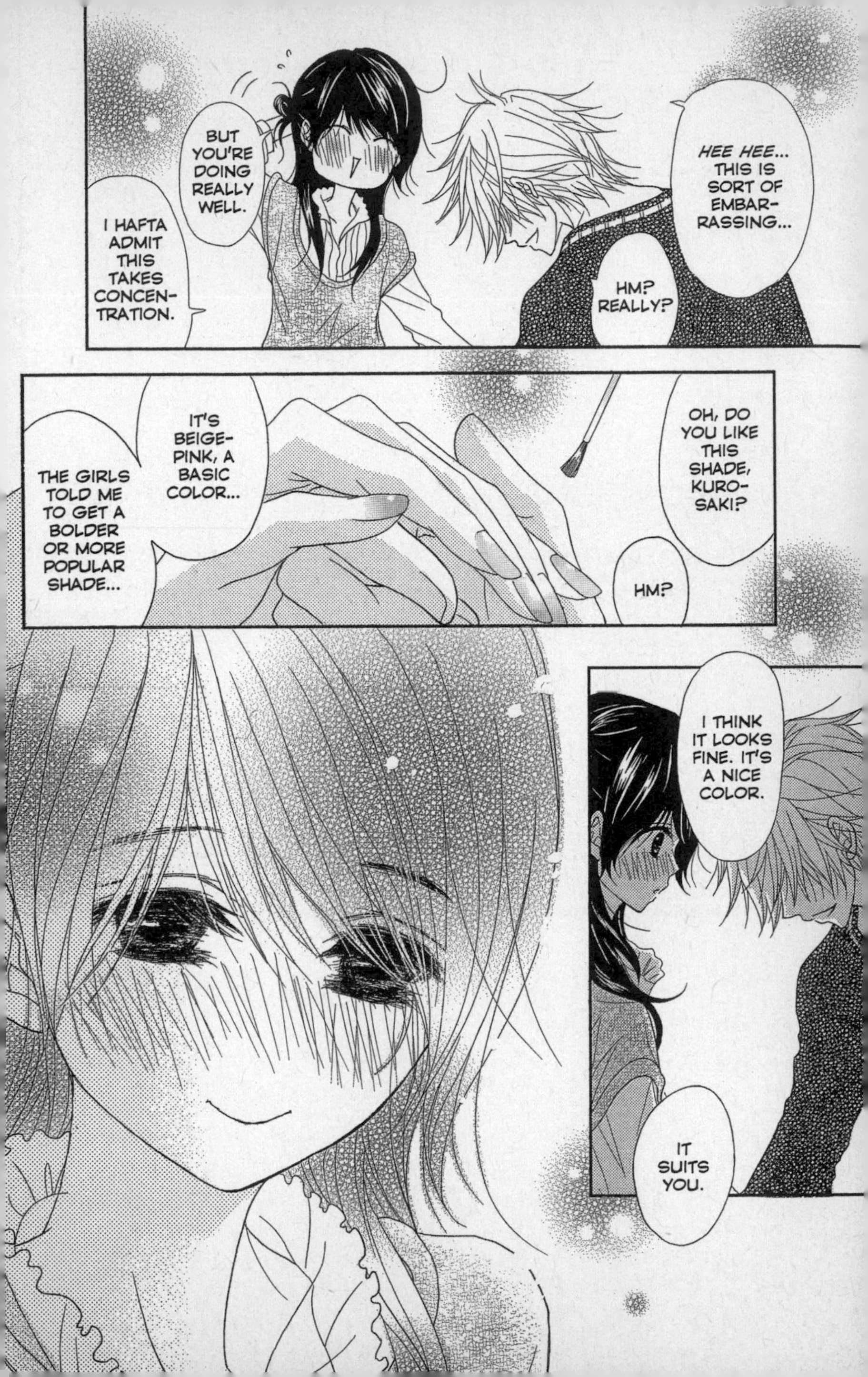

HEE HEE... THIS IS SORT OF EMBAR-RASSING...
HM? REALLY?
BUT YOU'RE DOING REALLY WELL.
I HAFTA ADMIT THIS TAKES CONCEN-TRATION.
OH, DO YOU LIKE THIS SHADE, KURO-SAKI?
HM?
IT'S BEIGE-PINK, A BASIC COLOR...
THE GIRLS TOLD ME TO GET A BOLDER OR MORE POPULAR SHADE...
I THINK IT LOOKS FINE. IT'S A NICE COLOR.
IT SUITS YOU.

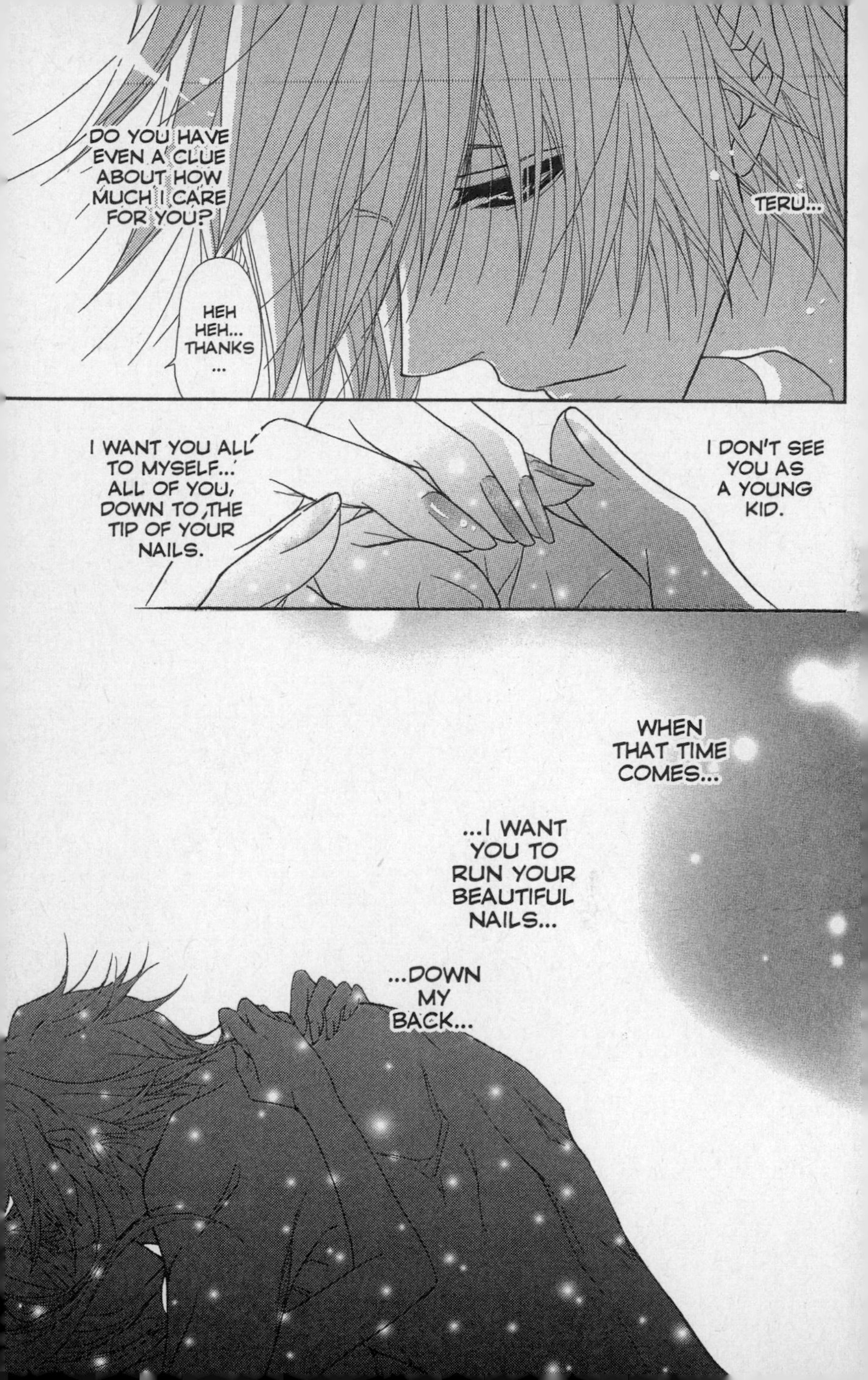
TERU...
DO YOU HAVE EVEN A CLUE ABOUT HOW MUCH I CARE FOR YOU?
HEH HEH... THANKS...
I DON'T SEE YOU AS A YOUNG KID.
I WANT YOU ALL TO MYSELF... ALL OF YOU, DOWN TO THE TIP OF YOUR NAILS.
WHEN THAT TIME COMES...
...I WANT YOU TO RUN YOUR BEAUTIFUL NAILS...
...DOWN MY BACK...

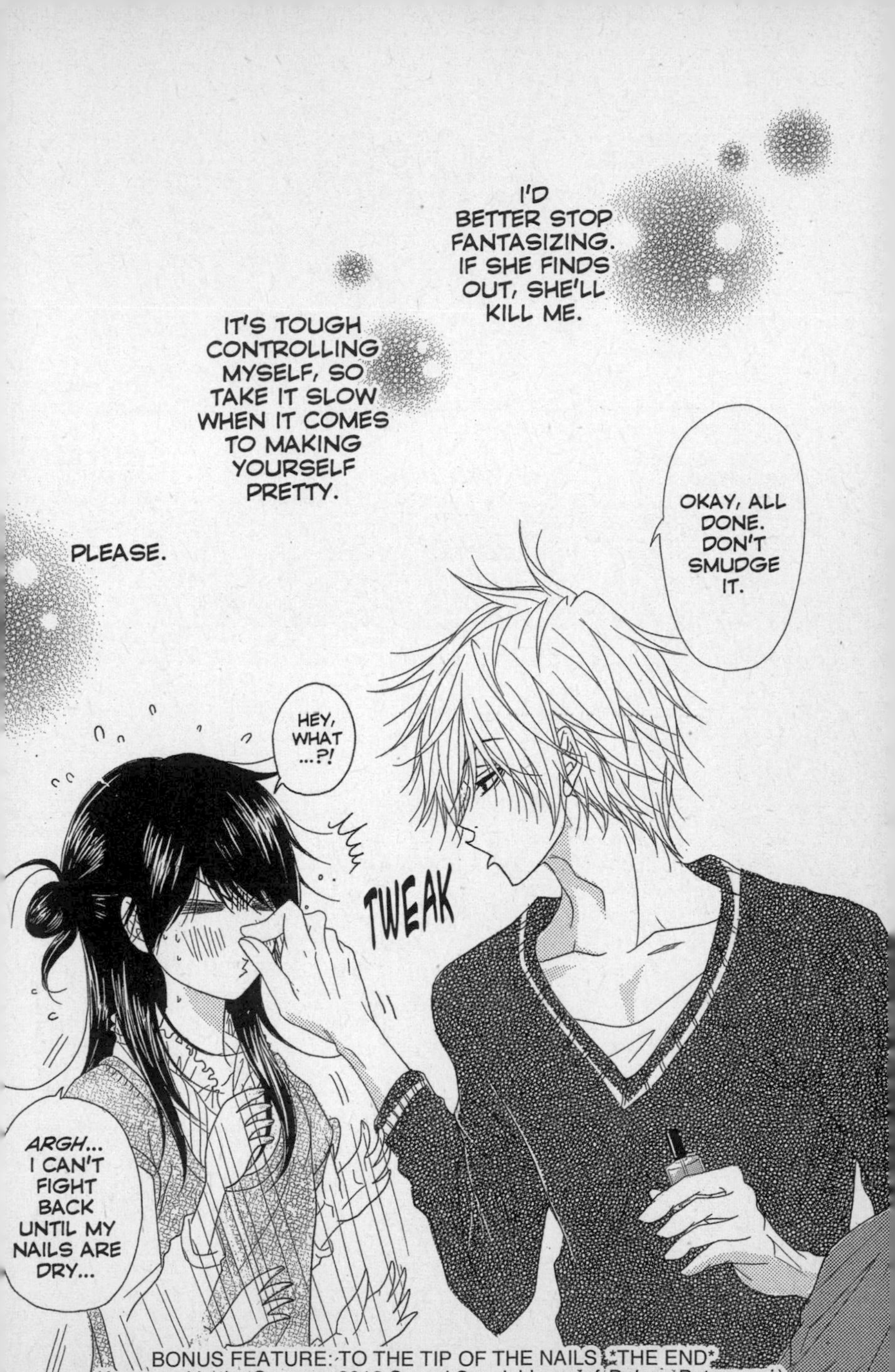
I'D BETTER STOP FANTASIZING. IF SHE FINDS OUT, SHE'LL KILL ME.
IT'S TOUGH CONTROLLING MYSELF, SO TAKE IT SLOW WHEN IT COMES TO MAKING YOURSELF PRETTY.
OKAY, ALL DONE. DON'T SMUDGE IT.
PLEASE.
HEY, WHAT ...?!
TWEAK
ARGH... I CAN'T FIGHT BACK UNTIL MY NAILS ARE DRY...

BONUS FEATURE: TO THE TIP OF THE NAILS *THE END*
(Appeared in the Summer 2012 Super! Special Issue of *Deluxe Betsucomi*)

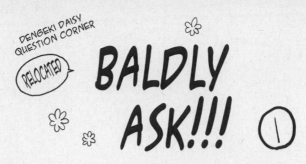

DENGEKI DAISY QUESTION CORNER

RELOCATED

BALDLY ASK!!! ①

OH DEAR! THIS IS THE LAST INSTALLMENT OF THE QUESTION CORNER WHICH SPROUTED FROM THE KINDNESS OF ALL YOU KIND READERS AND OFTEN HAD ME BITING MY NAILS IN APPREHENSION!

BUT LET'S KEEP GOING WITH THE RIDICULOUS UNTIL THE VERY LAST QUESTION!!!

THERE'S A SCENE IN CHAPTER 74 OF VOLUME 15 WHERE KUROSAKI PUTS HIS EAR CLOSE TO TERU, WHO IS UNCONSCIOUS. I ASSUMED HE WAS LISTENING FOR A HEARTBEAT...BUT AFTER READING THE LAST CHAPTER, I GOT TO THINKING...WAS HE LISTENING FOR HUNGER PAINS? DID HE PERHAPS SMILE BECAUSE HE HEARD TERU'S STOMACH GROWLING SOFTLY?

(I LOVE TUNA-FILLED RICE BALLS, KANAGAWA PREFECTURE)

YES! YOU ARE SO RIGHT!!!

GROWL GROWL GROWL

THANK YOU FOR PICKING UP ON THAT. IT WAS WORTH THE EXTRA PLANNING. NEEDLESS TO SAY, THAT FLOWS INTO THE RICE BALL SCENE IN THE FINAL CHAPTER.

AND BY THE WAY, TERU'S HUNGER PAINS ARE BY NO MEANS CUTE LITTLE SOUNDS. THINK LOUD HARD ROCK. SHE DID TRAIN A LOT, AFTER ALL. IT'S NO WONDER SHE GETS HUNGRY.

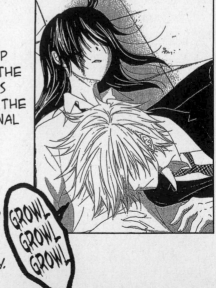

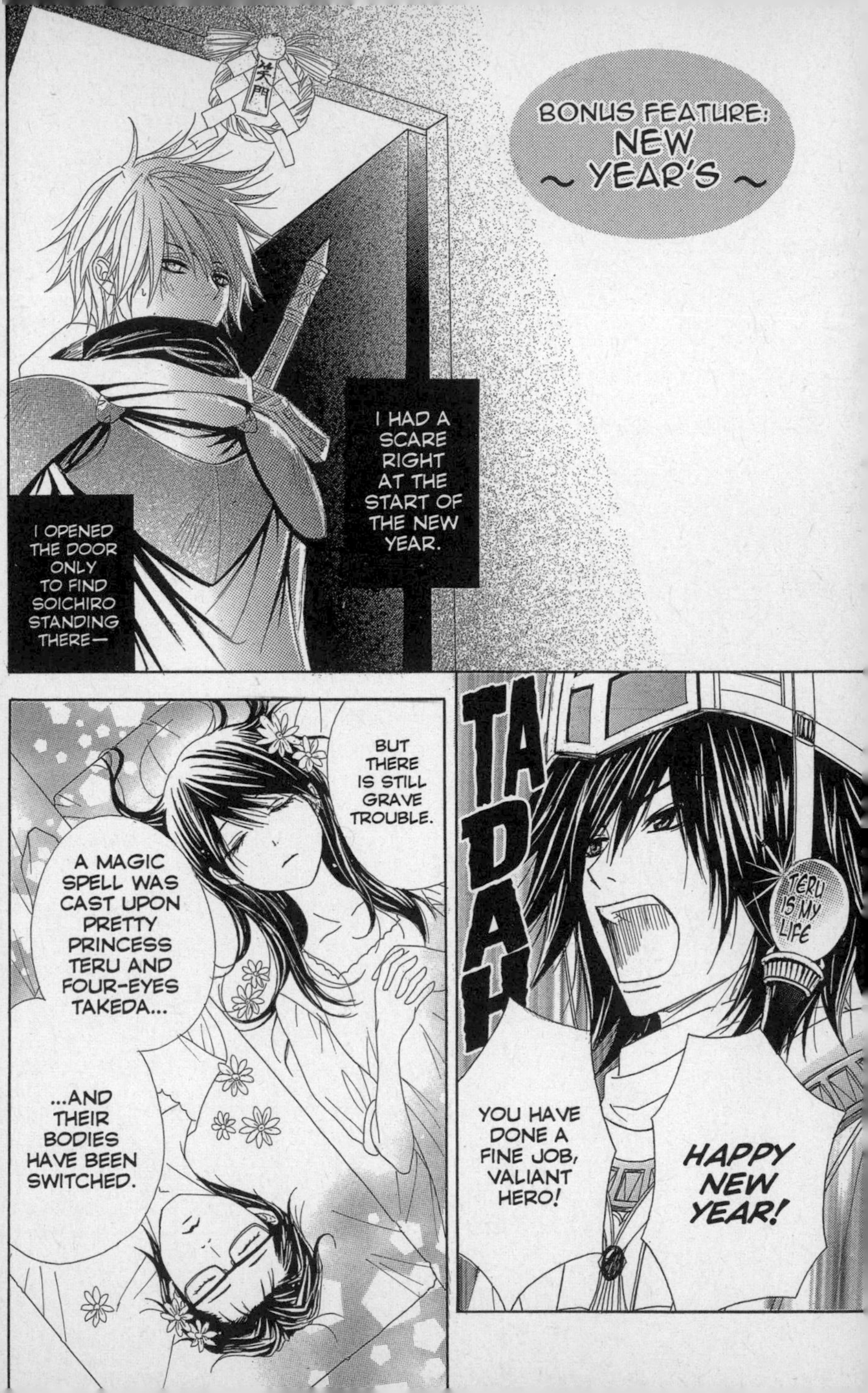
BONUS FEATURE: NEW ~ YEAR'S ~
笑門
I HAD A SCARE RIGHT AT THE START OF THE NEW YEAR.
I OPENED THE DOOR ONLY TO FIND SOICHIRO STANDING THERE—
TA DA
TERU IS MY LIFE
HAPPY NEW YEAR!
YOU HAVE DONE A FINE JOB, VALIANT HERO!
BUT THERE IS STILL GRAVE TROUBLE.
A MAGIC SPELL WAS CAST UPON PRETTY PRINCESS TERU AND FOUR-EYES TAKEDA...
...AND THEIR BODIES HAVE BEEN SWITCHED.

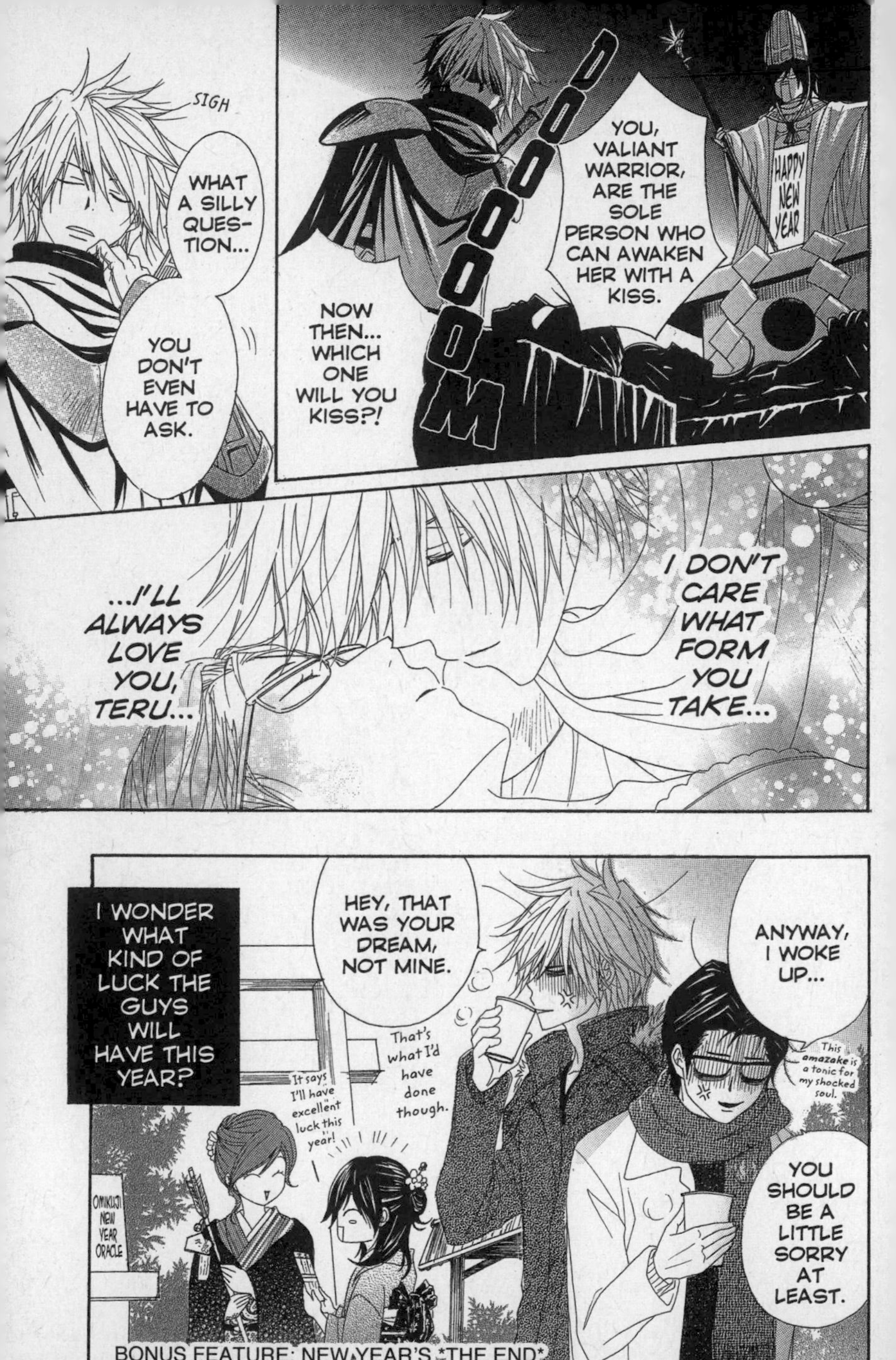
HAPPY NEW YEAR
YOU, VALIANT WARRIOR, ARE THE SOLE PERSON WHO CAN AWAKEN HER WITH A KISS.
DOOOOOOM
NOW THEN... WHICH ONE WILL YOU KISS?!
SIGH
WHAT A SILLY QUES-TION...
YOU DON'T EVEN HAVE TO ASK.
I DON'T CARE WHAT FORM YOU TAKE...
...I'LL ALWAYS LOVE YOU, TERU...
ANYWAY, I WOKE UP...
This amazake is a tonic for my shocked soul.
YOU SHOULD BE A LITTLE SORRY AT LEAST.
HEY, THAT WAS YOUR DREAM, NOT MINE.
That's what I'd have done though.
It says I'll have excellent luck this year!
I WONDER WHAT KIND OF LUCK THE GUYS WILL HAVE THIS YEAR?
OMIKUJI NEW YEAR ORACLE

BONUS FEATURE: NEW YEAR'S *THE END*
(Appeared in the January 2011 Issue of *Betsucomi*)

DENGEKI DAISY QUESTION CORNER

RELOCATED

BALDLY ASK!!! ②

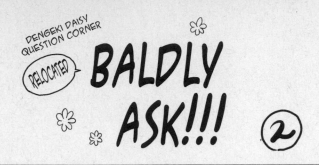

- WHAT'S WITH BOSS'S HEAD THAT HE ALWAYS KEEPS UNDER WRAPS?
- IN PAST CHAPTERS, ANDY'S ACTIONS SEEMED A BIT SHADY. WHAT WAS HE INVOLVED IN?

(FROM VARIOUS PEOPLE)

THESE TWO QUESTIONS WERE ASKED QUITE OFTEN, SO I'LL ANSWER THEM BOTH NOW.

REGARDING BOSS, I MENTIONED IN VOLUME 15 THAT HE ONCE BELONGED TO SPECIAL FORCES. HE SUSTAINED SERIOUS WOUNDS ON A MISSION AND RETIRED. THEN HE WAS RECRUITED FOR HIS CURRENT OCCUPATION. (NISHIDA OF THE MINISTRY IS HIS FORMER SUPERIOR AND SHIBAYAMA WAS A FELLOW UNIT MEMBER.) BOSS IS BLIND IN HIS RIGHT EYE, AND HE HAS SCARS FROM AN INJURY AND THE SUBSEQUENT BRAIN SURGERY.

BEFORE JOINING TEAM KUREBAYASHI, ANDY WORKED IN ELITE CIRCLES DOING RESEARCH. HOWEVER, THE WORK WAS SO DEMANDING THAT HE WAS ON THE VERGE OF BURNING OUT. THEN HIS SUBORDINATE PASSED AWAY DUE TO OVERWORK. IN ORDER TO HAVE HIS DEATH RULED AS A RESULT OF HARSH WORK CONDITIONS, ANDY RESORTED TO SOME EXTREME METHODS AND ENDED UP OWING A FAVOR TO A RATHER NASTY PERSON... THAT WAS THE SCENARIO I HAD PREPARED BUT NEVER INTRODUCED. SO ANYWAY, YES, ANDY WAS A PLAIN OLD SHADY PERSON. SORRY, ANDY... AS A MATTER OF FACT, SOICHIRO AND HIS TEAM KNEW ALL ABOUT IT. REST ASSURED, THE ISSUE HAD BEEN ADDRESSED.

I MEANT TO TIE IT ALL UP IN THE MAIN STORY BUT ENDED UP SUMMARIZING IT HERE. SORRY.

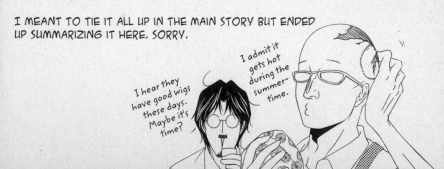

I admit it gets hot during the summertime.
I hear they have good wigs these days. Maybe it's time?

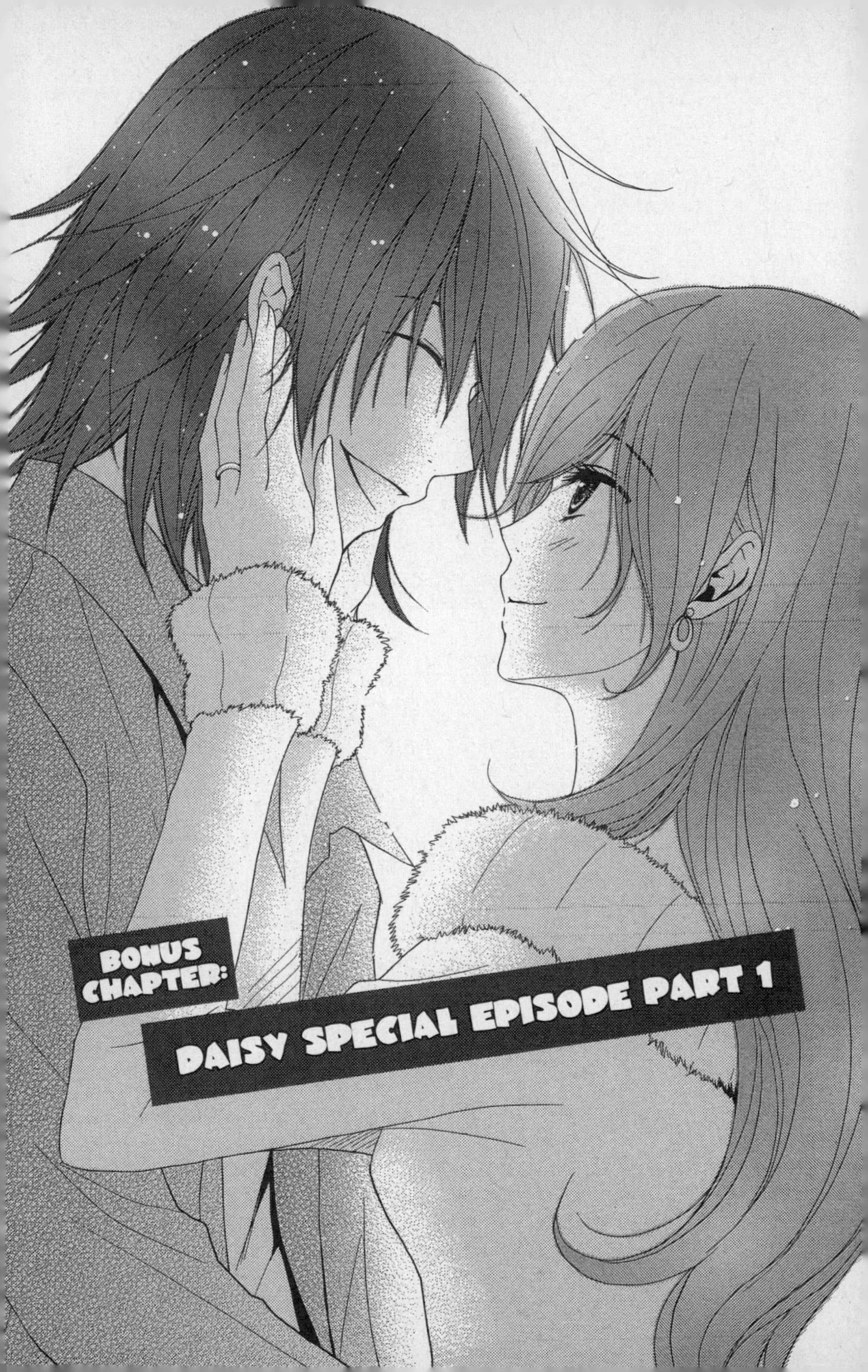
BONUS CHAPTER:
DAISY SPECIAL EPISODE PART 1

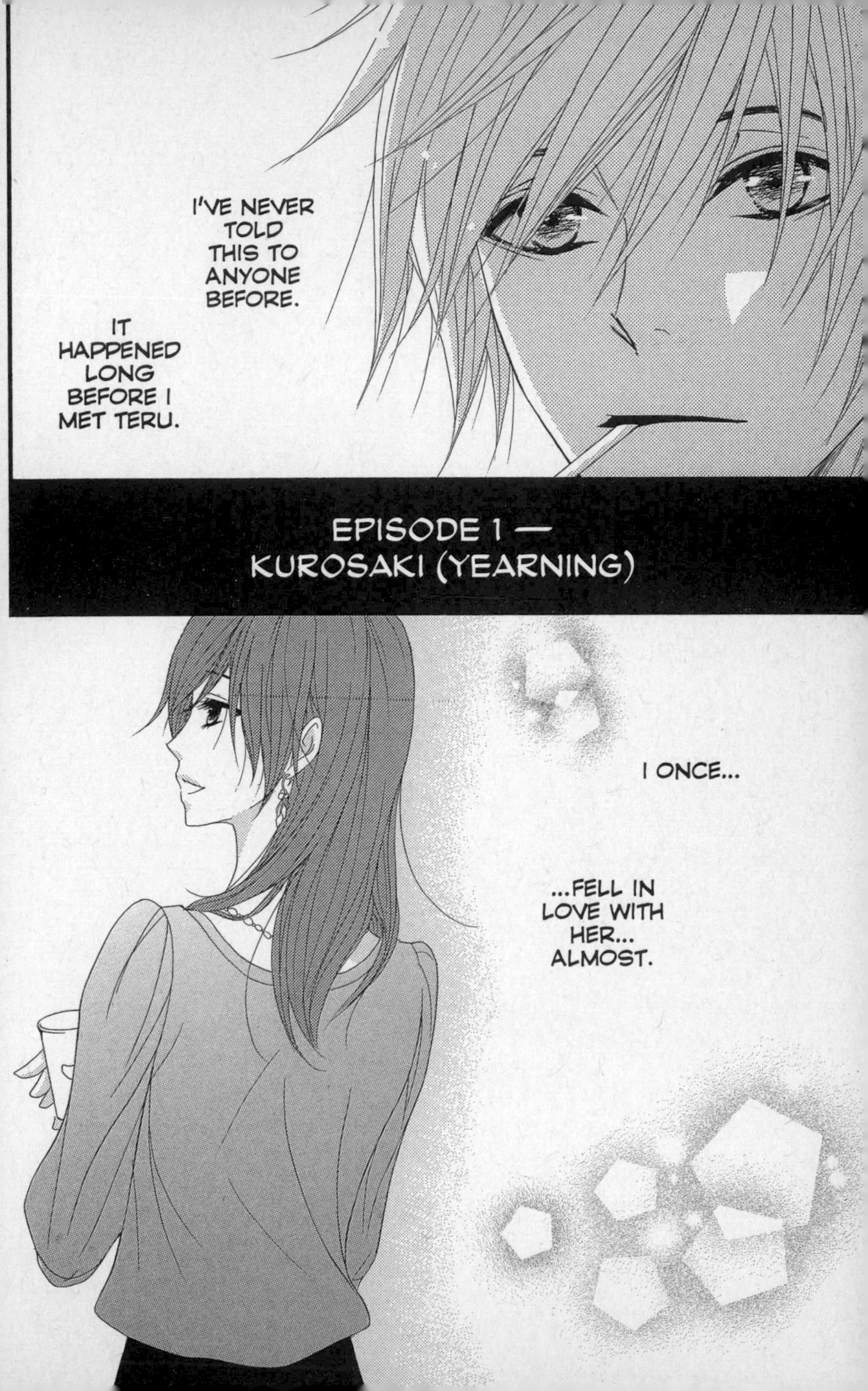
I'VE NEVER TOLD THIS TO ANYONE BEFORE.
IT HAPPENED LONG BEFORE I MET TERU.
EPISODE 1 — KUROSAKI (YEARNING)
I ONCE...
...FELL IN LOVE WITH HER... ALMOST.

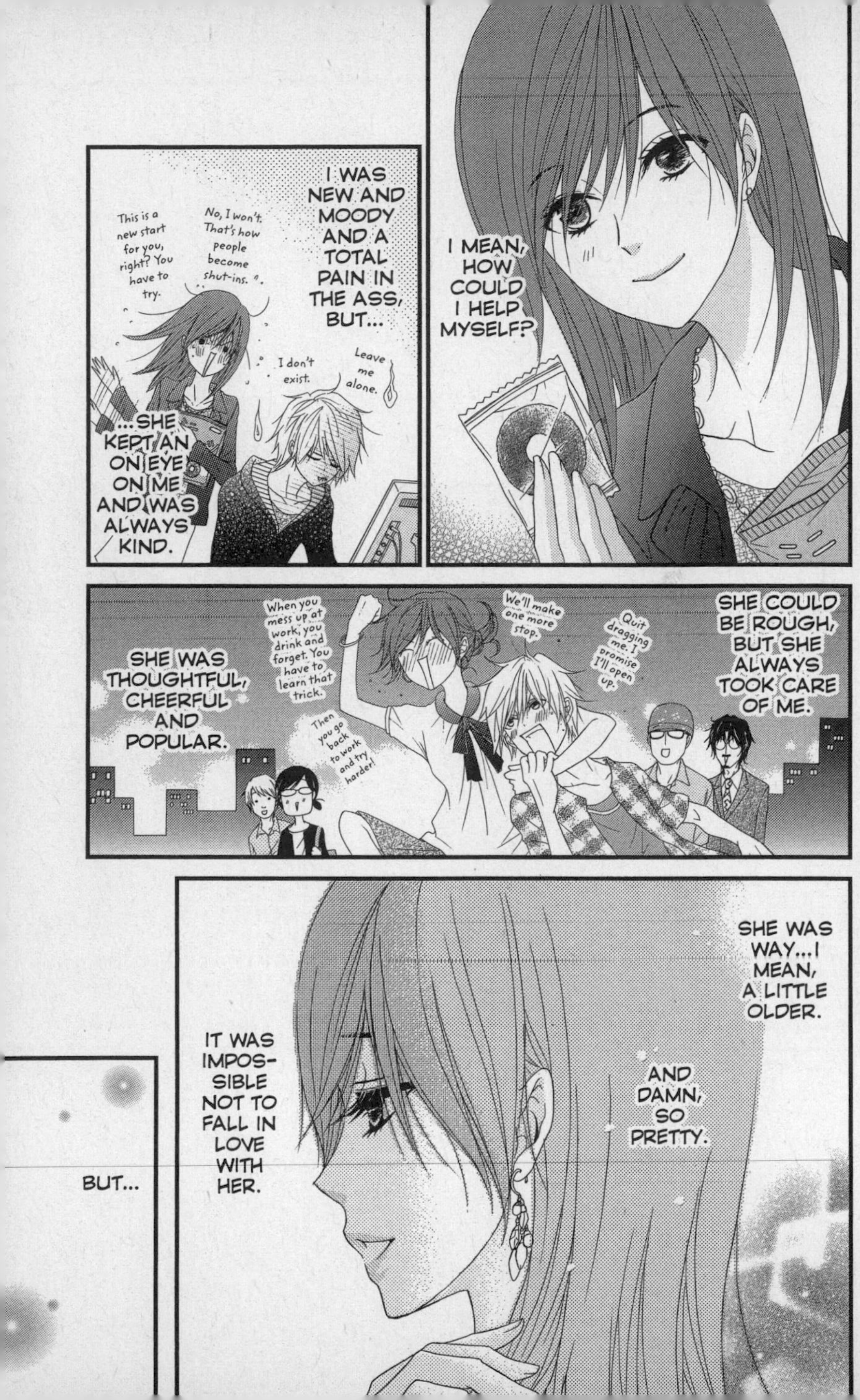
I MEAN, HOW COULD I HELP MYSELF?
I WAS NEW AND MOODY AND A TOTAL PAIN IN THE ASS, BUT...
No, I won't. That's how people become shut-ins.
This is a new start for you, right? You have to try.
Leave me alone.
I don't exist.
...SHE KEPT AN EYE ON ME AND WAS ALWAYS KIND.
SHE COULD BE ROUGH, BUT SHE ALWAYS TOOK CARE OF ME.
Quit dragging me. I promise I'll open up.
We'll make one more stop.
When you mess up at work, you drink and forget. You have to learn that trick.
Then you go back to work and try harder!
SHE WAS THOUGHTFUL, CHEERFUL AND POPULAR.
SHE WAS WAY...I MEAN, A LITTLE OLDER.
AND DAMN, SO PRETTY.
IT WAS IMPOSSIBLE NOT TO FALL IN LOVE WITH HER.
BUT...

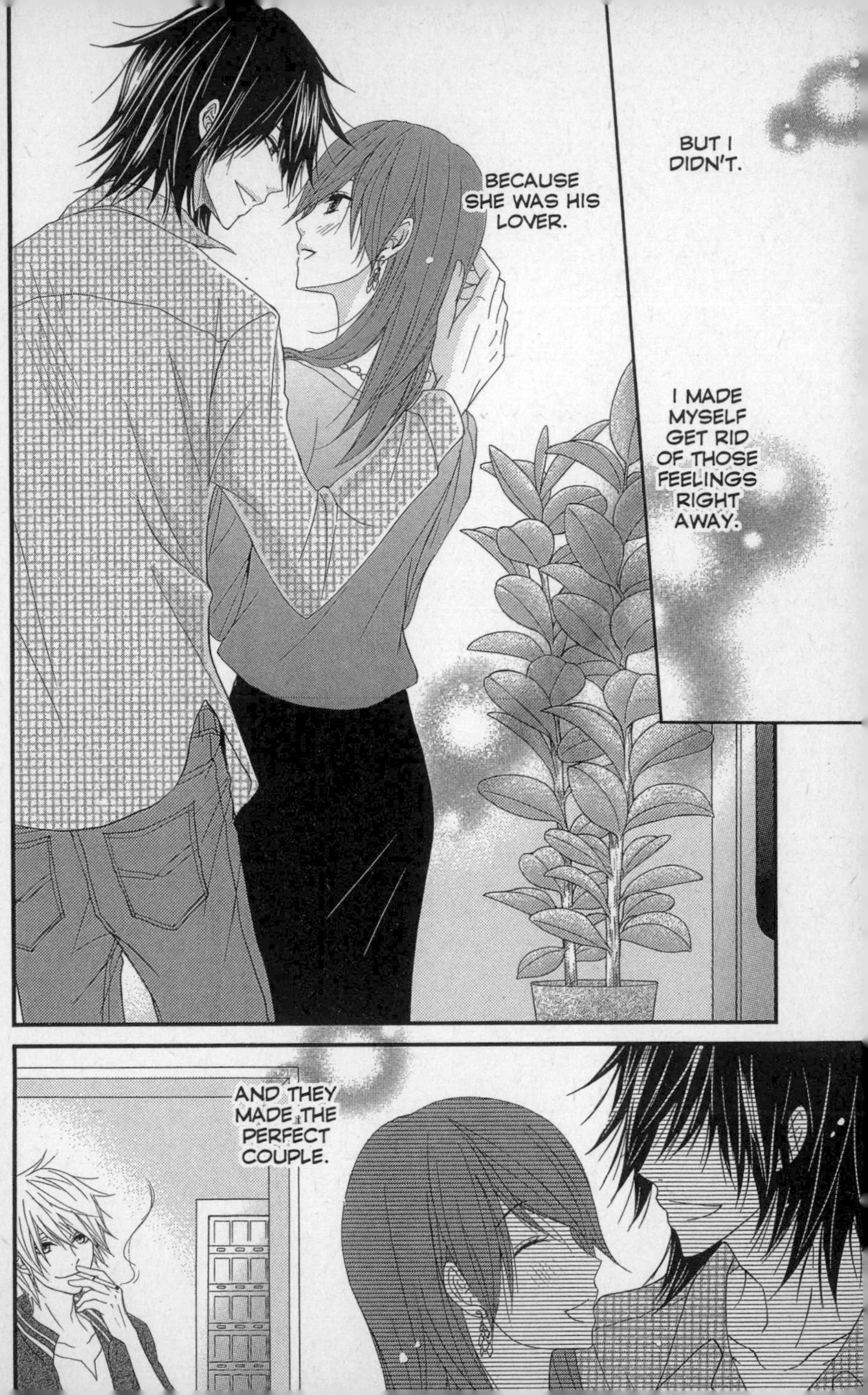
BUT I DIDN'T.
I MADE MYSELF GET RID OF THOSE FEELINGS RIGHT AWAY.
BECAUSE SHE WAS HIS LOVER.
AND THEY MADE THE PERFECT COUPLE.

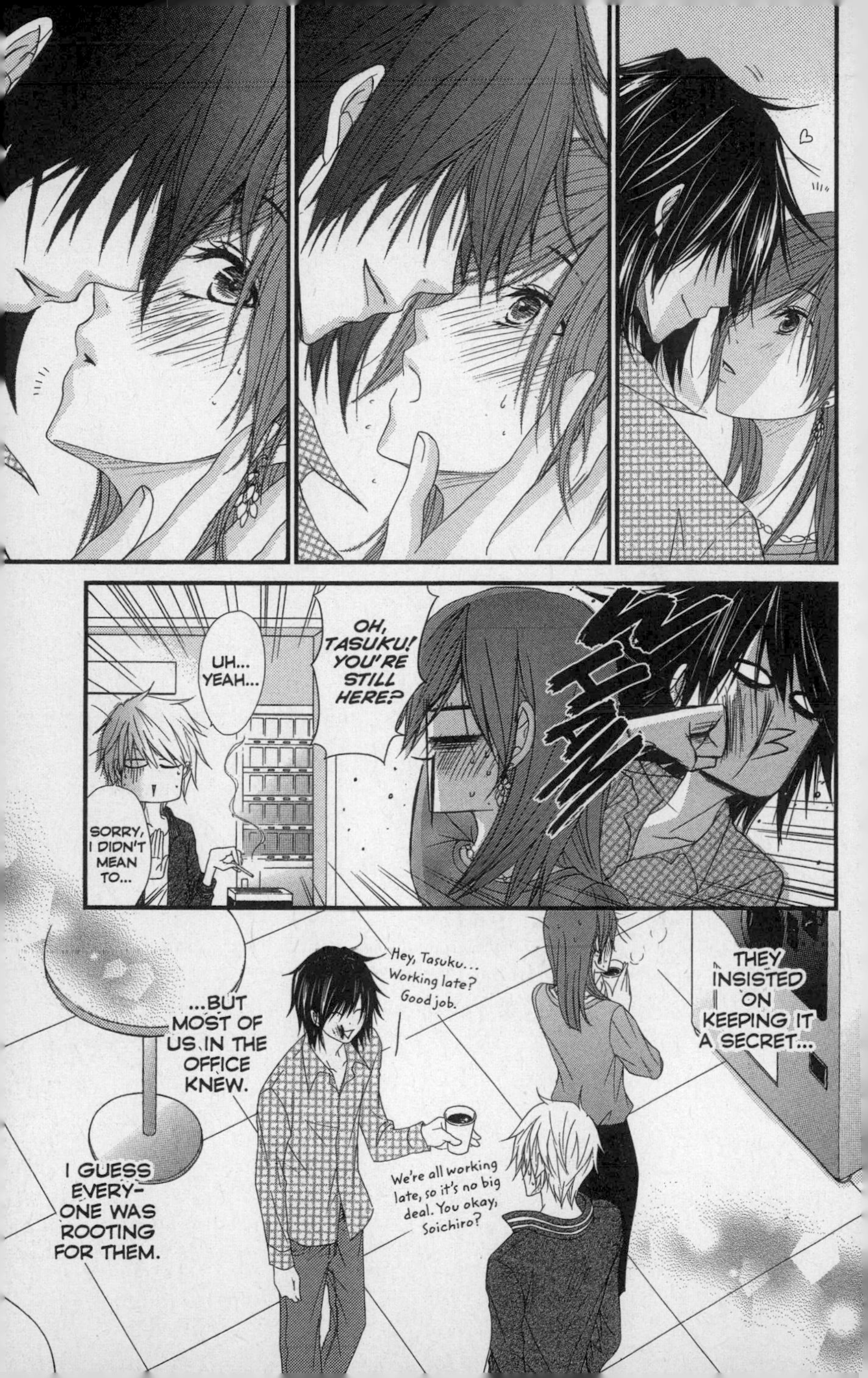
WHAM
OH, TASUKU! YOU'RE STILL HERE?
UH... YEAH...
SORRY, I DIDN'T MEAN TO...
THEY INSISTED ON KEEPING IT A SECRET...
Hey, Tasuku... Working late? Good job.
...BUT MOST OF US IN THE OFFICE KNEW.
We're all working late, so it's no big deal. You okay, Soichiro?
I GUESS EVERY-ONE WAS ROOTING FOR THEM.

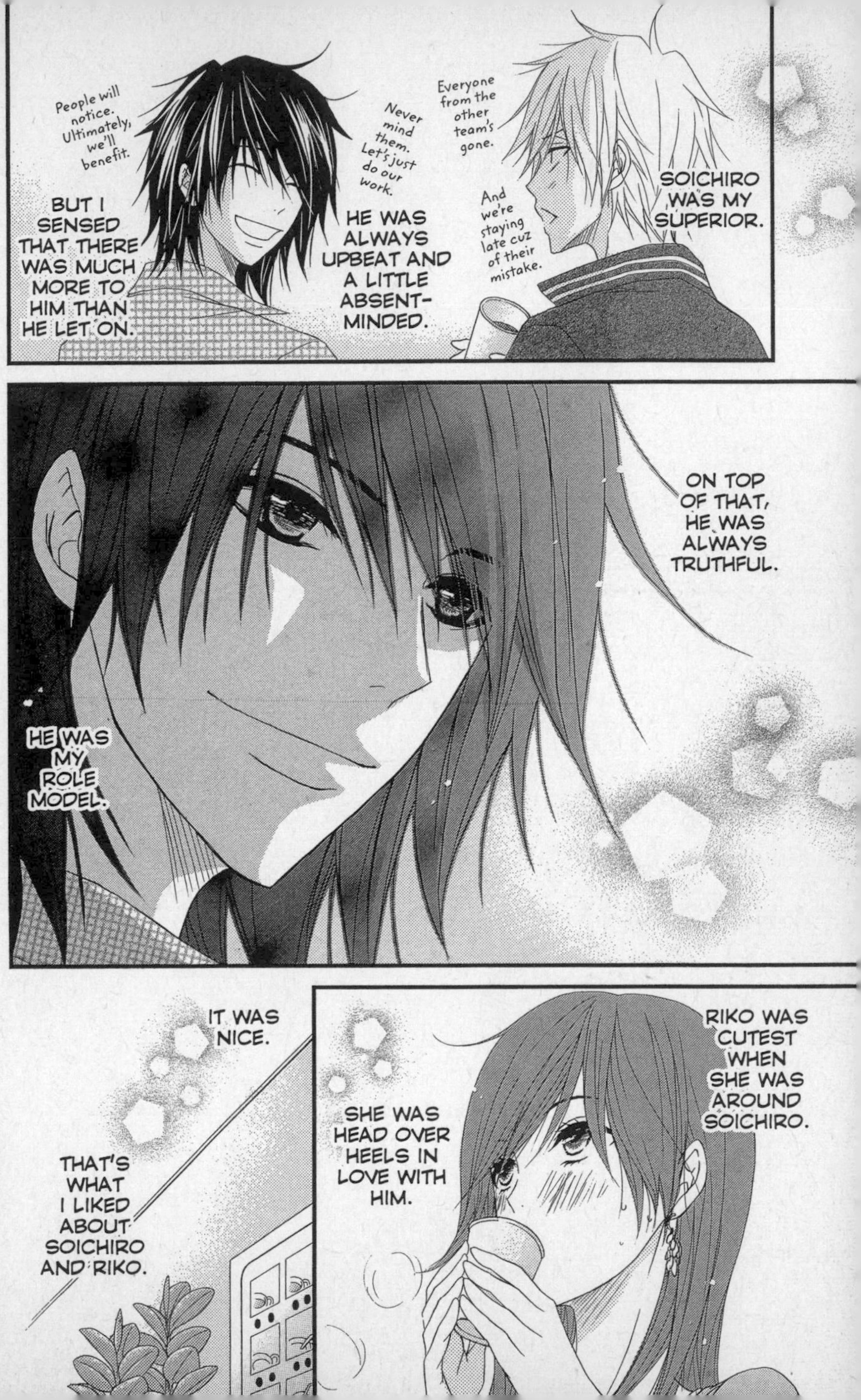
SOICHIRO WAS MY SUPERIOR.
Everyone from the other team's gone.
And we're staying late cuz of their mistake.
Never mind them. Let's just do our work.
HE WAS ALWAYS UPBEAT AND A LITTLE ABSENT-MINDED.
People will notice. Ultimately, we'll benefit.
BUT I SENSED THAT THERE WAS MUCH MORE TO HIM THAN HE LET ON.
ON TOP OF THAT, HE WAS ALWAYS TRUTHFUL.
HE WAS MY ROLE MODEL.
RIKO WAS CUTEST WHEN SHE WAS AROUND SOICHIRO.
SHE WAS HEAD OVER HEELS IN LOVE WITH HIM.
IT WAS NICE.
THAT'S WHAT I LIKED ABOUT SOICHIRO AND RIKO.

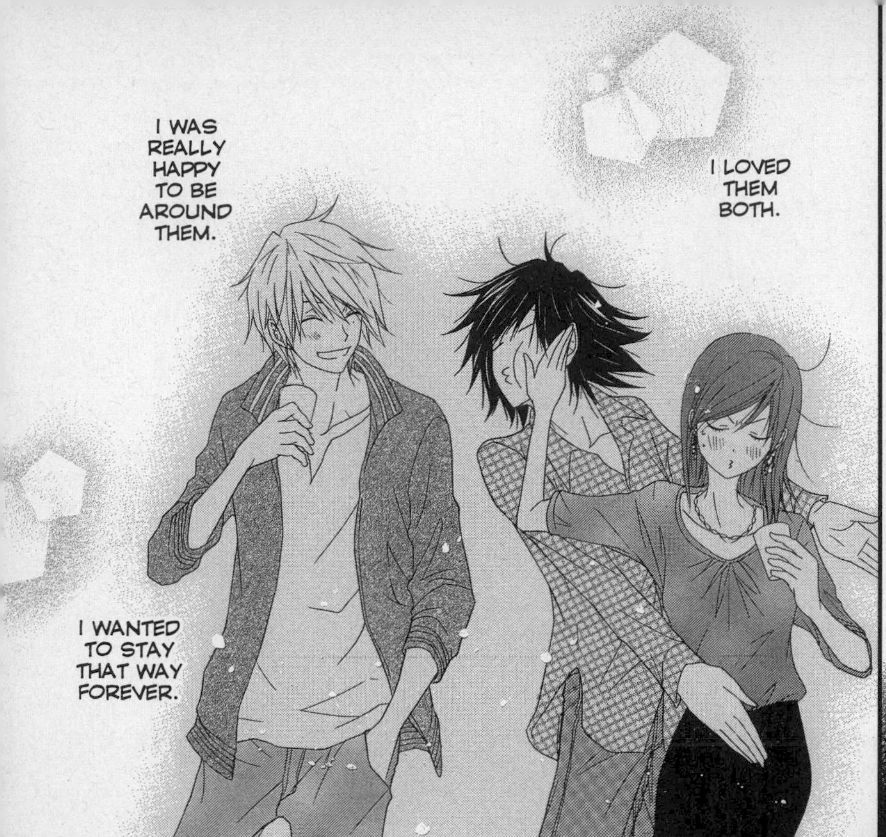
I LOVED THEM BOTH.
I WAS REALLY HAPPY TO BE AROUND THEM.
I WANTED TO STAY THAT WAY FOREVER.

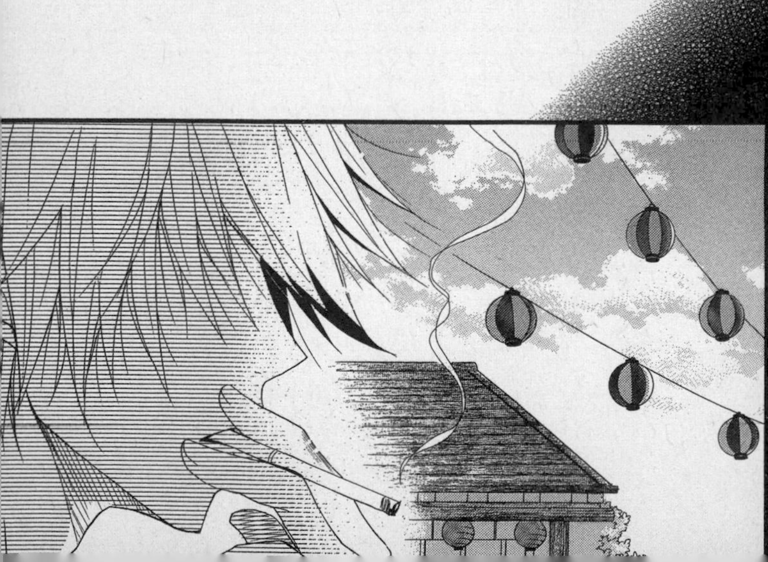

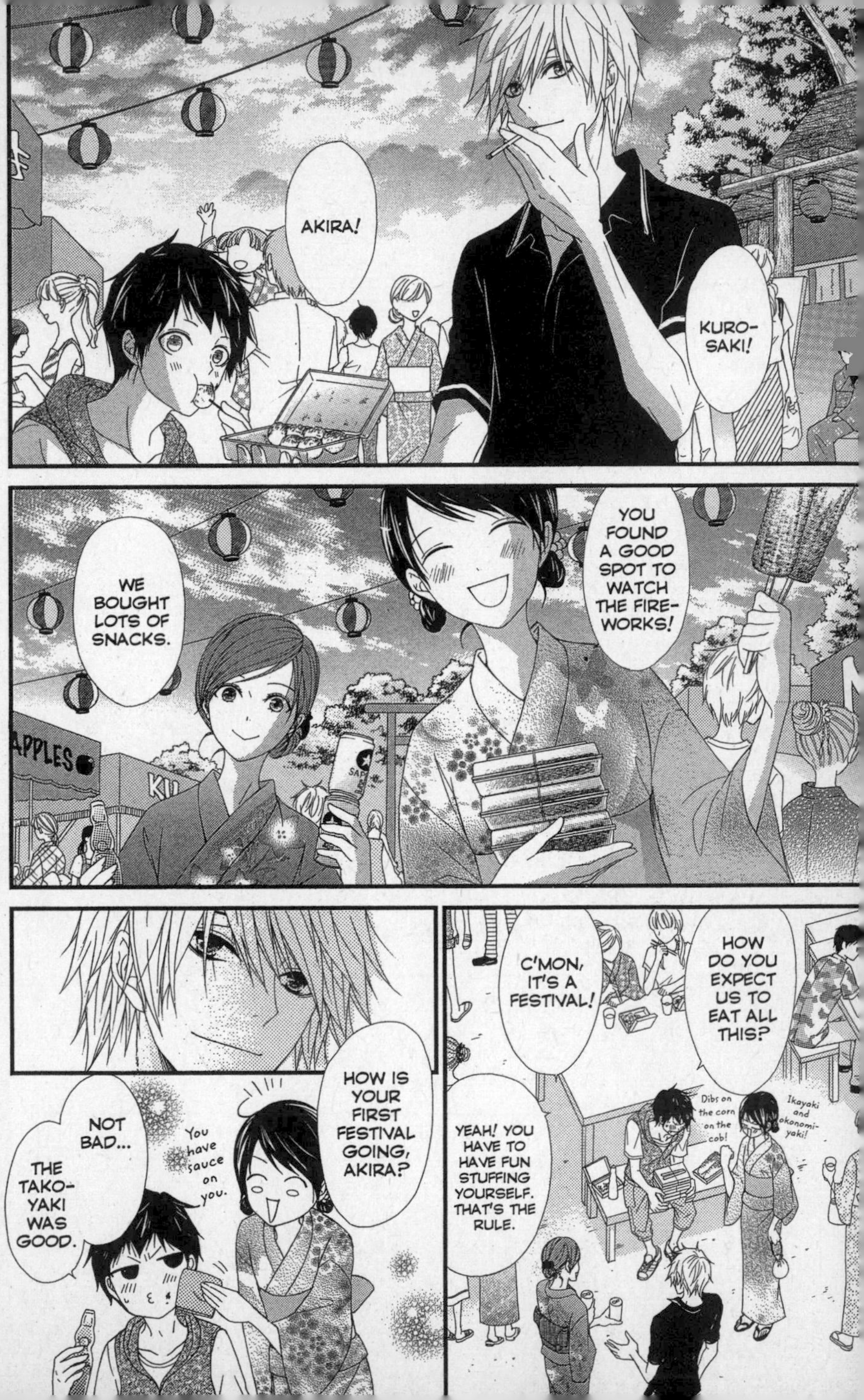
KURO-SAKI!
AKIRA!
YOU FOUND A GOOD SPOT TO WATCH THE FIRE-WORKS!
WE BOUGHT LOTS OF SNACKS.
APPLES
HOW DO YOU EXPECT US TO EAT ALL THIS?
C'MON, IT'S A FESTIVAL!
YEAH! YOU HAVE TO HAVE FUN STUFFING YOURSELF. THAT'S THE RULE.
Ikayaki and okonomi-yaki!
Dibs on the corn on the cob!
HOW IS YOUR FIRST FESTIVAL GOING, AKIRA?
You have sauce on you.
NOT BAD...
THE TAKO-YAKI WAS GOOD.

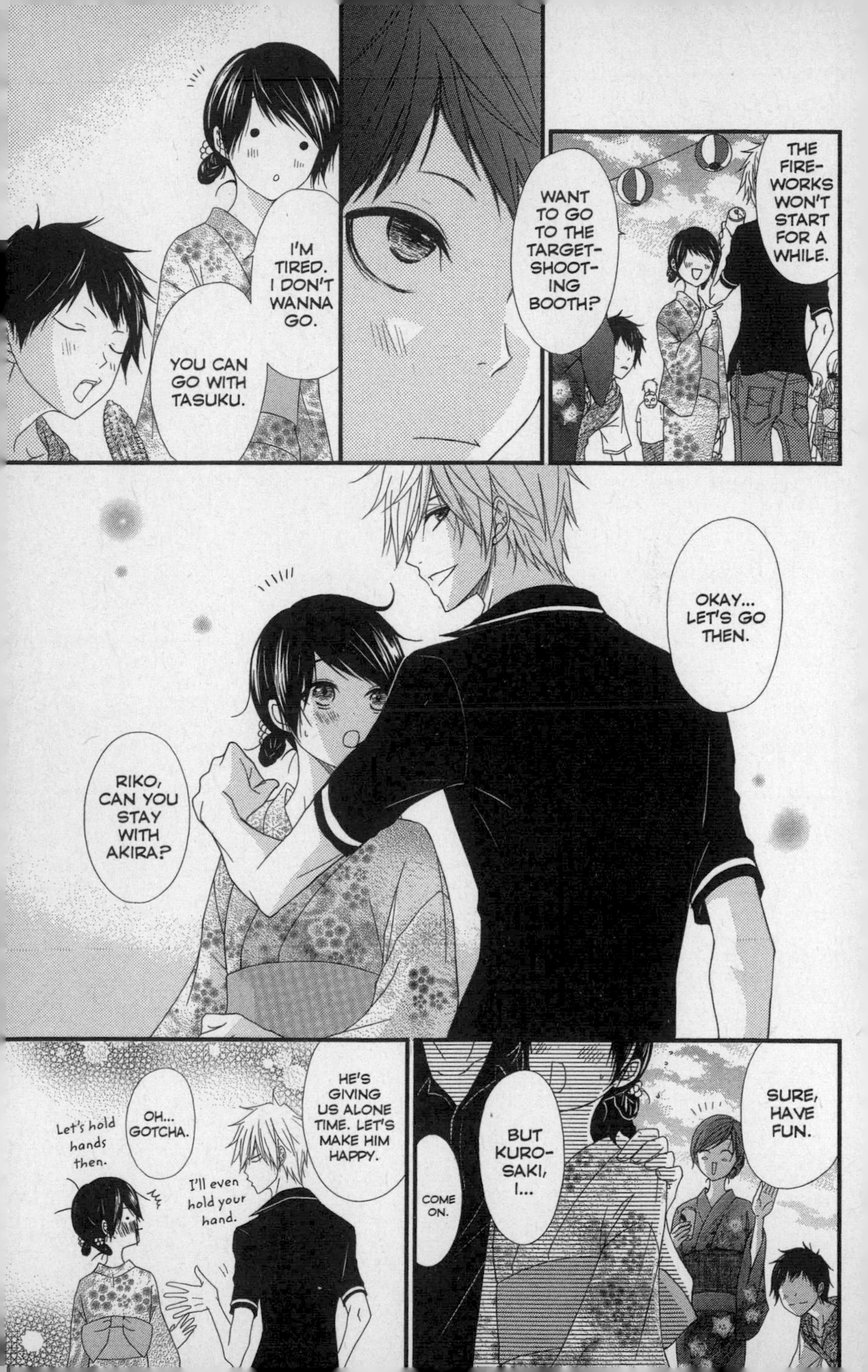
THE FIRE-WORKS WON'T START FOR A WHILE.
WANT TO GO TO THE TARGET-SHOOTING BOOTH?
I'M TIRED. I DON'T WANNA GO.
YOU CAN GO WITH TASUKU.
OKAY... LET'S GO THEN.
RIKO, CAN YOU STAY WITH AKIRA?
SURE, HAVE FUN.
BUT KURO-SAKI, I...
COME ON.
HE'S GIVING US ALONE TIME. LET'S MAKE HIM HAPPY.
OH... GOTCHA.
Let's hold hands then.
I'll even hold your hand.

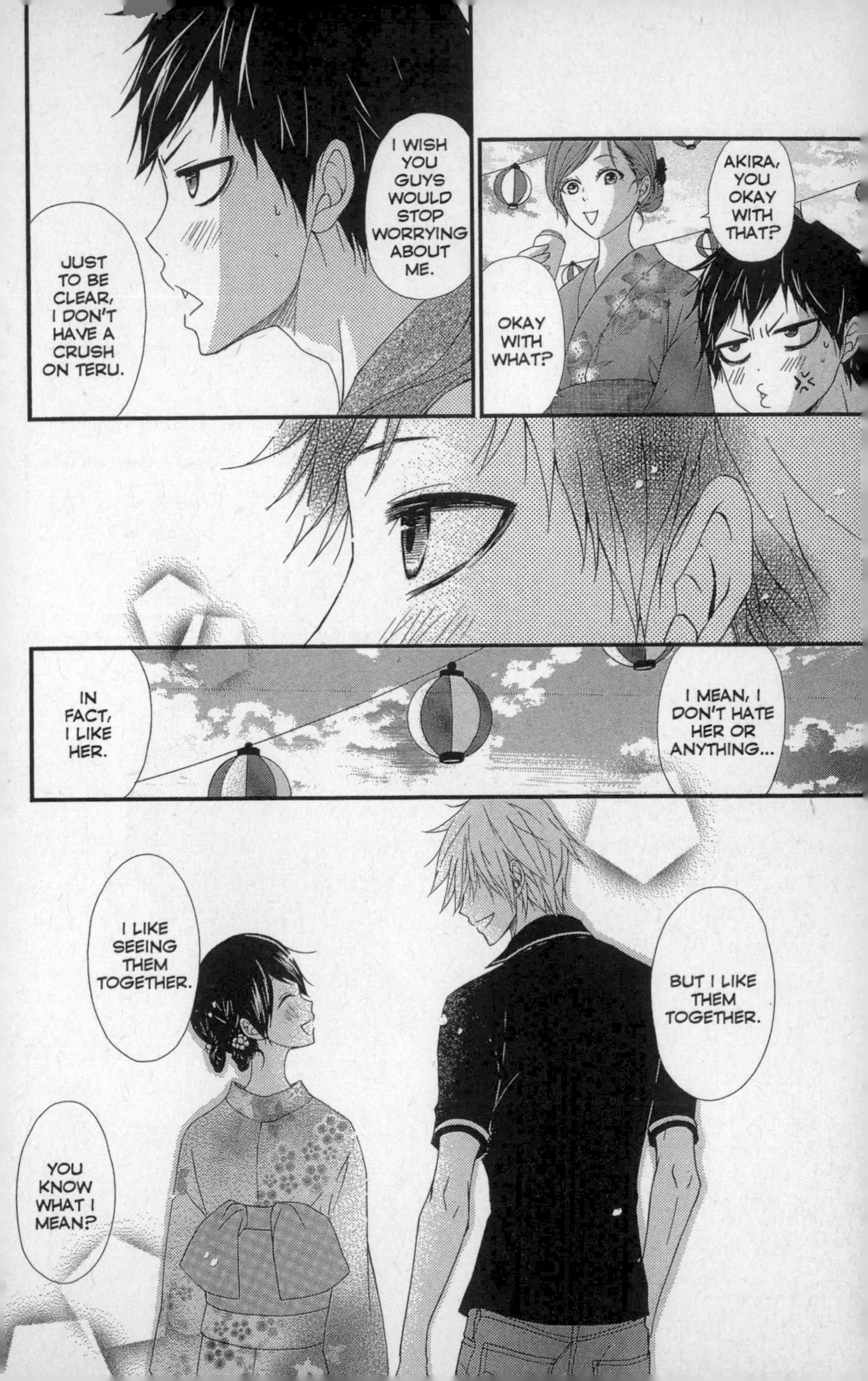
AKIRA, YOU OKAY WITH THAT?
OKAY WITH WHAT?
I WISH YOU GUYS WOULD STOP WORRYING ABOUT ME.
JUST TO BE CLEAR, I DON'T HAVE A CRUSH ON TERU.
I MEAN, I DON'T HATE HER OR ANYTHING...
IN FACT, I LIKE HER.
BUT I LIKE THEM TOGETHER.
I LIKE SEEING THEM TOGETHER.
YOU KNOW WHAT I MEAN?

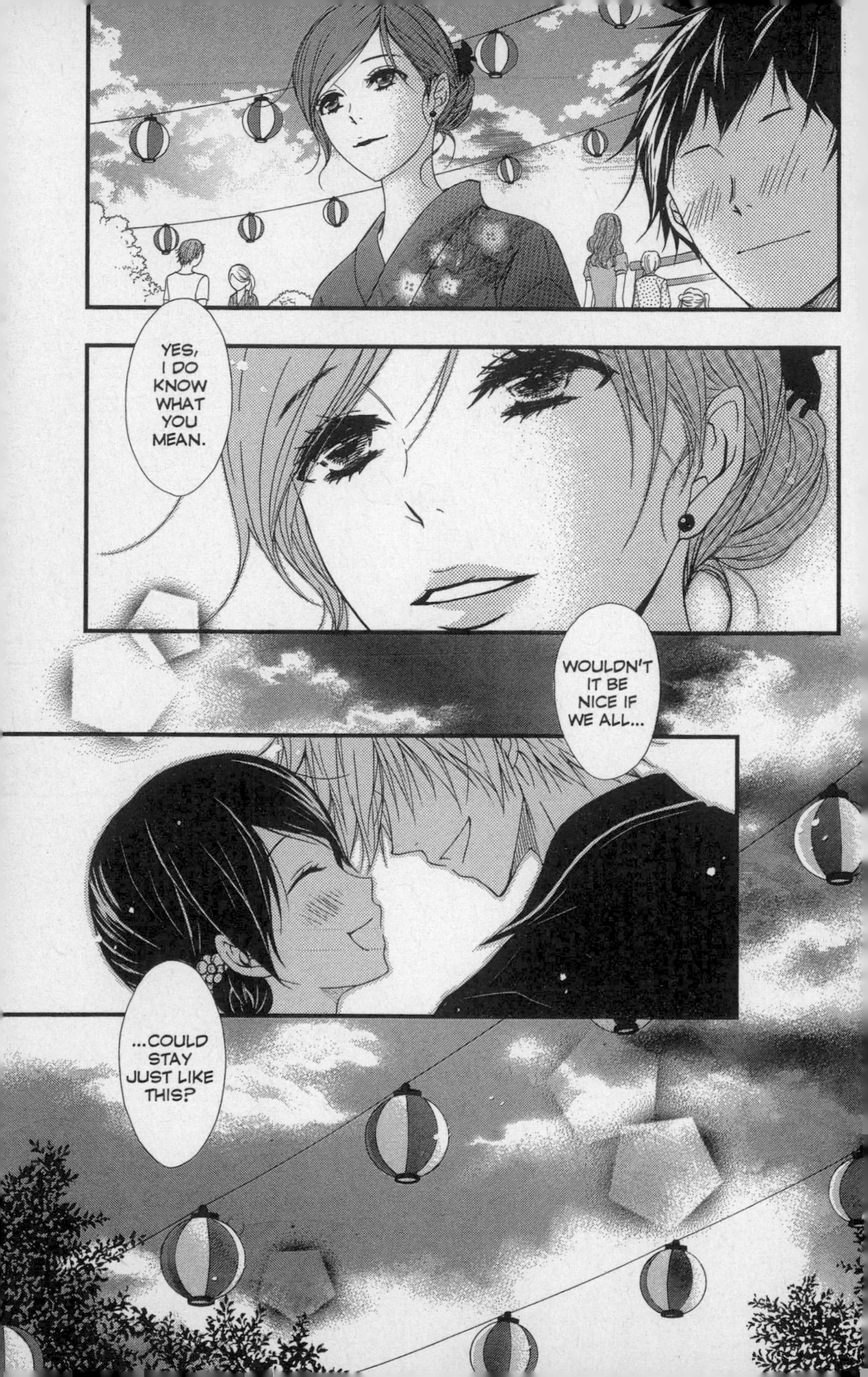
YES, I DO KNOW WHAT YOU MEAN.
WOULDN'T IT BE NICE IF WE ALL...
...COULD STAY JUST LIKE THIS?

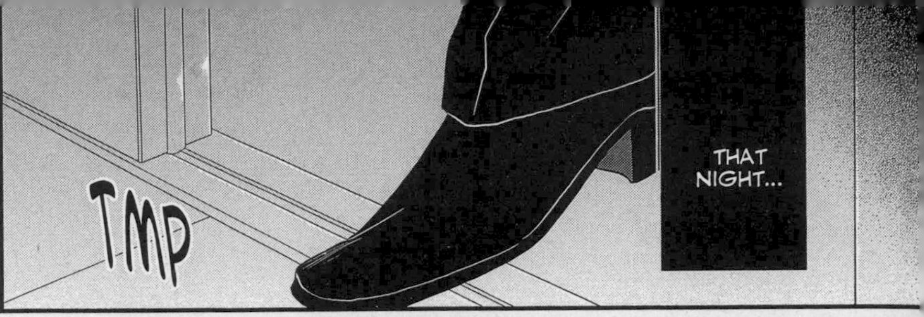
THAT NIGHT...
TMP

EPISODE 2 — ANTLER (ABYSS)

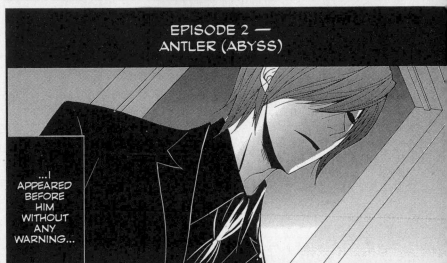

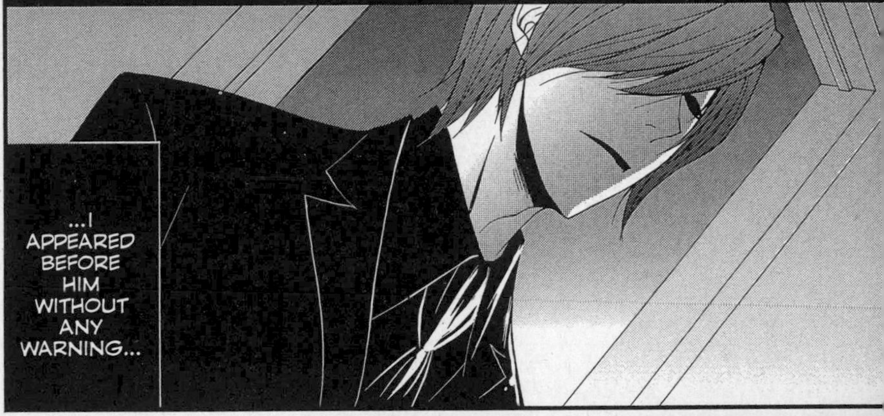
...I APPEARED BEFORE HIM WITHOUT ANY WARNING...

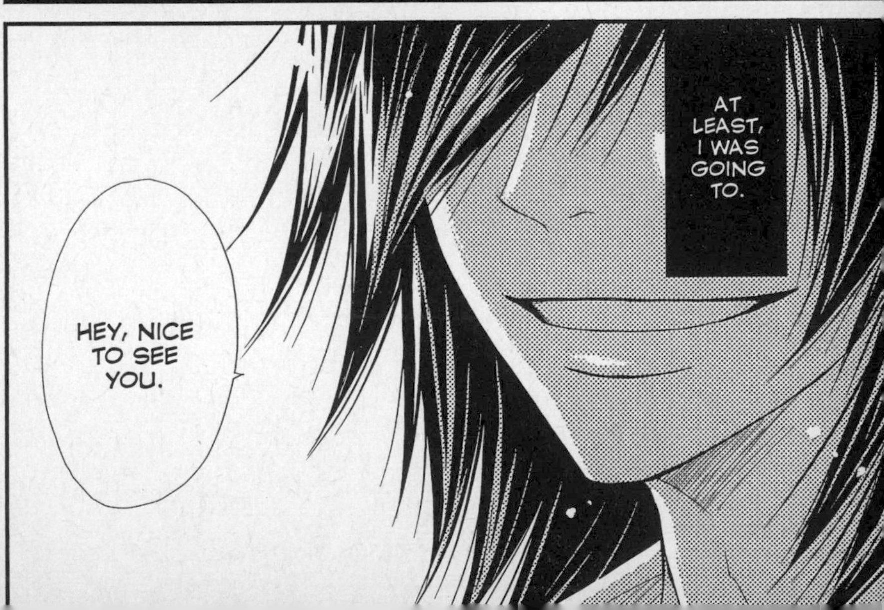
AT LEAST, I WAS GOING TO.
HEY, NICE TO SEE YOU.

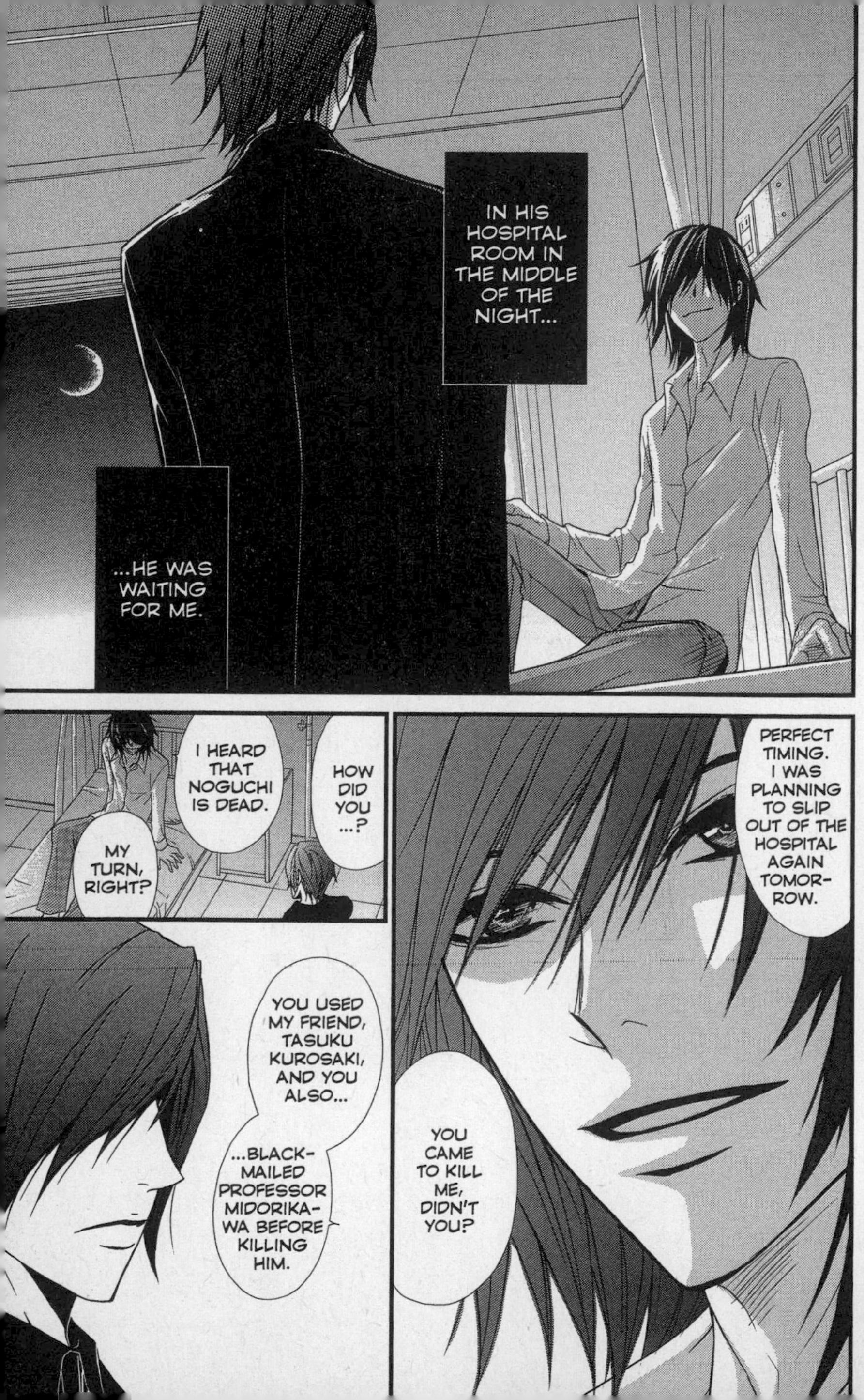
IN HIS HOSPITAL ROOM IN THE MIDDLE OF THE NIGHT...
...HE WAS WAITING FOR ME.
I HEARD THAT NOGUCHI IS DEAD.
MY TURN, RIGHT?
HOW DID YOU ...?
PERFECT TIMING. I WAS PLANNING TO SLIP OUT OF THE HOSPITAL AGAIN TOMOR-ROW.
YOU CAME TO KILL ME, DIDN'T YOU?
YOU USED MY FRIEND, TASUKU KUROSAKI, AND YOU ALSO...
...BLACK-MAILED PROFESSOR MIDORIKA-WA BEFORE KILLING HIM.

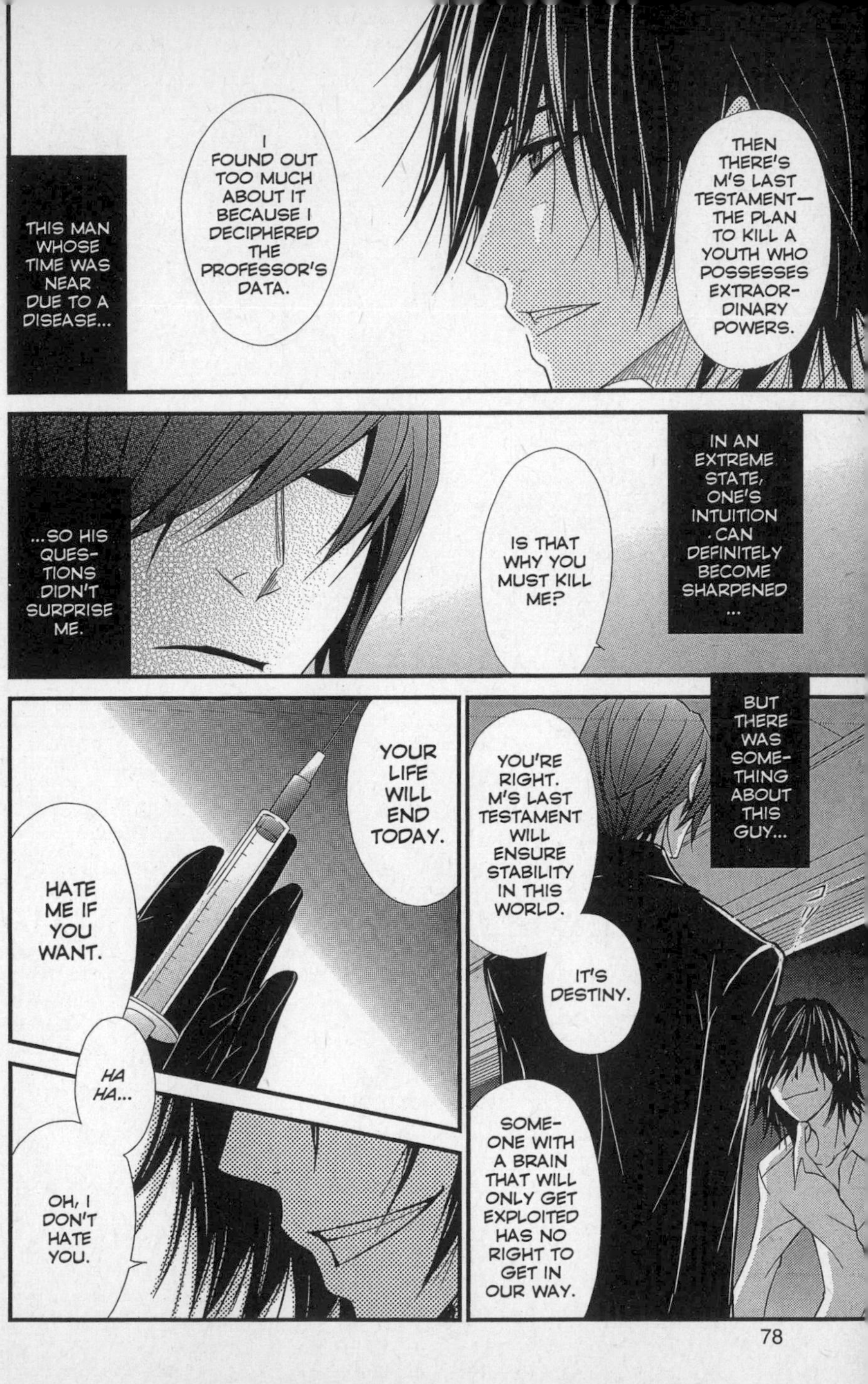
THEN THERE'S M'S LAST TESTAMENT—THE PLAN TO KILL A YOUTH WHO POSSESSES EXTRAORDINARY POWERS.
I FOUND OUT TOO MUCH ABOUT IT BECAUSE I DECIPHERED THE PROFESSOR'S DATA.
THIS MAN WHOSE TIME WAS NEAR DUE TO A DISEASE...
IN AN EXTREME STATE, ONE'S INTUITION CAN DEFINITELY BECOME SHARPENED...
IS THAT WHY YOU MUST KILL ME?
...SO HIS QUESTIONS DIDN'T SURPRISE ME.
BUT THERE WAS SOMETHING ABOUT THIS GUY...
YOU'RE RIGHT. M'S LAST TESTAMENT WILL ENSURE STABILITY IN THIS WORLD.
IT'S DESTINY.
SOMEONE WITH A BRAIN THAT WILL ONLY GET EXPLOITED HAS NO RIGHT TO GET IN OUR WAY.
YOUR LIFE WILL END TODAY.
HATE ME IF YOU WANT.
HA HA...
OH, I DON'T HATE YOU.

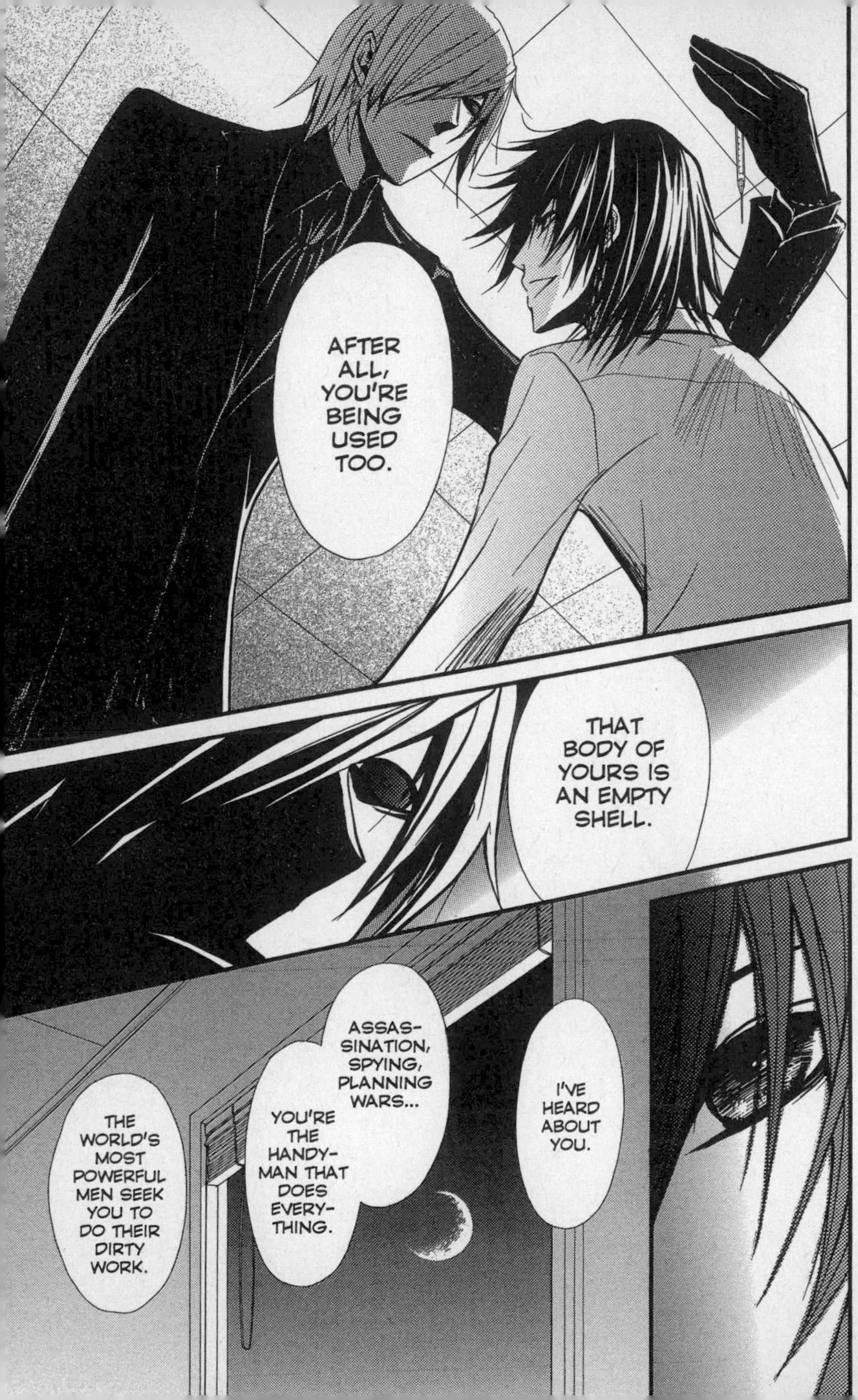
AFTER ALL, YOU'RE BEING USED TOO.
THAT BODY OF YOURS IS AN EMPTY SHELL.
I'VE HEARD ABOUT YOU.
ASSAS-SINATION, SPYING, PLANNING WARS...
YOU'RE THE HANDY-MAN THAT DOES EVERY-THING.
THE WORLD'S MOST POWERFUL MEN SEEK YOU TO DO THEIR DIRTY WORK.

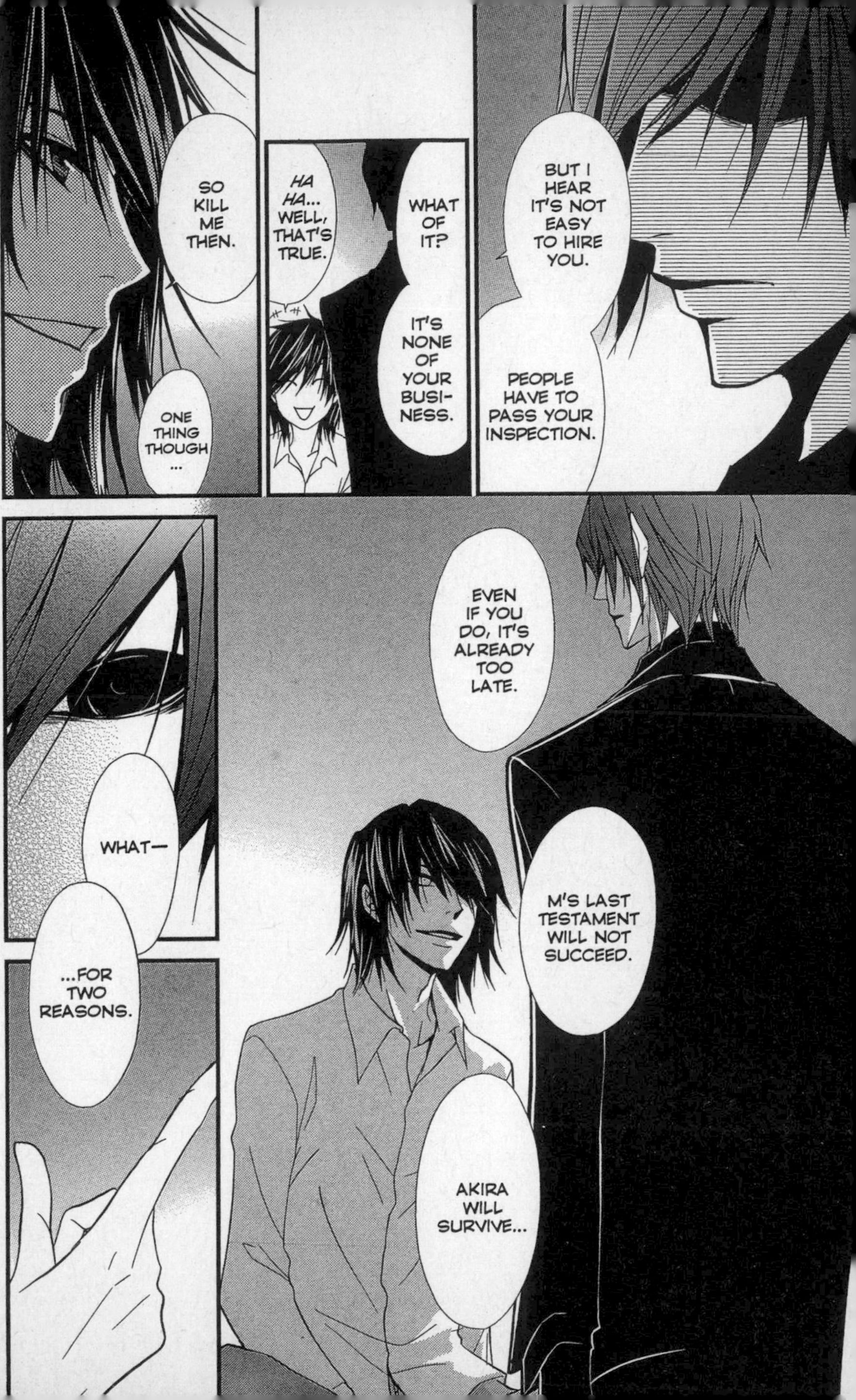
BUT I HEAR IT'S NOT EASY TO HIRE YOU.
PEOPLE HAVE TO PASS YOUR INSPECTION.
WHAT OF IT?
IT'S NONE OF YOUR BUSI-NESS.
HA HA... WELL, THAT'S TRUE.
SO KILL ME THEN.
ONE THING THOUGH ...
EVEN IF YOU DO, IT'S ALREADY TOO LATE.
WHAT—
...FOR TWO REASONS.
M'S LAST TESTAMENT WILL NOT SUCCEED.
AKIRA WILL SURVIVE...

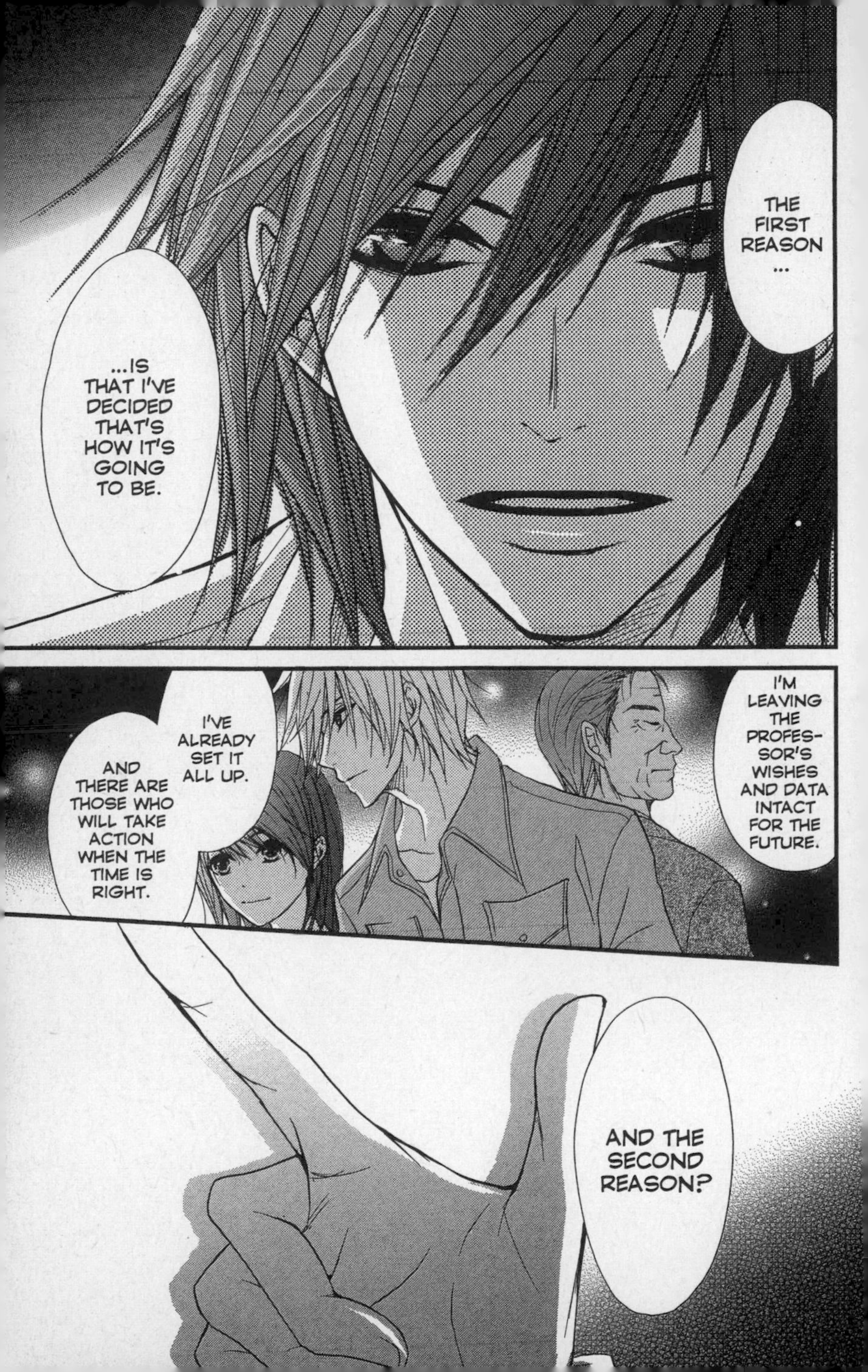
THE FIRST REASON ...
...IS THAT I'VE DECIDED THAT'S HOW IT'S GOING TO BE.
I'M LEAVING THE PROFES-SOR'S WISHES AND DATA INTACT FOR THE FUTURE.
I'VE ALREADY SET IT ALL UP.
AND THERE ARE THOSE WHO WILL TAKE ACTION WHEN THE TIME IS RIGHT.
AND THE SECOND REASON?

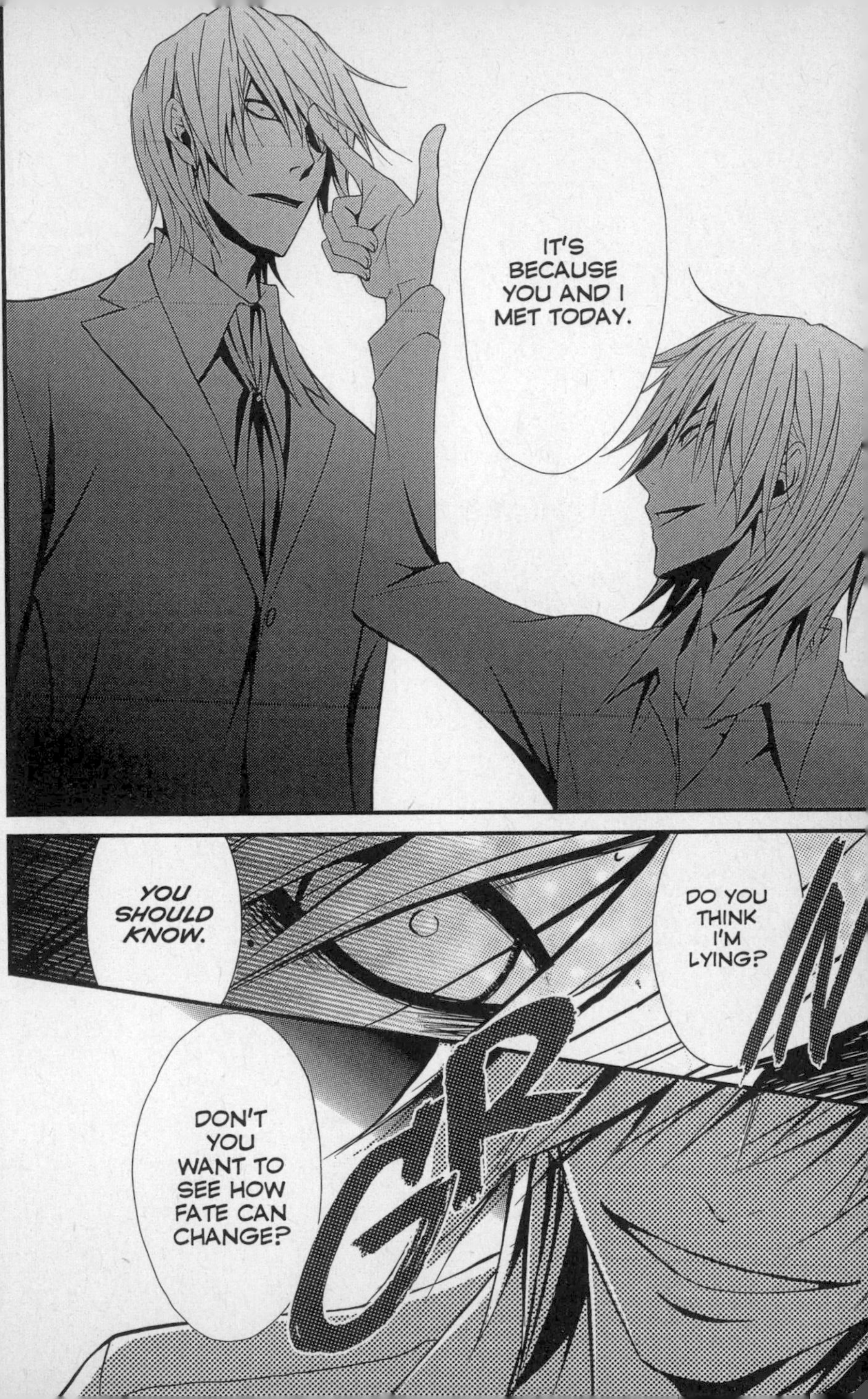
IT'S BECAUSE YOU AND I MET TODAY.
DO YOU THINK I'M LYING?
YOU SHOULD KNOW.
DON'T YOU WANT TO SEE HOW FATE CAN CHANGE?
GRIN

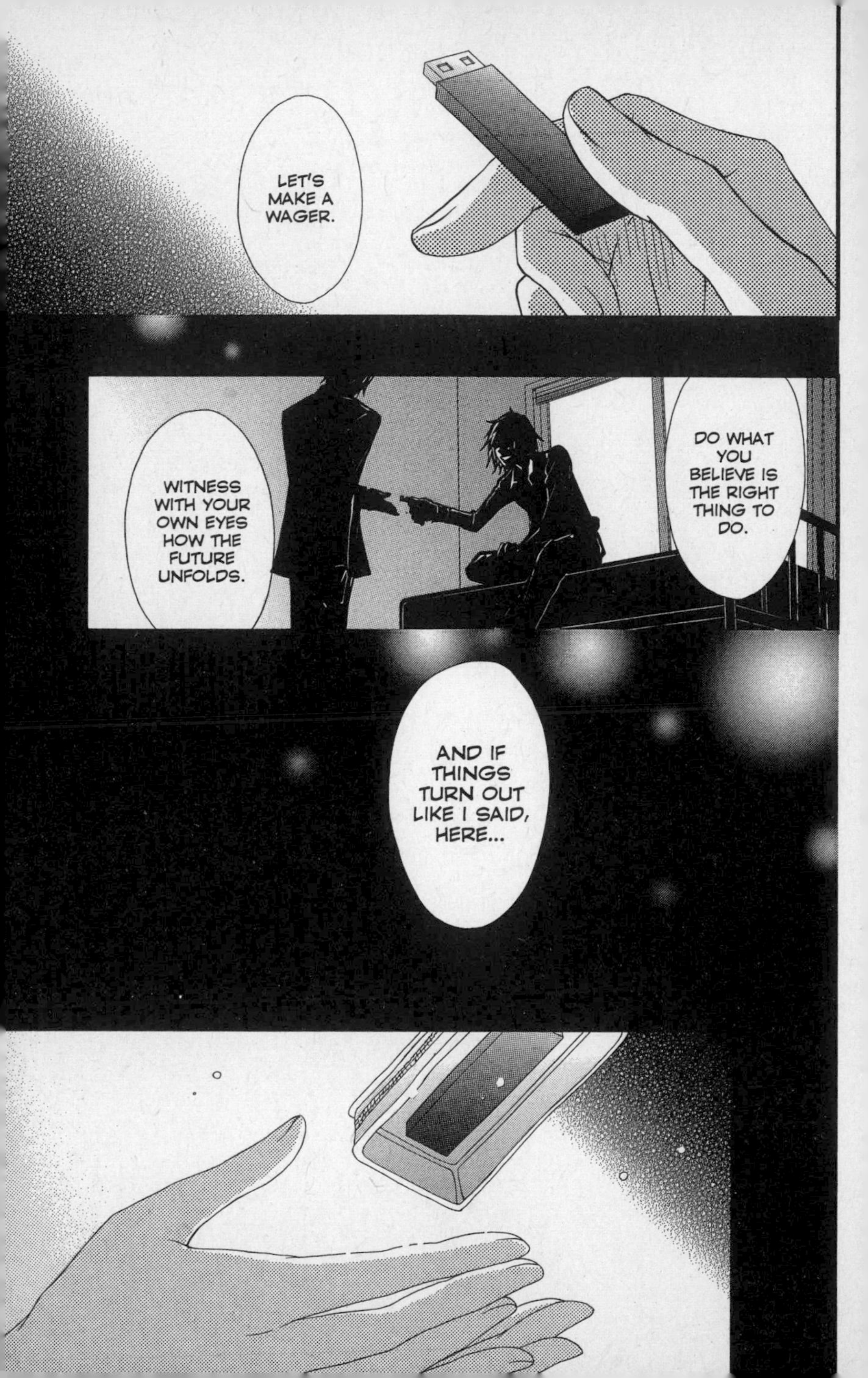
LET'S MAKE A WAGER.
DO WHAT YOU BELIEVE IS THE RIGHT THING TO DO.
WITNESS WITH YOUR OWN EYES HOW THE FUTURE UNFOLDS.
AND IF THINGS TURN OUT LIKE I SAID, HERE...

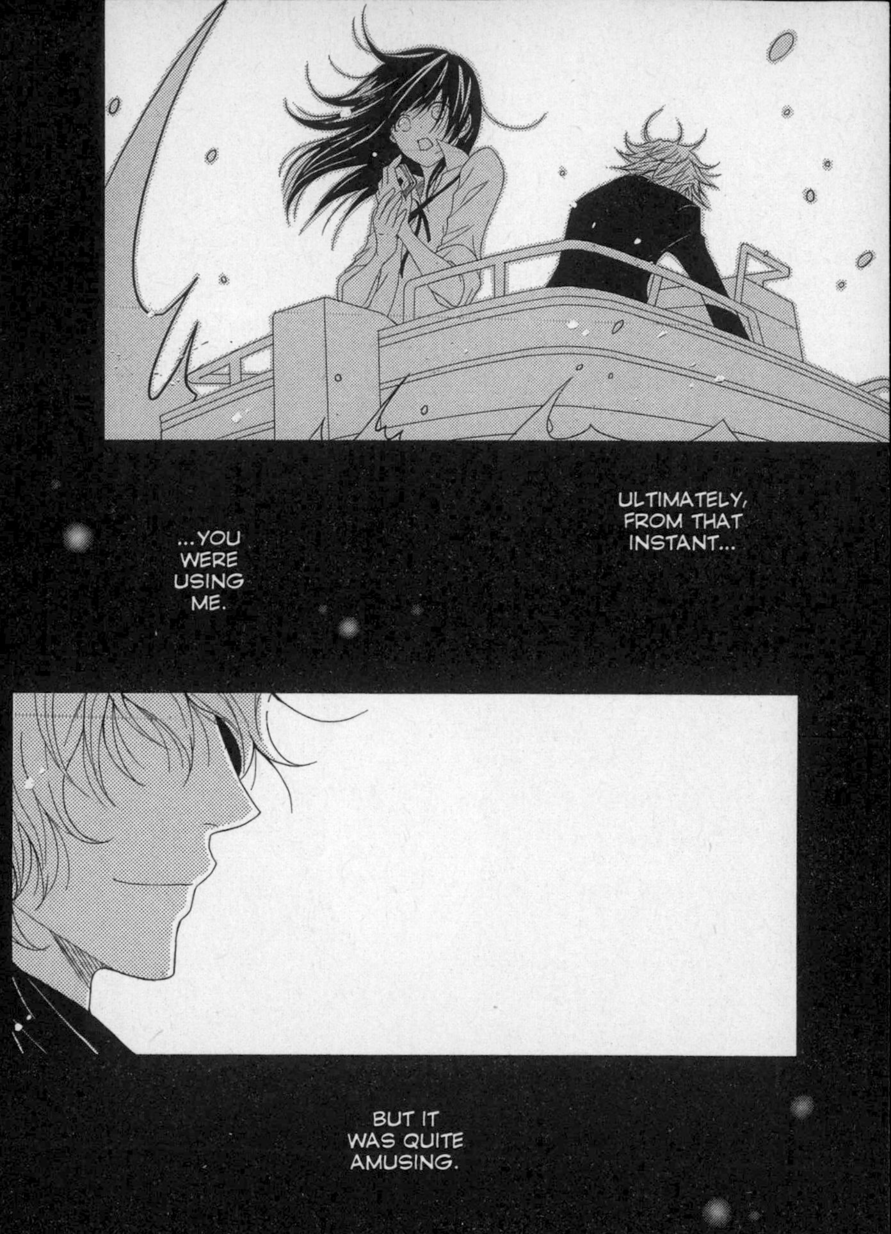
ULTIMATELY, FROM THAT INSTANT...
...YOU WERE USING ME.
BUT IT WAS QUITE AMUSING.

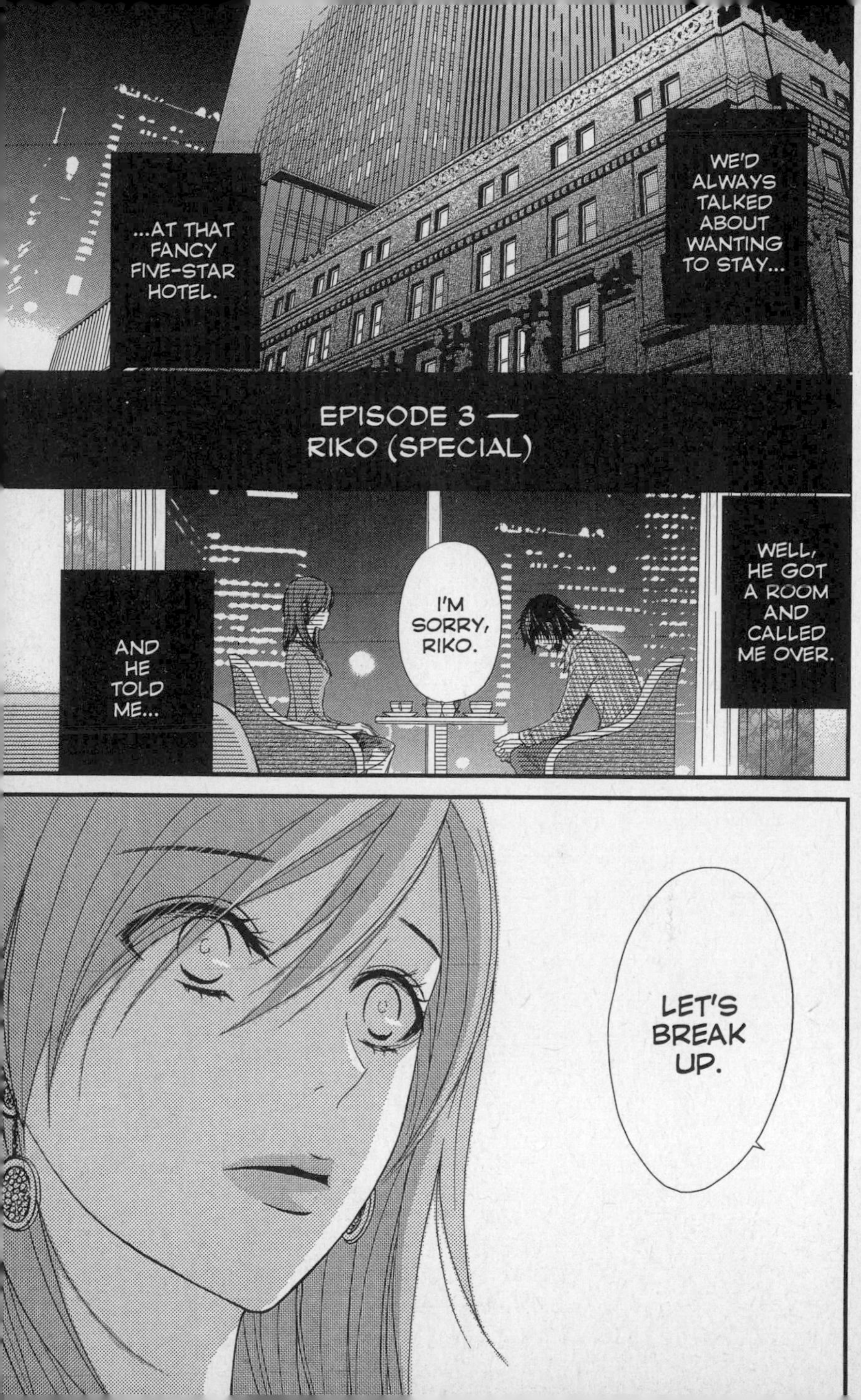
WE'D ALWAYS TALKED ABOUT WANTING TO STAY...
...AT THAT FANCY FIVE-STAR HOTEL.
EPISODE 3 — RIKO (SPECIAL)
WELL, HE GOT A ROOM AND CALLED ME OVER.
I'M SORRY, RIKO.
AND HE TOLD ME...
LET'S BREAK UP.

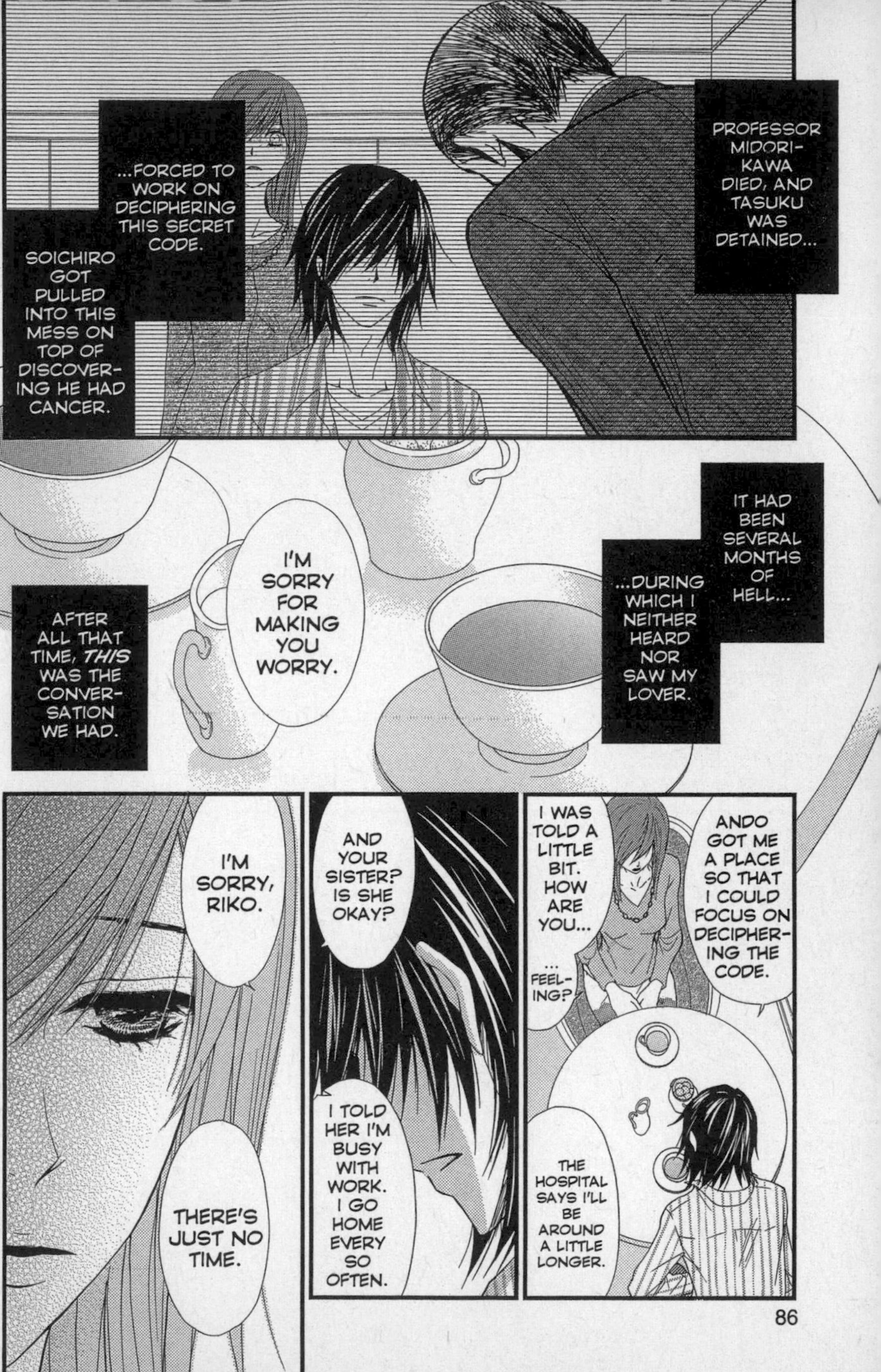
PROFESSOR MIDORI-KAWA DIED, AND TASUKU WAS DETAINED...
SOICHIRO GOT PULLED INTO THIS MESS ON TOP OF DISCOVER-ING HE HAD CANCER.
...FORCED TO WORK ON DECIPHERING THIS SECRET CODE.
IT HAD BEEN SEVERAL MONTHS OF HELL...
...DURING WHICH I NEITHER HEARD NOR SAW MY LOVER.
I'M SORRY FOR MAKING YOU WORRY.
AFTER ALL THAT TIME, *THIS* WAS THE CONVER-SATION WE HAD.
ANDO GOT ME A PLACE SO THAT I COULD FOCUS ON DECIPHER-ING THE CODE.
I WAS TOLD A LITTLE BIT. HOW ARE YOU...
...FEEL-ING?
THE HOSPITAL SAYS I'LL BE AROUND A LITTLE LONGER.
AND YOUR SISTER? IS SHE OKAY?
I TOLD HER I'M BUSY WITH WORK. I GO HOME EVERY SO OFTEN.
I'M SORRY, RIKO.
THERE'S JUST NO TIME.

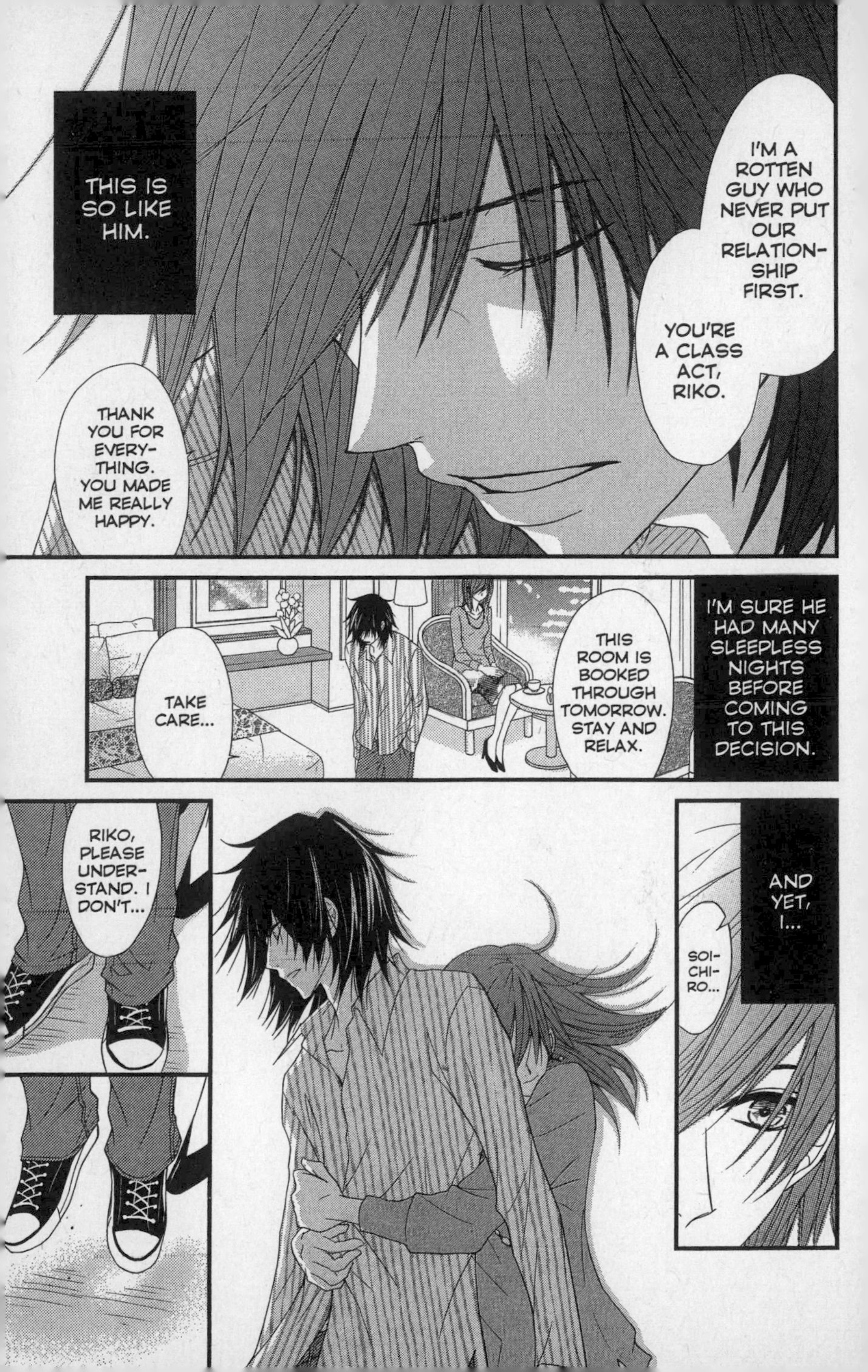
I'M A ROTTEN GUY WHO NEVER PUT OUR RELATIONSHIP FIRST.
YOU'RE A CLASS ACT, RIKO.
THIS IS SO LIKE HIM.
THANK YOU FOR EVERYTHING. YOU MADE ME REALLY HAPPY.
I'M SURE HE HAD MANY SLEEPLESS NIGHTS BEFORE COMING TO THIS DECISION.
THIS ROOM IS BOOKED THROUGH TOMORROW. STAY AND RELAX.
TAKE CARE...
AND YET, I...
SOI-CHI-RO...
RIKO, PLEASE UNDER-STAND. I DON'T...

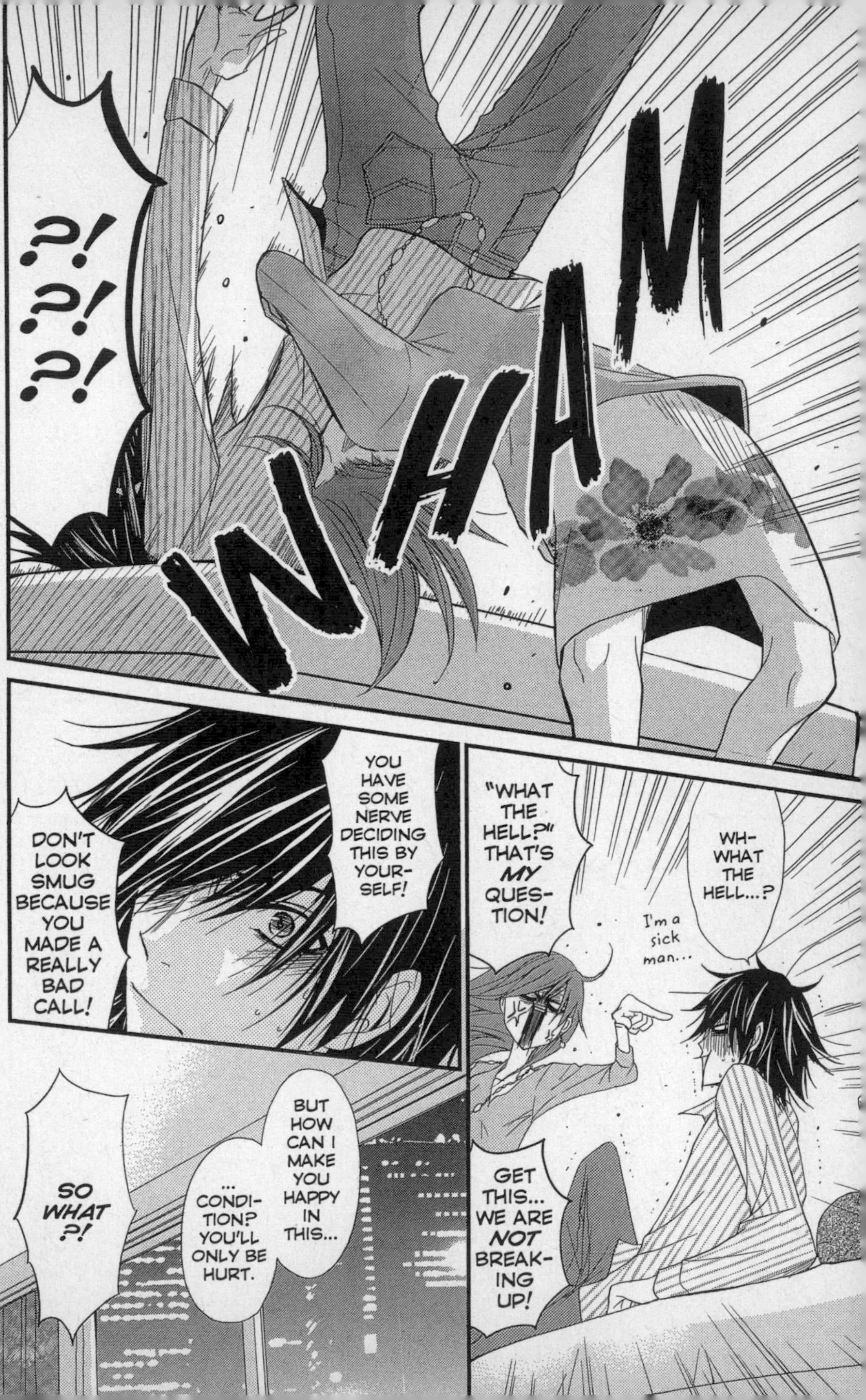
WHAM
?! ?! ?!
WH- WHAT THE HELL...?
I'm a sick man...
"WHAT THE HELL?" THAT'S *MY* QUESTION!
GET THIS... WE ARE *NOT* BREAKING UP!
YOU HAVE SOME NERVE DECIDING THIS BY YOURSELF!
DON'T LOOK SMUG BECAUSE YOU MADE A REALLY BAD CALL!
BUT HOW CAN I MAKE YOU HAPPY IN THIS...
... CONDITION? YOU'LL ONLY BE HURT.
SO *WHAT* ?!

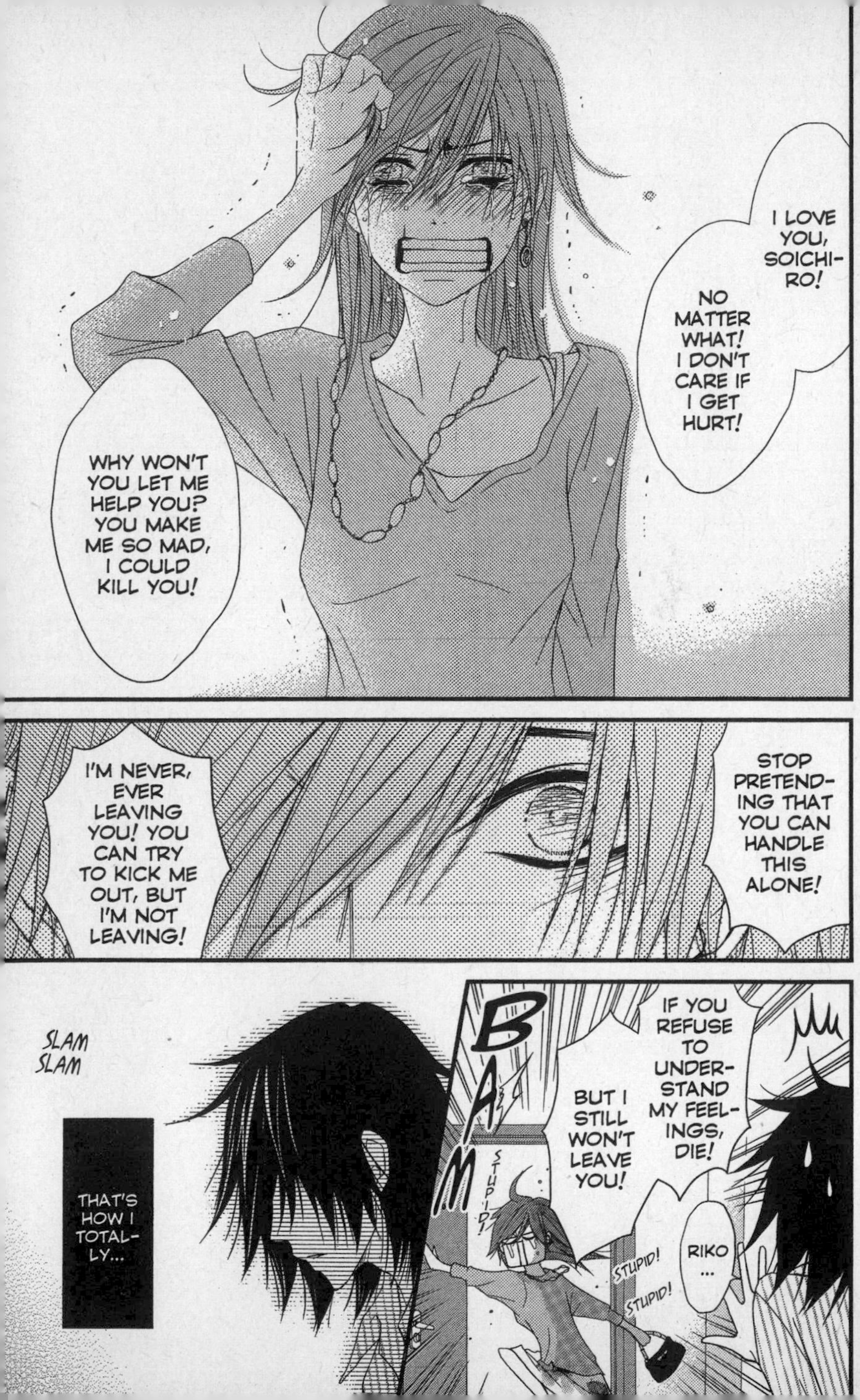
I LOVE YOU, SOICHIRO!
NO MATTER WHAT! I DON'T CARE IF I GET HURT!
WHY WON'T YOU LET ME HELP YOU? YOU MAKE ME SO MAD, I COULD KILL YOU!
STOP PRETENDING THAT YOU CAN HANDLE THIS ALONE!
I'M NEVER, EVER LEAVING YOU! YOU CAN TRY TO KICK ME OUT, BUT I'M NOT LEAVING!
IF YOU REFUSE TO UNDERSTAND MY FEELINGS, DIE!
BUT I STILL WON'T LEAVE YOU!
BAM
STUPID!
RIKO...
STUPID!
STUPID!
SLAM SLAM
THAT'S HOW I TOTALLY...

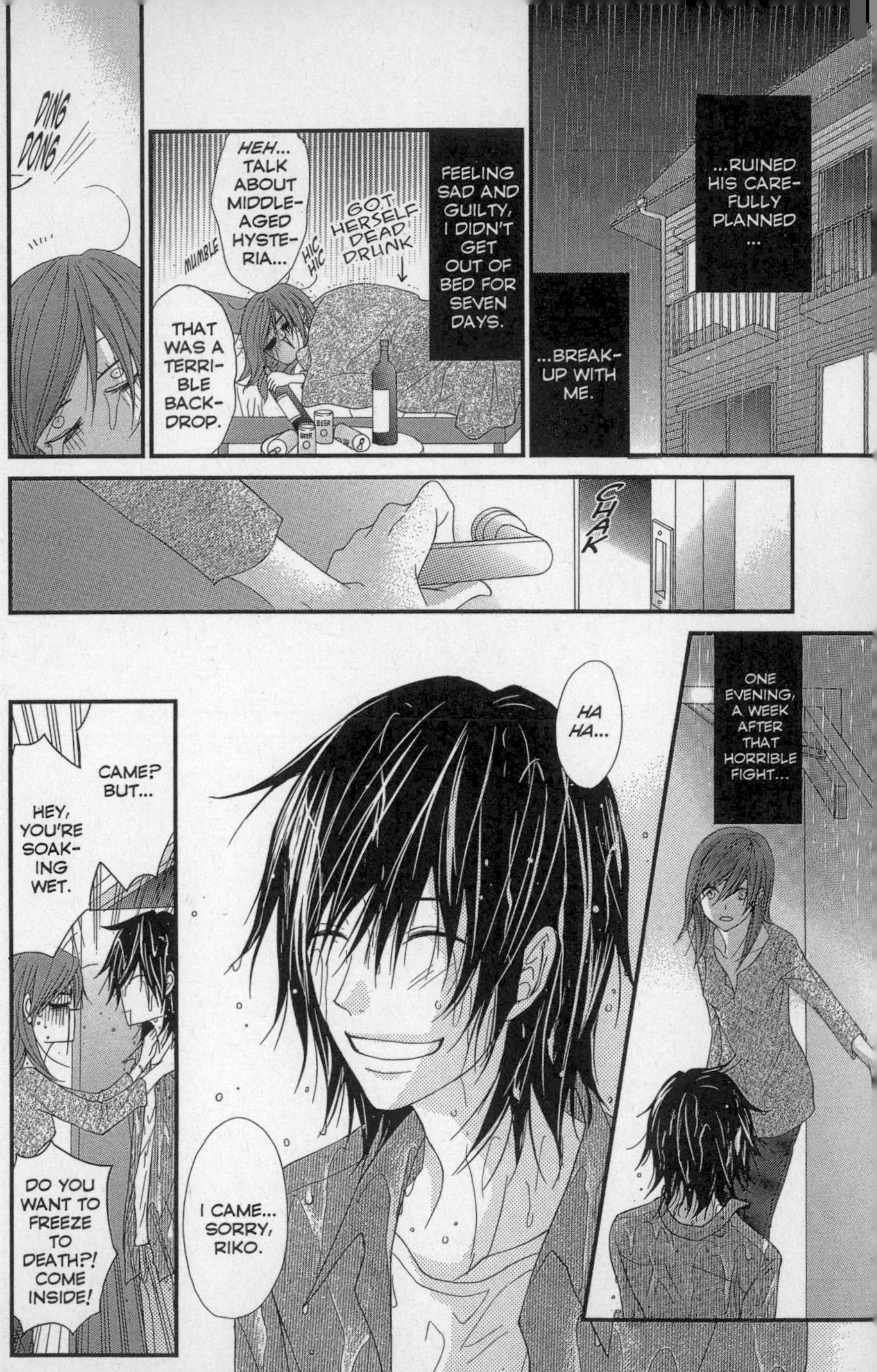
...RUINED HIS CAREFULLY PLANNED ...
...BREAK-UP WITH ME.
FEELING SAD AND GUILTY, I DIDN'T GET OUT OF BED FOR SEVEN DAYS.
GOT HERSELF DEAD DRUNK
HEH... TALK ABOUT MIDDLE-AGED HYSTERIA...
MUMBLE
HIC HIC
THAT WAS A TERRIBLE BACKDROP.
DING DONG
CHAK
ONE EVENING, A WEEK AFTER THAT HORRIBLE FIGHT...
HA HA...
I CAME... SORRY, RIKO.
CAME? BUT...
HEY, YOU'RE SOAKING WET.
DO YOU WANT TO FREEZE TO DEATH?! COME INSIDE!

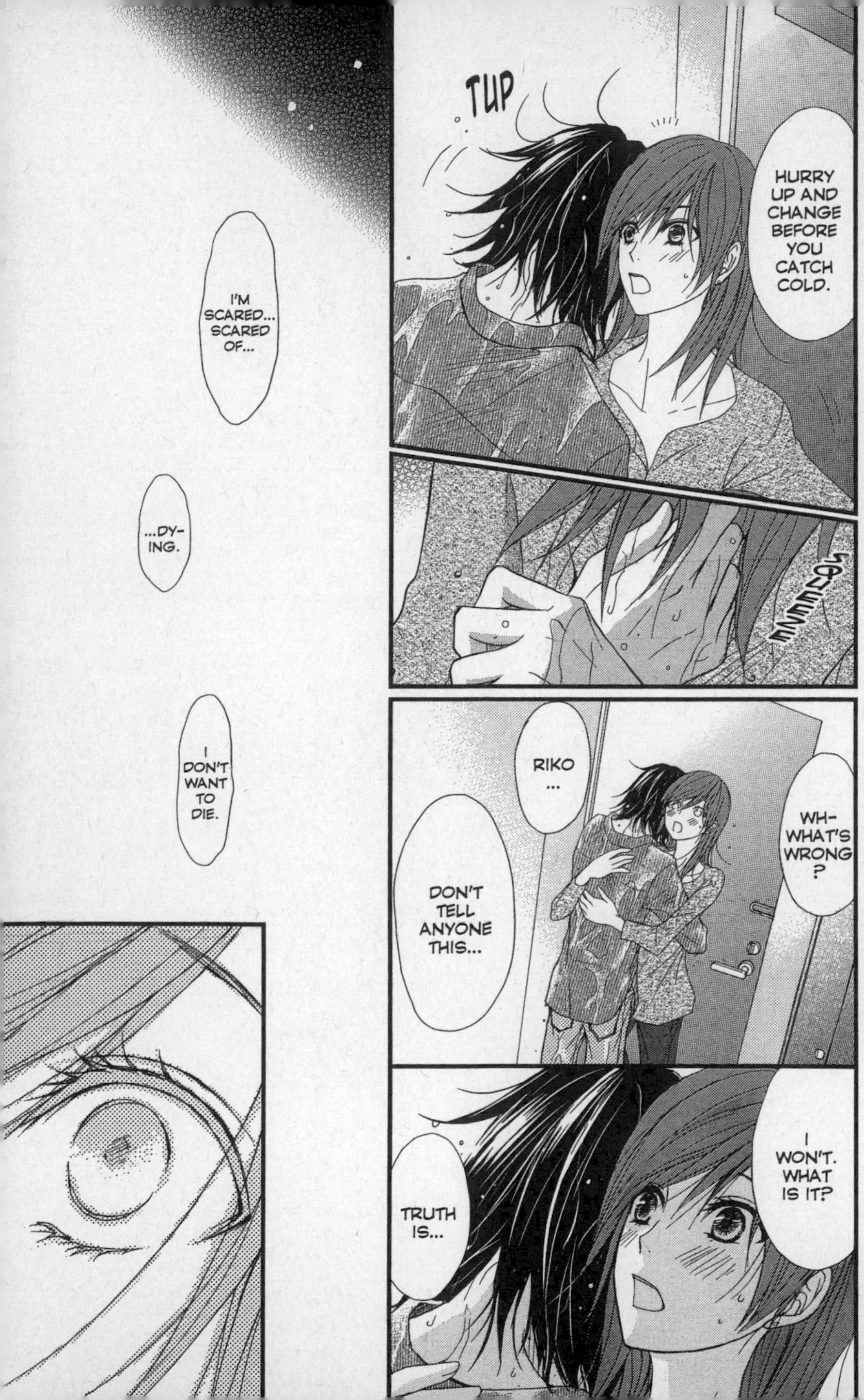
TUP
HURRY UP AND CHANGE BEFORE YOU CATCH COLD.
SQUEEZE
WH-WHAT'S WRONG?
RIKO...
DON'T TELL ANYONE THIS...
I WON'T. WHAT IS IT?
TRUTH IS...
I'M SCARED... SCARED OF...
...DY-ING.
I DON'T WANT TO DIE.

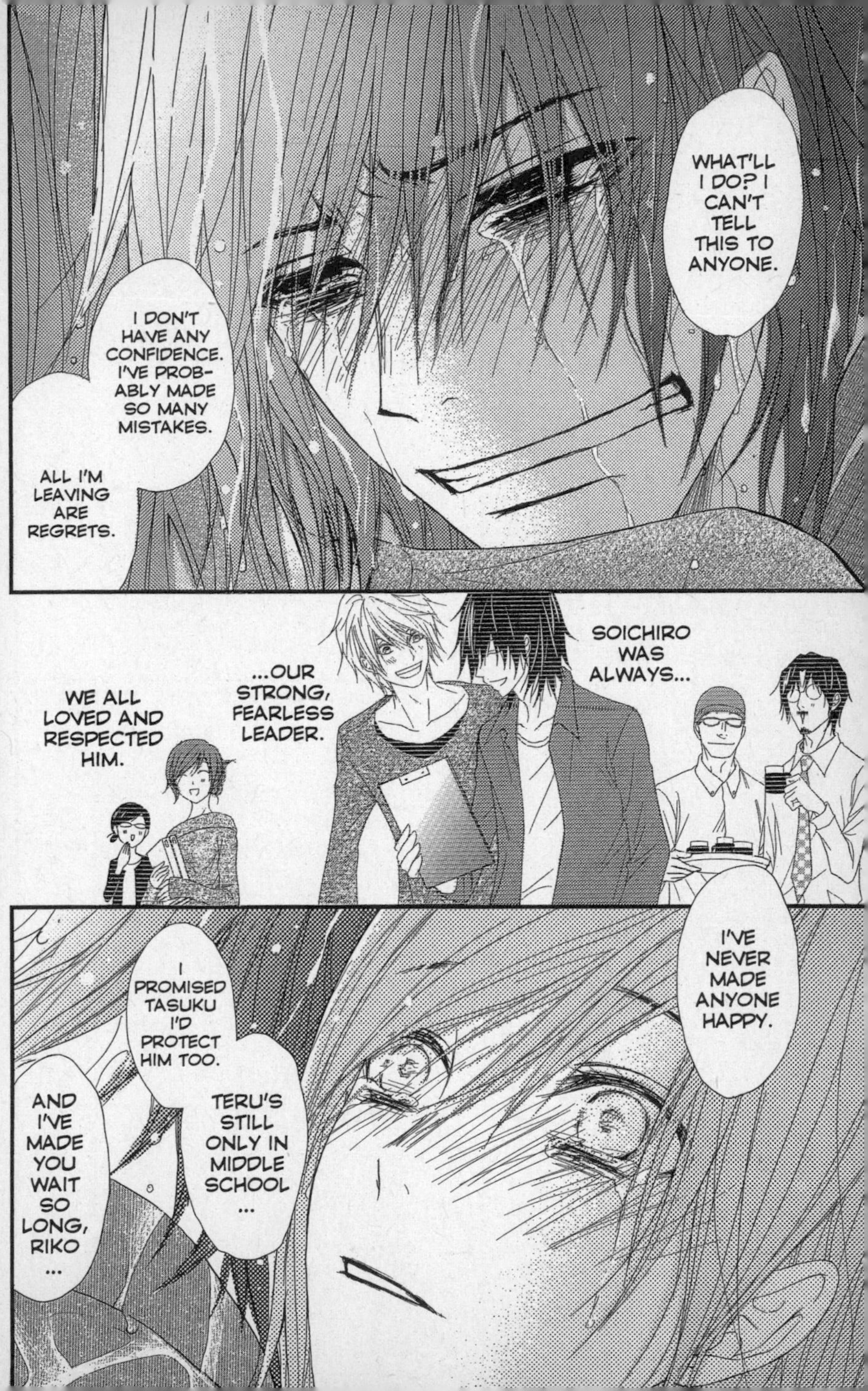
WHAT'LL I DO? I CAN'T TELL THIS TO ANYONE.
I DON'T HAVE ANY CONFIDENCE. I'VE PROB-ABLY MADE SO MANY MISTAKES.
ALL I'M LEAVING ARE REGRETS.
SOICHIRO WAS ALWAYS...
...OUR STRONG, FEARLESS LEADER.
WE ALL LOVED AND RESPECTED HIM.
I'VE NEVER MADE ANYONE HAPPY.
I PROMISED TASUKU I'D PROTECT HIM TOO.
TERU'S STILL ONLY IN MIDDLE SCHOOL ...
AND I'VE MADE YOU WAIT SO LONG, RIKO ...

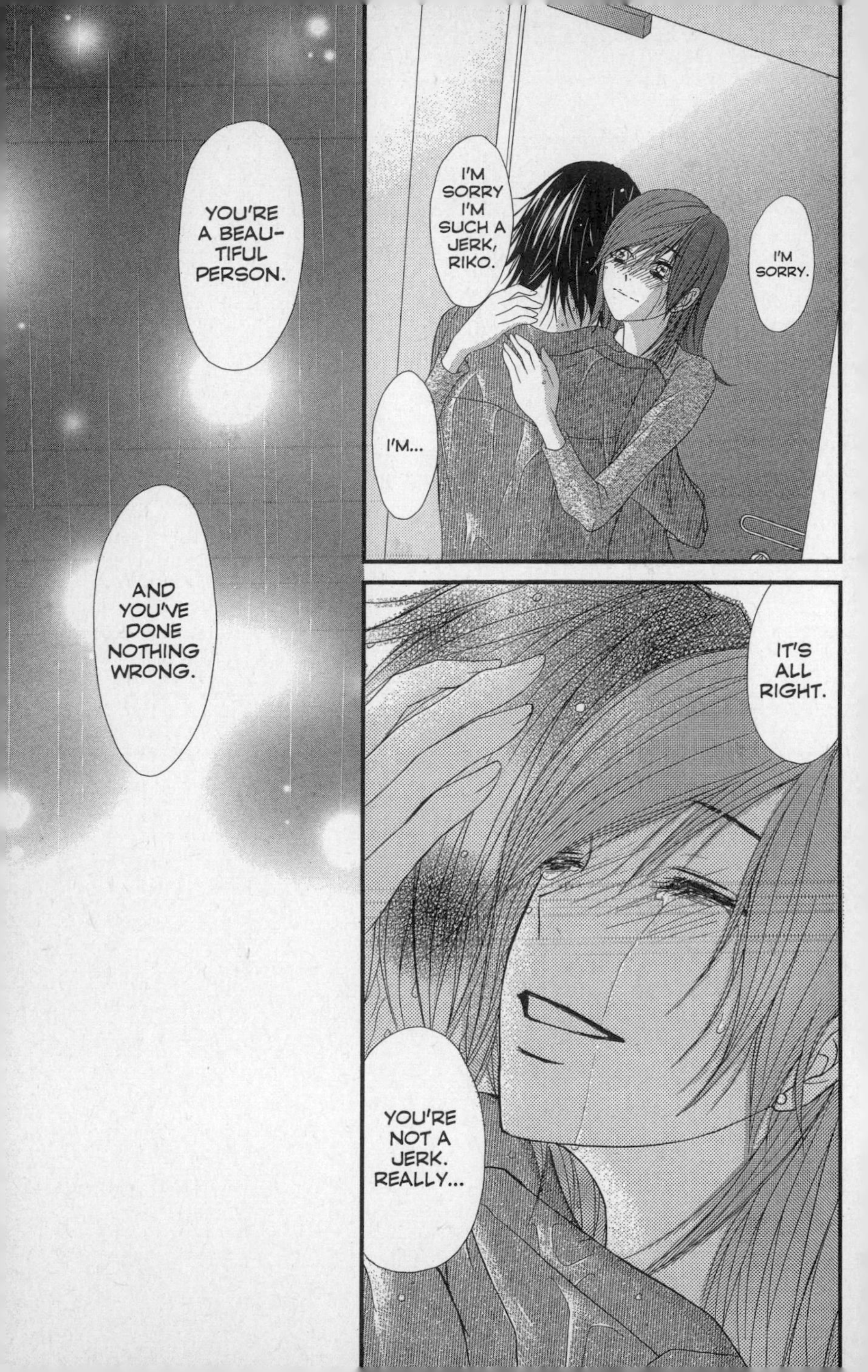
I'M SORRY.
I'M SORRY I'M SUCH A JERK, RIKO.
I'M...
IT'S ALL RIGHT.
YOU'RE NOT A JERK. REALLY...
YOU'RE A BEAU-TIFUL PERSON.
AND YOU'VE DONE NOTHING WRONG.

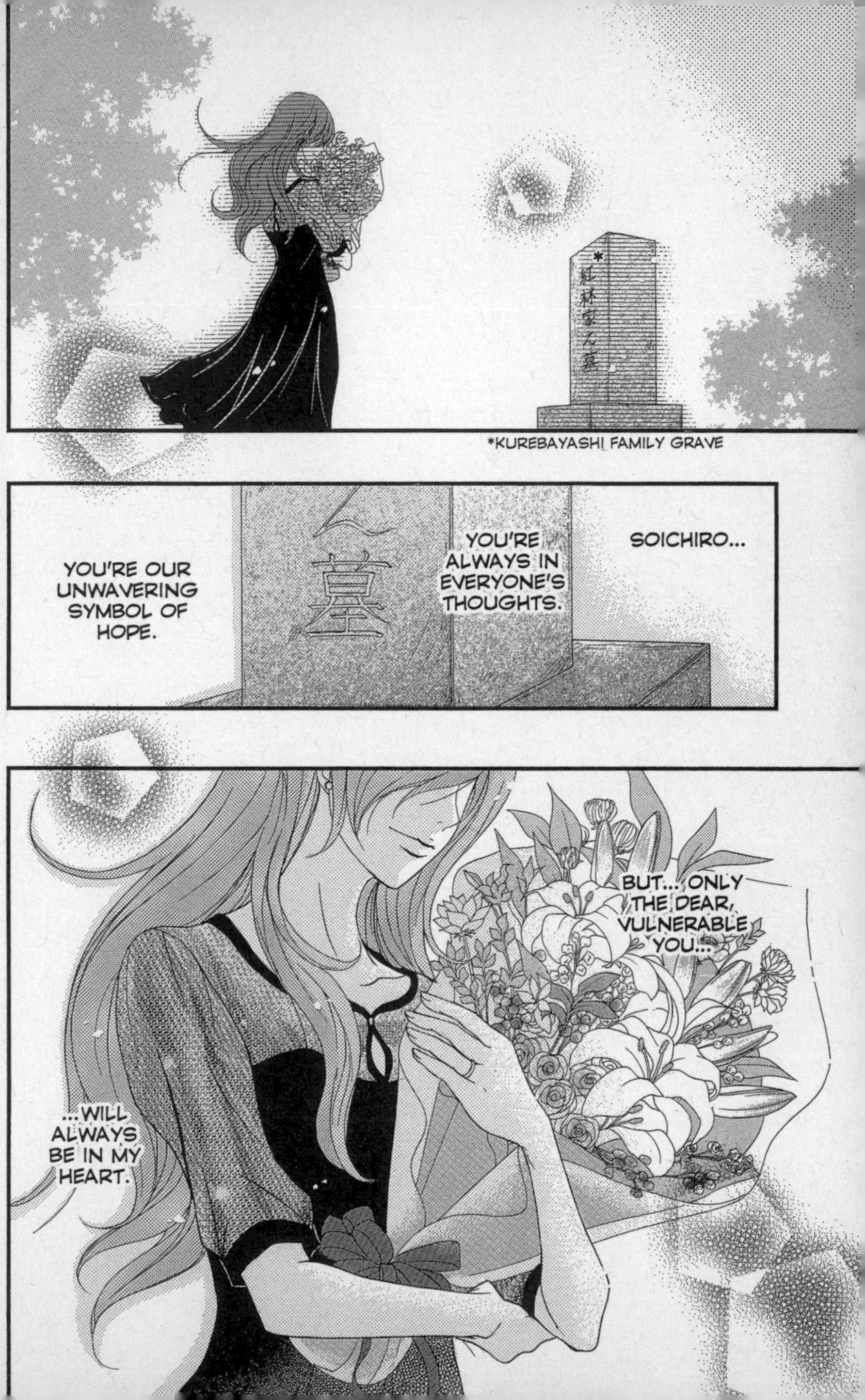
*KUREBAYASHI FAMILY GRAVE
SOICHIRO...
YOU'RE ALWAYS IN EVERYONE'S THOUGHTS.
YOU'RE OUR UNWAVERING SYMBOL OF HOPE.
BUT... ONLY THE DEAR, VULNERABLE YOU...
...WILL ALWAYS BE IN MY HEART.

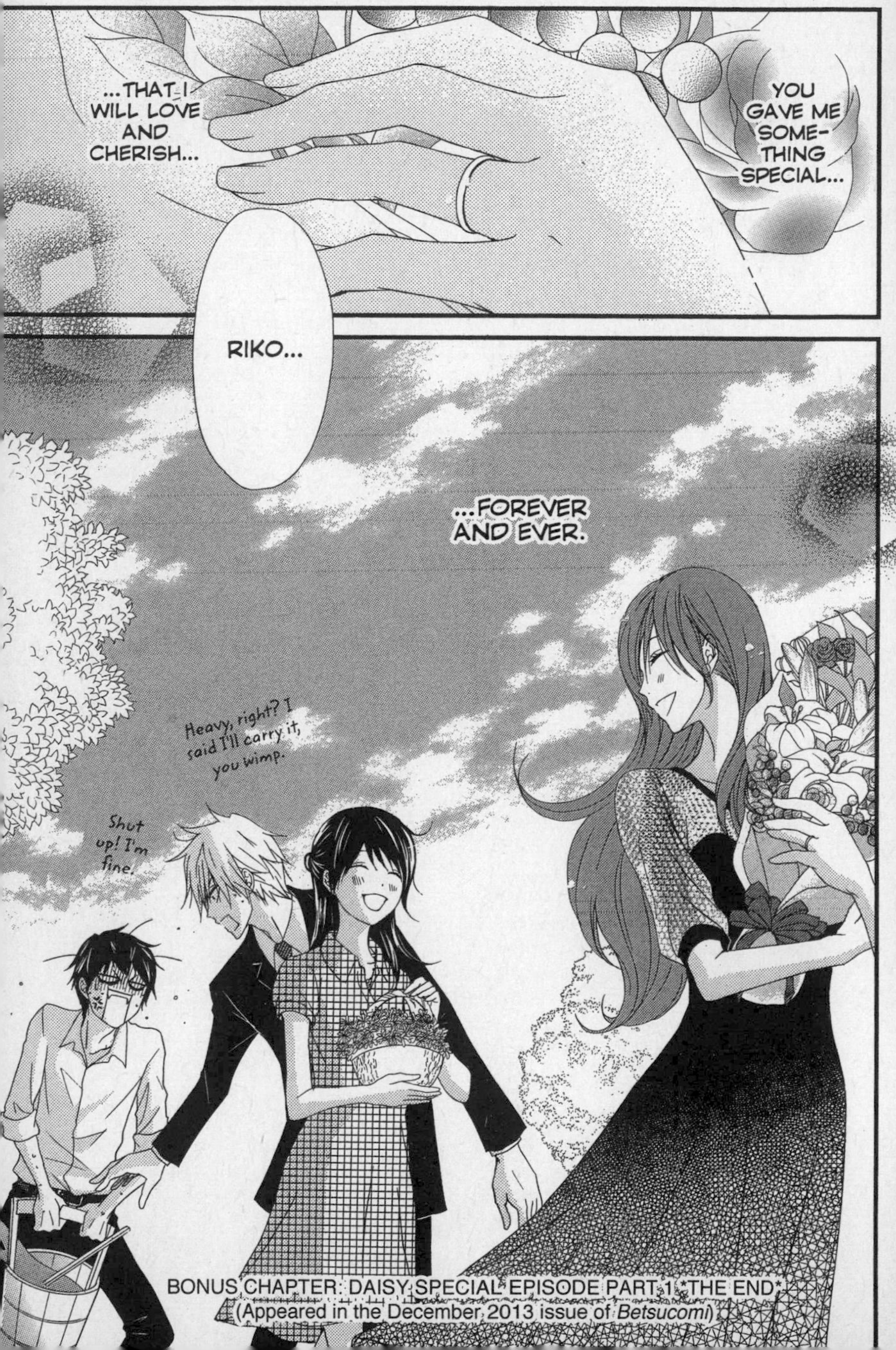
YOU GAVE ME SOMETHING SPECIAL...
...THAT I WILL LOVE AND CHERISH...
RIKO...
...FOREVER AND EVER.
Heavy, right? I said I'll carry it, you wimp.
Shut up! I'm fine.

BONUS CHAPTER: DAISY SPECIAL EPISODE PART 1 *THE END*
(Appeared in the December 2013 issue of *Betsucomi*)

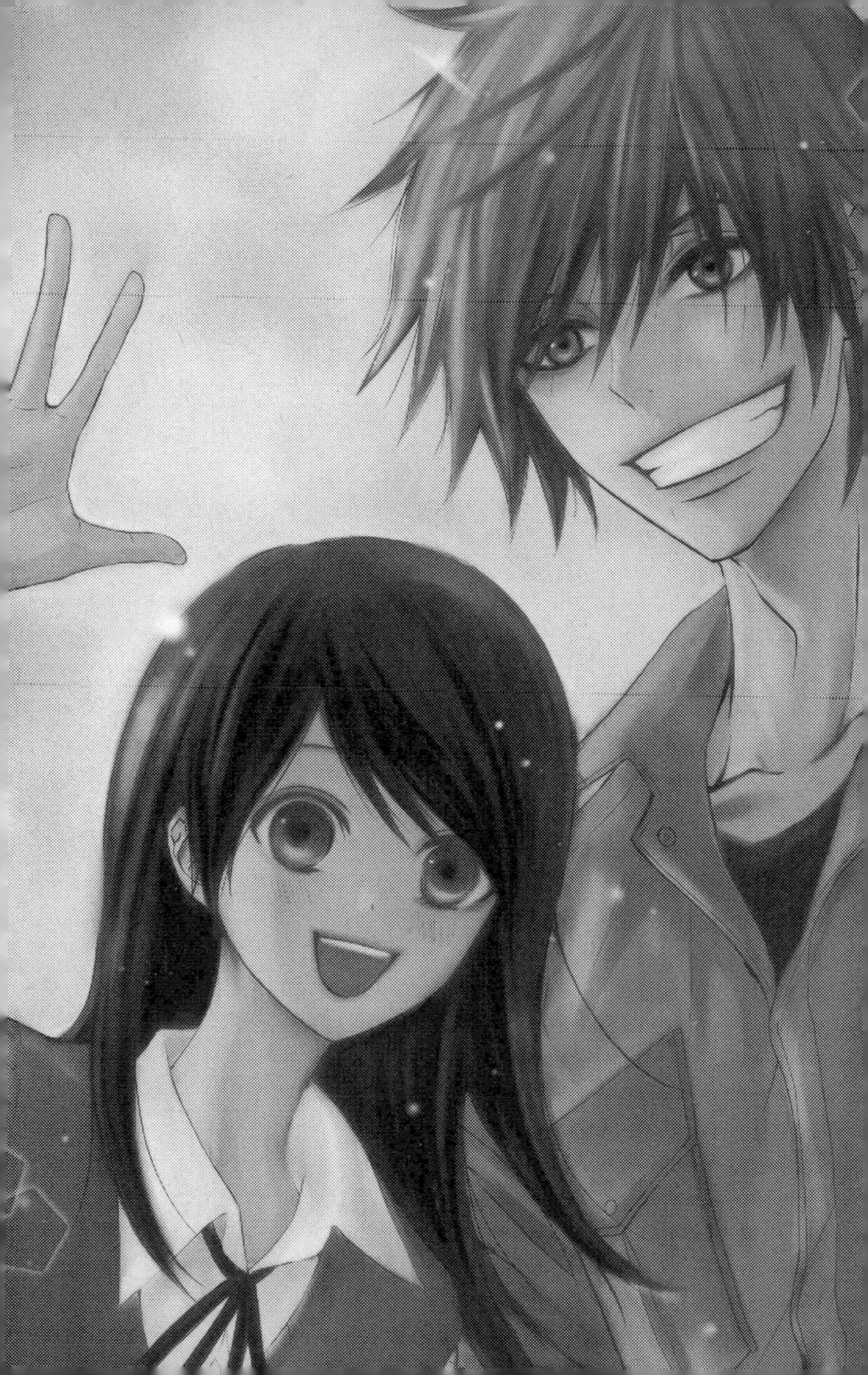

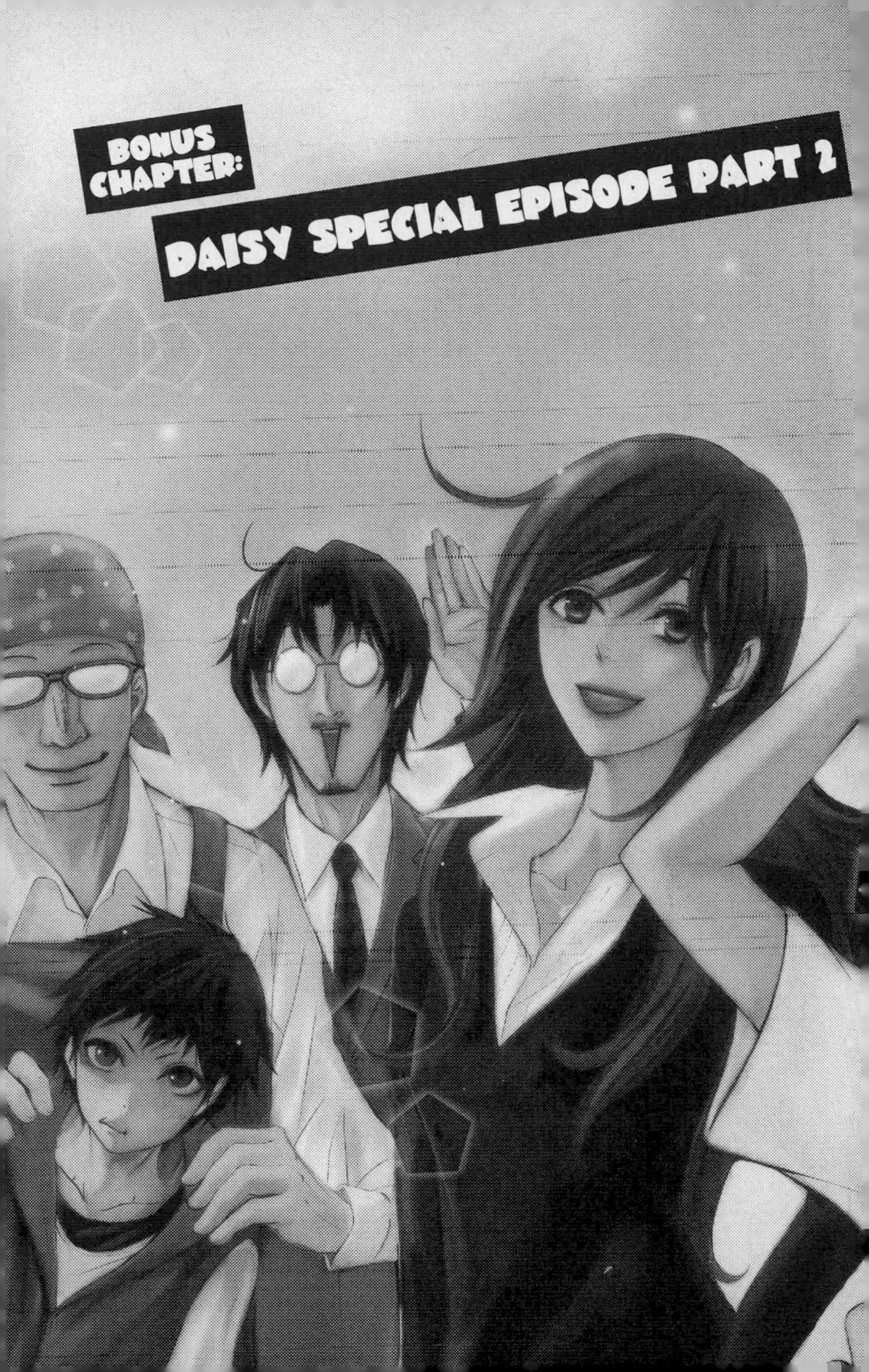
BONUS CHAPTER:
DAISY SPECIAL EPISODE PART 2

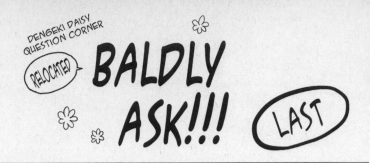

DENGEKI DAISY QUESTION CORNER

(RELOCATED) BALDLY ASK!!! (LAST)

JUST WHAT WAS ANTLER'S GOAL?

(YUKIKO)

I THINK IT BECAME QUITE CLEAR IN THE EXTRA SOICHIRO FEATURE. SO NEVER MIND ABOUT ANTLER. IT WAS SOICHIRO, JUST SOICHIRO.

I'VE ALREADY SET IT ALL UP.

I'M GOING TO LEAVE THE PROFESSOR'S WISHES AND CRITICAL DATA INTACT FOR THE FUTURE.

HE LOOKED AND SOUNDED SO SERIOUS, BUT WHAT HE'D "SET UP" WAS THAT... →

(CHAPTER 64 IN VOLUME 13)

SO WILL KUROSAKI LOSE HIS HAIR OR NOT?

(SO MANY READERS)

THANK YOU VERY MUCH FOR CONTINUING TO ASK ABOUT THIS!! THANKS TO ALL YOUR CONCERN, HE WAS ABLE TO KEEP HIS BLEACH-BLOND HAIR.

EVEN THOUGH THE STORY HAS ENDED, I'M SURE KUROSAKI WILL CONTINUE TO MASSAGE HIS SCALP!

THIS IS THE END OF THE "BALDLY ASK" CORNER!!! THANK YOU VERY MUCH!!!

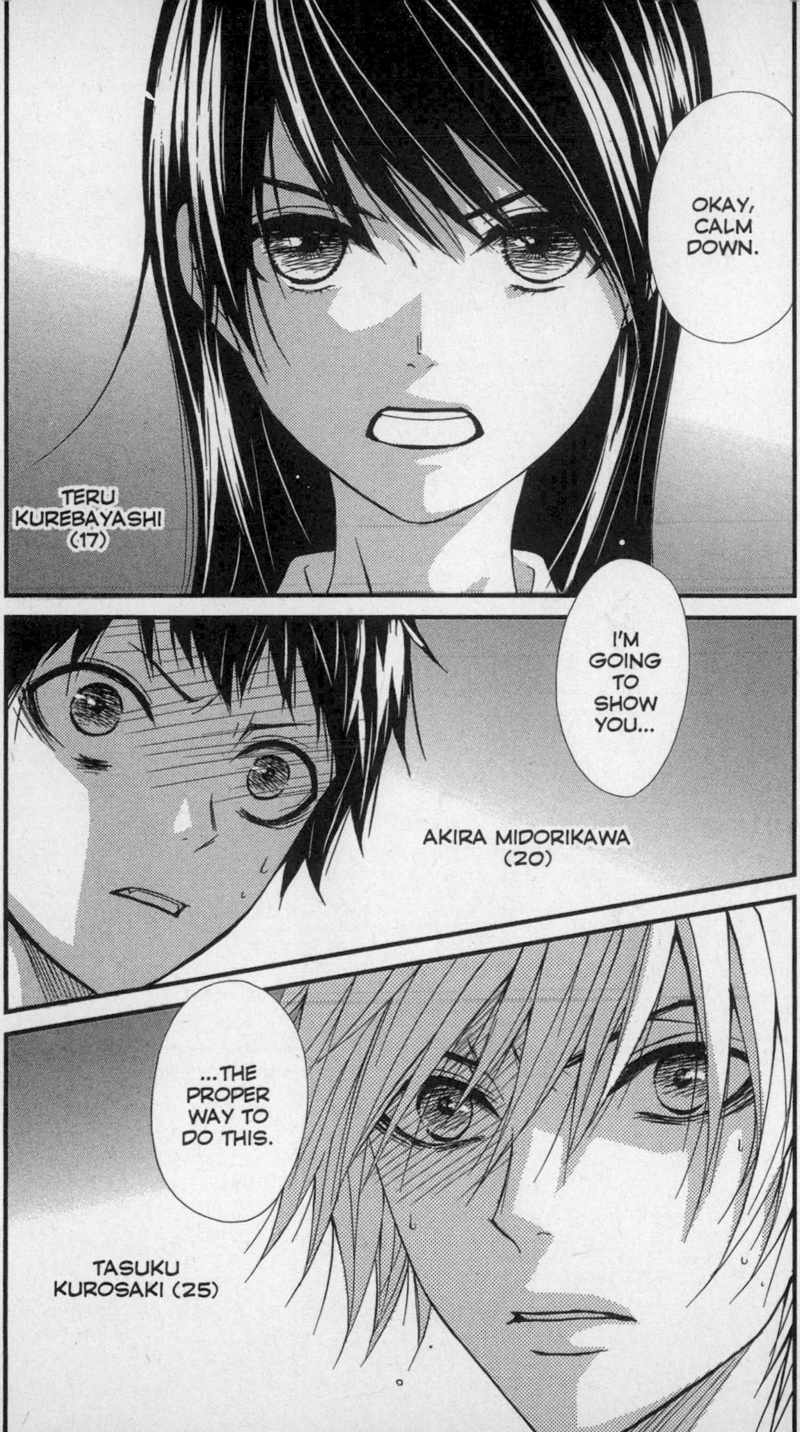
OKAY, CALM DOWN.
TERU KUREBAYASHI (17)
I'M GOING TO SHOW YOU...
AKIRA MIDORIKAWA (20)
...THE PROPER WAY TO DO THIS.
TASUKU KUROSAKI (25)

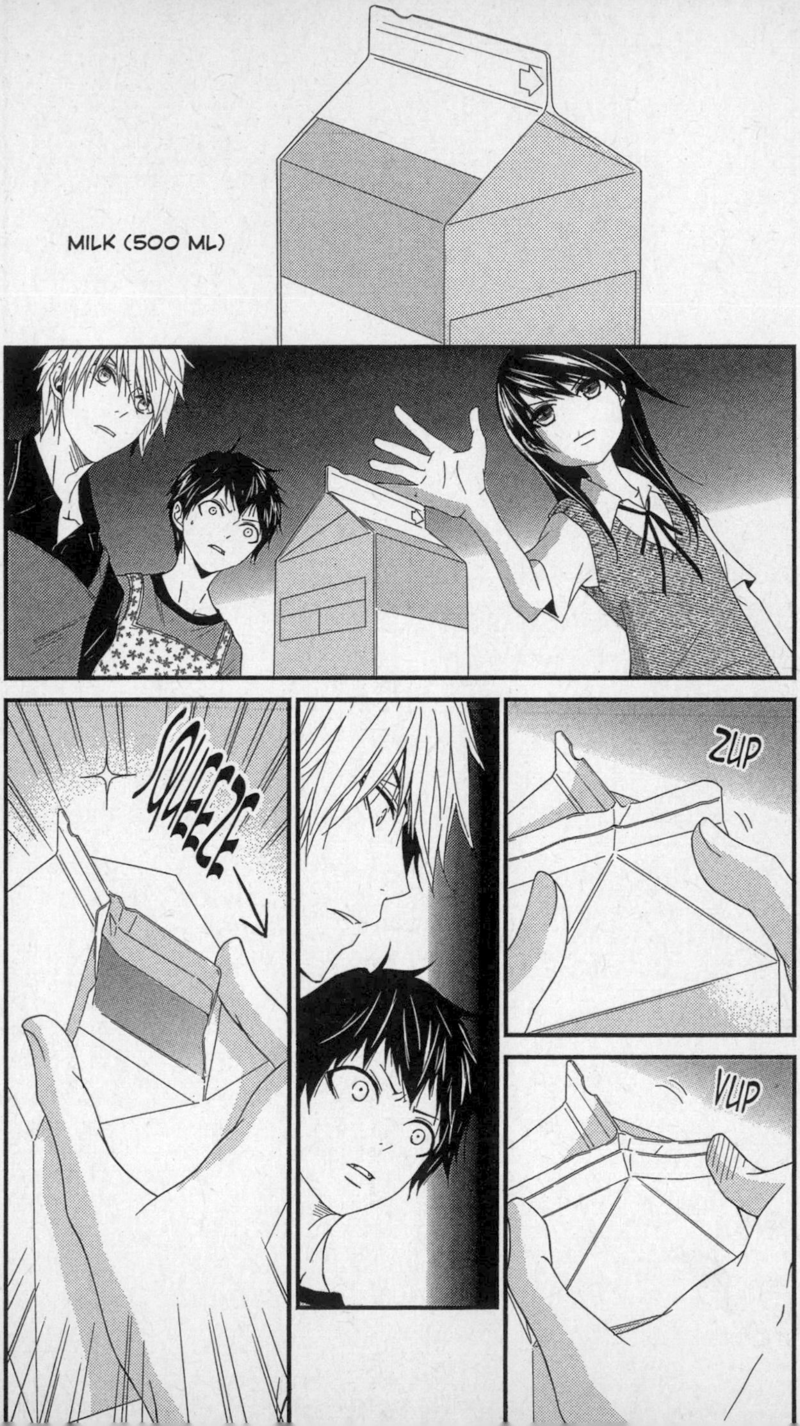
MILK (500 ML)
ZUP
SQUEEZE
VUP

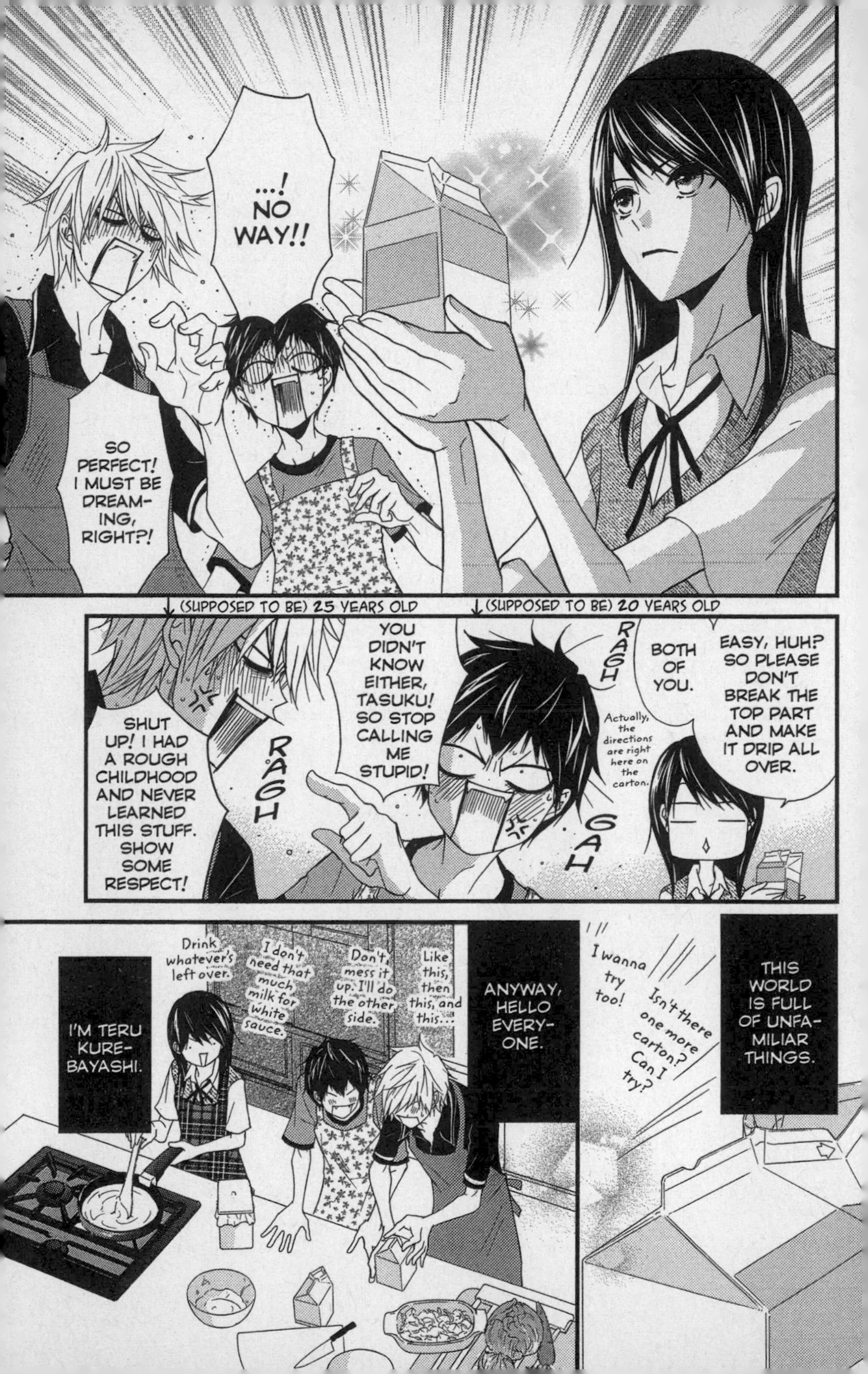
...! NO WAY!!
SO PERFECT! I MUST BE DREAMING, RIGHT?!
(SUPPOSED TO BE) 20 YEARS OLD
(SUPPOSED TO BE) 25 YEARS OLD
EASY, HUH? SO PLEASE DON'T BREAK THE TOP PART AND MAKE IT DRIP ALL OVER.
BOTH OF YOU.
Actually, the directions are right here on the carton.
RAGH
GAH
YOU DIDN'T KNOW EITHER, TASUKU! SO STOP CALLING ME STUPID!
RAGH
SHUT UP! I HAD A ROUGH CHILDHOOD AND NEVER LEARNED THIS STUFF. SHOW SOME RESPECT!
THIS WORLD IS FULL OF UNFAMILIAR THINGS.
Isn't there one more carton? Can I try?
I wanna try too!
ANYWAY, HELLO EVERYONE.
Like this, then this, and this...
Don't mess it up. I'll do the other side.
I don't need that much milk for white sauce.
Drink whatever's left over.
I'M TERU KUREBAYASHI.

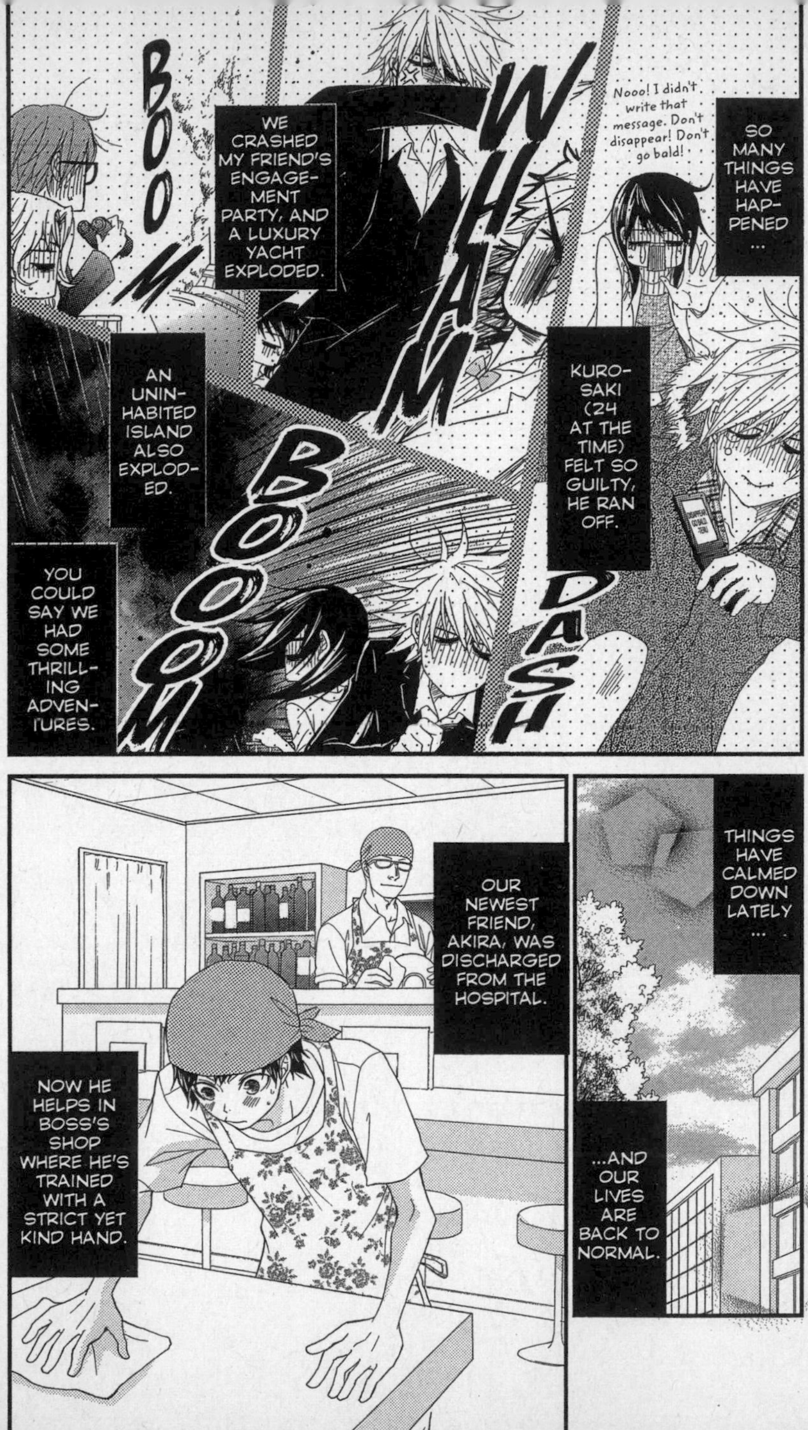
SO MANY THINGS HAVE HAPPENED...
Nooo! I didn't write that message. Don't disappear! Don't go bald!
WHAM
WE CRASHED MY FRIEND'S ENGAGEMENT PARTY, AND A LUXURY YACHT EXPLODED.
BOOM
KUROSAKI (24 AT THE TIME) FELT SO GUILTY, HE RAN OFF.
DASH
AN UNINHABITED ISLAND ALSO EXPLODED.
BOOOOM
YOU COULD SAY WE HAD SOME THRILLING ADVENTURES.
THINGS HAVE CALMED DOWN LATELY...
...AND OUR LIVES ARE BACK TO NORMAL.
OUR NEWEST FRIEND, AKIRA, WAS DISCHARGED FROM THE HOSPITAL.
NOW HE HELPS IN BOSS'S SHOP WHERE HE'S TRAINED WITH A STRICT YET KIND HAND.

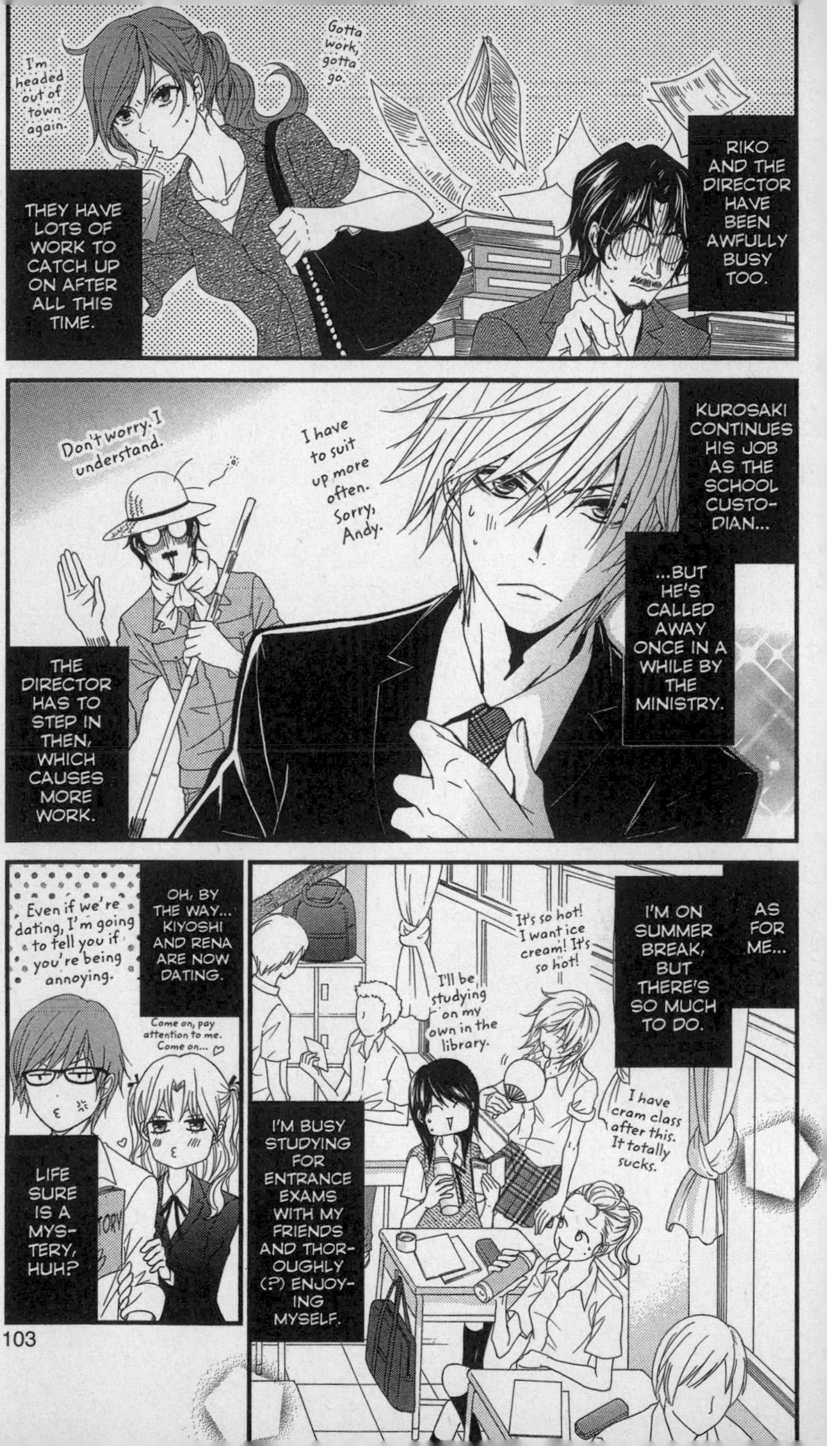

RIKO AND THE DIRECTOR HAVE BEEN AWFULLY BUSY TOO.
Gotta work, gotta go.
I'm headed out of town again.
THEY HAVE LOTS OF WORK TO CATCH UP ON AFTER ALL THIS TIME.
KUROSAKI CONTINUES HIS JOB AS THE SCHOOL CUSTO-DIAN...
...BUT HE'S CALLED AWAY ONCE IN A WHILE BY THE MINISTRY.
I have to suit up more often. Sorry, Andy.
Don't worry. I understand.
THE DIRECTOR HAS TO STEP IN THEN, WHICH CAUSES MORE WORK.
AS FOR ME...
I'M ON SUMMER BREAK, BUT THERE'S SO MUCH TO DO.
It's so hot! I want ice cream! It's so hot!
I'll be studying on my own in the library.
I have cram class after this. It totally sucks.
I'M BUSY STUDYING FOR ENTRANCE EXAMS WITH MY FRIENDS AND THOR-OUGHLY (?) ENJOY-ING MYSELF.
OH, BY THE WAY... KIYOSHI AND RENA ARE NOW DATING.
Even if we're dating, I'm going to tell you if you're being annoying.
Come on, pay attention to me. Come on...
LIFE SURE IS A MYS-TERY, HUH?

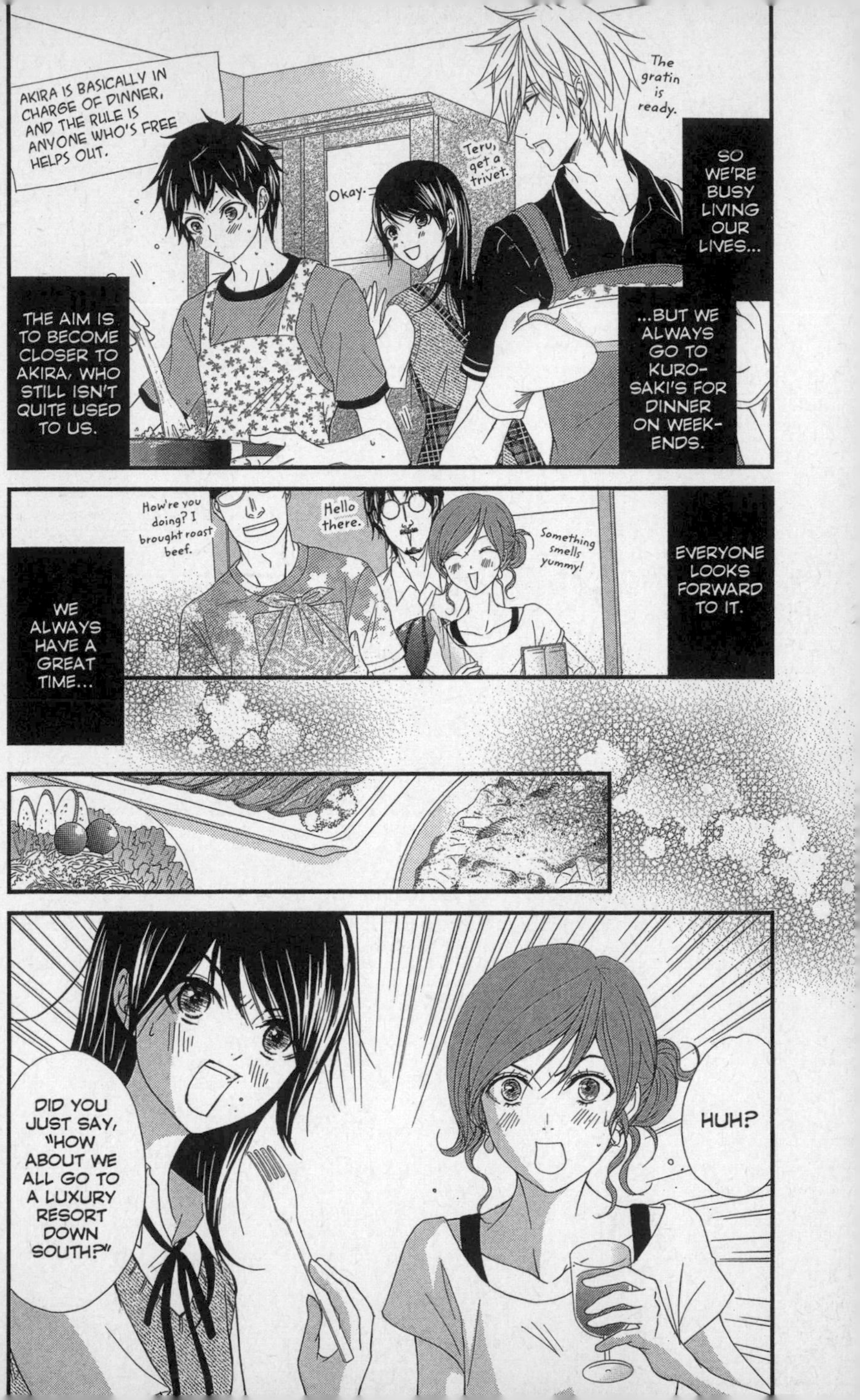
The gratin is ready.
SO WE'RE BUSY LIVING OUR LIVES...
...BUT WE ALWAYS GO TO KURO-SAKI'S FOR DINNER ON WEEK-ENDS.
Teru, get a trivet.
Okay.
AKIRA IS BASICALLY IN CHARGE OF DINNER, AND THE RULE IS ANYONE WHO'S FREE HELPS OUT.
THE AIM IS TO BECOME CLOSER TO AKIRA, WHO STILL ISN'T QUITE USED TO US.
EVERYONE LOOKS FORWARD TO IT.
Something smells yummy!
Hello there.
How're you doing? I brought roast beef.
WE ALWAYS HAVE A GREAT TIME...
HUH?
DID YOU JUST SAY, "HOW ABOUT WE ALL GO TO A LUXURY RESORT DOWN SOUTH?"

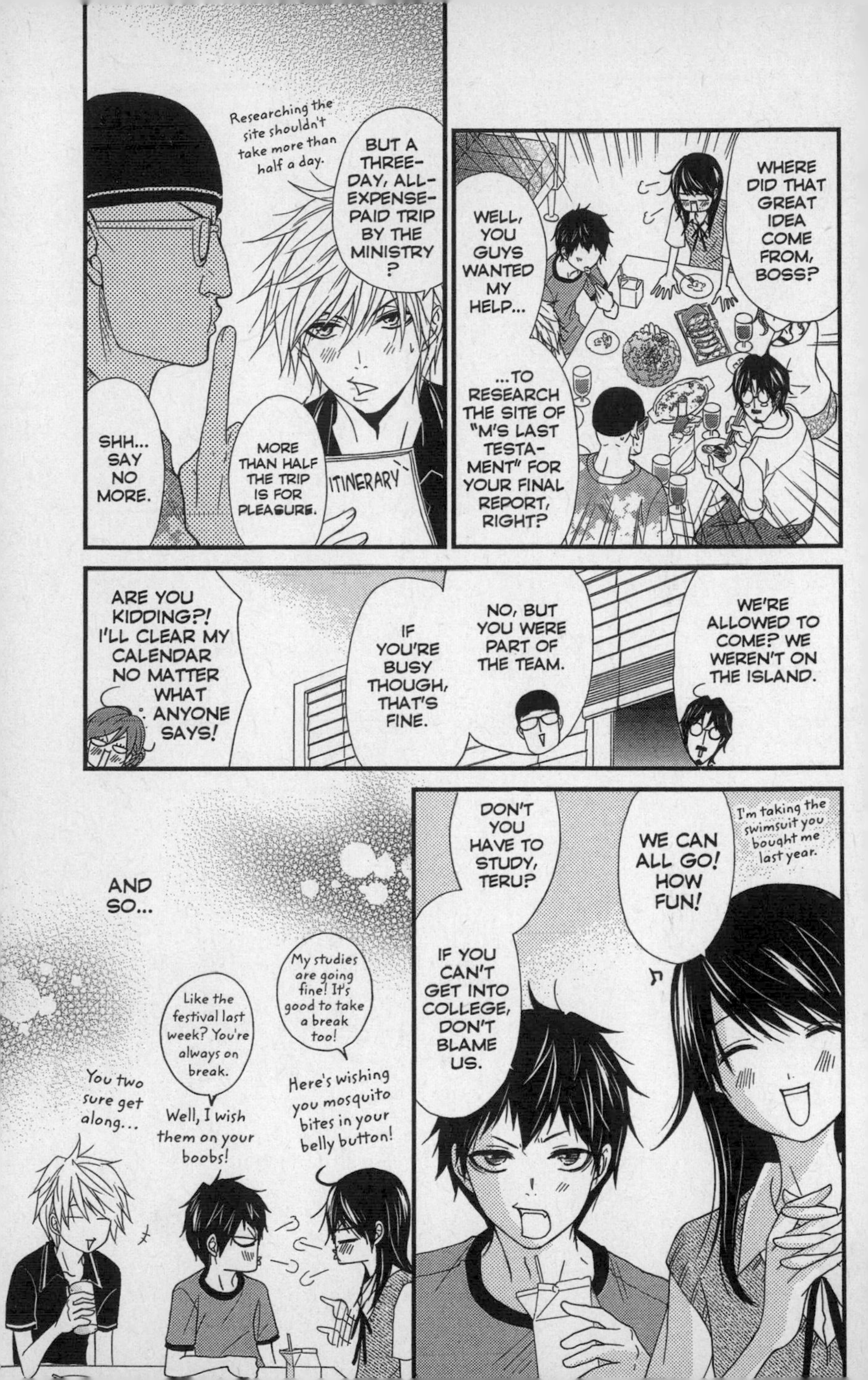
WHERE DID THAT GREAT IDEA COME FROM, BOSS?
WELL, YOU GUYS WANTED MY HELP...
...TO RESEARCH THE SITE OF "M'S LAST TESTAMENT" FOR YOUR FINAL REPORT, RIGHT?
BUT A THREE-DAY, ALL-EXPENSE-PAID TRIP BY THE MINISTRY?
Researching the site shouldn't take more than half a day.
MORE THAN HALF THE TRIP IS FOR PLEASURE.
ITINERARY
SHH... SAY NO MORE.
WE'RE ALLOWED TO COME? WE WEREN'T ON THE ISLAND.
NO, BUT YOU WERE PART OF THE TEAM.
IF YOU'RE BUSY THOUGH, THAT'S FINE.
ARE YOU KIDDING?! I'LL CLEAR MY CALENDAR NO MATTER WHAT ANYONE SAYS!
I'm taking the swimsuit you bought me last year.
WE CAN ALL GO! HOW FUN!
DON'T YOU HAVE TO STUDY, TERU?
IF YOU CAN'T GET INTO COLLEGE, DON'T BLAME US.
AND SO...
My studies are going fine! It's good to take a break too!
Like the festival last week? You're always on break.
Here's wishing you mosquito bites in your belly button!
Well, I wish them on your boobs!
You two sure get along...

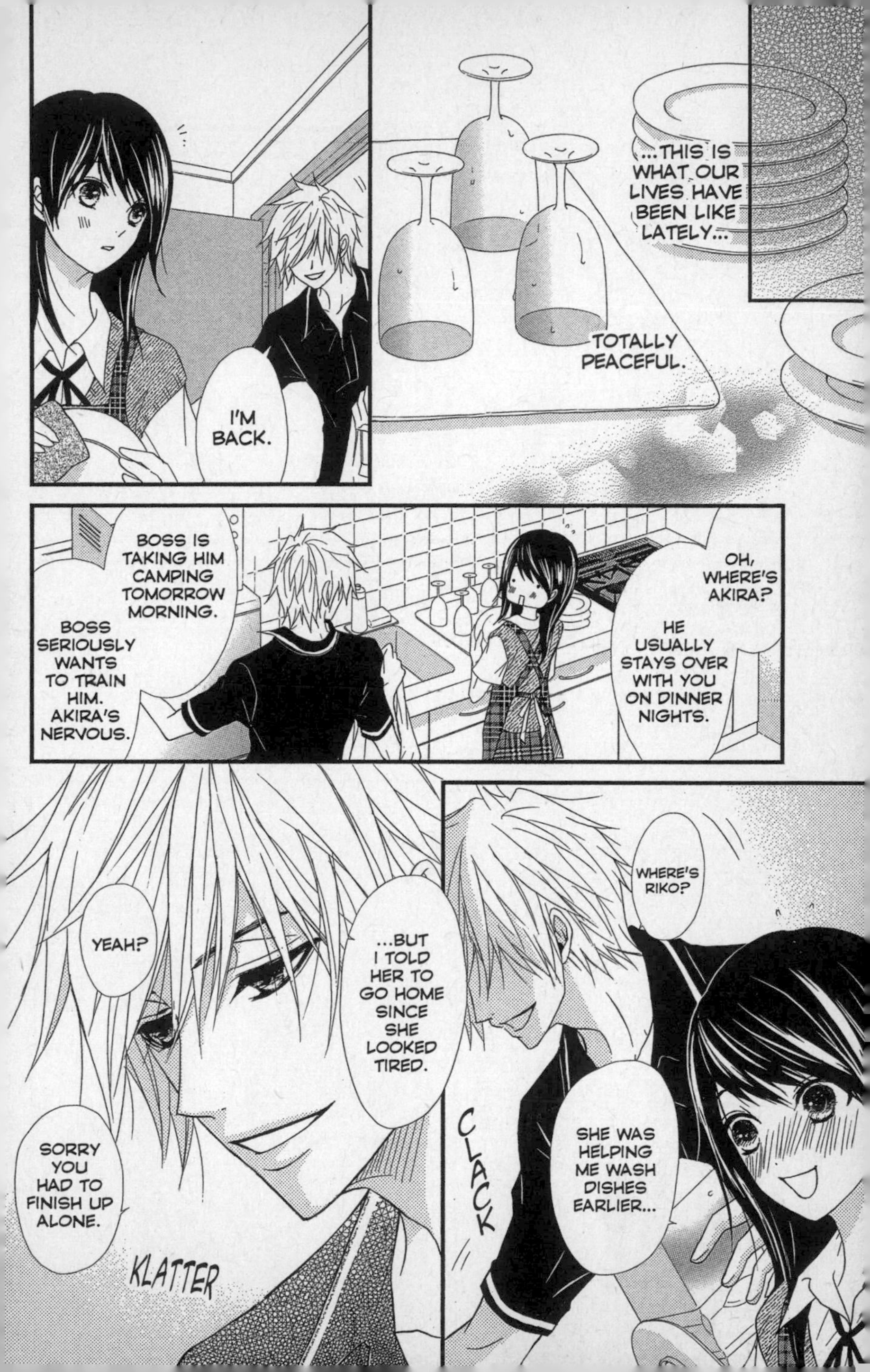
...THIS IS WHAT OUR LIVES HAVE BEEN LIKE LATELY...
TOTALLY PEACEFUL.
I'M BACK.
OH, WHERE'S AKIRA?
HE USUALLY STAYS OVER WITH YOU ON DINNER NIGHTS.
BOSS IS TAKING HIM CAMPING TOMORROW MORNING.
BOSS SERIOUSLY WANTS TO TRAIN HIM. AKIRA'S NERVOUS.
WHERE'S RIKO?
SHE WAS HELPING ME WASH DISHES EARLIER...
CLACK
...BUT I TOLD HER TO GO HOME SINCE SHE LOOKED TIRED.
YEAH?
SORRY YOU HAD TO FINISH UP ALONE.
KLATTER

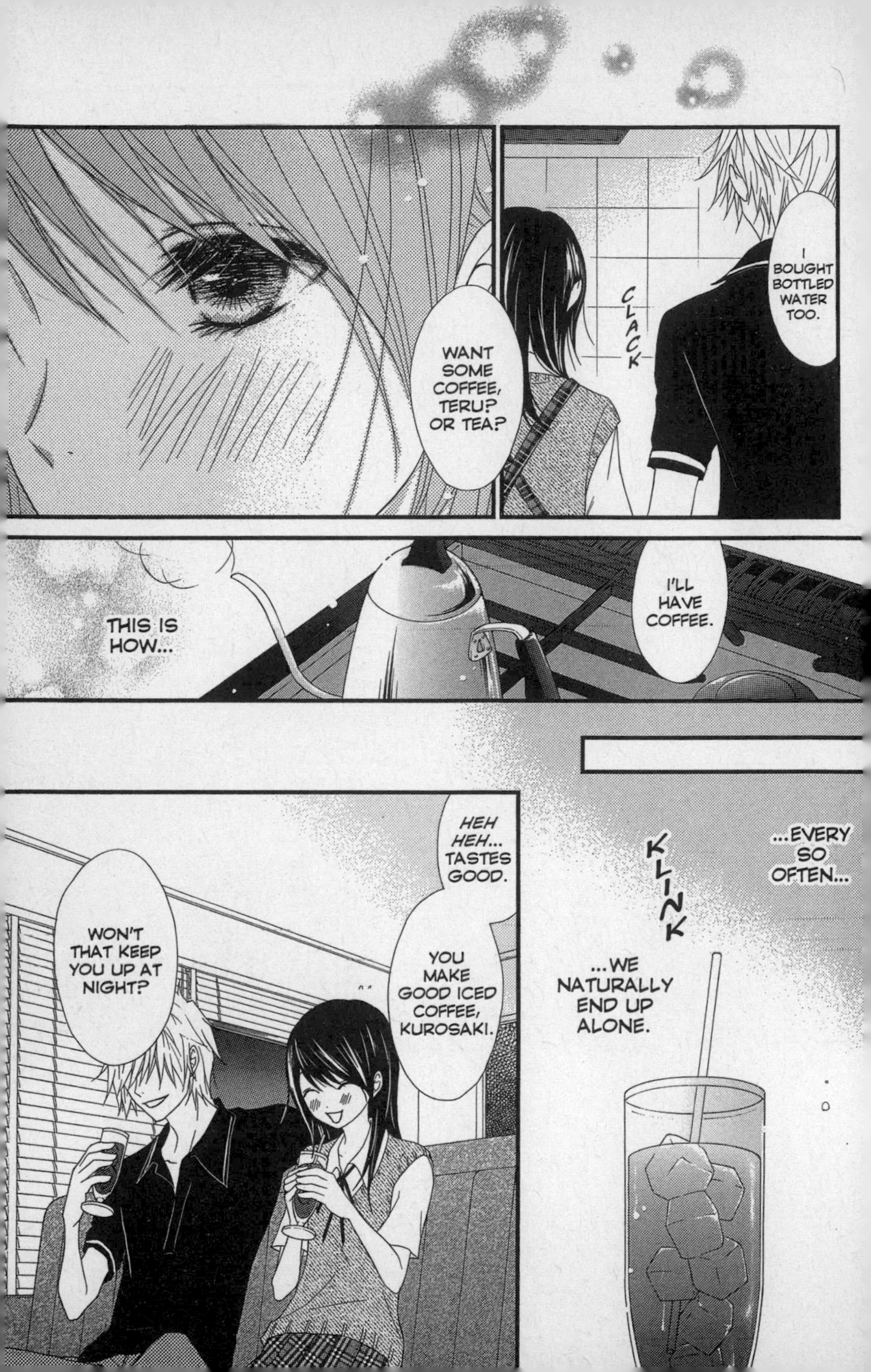
I BOUGHT BOTTLED WATER TOO.
CLACK
WANT SOME COFFEE, TERU? OR TEA?
I'LL HAVE COFFEE.
THIS IS HOW...
...EVERY SO OFTEN...
KLINK
...WE NATURALLY END UP ALONE.
HEH HEH... TASTES GOOD.
YOU MAKE GOOD ICED COFFEE, KUROSAKI.
WON'T THAT KEEP YOU UP AT NIGHT?

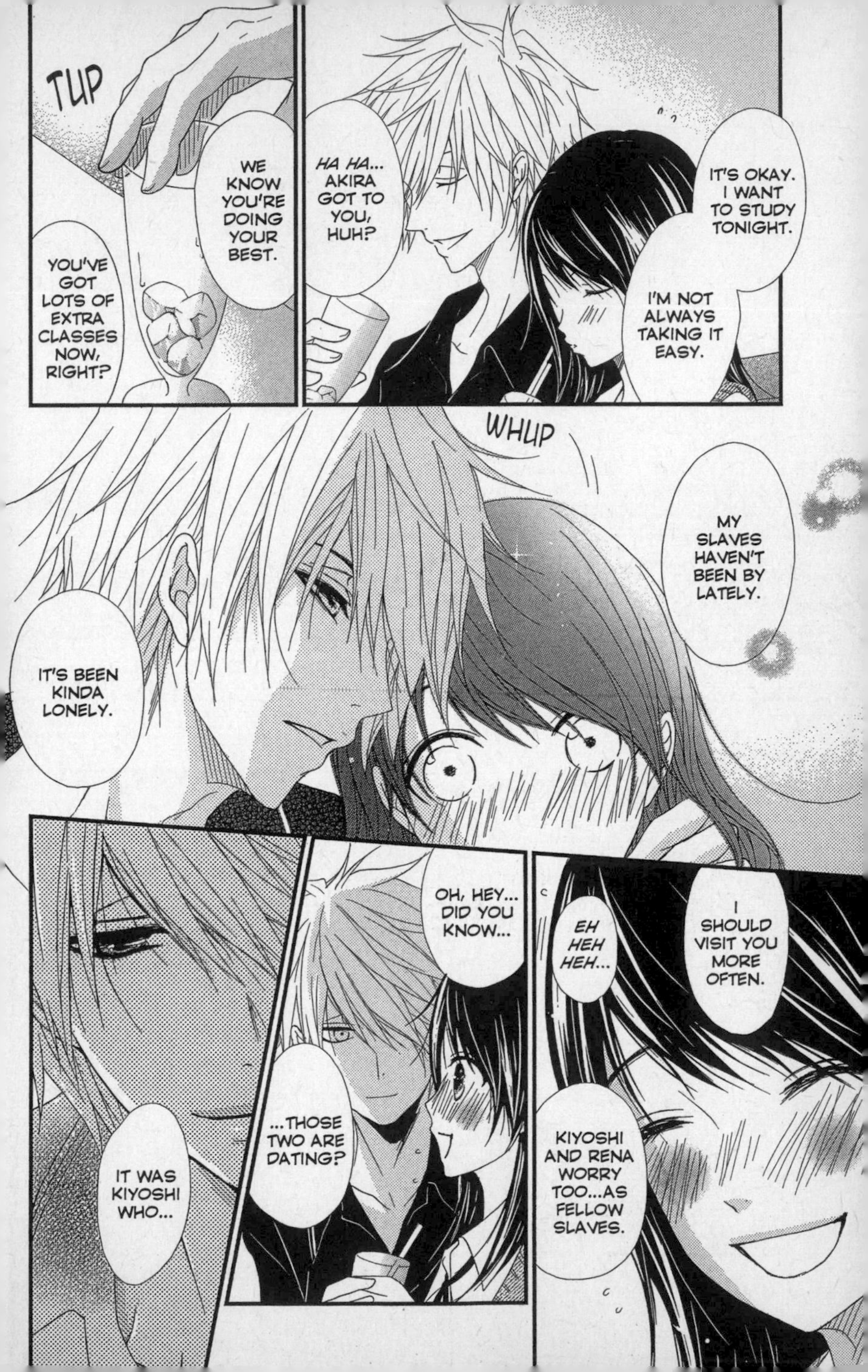
IT'S OKAY. I WANT TO STUDY TONIGHT.
I'M NOT ALWAYS TAKING IT EASY.
HA HA... AKIRA GOT TO YOU, HUH?
TUP
WE KNOW YOU'RE DOING YOUR BEST.
YOU'VE GOT LOTS OF EXTRA CLASSES NOW, RIGHT?
WHUP
MY SLAVES HAVEN'T BEEN BY LATELY.
IT'S BEEN KINDA LONELY.
I SHOULD VISIT YOU MORE OFTEN.
EH HEH HEH...
KIYOSHI AND RENA WORRY TOO...AS FELLOW SLAVES.
OH, HEY... DID YOU KNOW...
...THOSE TWO ARE DATING?
IT WAS KIYOSHI WHO...

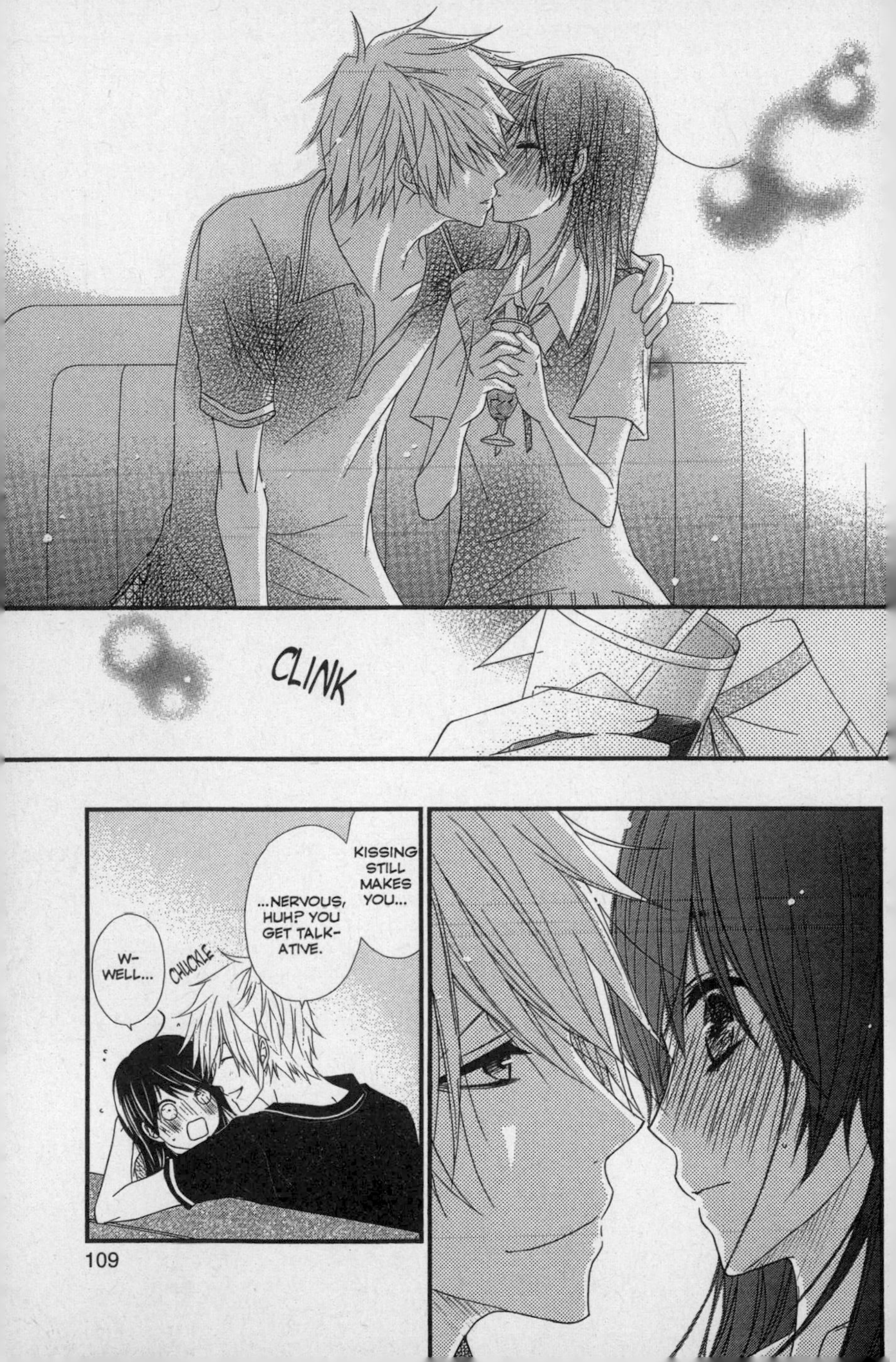
CLINK
KISSING STILL MAKES YOU...
...NERVOUS, HUH? YOU GET TALK-ATIVE.
CHUCKLE
W-WELL...

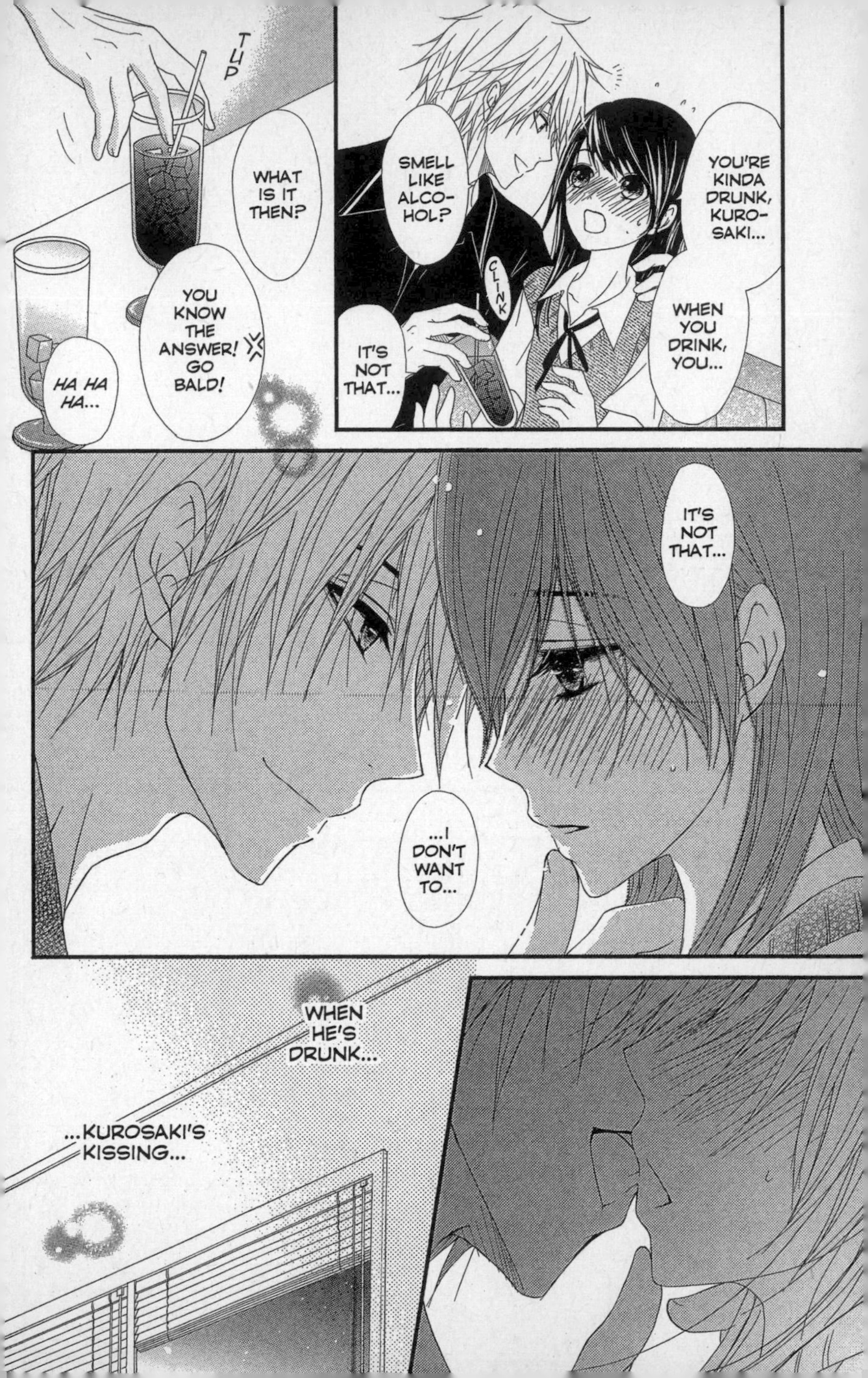
YOU'RE KINDA DRUNK, KUROSAKI...
SMELL LIKE ALCO-HOL?
WHEN YOU DRINK, YOU...
CLINK
IT'S NOT THAT...
TUP
WHAT IS IT THEN?
YOU KNOW THE ANSWER! GO BALD!
HA HA HA...
IT'S NOT THAT...
...I DON'T WANT TO...
WHEN HE'S DRUNK...
...KUROSAKI'S KISSING...

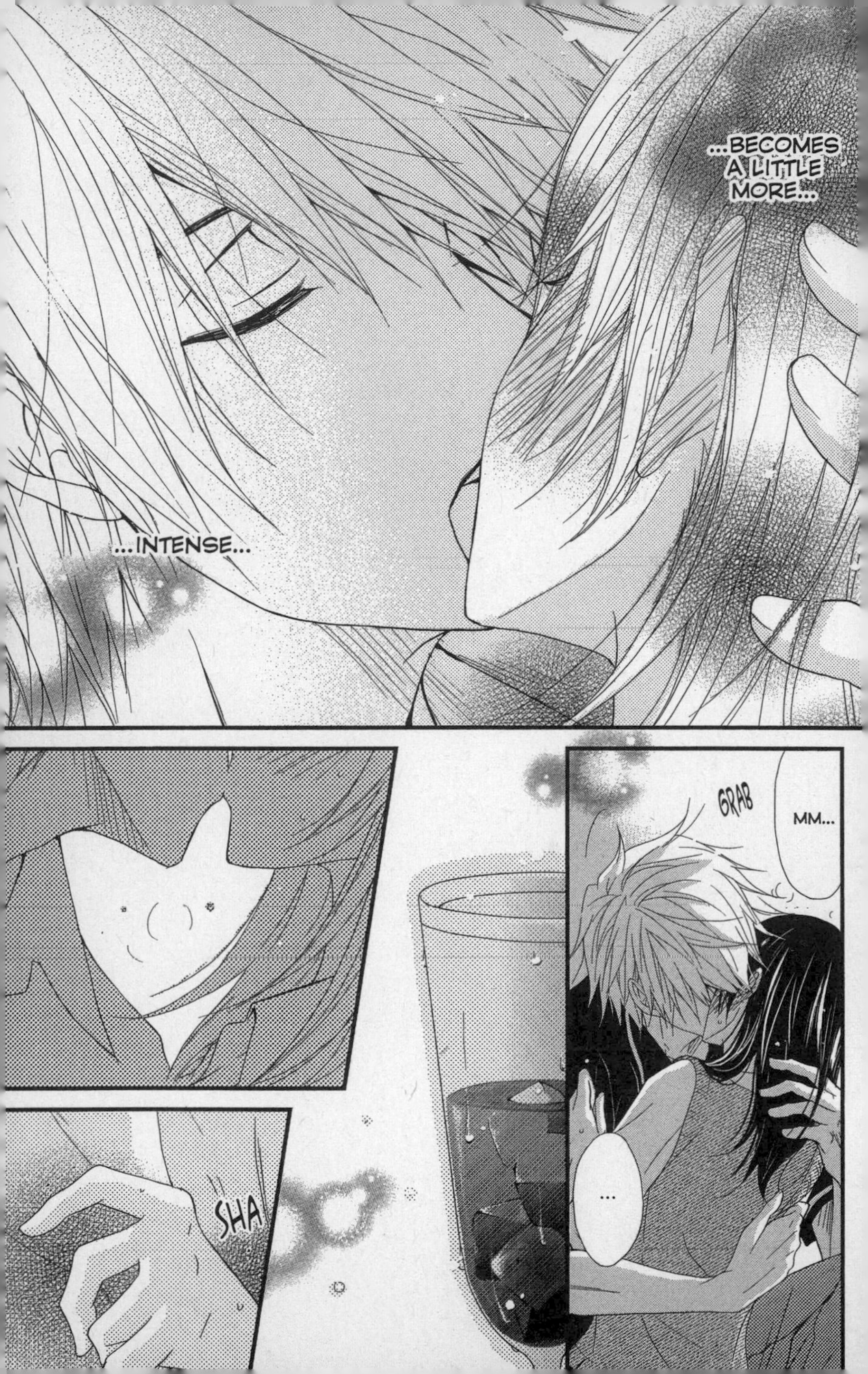
...BECOMES A LITTLE MORE...
...INTENSE...
MM...
GRAB
...
SHA

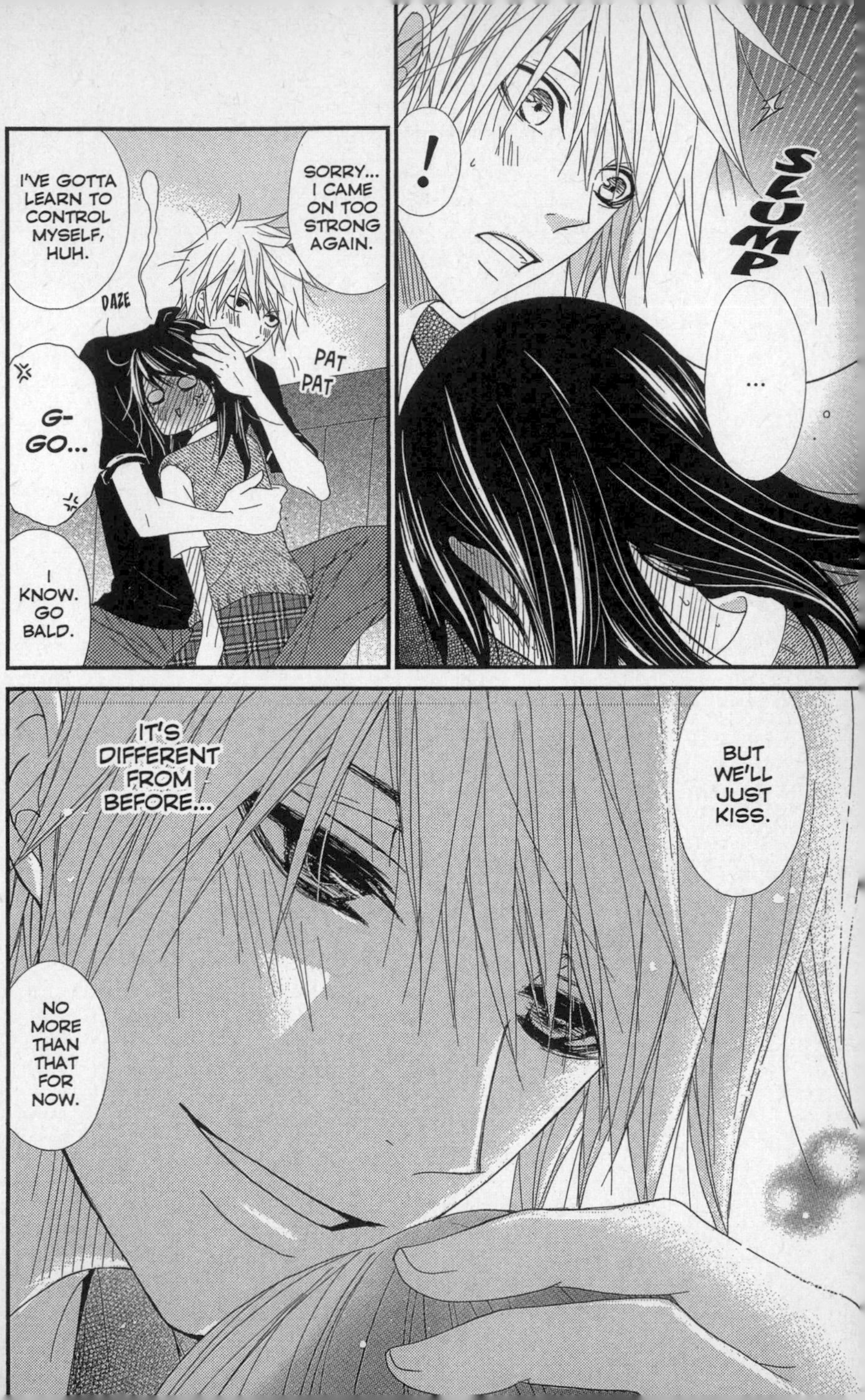
!
SLUMP
...
SORRY... I CAME ON TOO STRONG AGAIN.
I'VE GOTTA LEARN TO CONTROL MYSELF, HUH.
DAZE
PAT PAT
G- GO...
I KNOW. GO BALD.
BUT WE'LL JUST KISS.
IT'S DIFFERENT FROM BEFORE...
NO MORE THAN THAT FOR NOW.

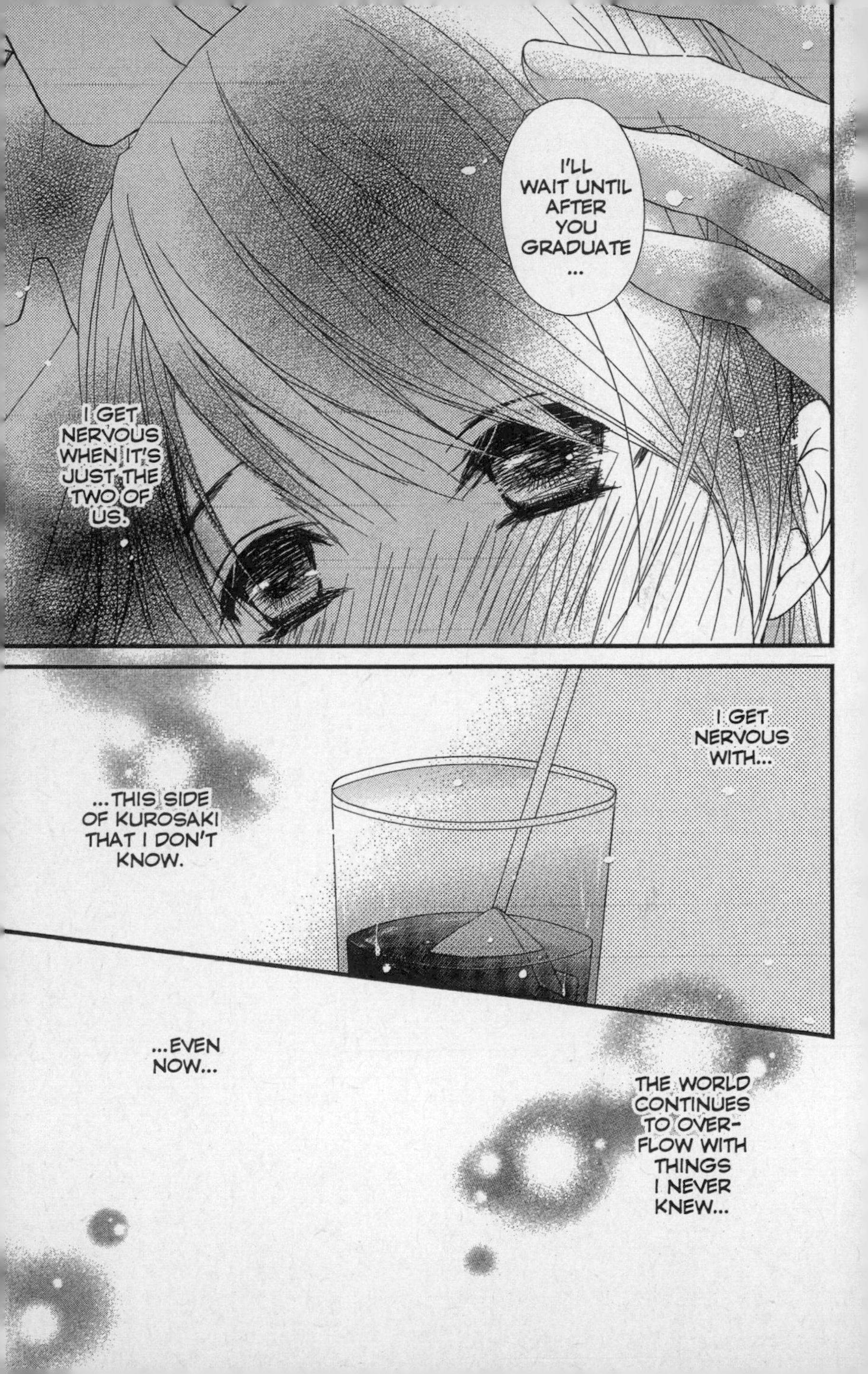
I'LL WAIT UNTIL AFTER YOU GRADUATE...
I GET NERVOUS WHEN IT'S JUST THE TWO OF US.
I GET NERVOUS WITH...
...THIS SIDE OF KUROSAKI THAT I DON'T KNOW.
...EVEN NOW...
THE WORLD CONTINUES TO OVER-FLOW WITH THINGS I NEVER KNEW...

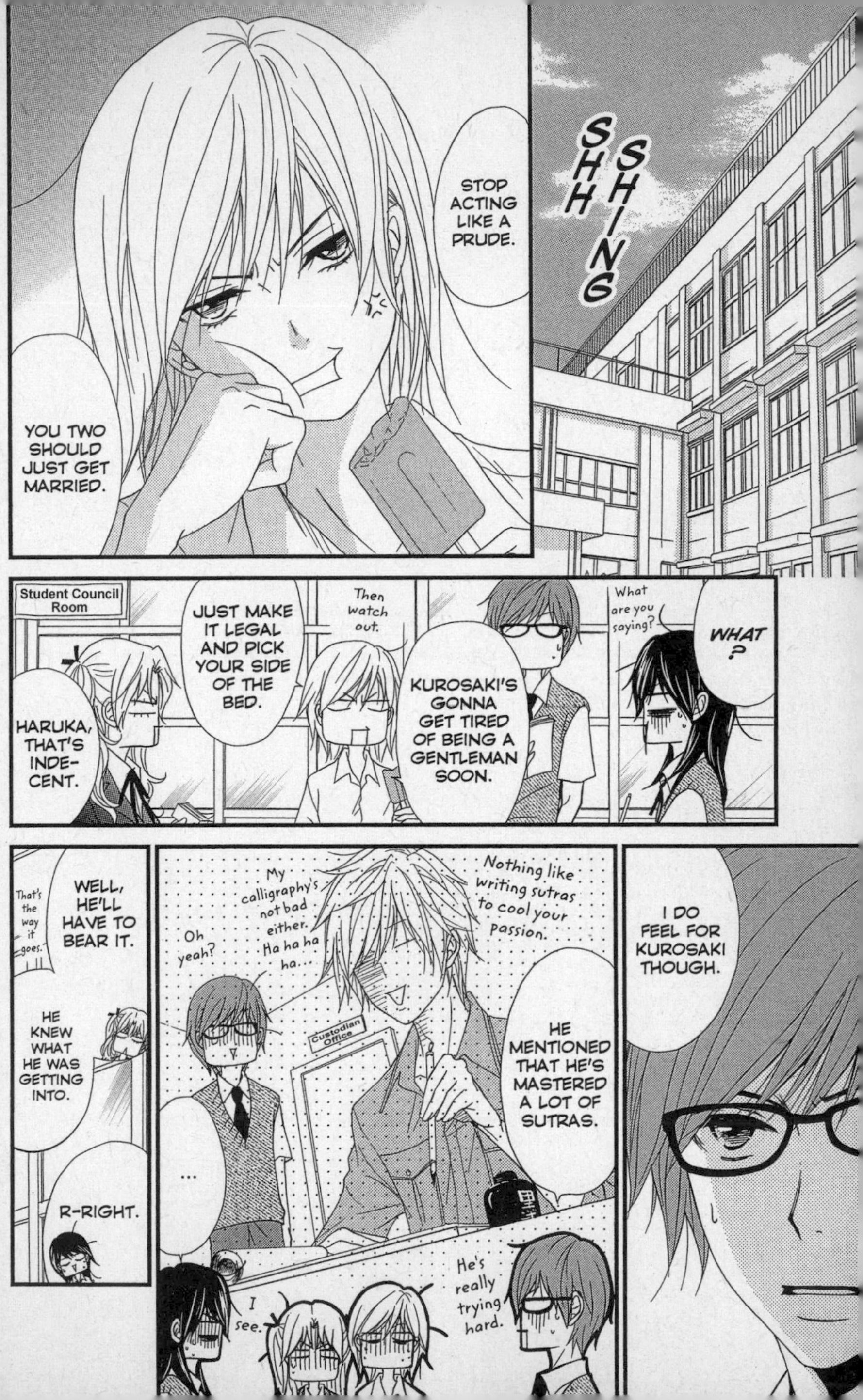
SHHH SHING
STOP ACTING LIKE A PRUDE.
YOU TWO SHOULD JUST GET MARRIED.
WHAT?
What are you saying?
KUROSAKI'S GONNA GET TIRED OF BEING A GENTLEMAN SOON.
Then watch out.
JUST MAKE IT LEGAL AND PICK YOUR SIDE OF THE BED.
Student Council Room
HARUKA, THAT'S INDECENT.
I DO FEEL FOR KUROSAKI THOUGH.
HE MENTIONED THAT HE'S MASTERED A LOT OF SUTRAS.
Nothing like writing sutras to cool your passion.
My calligraphy's not bad either. Ha ha ha ha...
Oh yeah?
Custodian Office
...
He's really trying hard.
I see.
WELL, HE'LL HAVE TO BEAR IT.
That's the way it goes.
HE KNEW WHAT HE WAS GETTING INTO.
R-RIGHT.

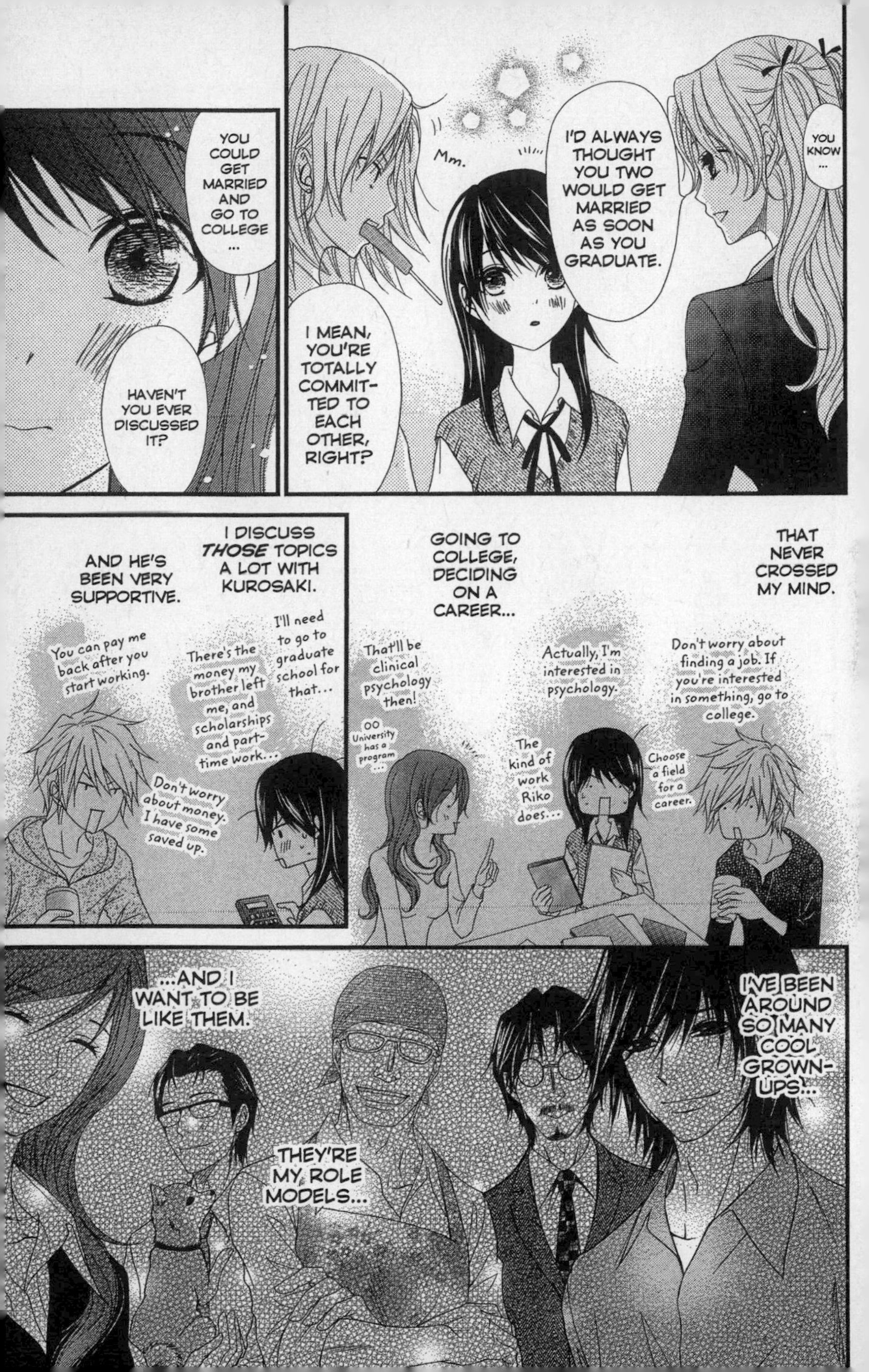
YOU KNOW...
I'D ALWAYS THOUGHT YOU TWO WOULD GET MARRIED AS SOON AS YOU GRADUATE.
Mm.
I MEAN, YOU'RE TOTALLY COMMITTED TO EACH OTHER, RIGHT?
YOU COULD GET MARRIED AND GO TO COLLEGE...
HAVEN'T YOU EVER DISCUSSED IT?
THAT NEVER CROSSED MY MIND.
GOING TO COLLEGE, DECIDING ON A CAREER...
Don't worry about finding a job. If you're interested in something, go to college.
Actually, I'm interested in psychology.
Choose a field for a career.
The kind of work Riko does...
That'll be clinical psychology then!
OO University has a program...
I DISCUSS *THOSE* TOPICS A LOT WITH KUROSAKI.
AND HE'S BEEN VERY SUPPORTIVE.
I'll need to go to graduate school for that...
There's the money my brother left me, and scholarships and part-time work...
You can pay me back after you start working.
Don't worry about money. I have some saved up.
I'VE BEEN AROUND SO MANY COOL GROWN-UPS...
...AND I WANT TO BE LIKE THEM.
THEY'RE MY ROLE MODELS...

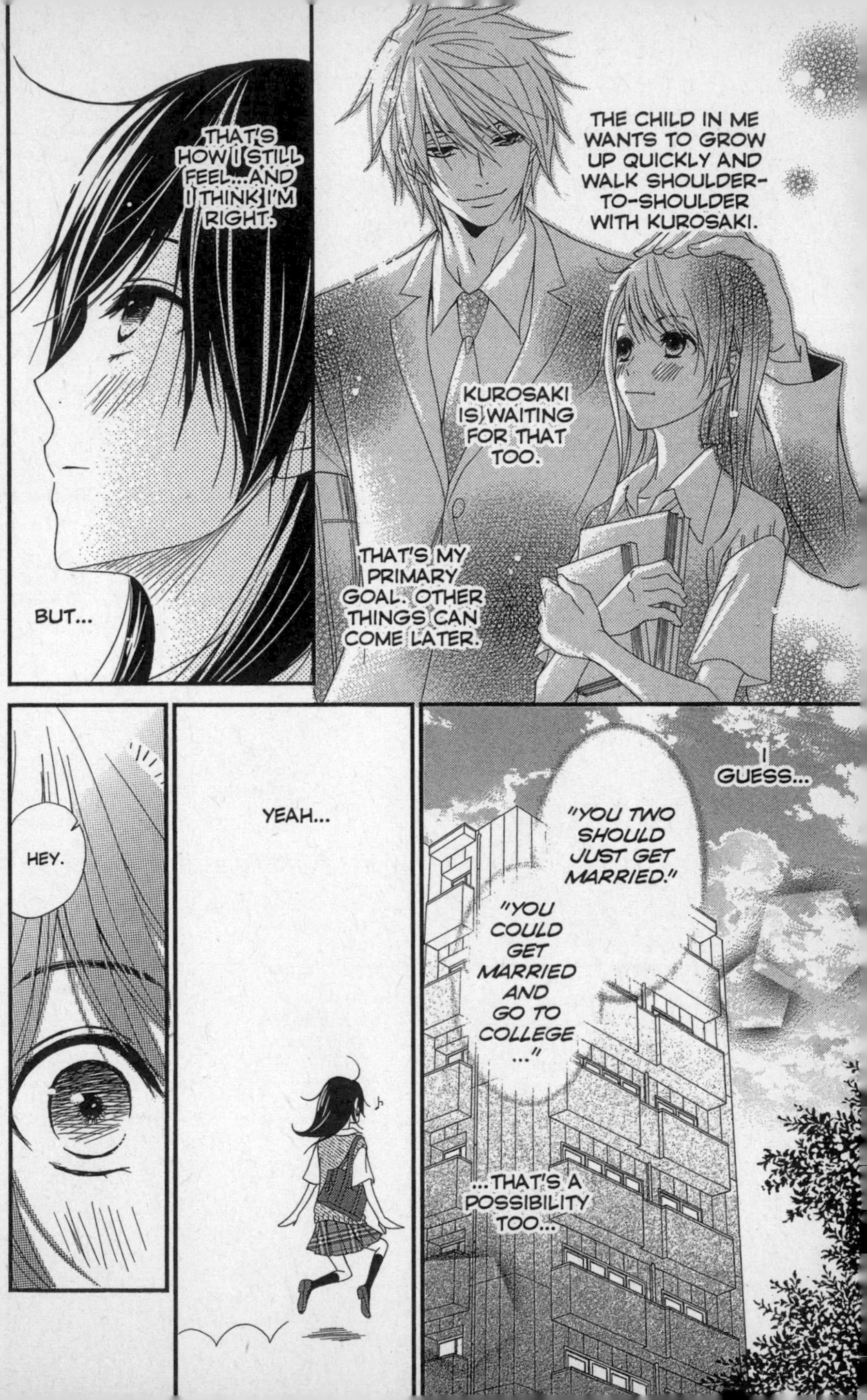
THE CHILD IN ME WANTS TO GROW UP QUICKLY AND WALK SHOULDER-TO-SHOULDER WITH KUROSAKI.
KUROSAKI IS WAITING FOR THAT TOO.
THAT'S MY PRIMARY GOAL. OTHER THINGS CAN COME LATER.
THAT'S HOW I STILL FEEL... AND I THINK I'M RIGHT.
BUT...
I GUESS...
"YOU TWO SHOULD JUST GET MARRIED."
"YOU COULD GET MARRIED AND GO TO COLLEGE ..."
...THAT'S A POSSIBILITY TOO...
YEAH...
HEY.

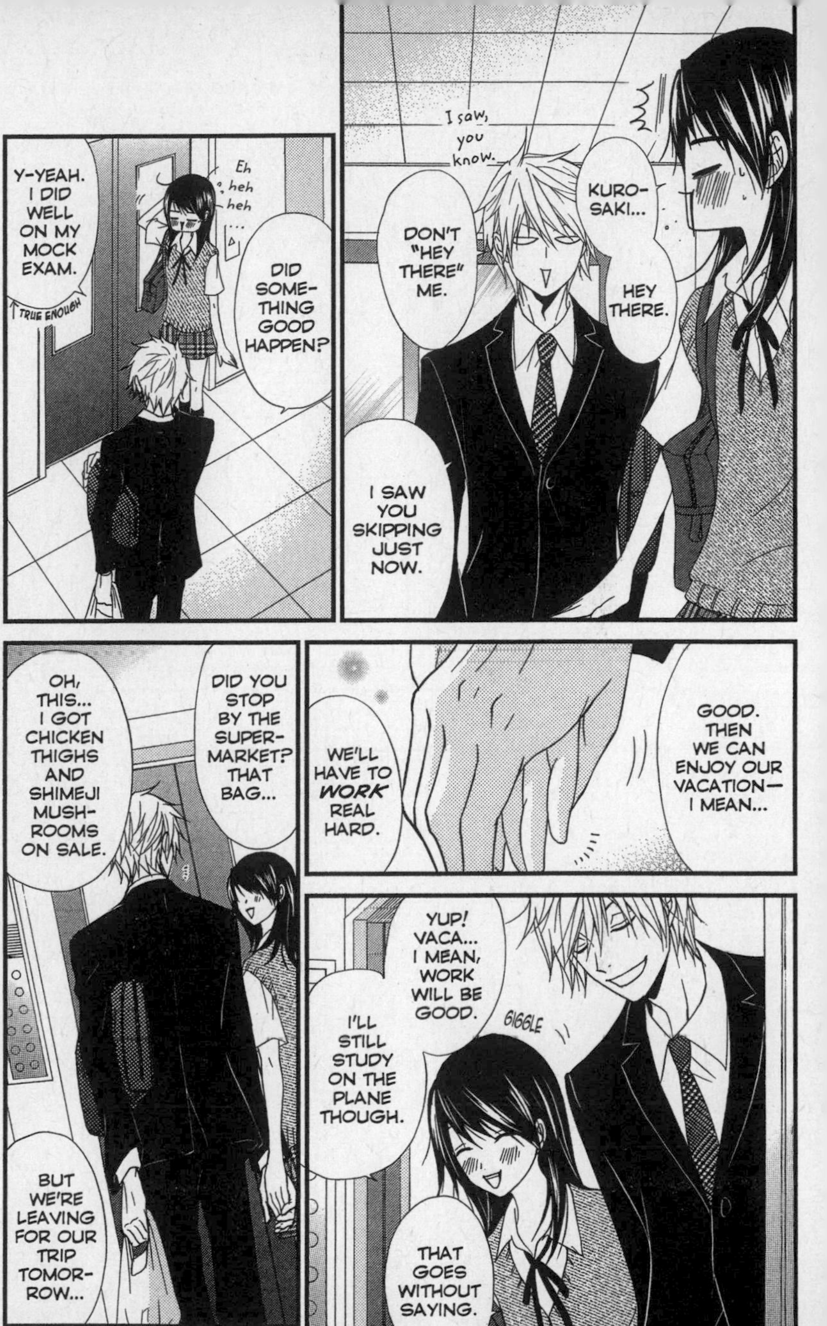
KURO-SAKI...
HEY THERE.
I saw, you know.
DON'T "HEY THERE" ME.
I SAW YOU SKIPPING JUST NOW.
DID SOMETHING GOOD HAPPEN?
Eh heh heh...
Y-YEAH. I DID WELL ON MY MOCK EXAM.
TRUE ENOUGH
GOOD. THEN WE CAN ENJOY OUR VACATION— I MEAN...
WE'LL HAVE TO WORK REAL HARD.
YUP! VACA... I MEAN, WORK WILL BE GOOD.
GIGGLE
I'LL STILL STUDY ON THE PLANE THOUGH.
THAT GOES WITHOUT SAYING.
DID YOU STOP BY THE SUPER-MARKET? THAT BAG...
OH, THIS... I GOT CHICKEN THIGHS AND SHIMEJI MUSH-ROOMS ON SALE.
BUT WE'RE LEAVING FOR OUR TRIP TOMOR-ROW...

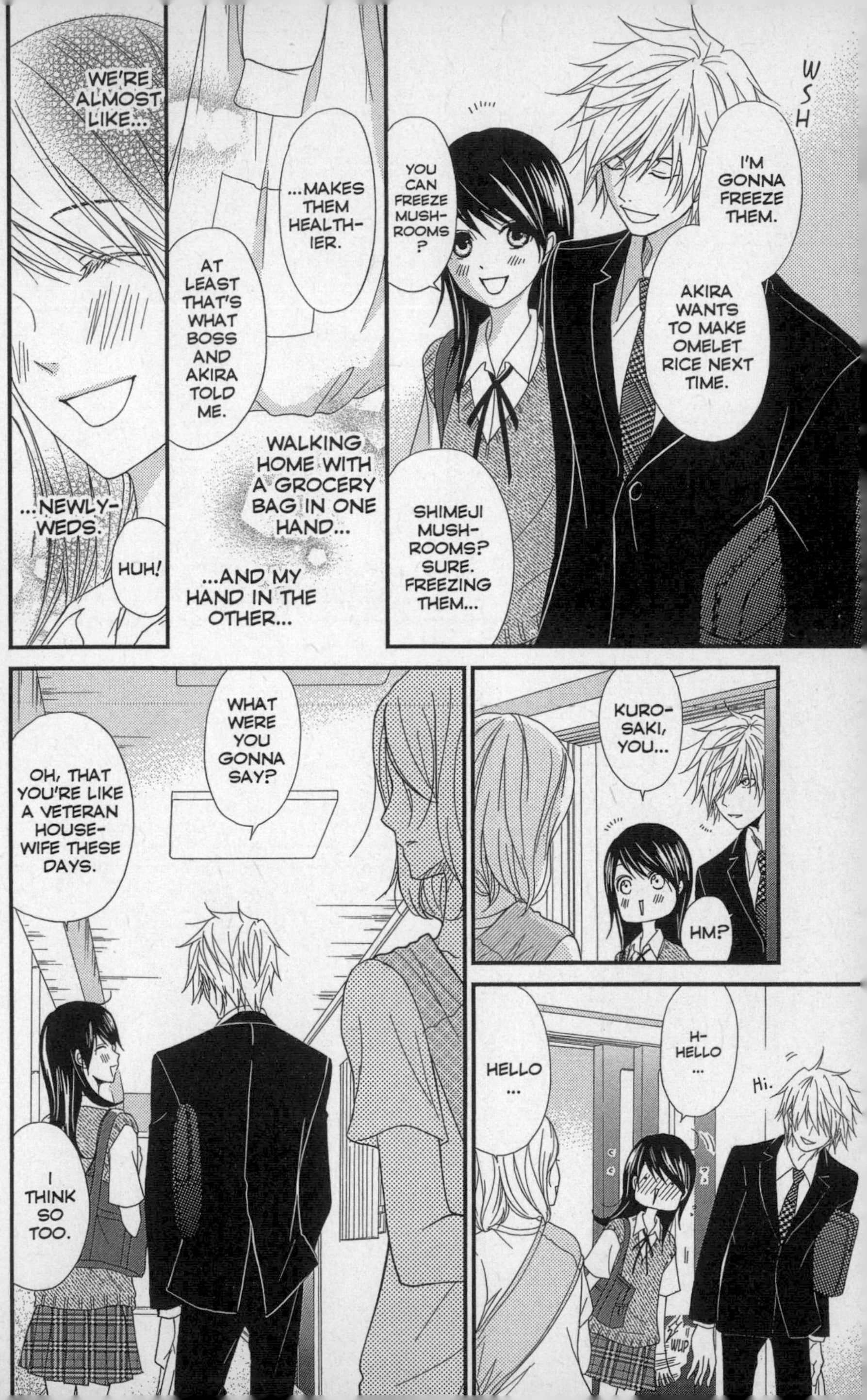
WSH
I'M GONNA FREEZE THEM.
AKIRA WANTS TO MAKE OMELET RICE NEXT TIME.
YOU CAN FREEZE MUSH-ROOMS?
SHIMEJI MUSH-ROOMS? SURE. FREEZING THEM...
...MAKES THEM HEALTH-IER.
AT LEAST THAT'S WHAT BOSS AND AKIRA TOLD ME.
WALKING HOME WITH A GROCERY BAG IN ONE HAND...
...AND MY HAND IN THE OTHER...
WE'RE ALMOST LIKE...
...NEWLY-WEDS.
HUH!
KURO-SAKI, YOU...
HM?
H-HELLO...
Hi.
HELLO...
WUP
WHAT WERE YOU GONNA SAY?
OH, THAT YOU'RE LIKE A VETERAN HOUSE-WIFE THESE DAYS.
I THINK SO TOO.

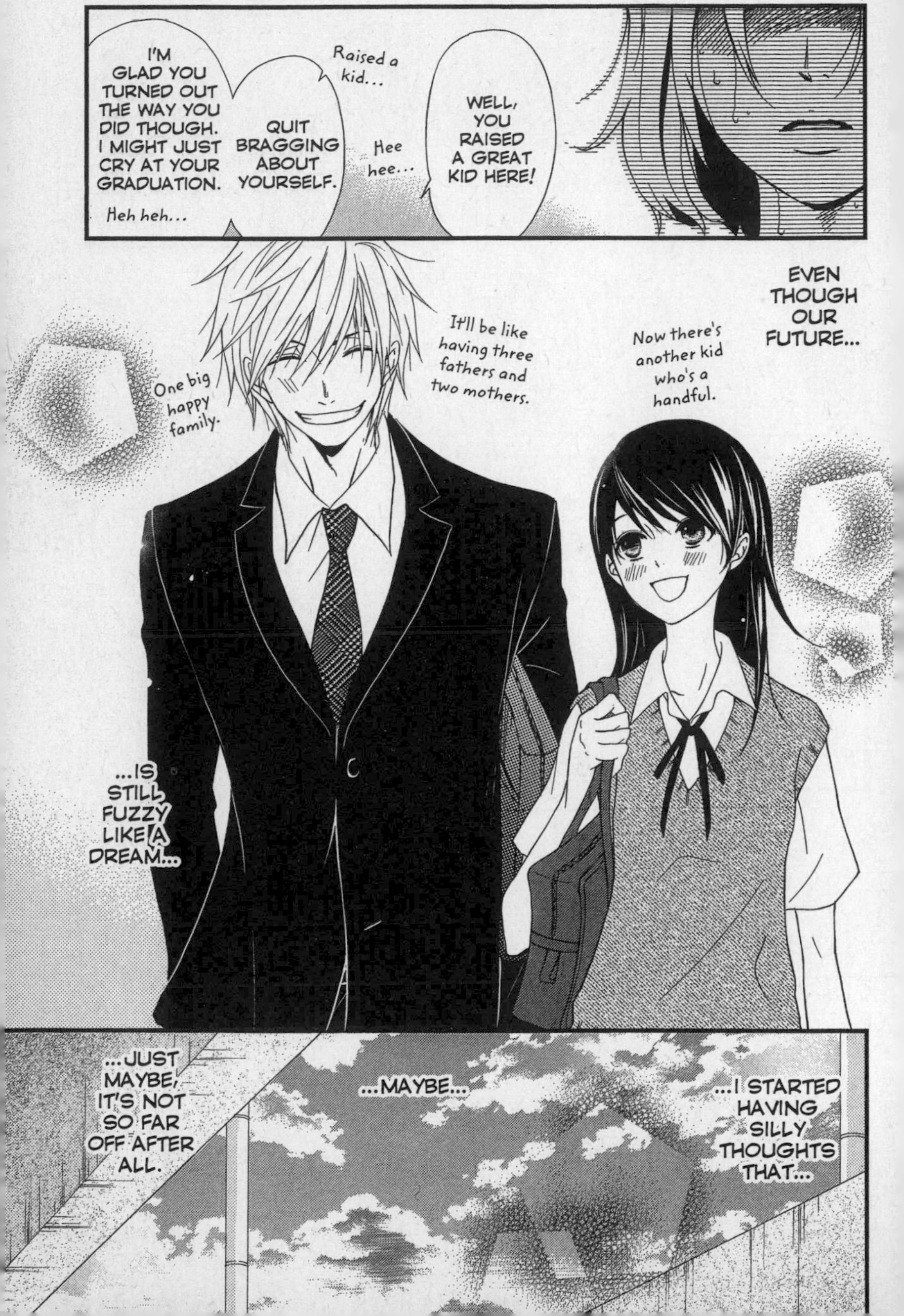
WELL, YOU RAISED A GREAT KID HERE!
Hee hee...
Raised a kid...
QUIT BRAGGING ABOUT YOURSELF.
I'M GLAD YOU TURNED OUT THE WAY YOU DID THOUGH. I MIGHT JUST CRY AT YOUR GRADUATION.
Heh heh...
EVEN THOUGH OUR FUTURE...
Now there's another kid who's a handful.
It'll be like having three fathers and two mothers.
One big happy family.
...IS STILL FUZZY LIKE A DREAM...
...I STARTED HAVING SILLY THOUGHTS THAT...
...MAYBE...
...JUST MAYBE, IT'S NOT SO FAR OFF AFTER ALL.

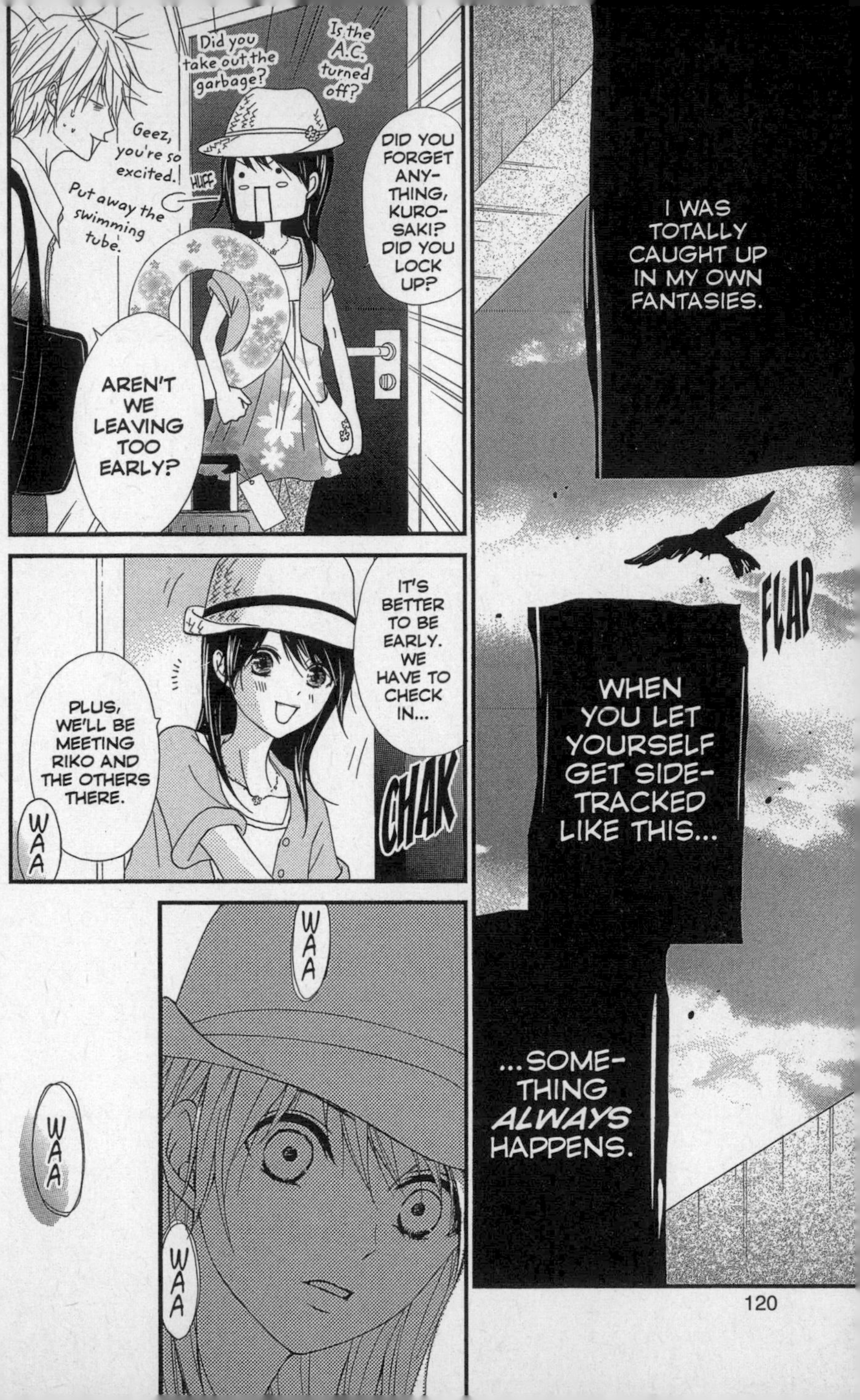
I WAS TOTALLY CAUGHT UP IN MY OWN FANTASIES.
FLAP
WHEN YOU LET YOURSELF GET SIDE-TRACKED LIKE THIS...
...SOMETHING ALWAYS HAPPENS.
Is the A.C. turned off?
Did you take out the garbage?
DID YOU FORGET ANYTHING, KUROSAKI? DID YOU LOCK UP?
Geez, you're so excited.
HUFF
Put away the swimming tube.
AREN'T WE LEAVING TOO EARLY?
IT'S BETTER TO BE EARLY. WE HAVE TO CHECK IN...
CHAK
PLUS, WE'LL BE MEETING RIKO AND THE OTHERS THERE.
WAA
WAA
WAA
WAA

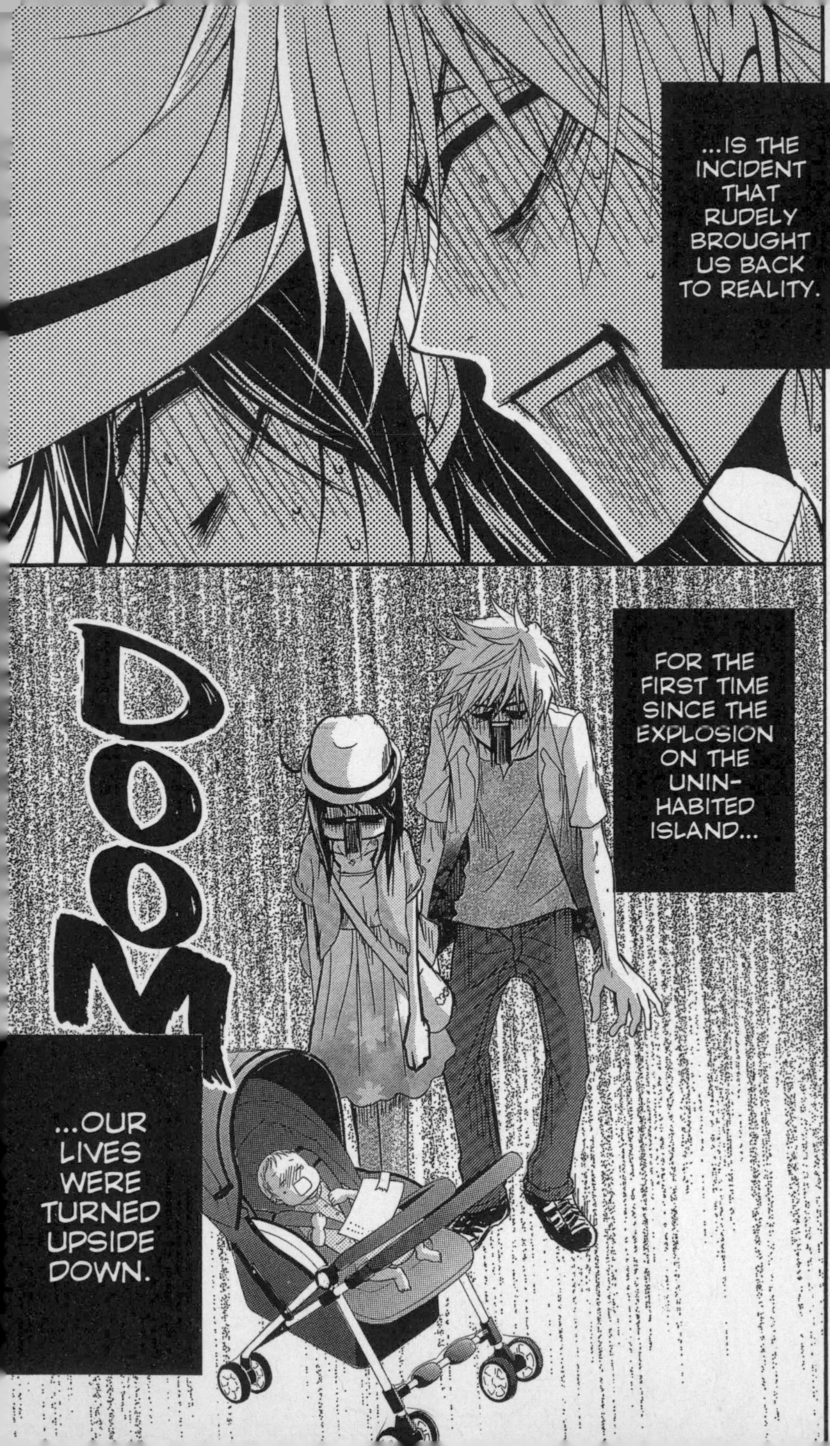
...IS THE INCIDENT THAT RUDELY BROUGHT US BACK TO REALITY.
FOR THE FIRST TIME SINCE THE EXPLOSION ON THE UNIN-HABITED ISLAND...
DOOM
...OUR LIVES WERE TURNED UPSIDE DOWN.

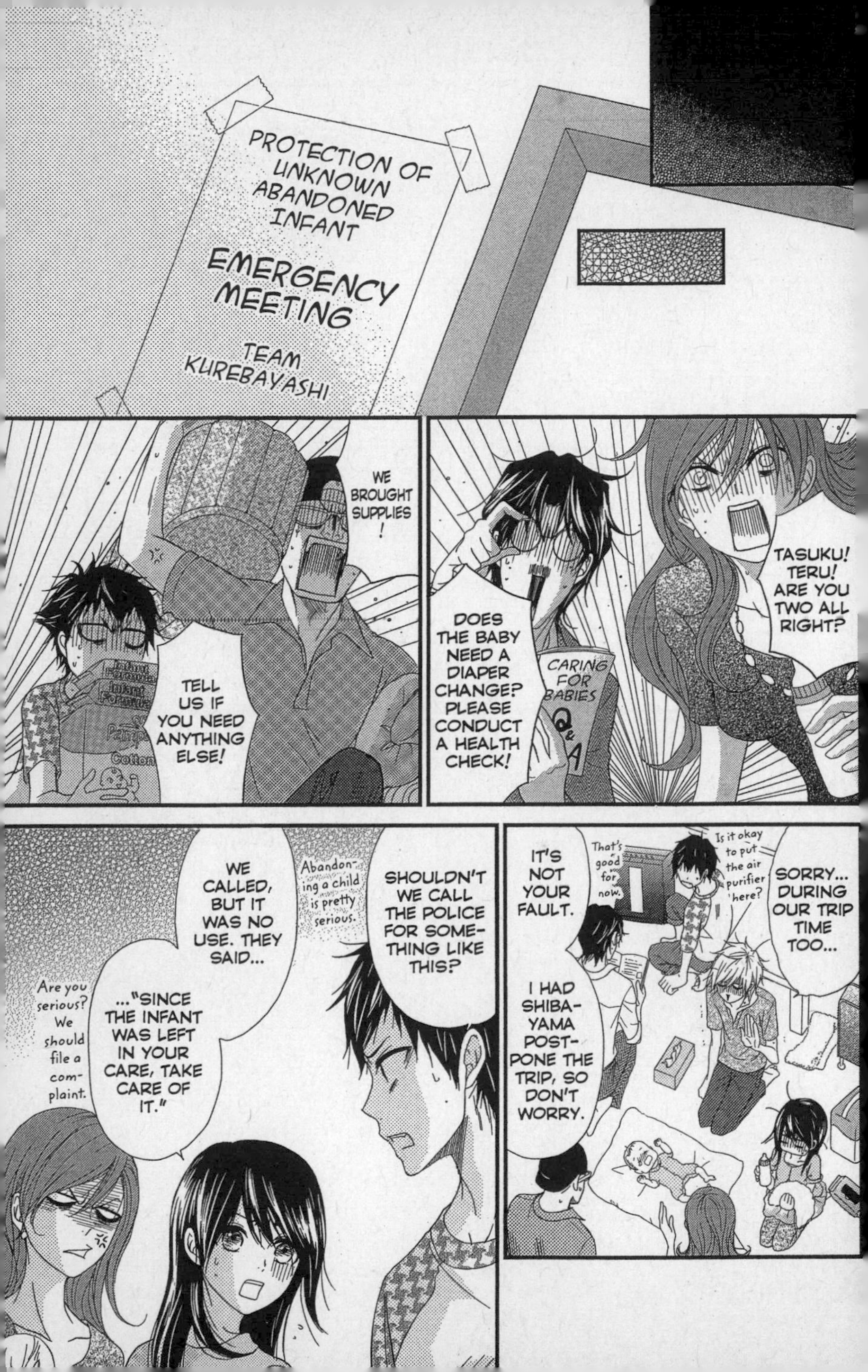
PROTECTION OF UNKNOWN ABANDONED INFANT
EMERGENCY MEETING
TEAM KUREBAYASHI
TASUKU! TERU! ARE YOU TWO ALL RIGHT?
DOES THE BABY NEED A DIAPER CHANGE? PLEASE CONDUCT A HEALTH CHECK!
CARING FOR BABIES Q&A
WE BROUGHT SUPPLIES!
TELL US IF YOU NEED ANYTHING ELSE!
SORRY... DURING OUR TRIP TIME TOO...
Is it okay to put the air purifier here?
IT'S NOT YOUR FAULT.
That's good for now.
I HAD SHIBAYAMA POSTPONE THE TRIP, SO DON'T WORRY.
SHOULDN'T WE CALL THE POLICE FOR SOMETHING LIKE THIS?
Abandoning a child is pretty serious.
WE CALLED, BUT IT WAS NO USE. THEY SAID...
..."SINCE THE INFANT WAS LEFT IN YOUR CARE, TAKE CARE OF IT."
Are you serious? We should file a complaint.

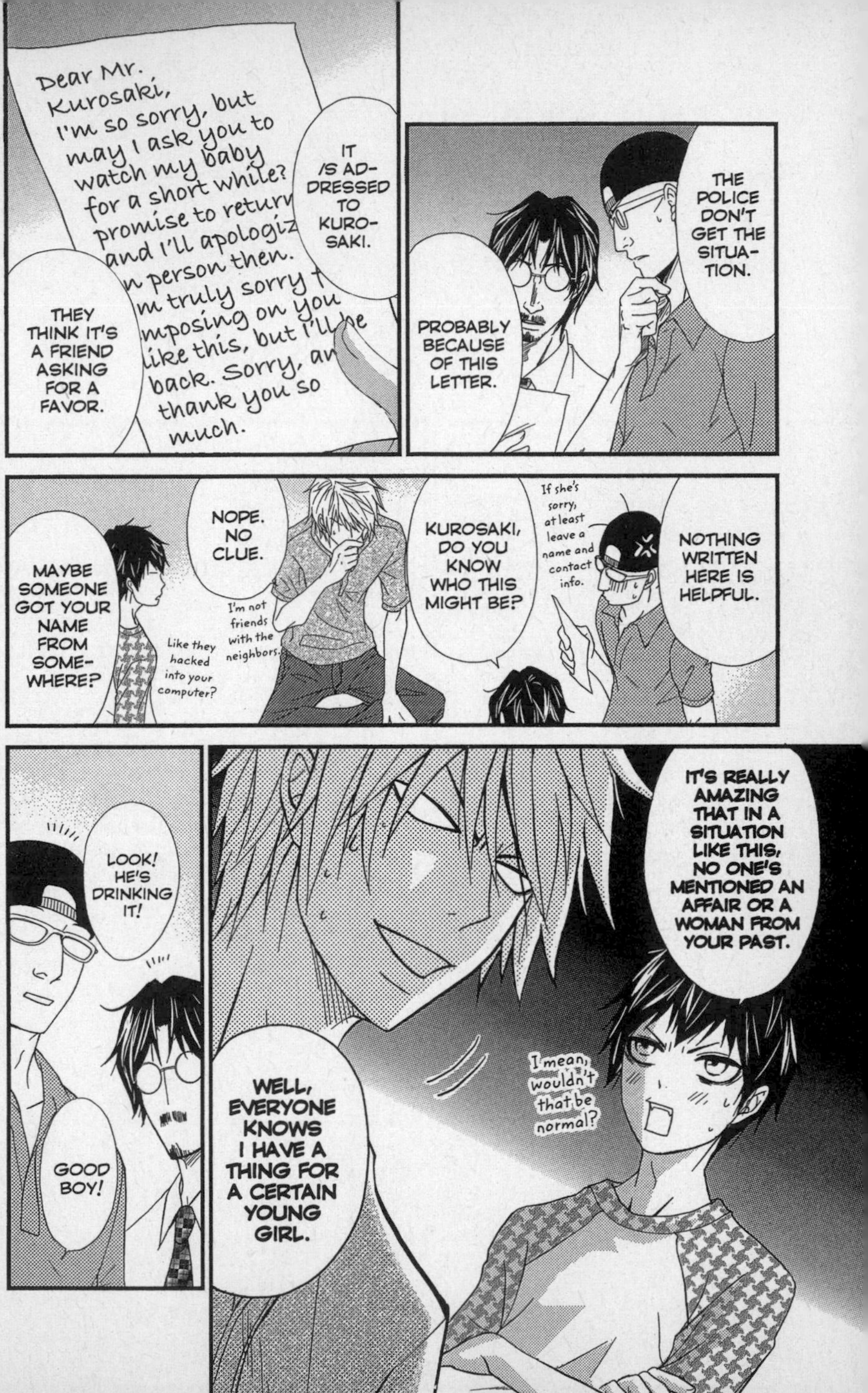
THE POLICE DON'T GET THE SITUATION.
PROBABLY BECAUSE OF THIS LETTER.
Dear Mr. Kurosaki,
I'm so sorry, but
may I ask you to
watch my baby
for a short while?
promise to retur
and I'll apologiz
n person then.
m truly sorry f
mposing on you
like this, but I'll be
back. Sorry, an
thank you so
much.
IT IS ADDRESSED TO KUROSAKI.
THEY THINK IT'S A FRIEND ASKING FOR A FAVOR.
NOTHING WRITTEN HERE IS HELPFUL.
If she's sorry, at least leave a name and contact info.
KUROSAKI, DO YOU KNOW WHO THIS MIGHT BE?
NOPE. NO CLUE.
I'm not friends with the neighbors.
MAYBE SOMEONE GOT YOUR NAME FROM SOMEWHERE?
Like they hacked into your computer?
IT'S REALLY AMAZING THAT IN A SITUATION LIKE THIS, NO ONE'S MENTIONED AN AFFAIR OR A WOMAN FROM YOUR PAST.
I mean, wouldn't that be normal?
WELL, EVERYONE KNOWS I HAVE A THING FOR A CERTAIN YOUNG GIRL.
LOOK! HE'S DRINKING IT!
GOOD BOY!

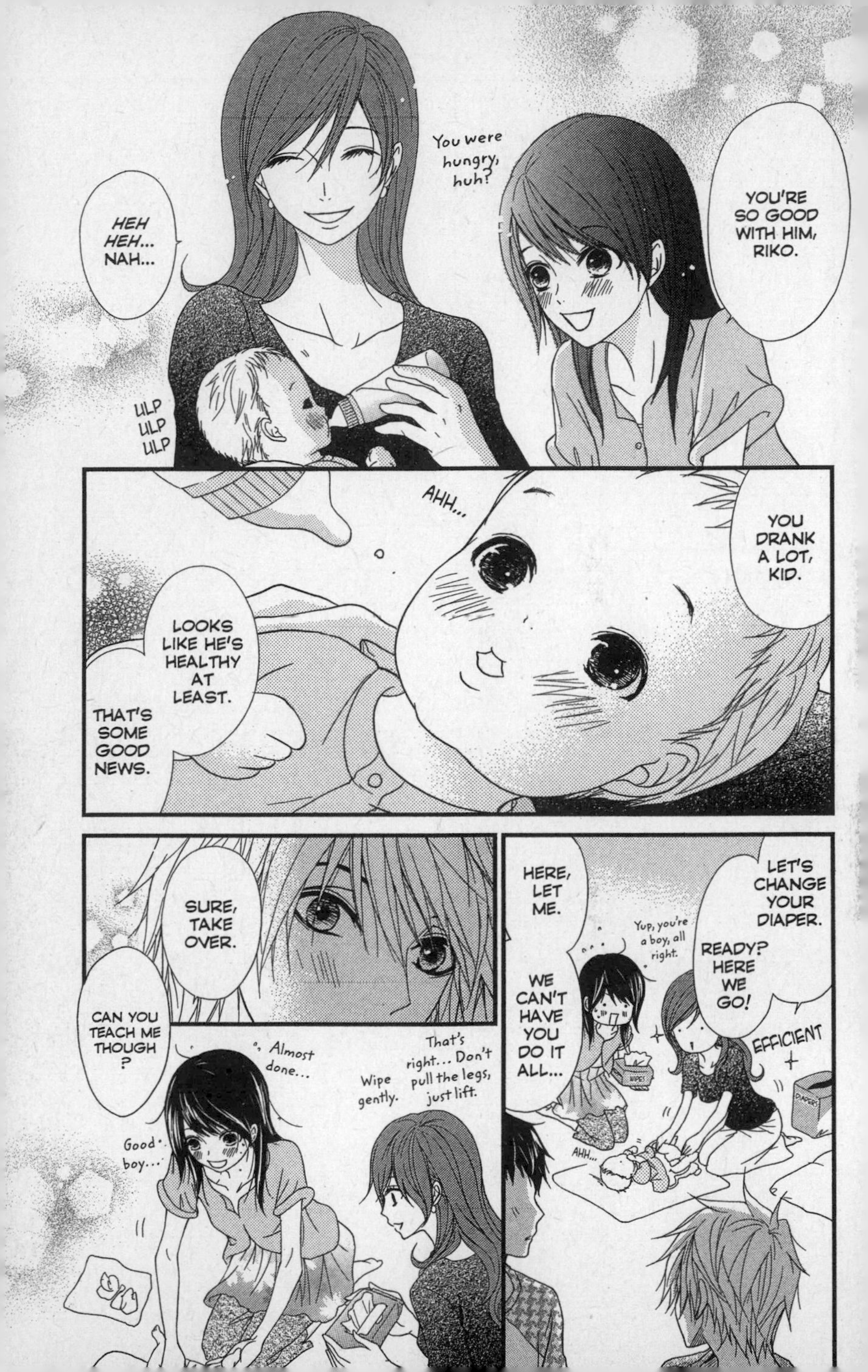
YOU'RE SO GOOD WITH HIM, RIKO.
You were hungry, huh?
HEH HEH... NAH...
ULP ULP ULP
AHH...
YOU DRANK A LOT, KID.
LOOKS LIKE HE'S HEALTHY AT LEAST.
THAT'S SOME GOOD NEWS.
LET'S CHANGE YOUR DIAPER.
READY? HERE WE GO!
EFFICIENT
DIAPERS
HERE, LET ME.
Yup, you're a boy, all right.
WE CAN'T HAVE YOU DO IT ALL...
WIPES
AHH...
SURE, TAKE OVER.
CAN YOU TEACH ME THOUGH?
That's right... Don't pull the legs, just lift.
Wipe gently.
Almost done...
Good boy...

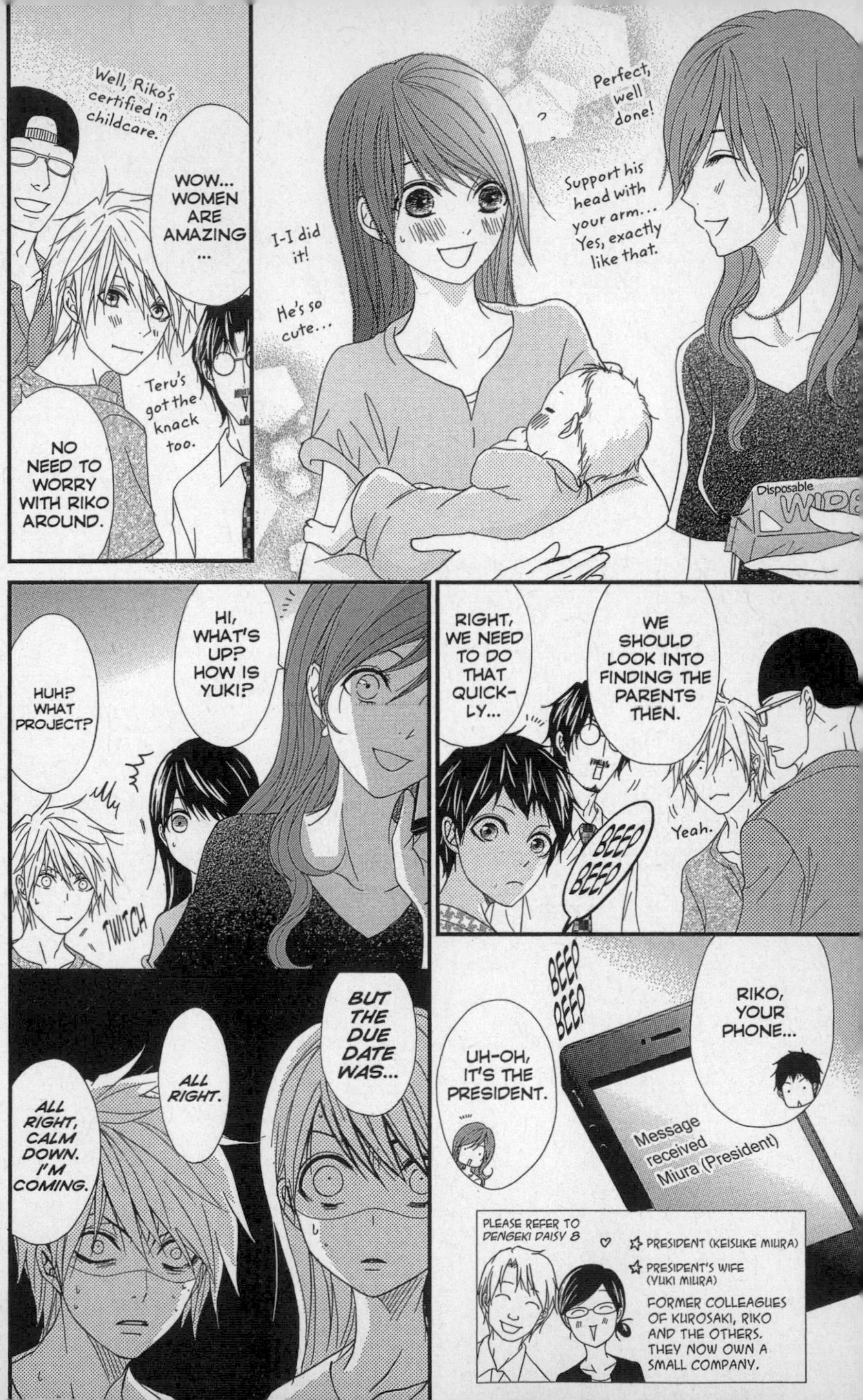
Perfect, well done!
Support his head with your arm... Yes, exactly like that.
I-I did it!
He's so cute...
Disposable
Well, Riko's certified in childcare.
WOW... WOMEN ARE AMAZING...
Teru's got the knack too.
NO NEED TO WORRY WITH RIKO AROUND.
WE SHOULD LOOK INTO FINDING THE PARENTS THEN.
RIGHT, WE NEED TO DO THAT QUICKLY...
Yeah.
BEEP BEEP
RIKO, YOUR PHONE...
BEEP BEEP
UH-OH, IT'S THE PRESIDENT.
Message received Miura (President)
PLEASE REFER TO DENGEKI DAISY 8
PRESIDENT (KEISUKE MIURA)
PRESIDENT'S WIFE (YUKI MIURA)
FORMER COLLEAGUES OF KUROSAKI, RIKO AND THE OTHERS. THEY NOW OWN A SMALL COMPANY.
HI, WHAT'S UP? HOW IS YUKI?
HUH? WHAT PROJECT?
TWITCH
BUT THE DUE DATE WAS...
ALL RIGHT.
ALL RIGHT, CALM DOWN. I'M COMING.

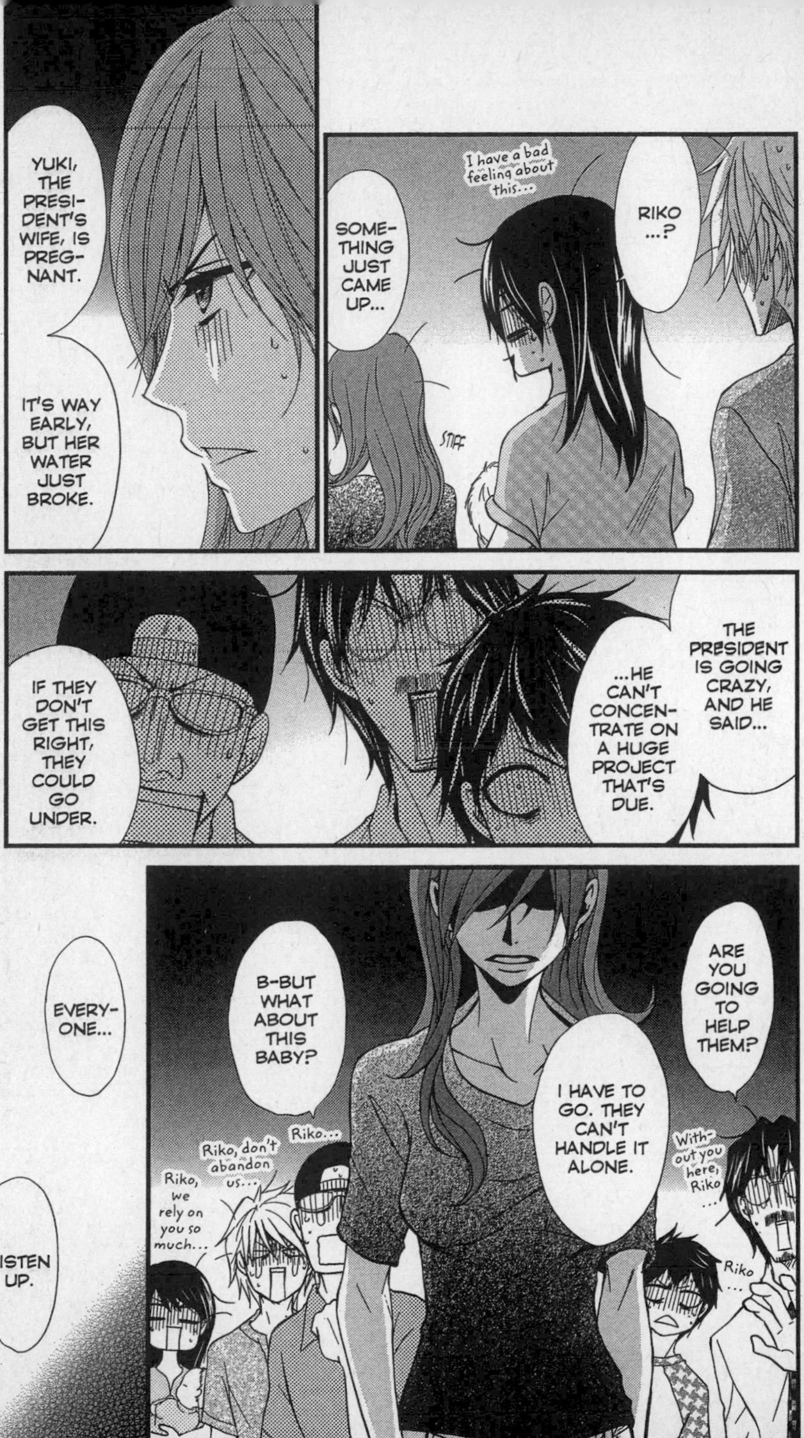
RIKO ...?
I have a bad feeling about this...
SOMETHING JUST CAME UP...
STIFF
YUKI, THE PRESIDENT'S WIFE, IS PREGNANT.
IT'S WAY EARLY, BUT HER WATER JUST BROKE.
THE PRESIDENT IS GOING CRAZY, AND HE SAID...
...HE CAN'T CONCENTRATE ON A HUGE PROJECT THAT'S DUE.
IF THEY DON'T GET THIS RIGHT, THEY COULD GO UNDER.
ARE YOU GOING TO HELP THEM?
I HAVE TO GO. THEY CAN'T HANDLE IT ALONE.
Without you here, Riko...
Riko...
B-BUT WHAT ABOUT THIS BABY?
Riko...
Riko, don't abandon us...
Riko, we rely on you so much...
EVERYONE...
LISTEN UP.

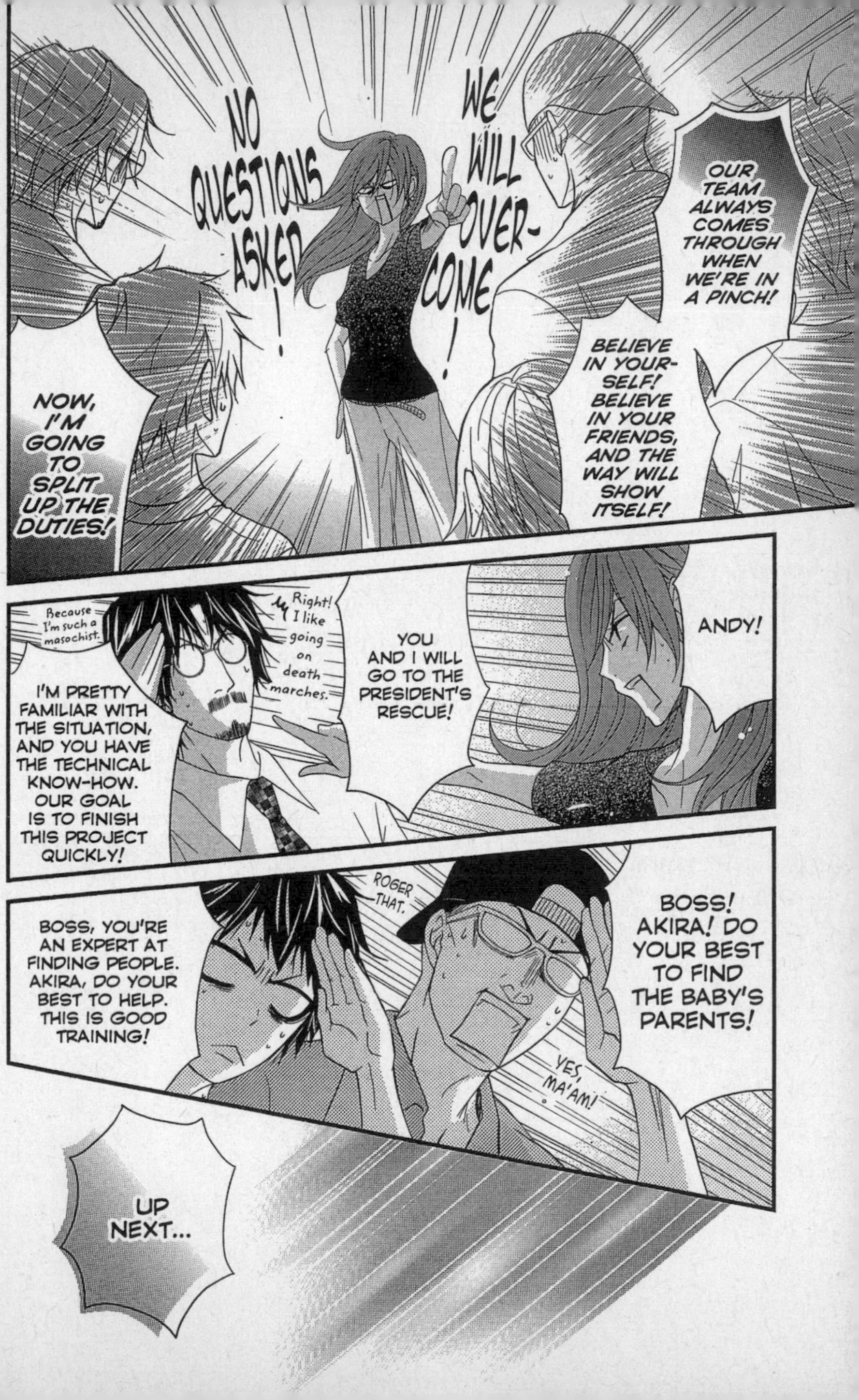
OUR TEAM ALWAYS COMES THROUGH WHEN WE'RE IN A PINCH!
WE WILL OVERCOME!
NO QUESTIONS ASKED!
BELIEVE IN YOURSELF! BELIEVE IN YOUR FRIENDS, AND THE WAY WILL SHOW ITSELF!
NOW, I'M GOING TO SPLIT UP THE DUTIES!
ANDY!
YOU AND I WILL GO TO THE PRESIDENT'S RESCUE!
Right! I like going on death marches.
Because I'm such a masochist.
I'M PRETTY FAMILIAR WITH THE SITUATION, AND YOU HAVE THE TECHNICAL KNOW-HOW. OUR GOAL IS TO FINISH THIS PROJECT QUICKLY!
BOSS! AKIRA! DO YOUR BEST TO FIND THE BABY'S PARENTS!
YES, MA'AM!
ROGER THAT.
BOSS, YOU'RE AN EXPERT AT FINDING PEOPLE. AKIRA, DO YOUR BEST TO HELP. THIS IS GOOD TRAINING!
UP NEXT...

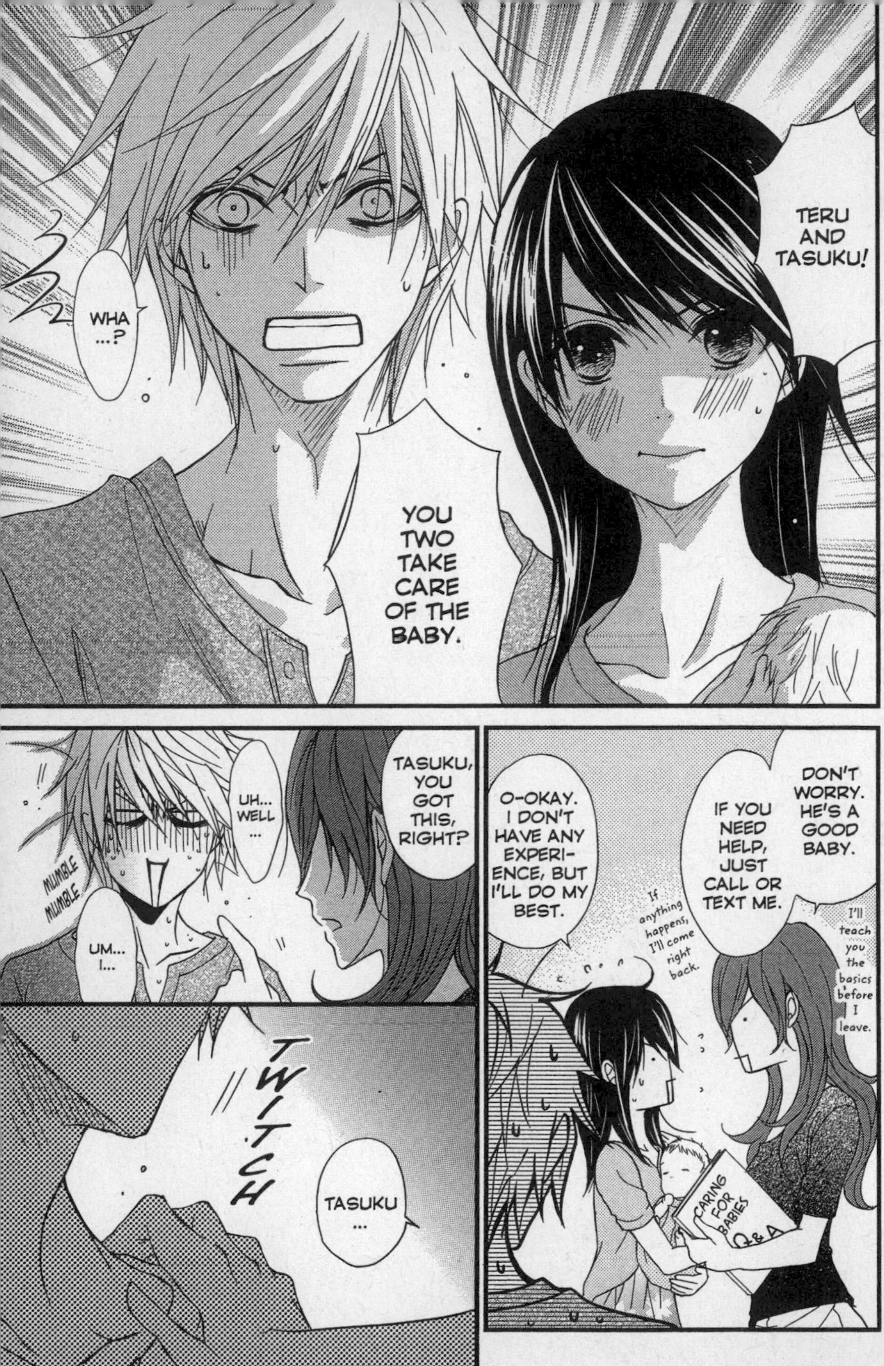
TERU AND TASUKU!
YOU TWO TAKE CARE OF THE BABY.
WHA ...?
DON'T WORRY. HE'S A GOOD BABY.
IF YOU NEED HELP, JUST CALL OR TEXT ME.
O-OKAY. I DON'T HAVE ANY EXPERI-ENCE, BUT I'LL DO MY BEST.
I'll teach you the basics before I leave.
If anything happens, I'll come right back.
CARING FOR BABIES Q&A
TASUKU, YOU GOT THIS, RIGHT?
UH... WELL ...
MUMBLE MUMBLE
UM... I...
TWITCH
TASUKU ...

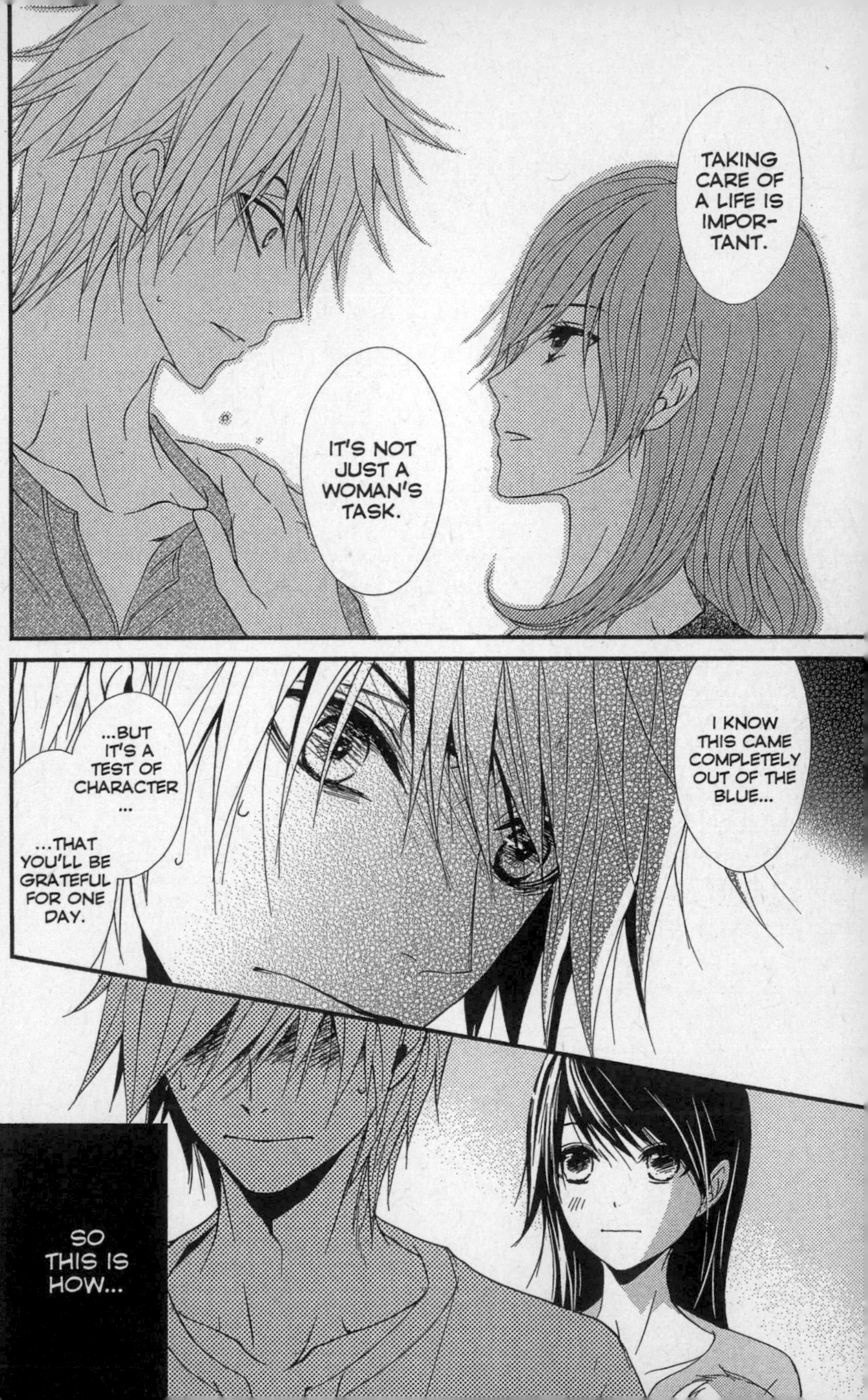
TAKING CARE OF A LIFE IS IMPOR-TANT.
IT'S NOT JUST A WOMAN'S TASK.
I KNOW THIS CAME COMPLETELY OUT OF THE BLUE...
...BUT IT'S A TEST OF CHARACTER ...
...THAT YOU'LL BE GRATEFUL FOR ONE DAY.
SO THIS IS HOW...

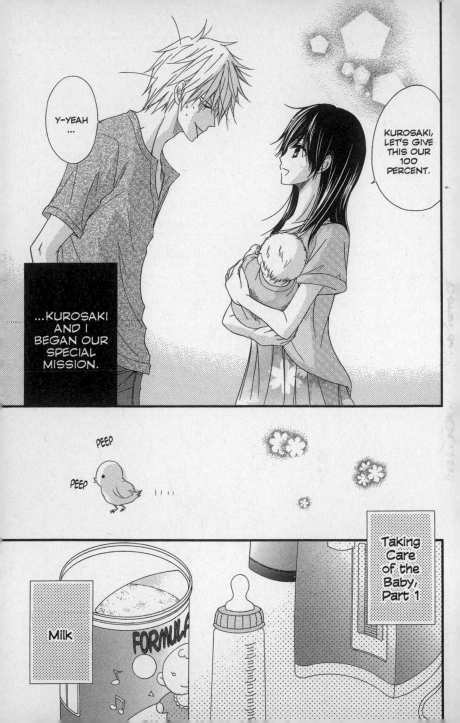

Y-YEAH...

KUROSAKI, LET'S GIVE THIS OUR 100 PERCENT.

...KUROSAKI AND I BEGAN OUR SPECIAL MISSION.

PEEP

PEEP

Taking Care of the Baby, Part 1

Milk

FORMULA

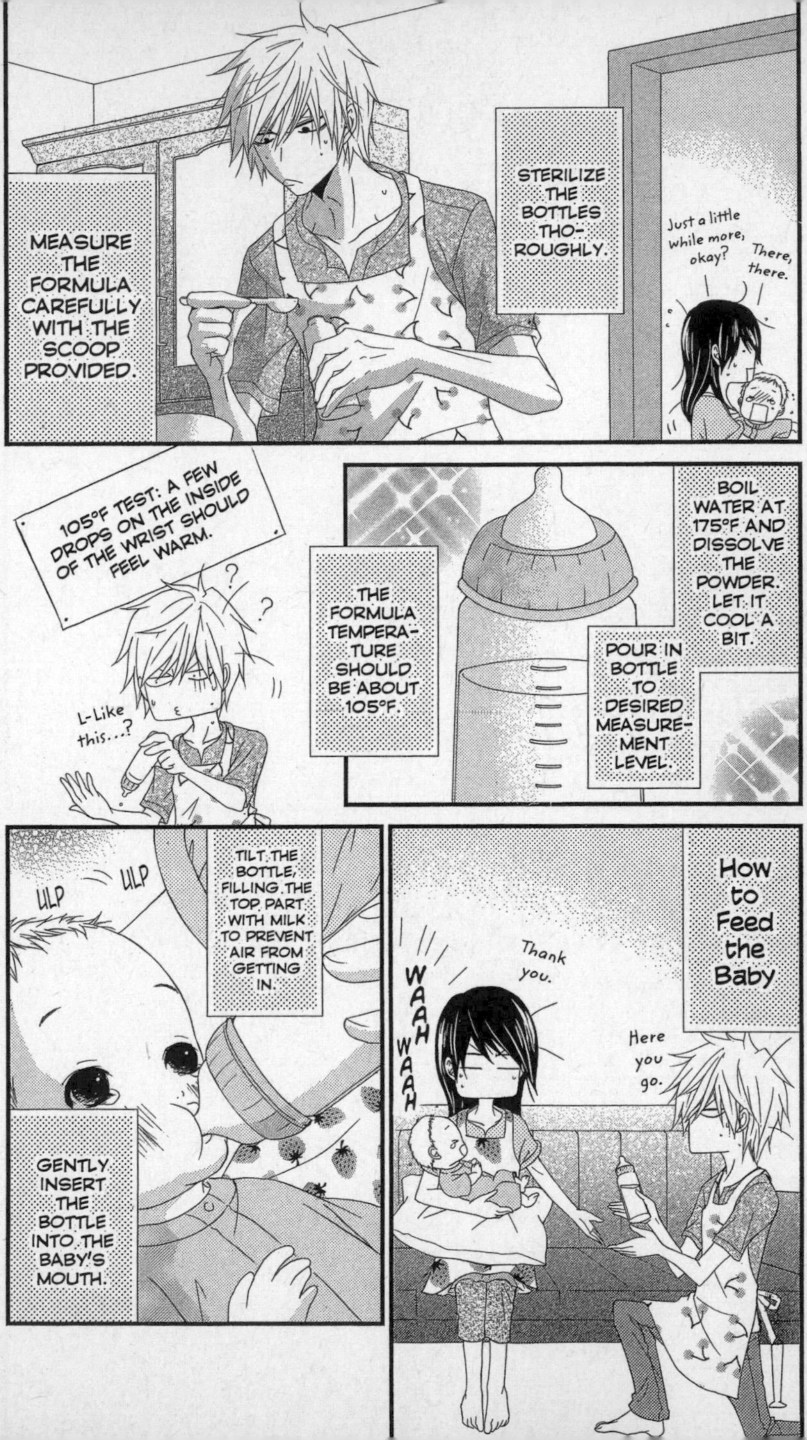
There, there.
Just a little while more, okay?
STERILIZE THE BOTTLES THO-ROUGHLY.
MEASURE THE FORMULA CAREFULLY WITH THE SCOOP PROVIDED.
BOIL WATER AT 175°F AND DISSOLVE THE POWDER. LET IT COOL A BIT.
POUR IN BOTTLE TO DESIRED MEASURE-MENT LEVEL.
THE FORMULA TEMPERA-TURE SHOULD BE ABOUT 105°F.
105°F TEST: A FEW DROPS ON THE INSIDE OF THE WRIST SHOULD FEEL WARM.
? ?
L-Like this...?
How to Feed the Baby
Here you go.
Thank you.
WAAH WAAH
TILT THE BOTTLE, FILLING THE TOP PART WITH MILK TO PREVENT AIR FROM GETTING IN.
ULP ULP
GENTLY INSERT THE BOTTLE INTO THE BABY'S MOUTH.

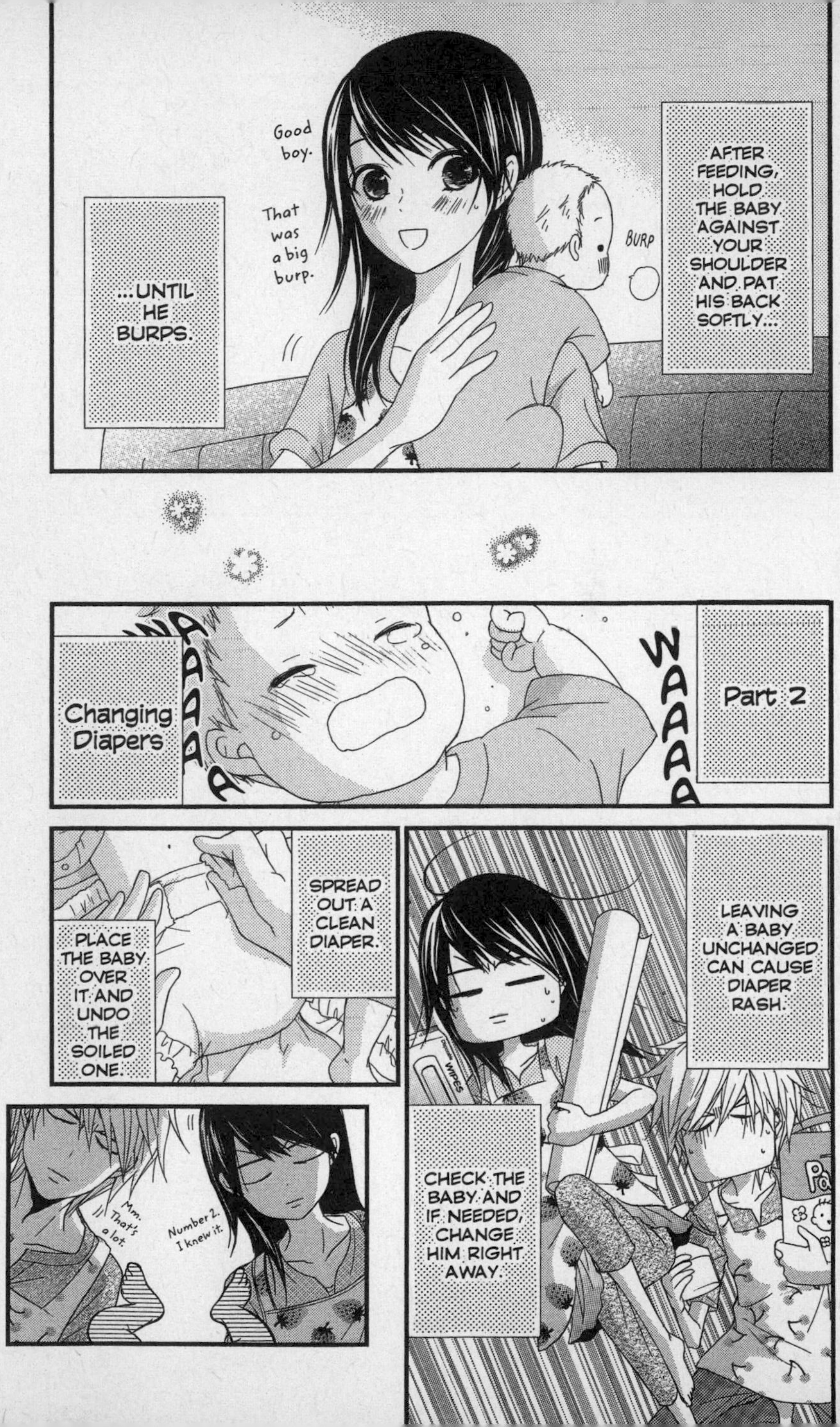
AFTER FEEDING, HOLD THE BABY AGAINST YOUR SHOULDER AND PAT HIS BACK SOFTLY...
BURP
Good boy.
That was a big burp.
...UNTIL HE BURPS.
Part 2
WAAAAA
Changing Diapers
WAAAAAA
LEAVING A BABY UNCHANGED CAN CAUSE DIAPER RASH.
WIPES
CHECK THE BABY AND IF NEEDED, CHANGE HIM RIGHT AWAY.
SPREAD OUT A CLEAN DIAPER.
PLACE THE BABY OVER IT AND UNDO THE SOILED ONE.
Number 2. I knew it.
Mm. That's a lot.

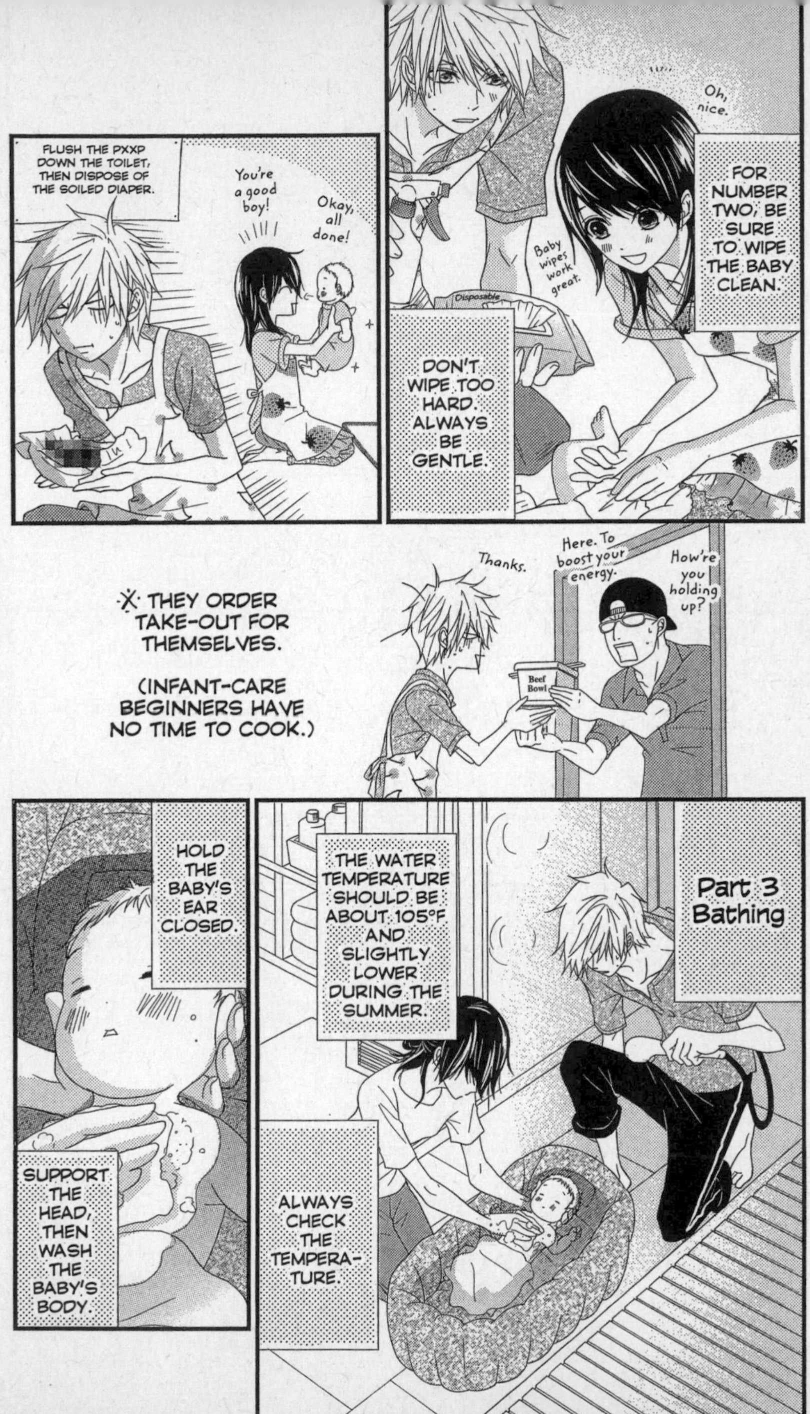
Oh, nice.
FOR NUMBER TWO, BE SURE TO WIPE THE BABY CLEAN.
Baby wipes work great.
Disposable
DON'T WIPE TOO HARD. ALWAYS BE GENTLE.
FLUSH THE PXXP DOWN THE TOILET, THEN DISPOSE OF THE SOILED DIAPER.
You're a good boy!
Okay, all done!
How're you holding up?
Here. To boost your energy.
Thanks.
Beef Bowl
※ THEY ORDER TAKE-OUT FOR THEMSELVES.
(INFANT-CARE BEGINNERS HAVE NO TIME TO COOK.)
Part 3 Bathing
THE WATER TEMPERATURE SHOULD BE ABOUT 105°F AND SLIGHTLY LOWER DURING THE SUMMER.
ALWAYS CHECK THE TEMPERA-TURE.
HOLD THE BABY'S EAR CLOSED.
SUPPORT THE HEAD, THEN WASH THE BABY'S BODY.

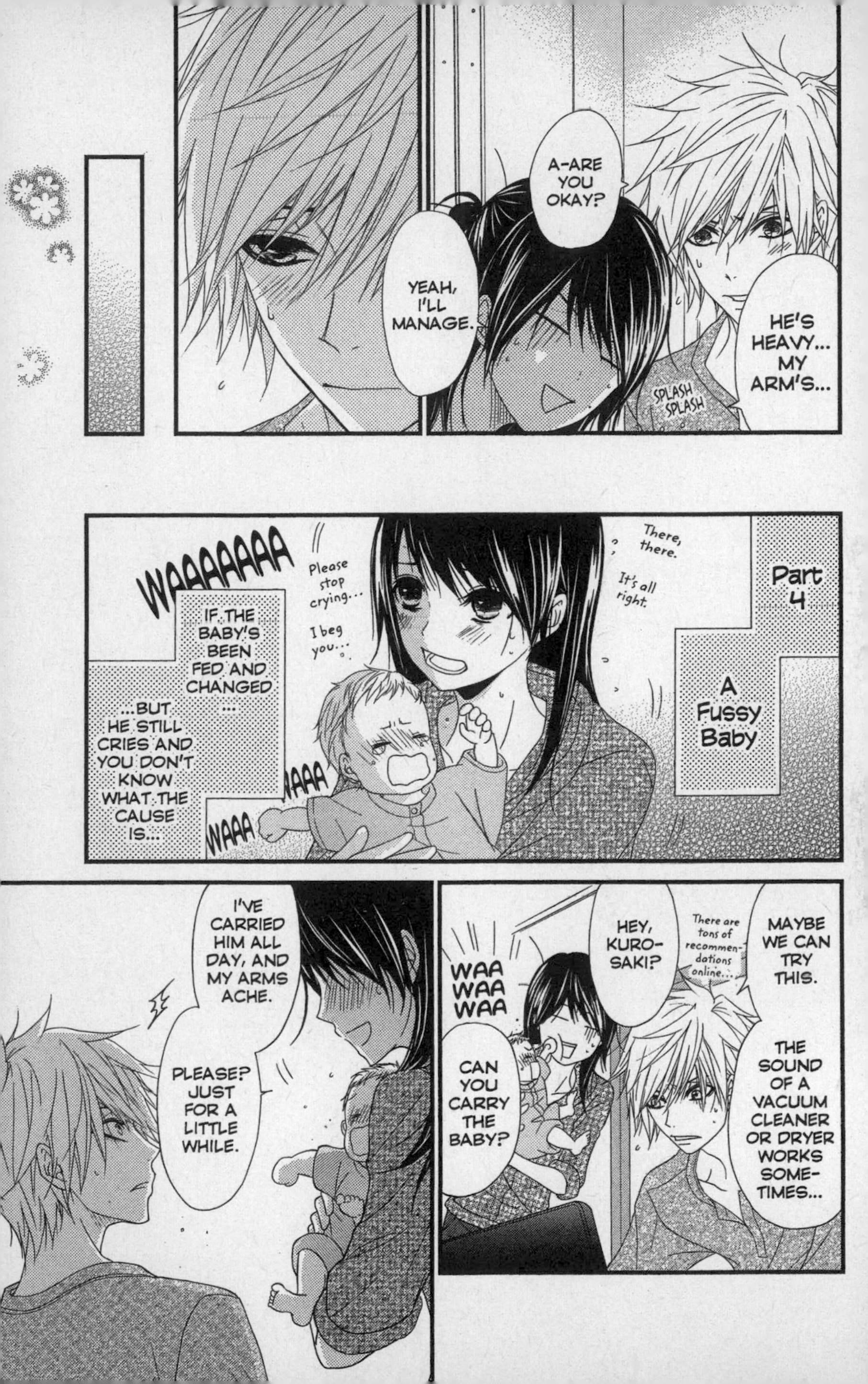
HE'S HEAVY... MY ARM'S...
SPLASH SPLASH
A-ARE YOU OKAY?
YEAH, I'LL MANAGE.
Part 4
A Fussy Baby
There, there.
It's all right.
Please stop crying...
I beg you...
WAAAAAAA
IF THE BABY'S BEEN FED AND CHANGED...
...BUT HE STILL CRIES AND YOU DON'T KNOW WHAT THE CAUSE IS...
WAAAA
WAAA
MAYBE WE CAN TRY THIS.
There are tons of recommen-dations online...
THE SOUND OF A VACUUM CLEANER OR DRYER WORKS SOME-TIMES...
HEY, KURO-SAKI?
WAA WAA WAA
CAN YOU CARRY THE BABY?
I'VE CARRIED HIM ALL DAY, AND MY ARMS ACHE.
PLEASE? JUST FOR A LITTLE WHILE.

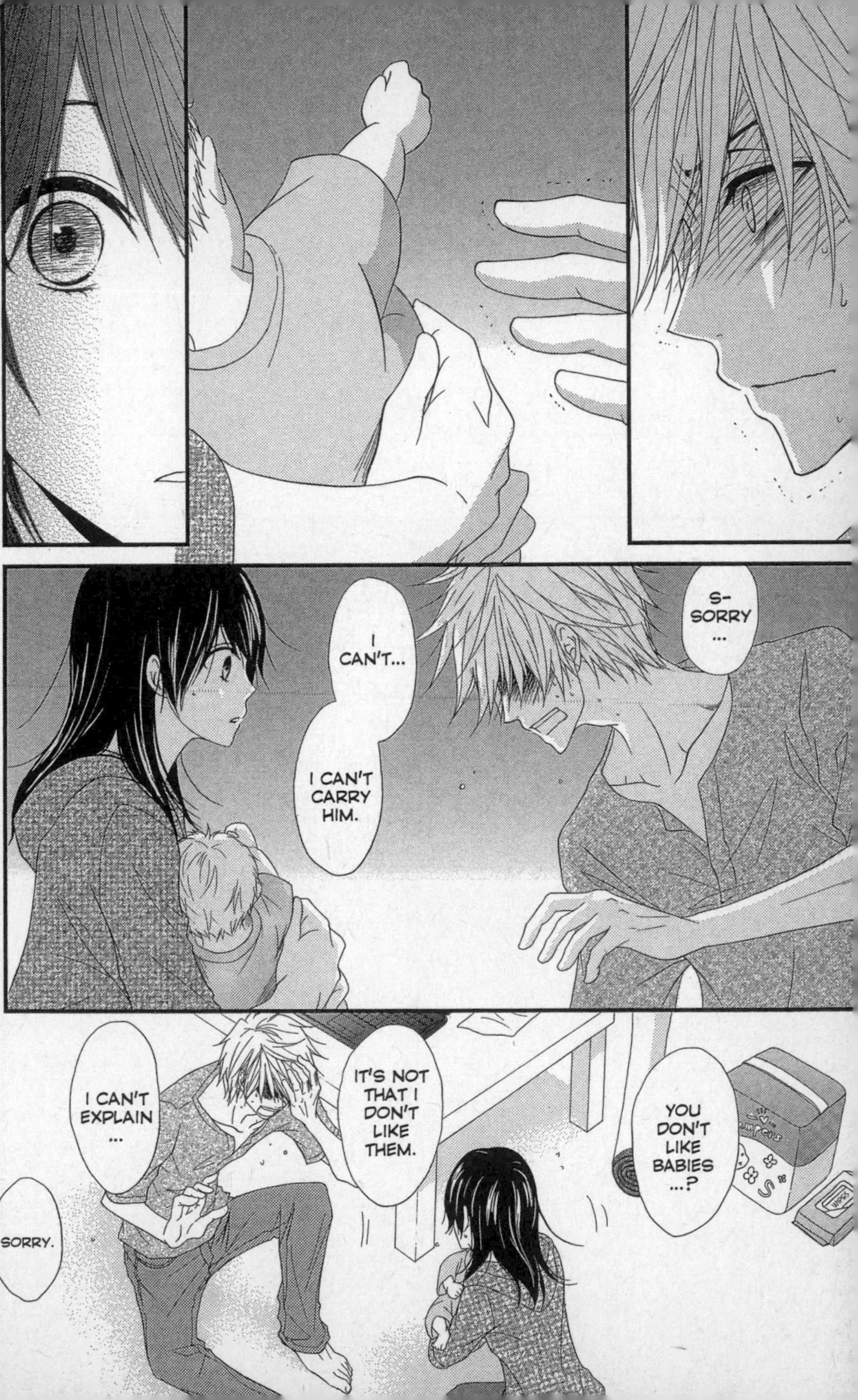
S-SORRY ...
I CAN'T...
I CAN'T CARRY HIM.
YOU DON'T LIKE BABIES ...?
IT'S NOT THAT I DON'T LIKE THEM.
I CAN'T EXPLAIN ...
SORRY.

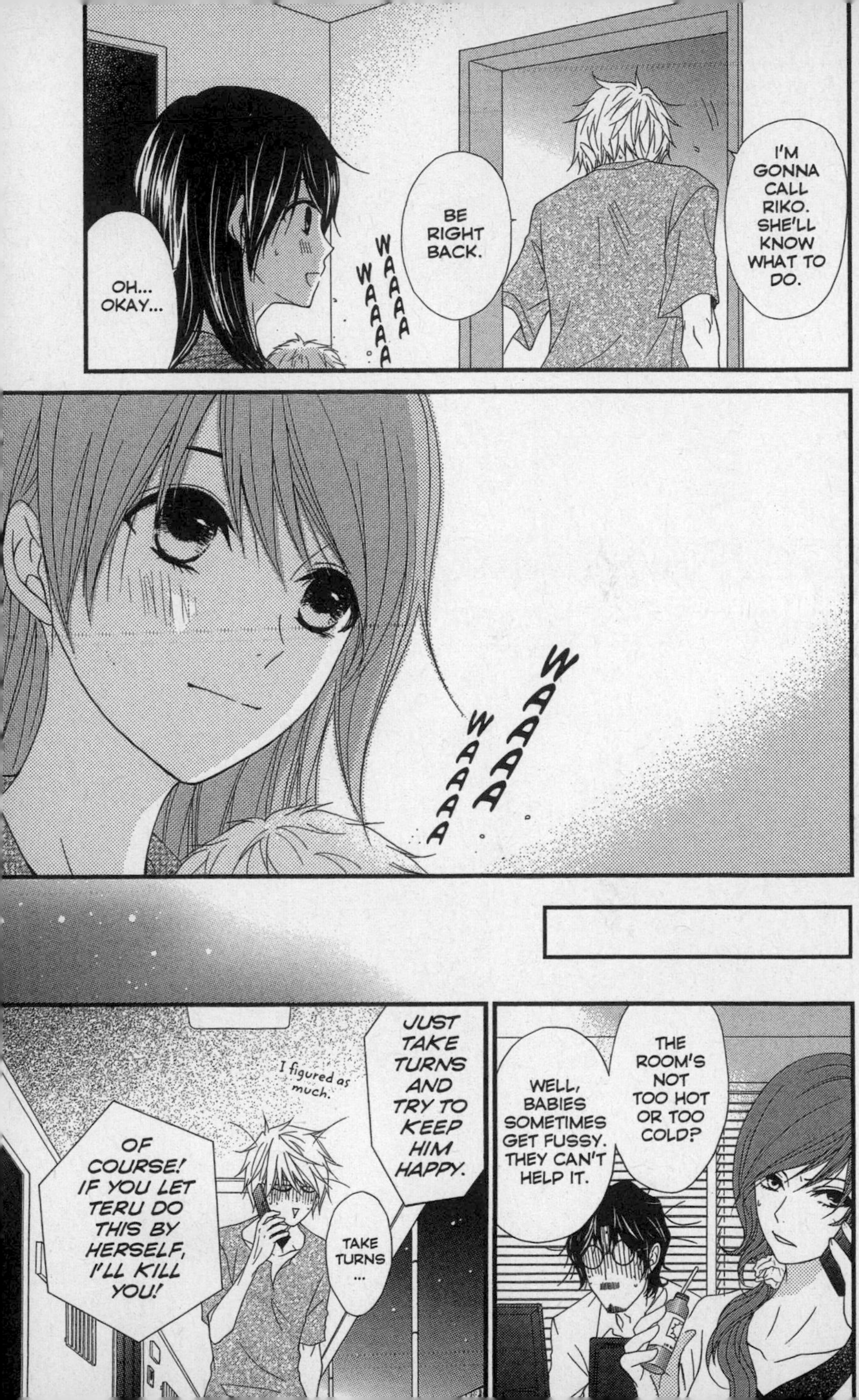
I'M GONNA CALL RIKO. SHE'LL KNOW WHAT TO DO.
BE RIGHT BACK.
WAAAAA
WAAAAA
OH... OKAY...
WAAAAA
WAAAAA
THE ROOM'S NOT TOO HOT OR TOO COLD?
WELL, BABIES SOMETIMES GET FUSSY. THEY CAN'T HELP IT.
JUST TAKE TURNS AND TRY TO KEEP HIM HAPPY.
TAKE TURNS...
I figured as much.
OF COURSE! IF YOU LET TERU DO THIS BY HERSELF, I'LL KILL YOU!

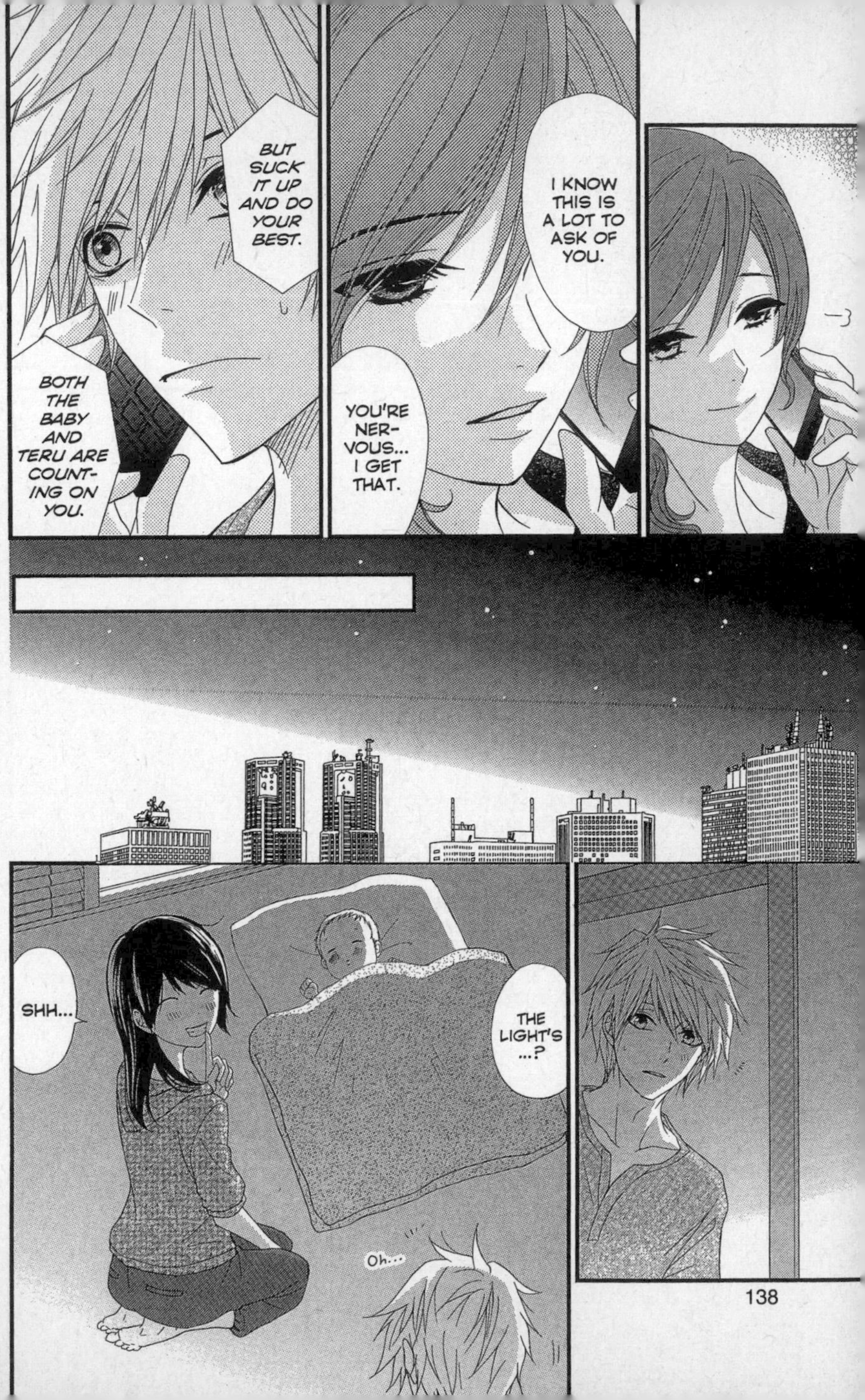
I KNOW THIS IS A LOT TO ASK OF YOU.
YOU'RE NERVOUS... I GET THAT.
BUT SUCK IT UP AND DO YOUR BEST.
BOTH THE BABY AND TERU ARE COUNTING ON YOU.
THE LIGHT'S ...?
SHH...
Oh...

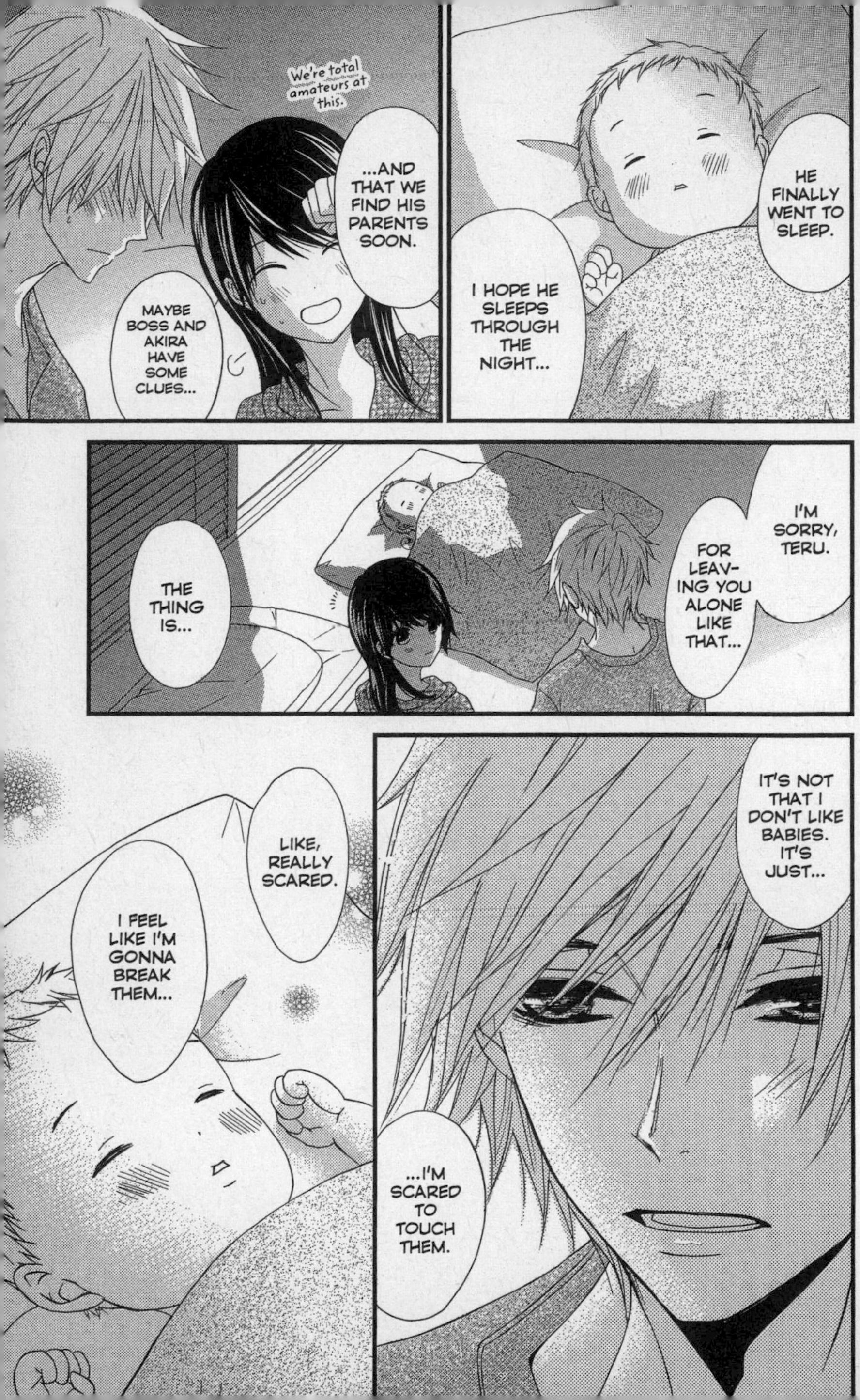
HE FINALLY WENT TO SLEEP.
I HOPE HE SLEEPS THROUGH THE NIGHT...
...AND THAT WE FIND HIS PARENTS SOON.
We're total amateurs at this.
MAYBE BOSS AND AKIRA HAVE SOME CLUES...
I'M SORRY, TERU.
FOR LEAV-ING YOU ALONE LIKE THAT...
THE THING IS...
IT'S NOT THAT I DON'T LIKE BABIES. IT'S JUST...
...I'M SCARED TO TOUCH THEM.
LIKE, REALLY SCARED.
I FEEL LIKE I'M GONNA BREAK THEM...

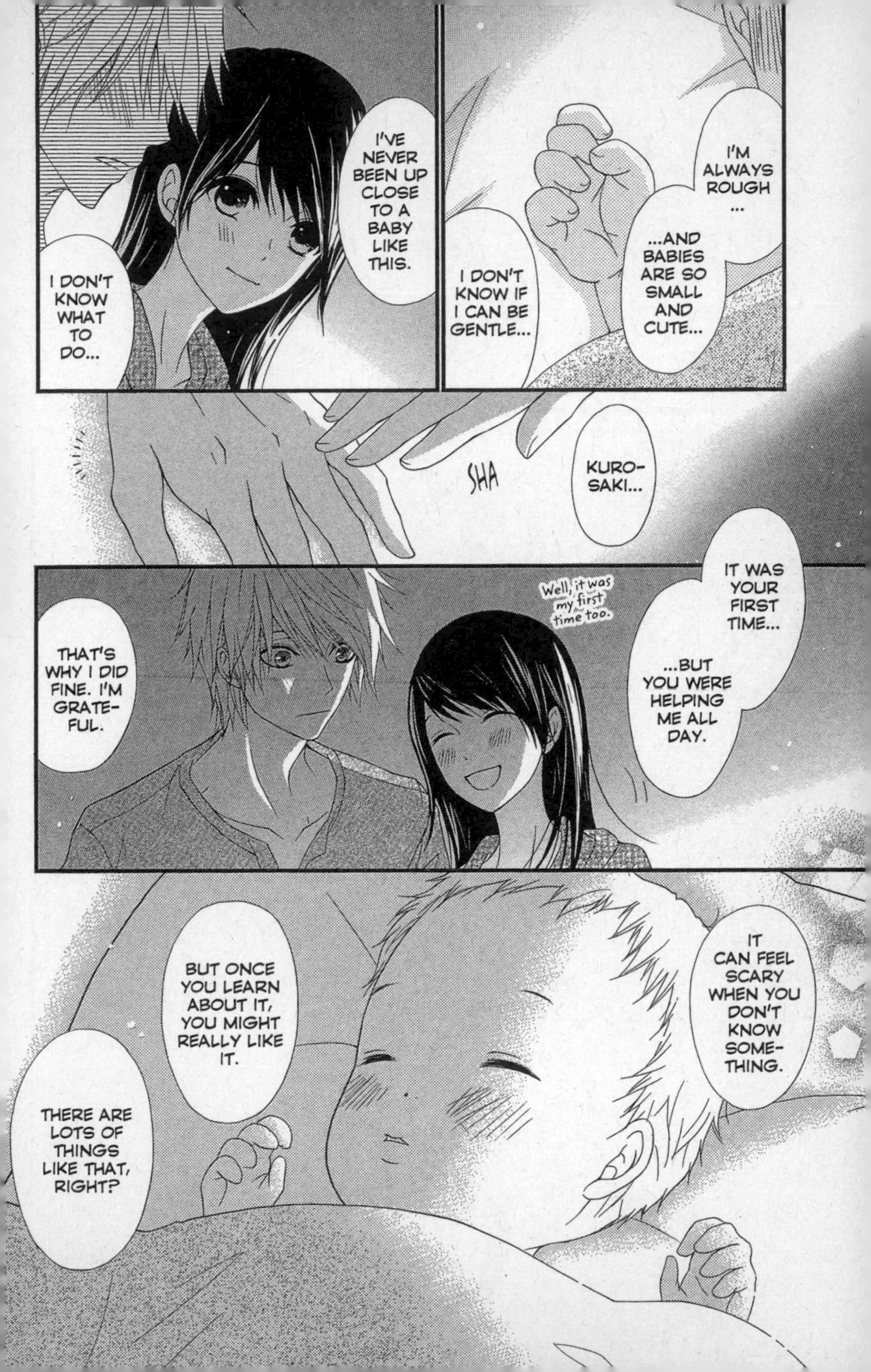
I'M ALWAYS ROUGH ...
...AND BABIES ARE SO SMALL AND CUTE...
I DON'T KNOW IF I CAN BE GENTLE...
I'VE NEVER BEEN UP CLOSE TO A BABY LIKE THIS.
I DON'T KNOW WHAT TO DO...
KURO-SAKI...
SHA
IT WAS YOUR FIRST TIME...
...BUT YOU WERE HELPING ME ALL DAY.
Well, it was my first time too.
THAT'S WHY I DID FINE. I'M GRATE-FUL.
IT CAN FEEL SCARY WHEN YOU DON'T KNOW SOME-THING.
BUT ONCE YOU LEARN ABOUT IT, YOU MIGHT REALLY LIKE IT.
THERE ARE LOTS OF THINGS LIKE THAT, RIGHT?

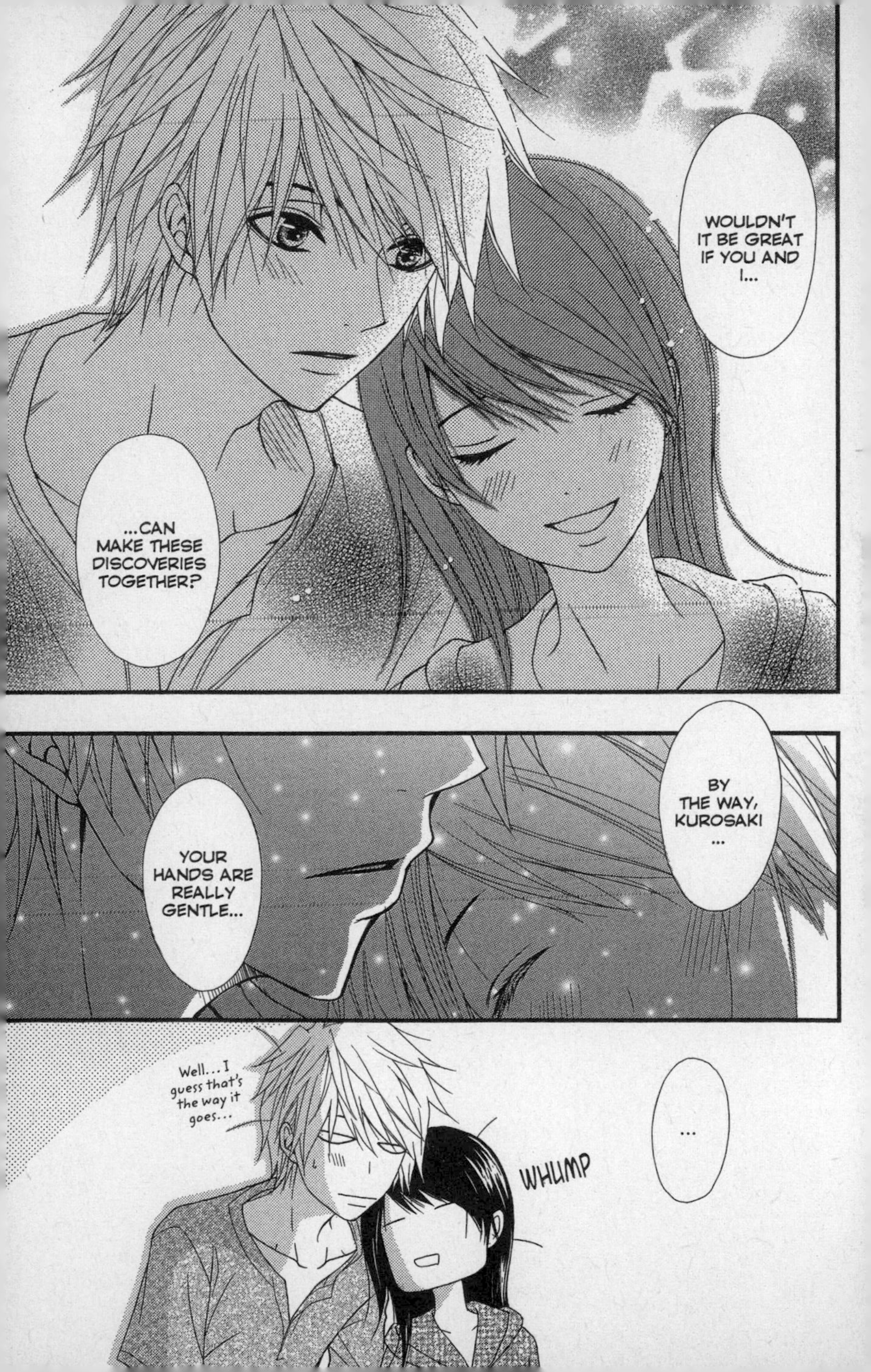
WOULDN'T IT BE GREAT IF YOU AND I...
...CAN MAKE THESE DISCOVERIES TOGETHER?
BY THE WAY, KUROSAKI ...
YOUR HANDS ARE REALLY GENTLE...
...
WHUMP
Well... I guess that's the way it goes...

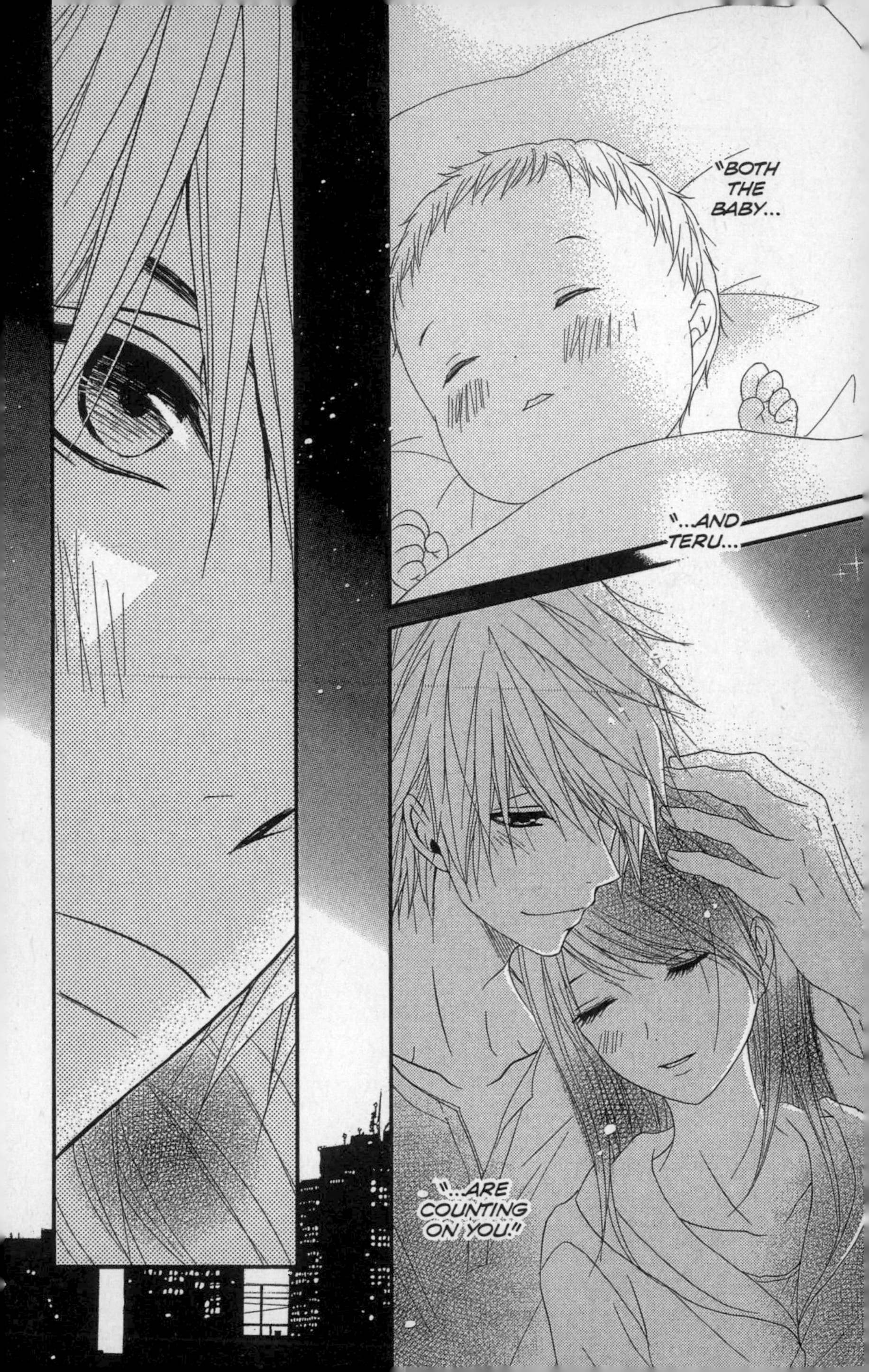
"BOTH THE BABY...
"...AND TERU...
"...ARE COUNTING ON YOU."

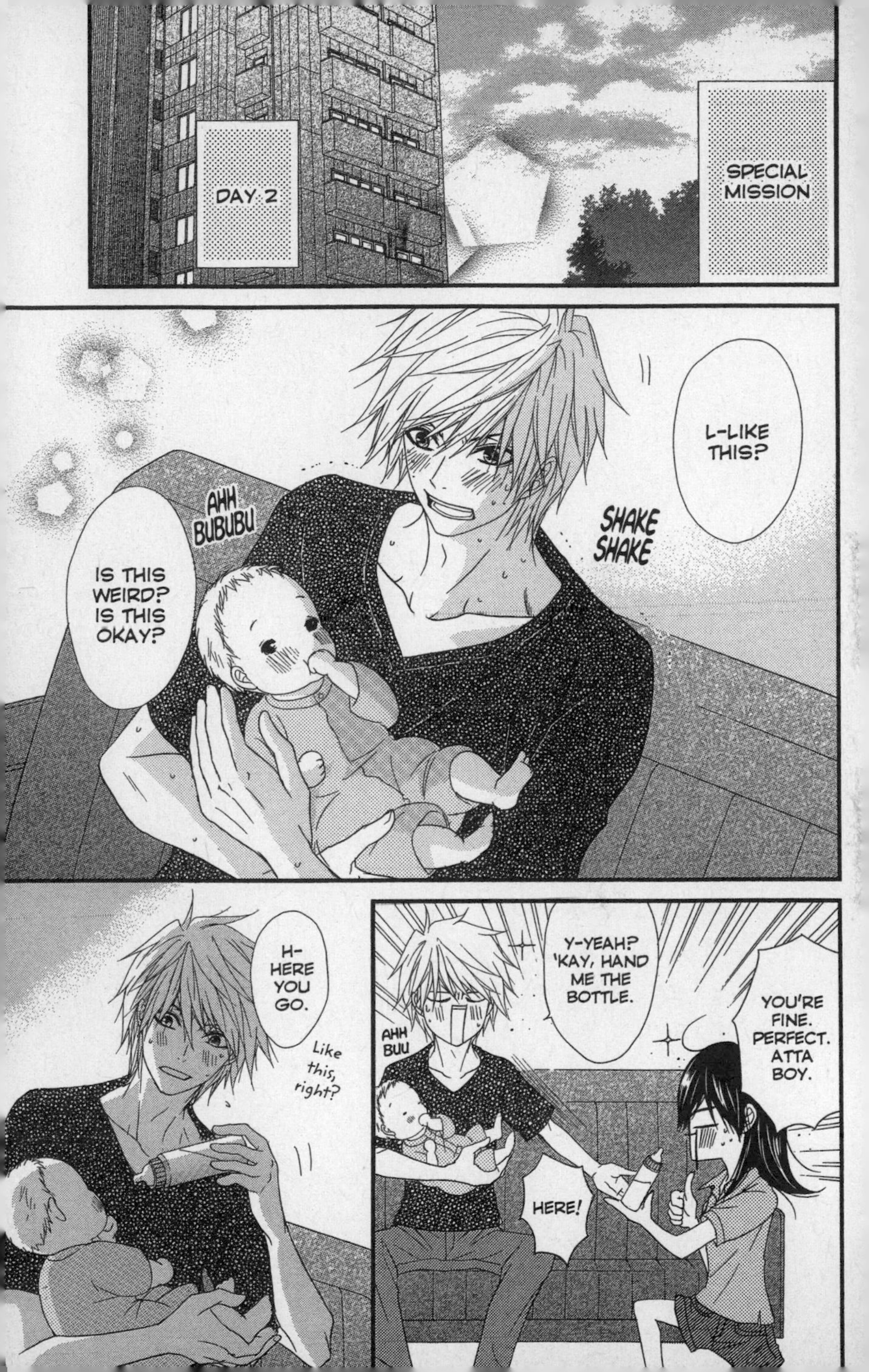
SPECIAL MISSION
DAY 2
L-LIKE THIS?
SHAKE SHAKE
AHH BUBUBU
IS THIS WEIRD? IS THIS OKAY?
YOU'RE FINE. PERFECT. ATTA BOY.
Y-YEAH? 'KAY, HAND ME THE BOTTLE.
AHH BUU
HERE!
H-HERE YOU GO.
Like this, right?

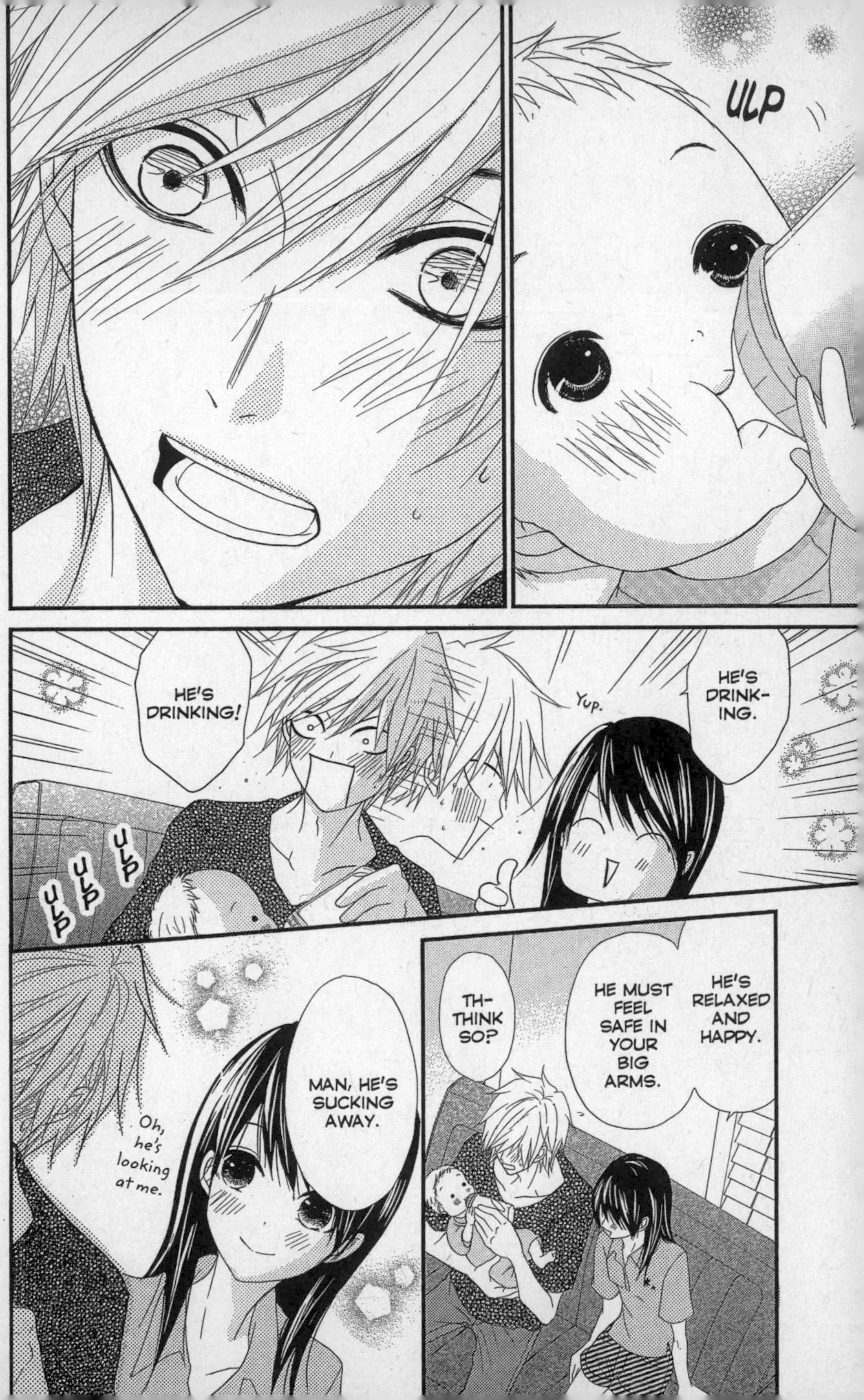
ULP
HE'S DRINK- ING.
Yup.
HE'S DRINKING!
ULP ULP ULP
HE'S RELAXED AND HAPPY.
HE MUST FEEL SAFE IN YOUR BIG ARMS.
TH- THINK SO?
MAN, HE'S SUCKING AWAY.
Oh, he's looking at me.

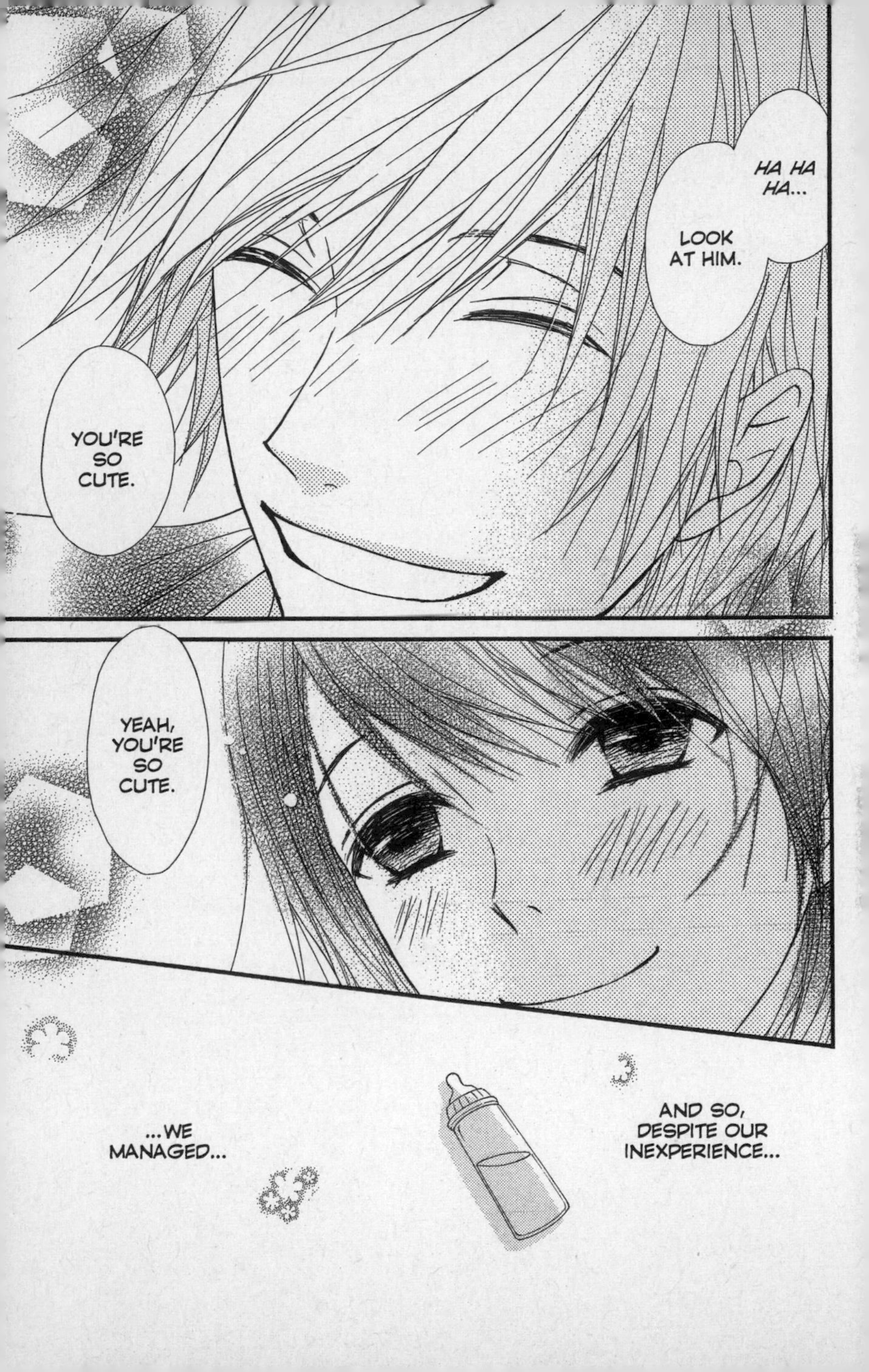
HA HA HA...
LOOK AT HIM.
YOU'RE SO CUTE.
YEAH, YOU'RE SO CUTE.
AND SO, DESPITE OUR INEXPERIENCE...
...WE MANAGED...

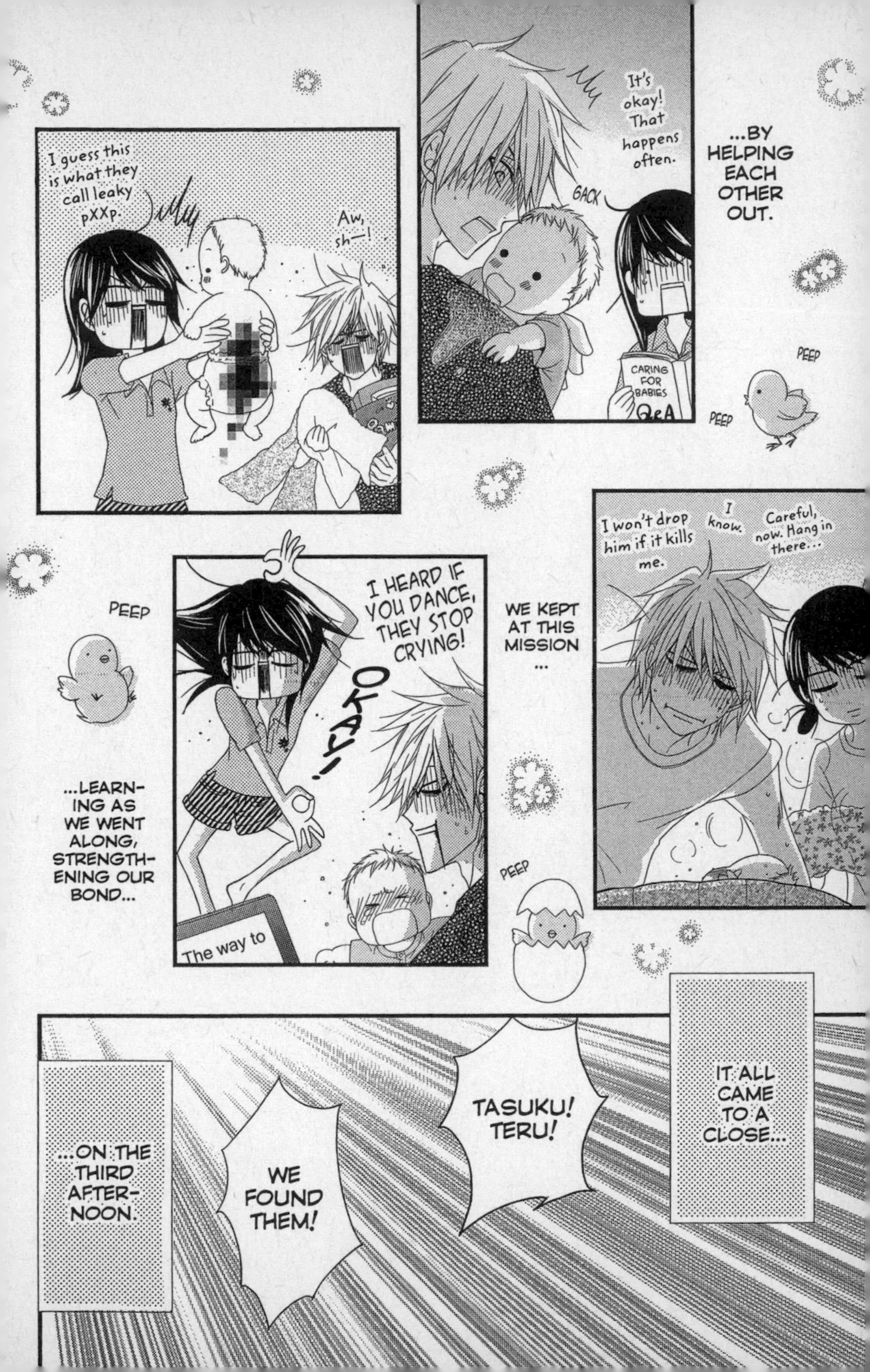
...BY HELPING EACH OTHER OUT.
It's okay! That happens often.
GACK
CARING FOR BABIES Q&A
PEEP
PEEP
Aw, sh—!
I guess this is what they call leaky pXXp.
Careful, now. Hang in there...
I know.
I won't drop him if it kills me.
PEEP
WE KEPT AT THIS MISSION ...
I HEARD IF YOU DANCE, THEY STOP CRYING!
OKAY!
The way to
PEEP
...LEARNING AS WE WENT ALONG, STRENGTHENING OUR BOND...
IT ALL CAME TO A CLOSE...
TASUKU! TERU!
WE FOUND THEM!
...ON THE THIRD AFTERNOON.

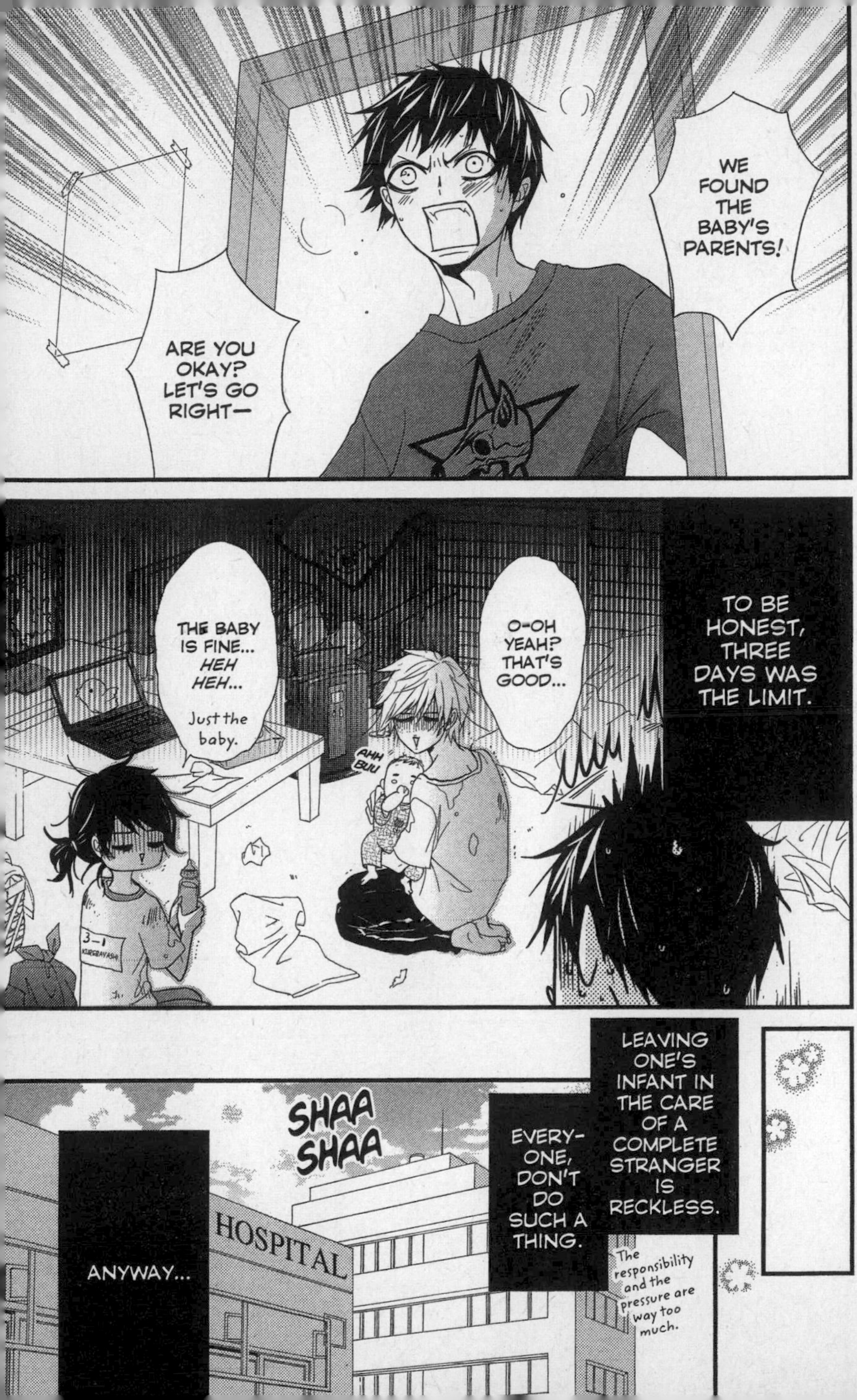
WE FOUND THE BABY'S PARENTS!
ARE YOU OKAY? LET'S GO RIGHT—
TO BE HONEST, THREE DAYS WAS THE LIMIT.
O-OH YEAH? THAT'S GOOD...
AHH BUU
THE BABY IS FINE... HEH HEH...
Just the baby.
LEAVING ONE'S INFANT IN THE CARE OF A COMPLETE STRANGER IS RECKLESS.
EVERY-ONE, DON'T DO SUCH A THING.
The responsibility and the pressure are way too much.
SHAA SHAA
HOSPITAL
ANYWAY...

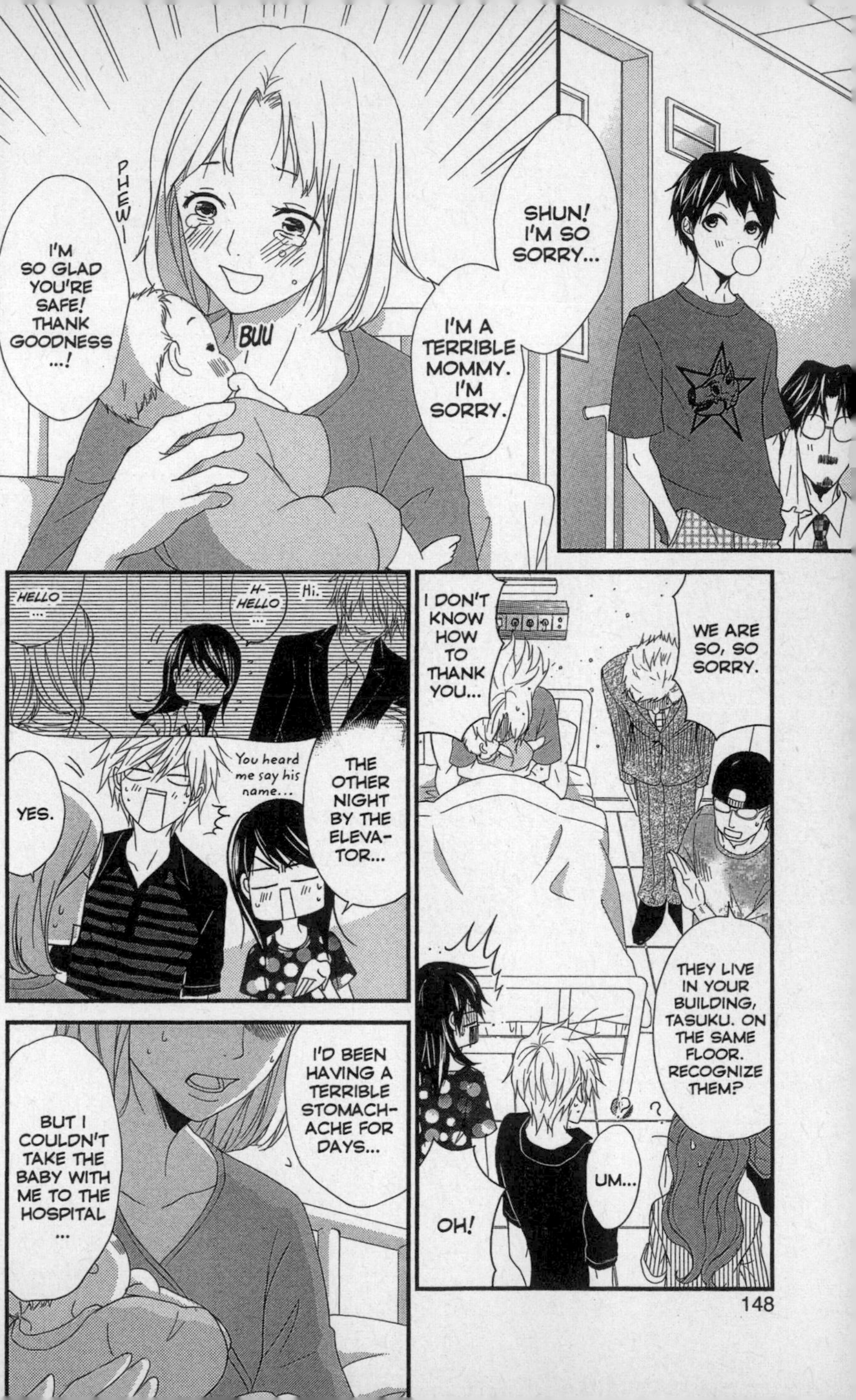
SHUN! I'M SO SORRY...
I'M A TERRIBLE MOMMY. I'M SORRY.
BUU
PHEW
I'M SO GLAD YOU'RE SAFE! THANK GOODNESS ...!
WE ARE SO, SO SORRY.
I DON'T KNOW HOW TO THANK YOU...
THEY LIVE IN YOUR BUILDING, TASUKU. ON THE SAME FLOOR. RECOGNIZE THEM?
UM...
OH!
Hi.
H-HELLO ...
HELLO ...
THE OTHER NIGHT BY THE ELEVATOR...
You heard me say his name...
YES.
I'D BEEN HAVING A TERRIBLE STOMACHACHE FOR DAYS...
BUT I COULDN'T TAKE THE BABY WITH ME TO THE HOSPITAL ...

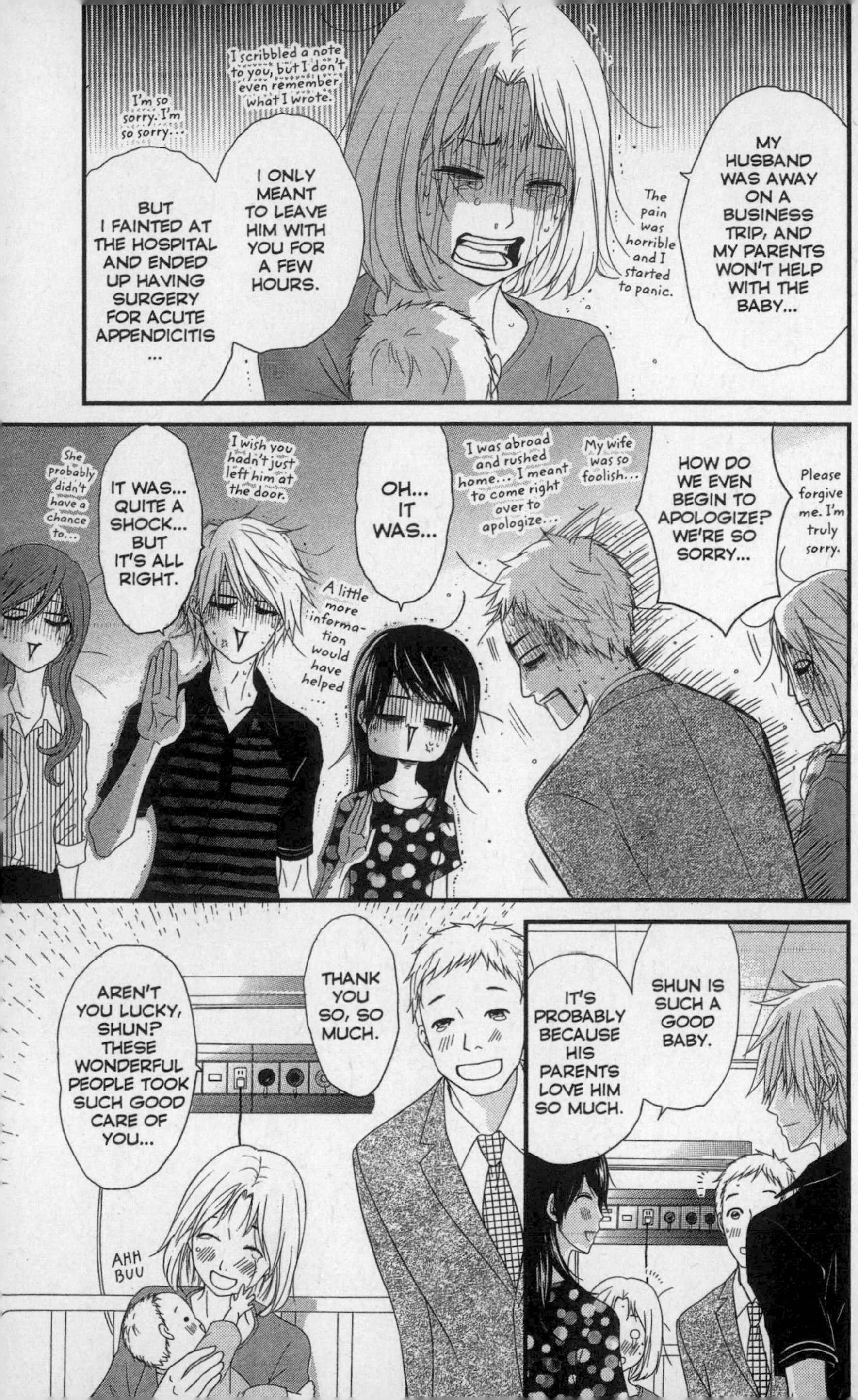
MY HUSBAND WAS AWAY ON A BUSINESS TRIP, AND MY PARENTS WON'T HELP WITH THE BABY...
The pain was horrible and I started to panic.
I ONLY MEANT TO LEAVE HIM WITH YOU FOR A FEW HOURS.
I scribbled a note to you, but I don't even remember what I wrote.
BUT I FAINTED AT THE HOSPITAL AND ENDED UP HAVING SURGERY FOR ACUTE APPENDICITIS ...
I'm so sorry. I'm so sorry...
Please forgive me. I'm truly sorry.
HOW DO WE EVEN BEGIN TO APOLOGIZE? WE'RE SO SORRY...
My wife was so foolish...
I was abroad and rushed home... I meant to come right over to apologize...
OH... IT WAS...
A little more information would have helped...
I wish you hadn't just left him at the door.
IT WAS... QUITE A SHOCK... BUT IT'S ALL RIGHT.
She probably didn't have a chance to...
SHUN IS SUCH A GOOD BABY.
IT'S PROBABLY BECAUSE HIS PARENTS LOVE HIM SO MUCH.
THANK YOU SO, SO MUCH.
AREN'T YOU LUCKY, SHUN? THESE WONDERFUL PEOPLE TOOK SUCH GOOD CARE OF YOU...
AHH BUU

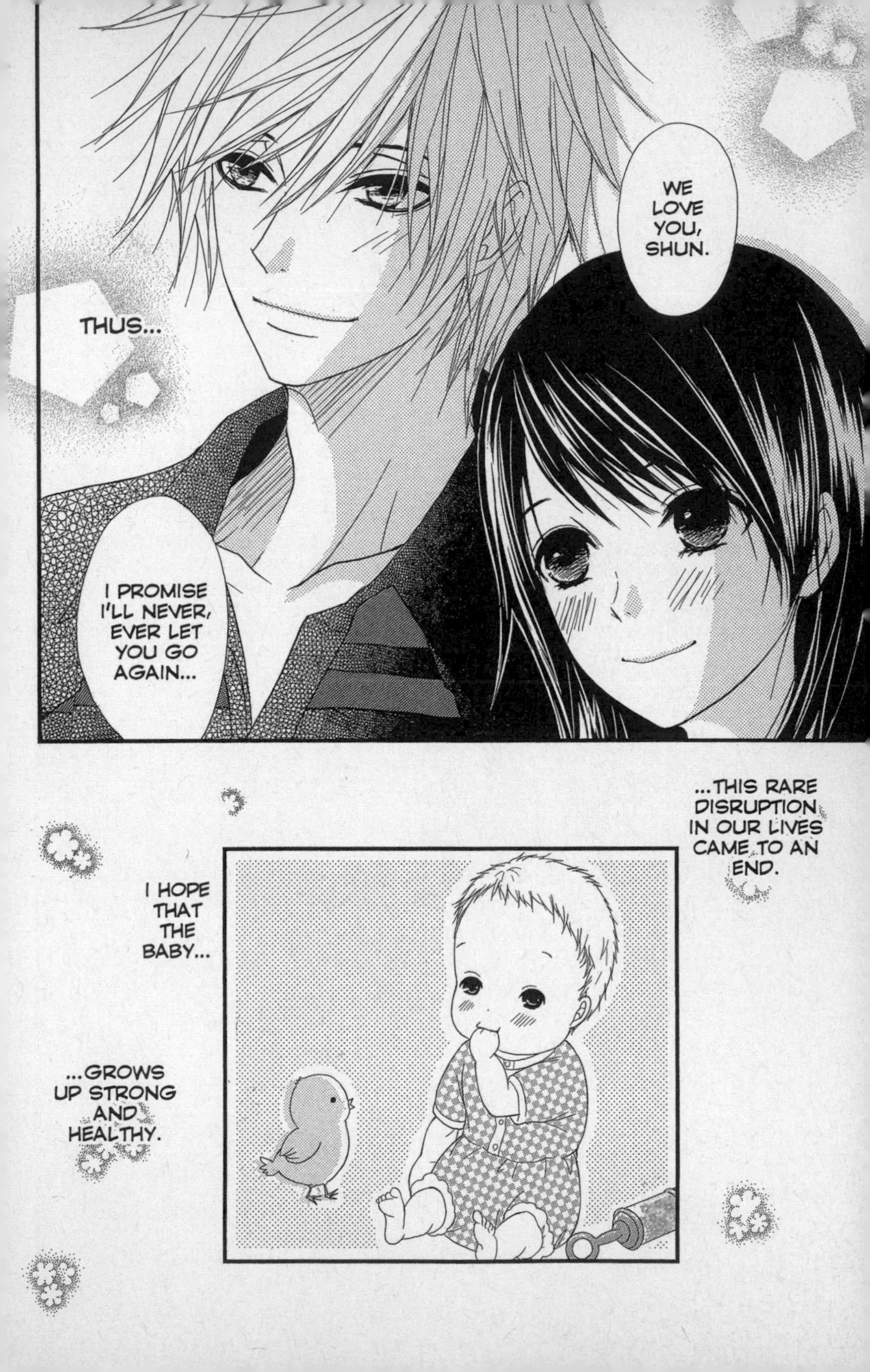
WE LOVE YOU, SHUN.
THUS...
I PROMISE I'LL NEVER, EVER LET YOU GO AGAIN...
...THIS RARE DISRUPTION IN OUR LIVES CAME TO AN END.
I HOPE THAT THE BABY...
...GROWS UP STRONG AND HEALTHY.

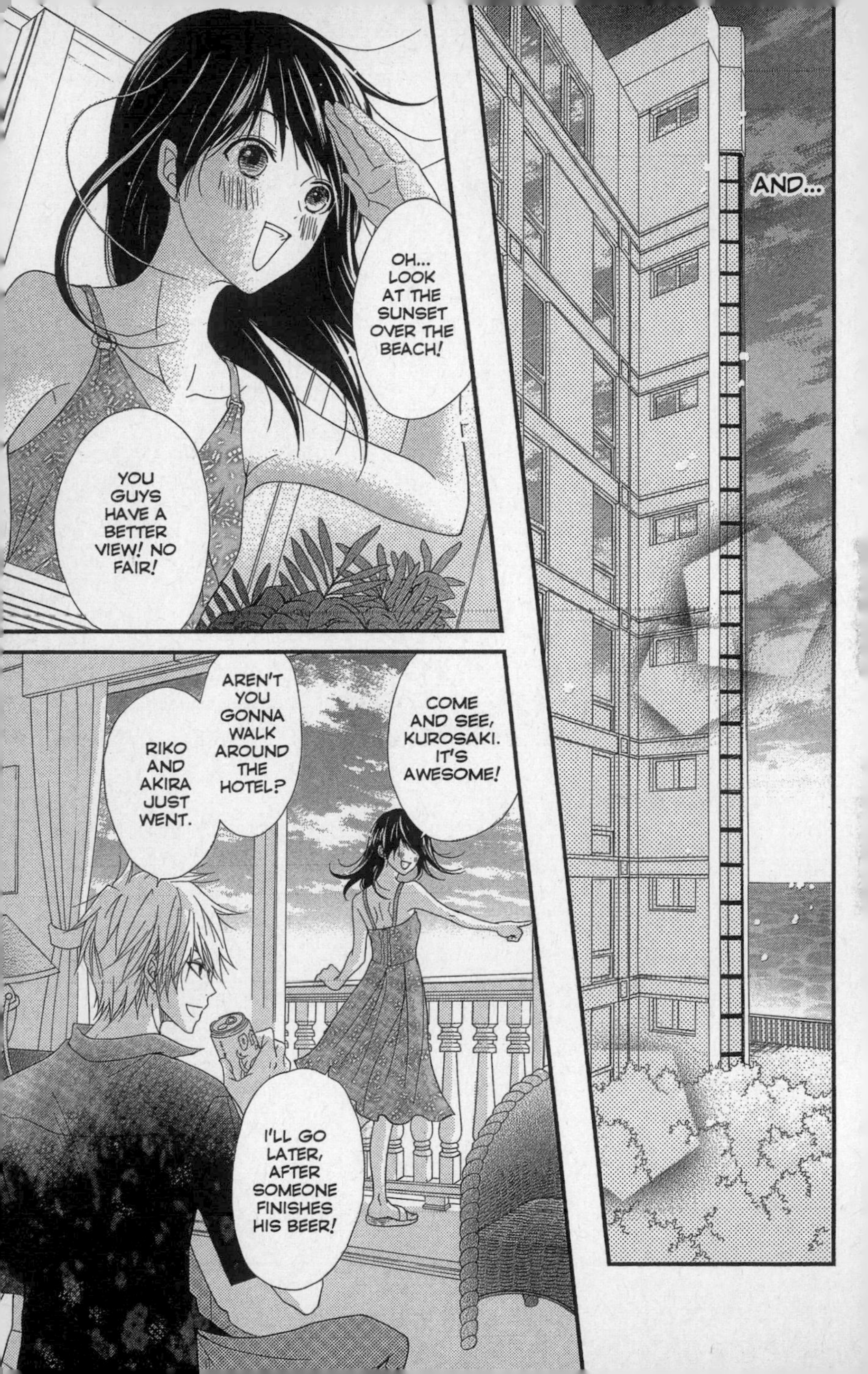
AND...
OH... LOOK AT THE SUNSET OVER THE BEACH!
YOU GUYS HAVE A BETTER VIEW! NO FAIR!
COME AND SEE, KUROSAKI. IT'S AWESOME!
AREN'T YOU GONNA WALK AROUND THE HOTEL?
RIKO AND AKIRA JUST WENT.
I'LL GO LATER, AFTER SOMEONE FINISHES HIS BEER!

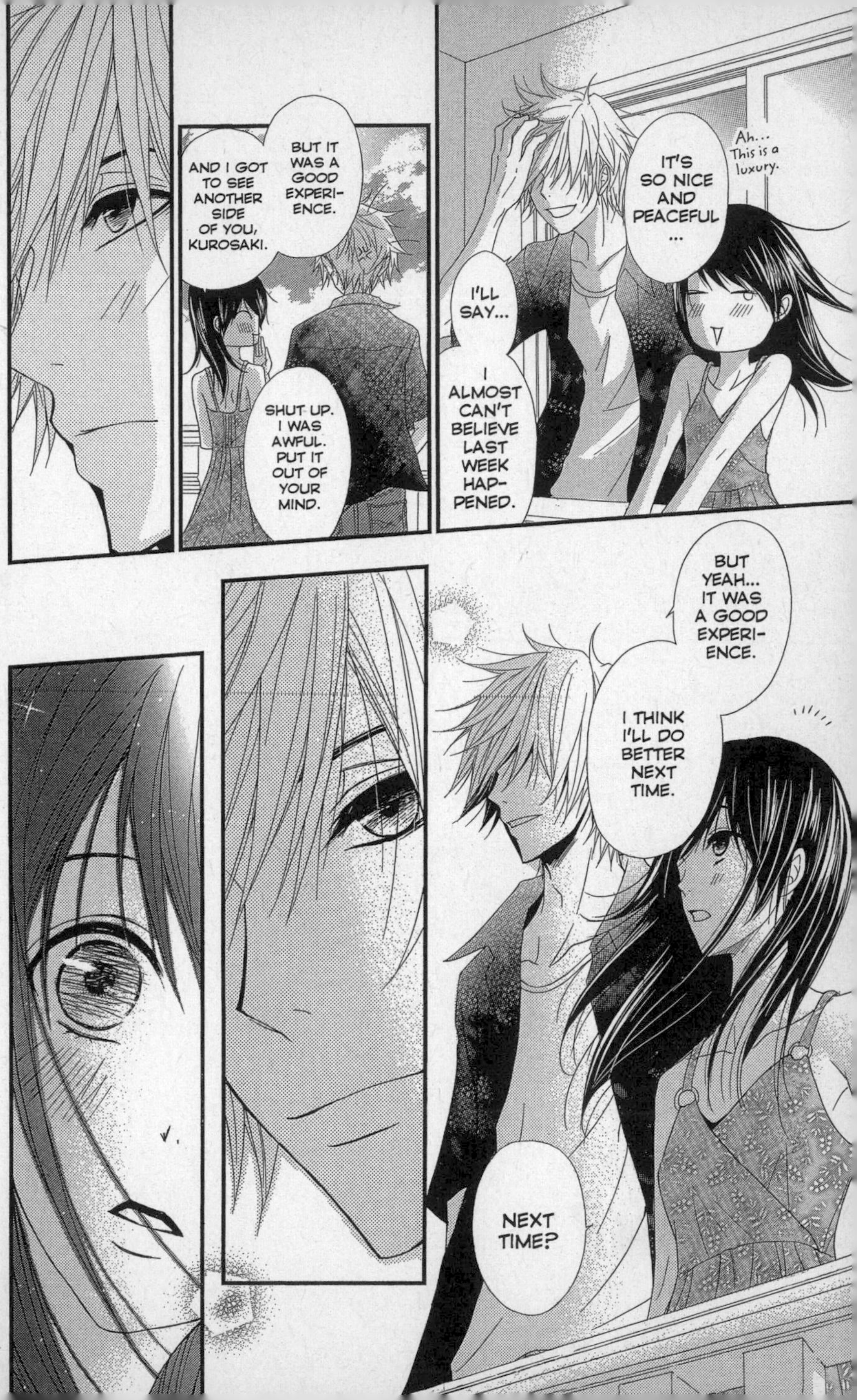
Ah... This is a luxury.
IT'S SO NICE AND PEACEFUL...
I'LL SAY...
I ALMOST CAN'T BELIEVE LAST WEEK HAPPENED.
BUT IT WAS A GOOD EXPERIENCE.
AND I GOT TO SEE ANOTHER SIDE OF YOU, KUROSAKI.
SHUT UP. I WAS AWFUL. PUT IT OUT OF YOUR MIND.
BUT YEAH... IT WAS A GOOD EXPERIENCE.
I THINK I'LL DO BETTER NEXT TIME.
NEXT TIME?

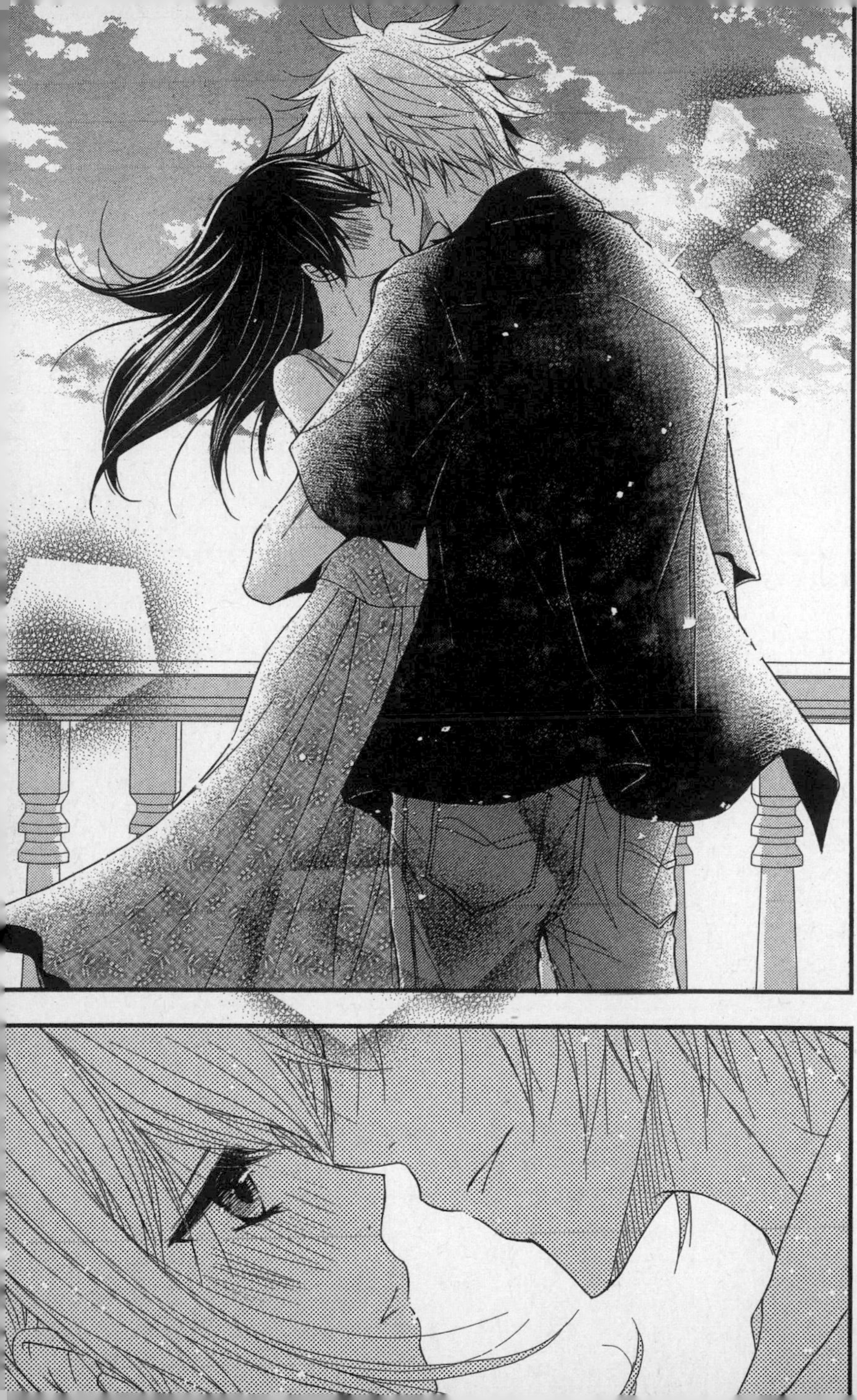

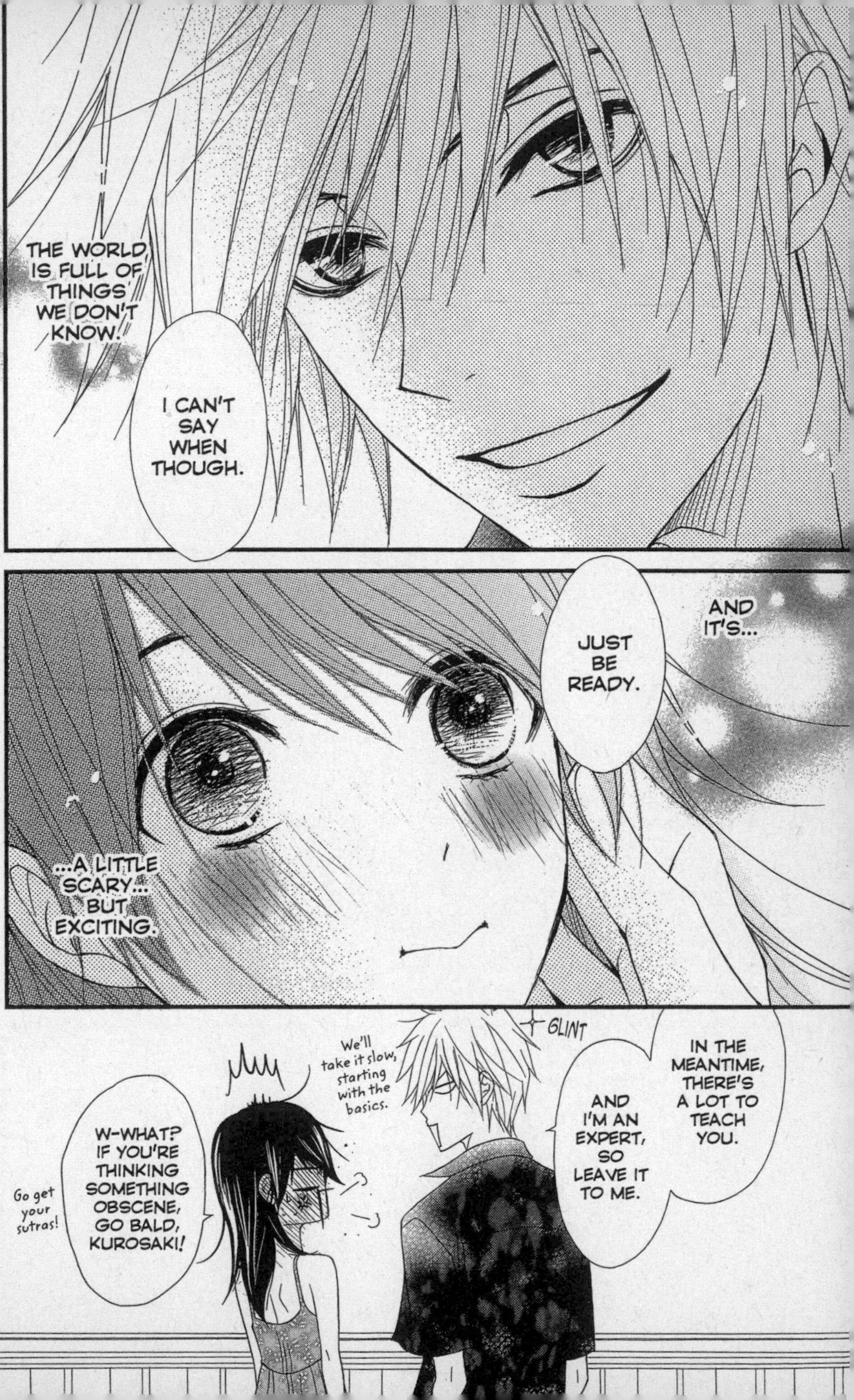
THE WORLD IS FULL OF THINGS WE DON'T KNOW.
I CAN'T SAY WHEN THOUGH.
AND IT'S...
JUST BE READY.
...A LITTLE SCARY... BUT EXCITING.
GLINT
IN THE MEANTIME, THERE'S A LOT TO TEACH YOU.
AND I'M AN EXPERT, SO LEAVE IT TO ME.
We'll take it slow, starting with the basics.
W-WHAT? IF YOU'RE THINKING SOMETHING OBSCENE, GO BALD, KUROSAKI!
Go get your sutras!

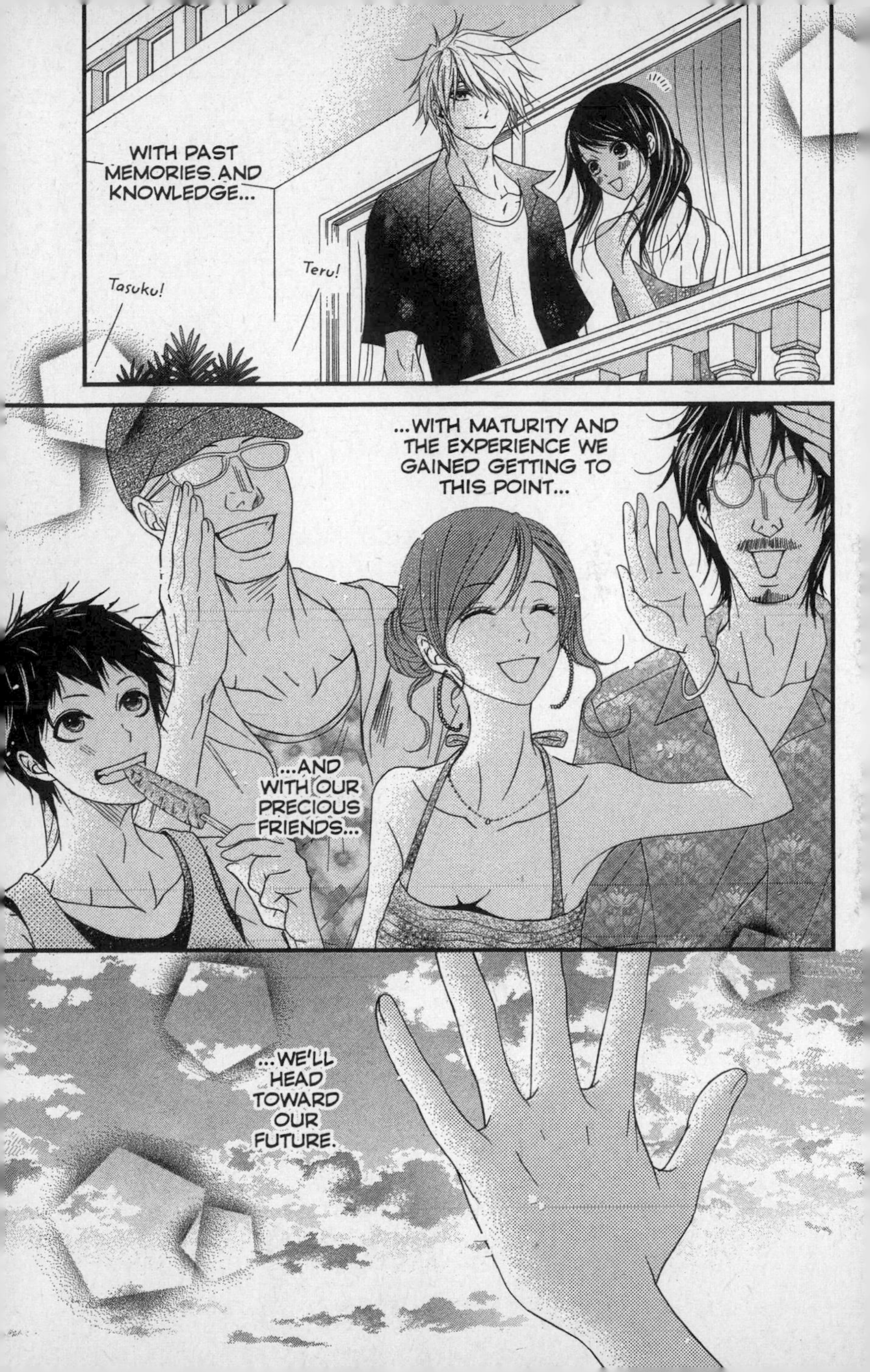
WITH PAST MEMORIES AND KNOWLEDGE...
Teru!
Tasuku!
...WITH MATURITY AND THE EXPERIENCE WE GAINED GETTING TO THIS POINT...
...AND WITH OUR PRECIOUS FRIENDS...
...WE'LL HEAD TOWARD OUR FUTURE.

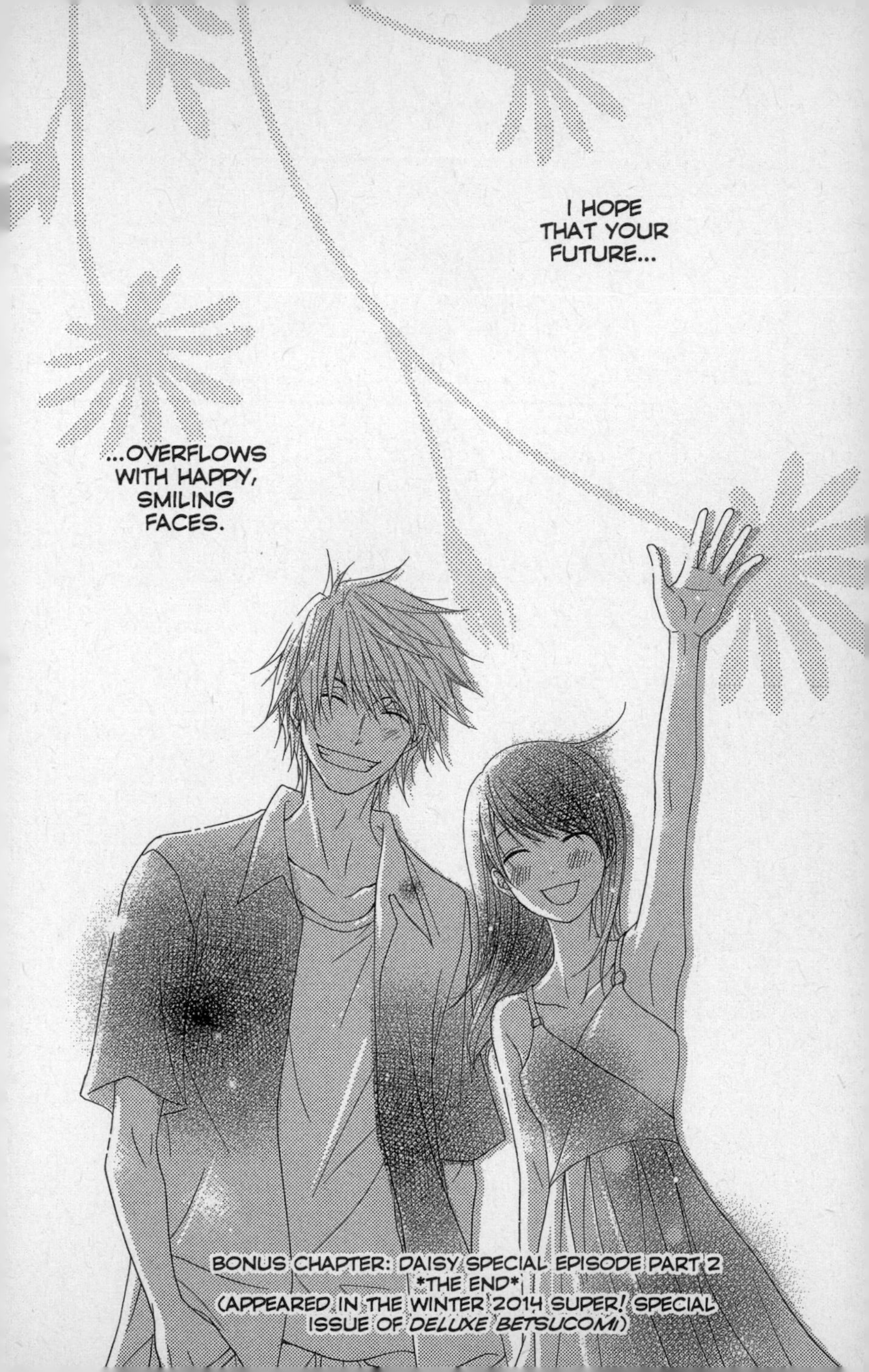
I HOPE THAT YOUR FUTURE...
...OVERFLOWS WITH HAPPY, SMILING FACES.
BONUS CHAPTER: DAISY SPECIAL EPISODE PART 2
THE END
(APPEARED IN THE WINTER 2014 SUPER! SPECIAL ISSUE OF *DELUXE BETSUCOMI*)

AFTERWORD

OKAY, SO DENGEKI DAISY COMES TO A CLOSE.

THANK YOU, THANK YOU FOR STAYING WITH IT UNTIL THE VERY END. AS THE AUTHOR, NOTHING WOULD PLEASE ME MORE THAN IF THERE WERE MOMENTS THAT MADE YOU LAUGH, MADE YOU FEEL GOOD OR GOT STORED AWAY IN YOUR HEART.

I POURED ALL OF MYSELF INTO THIS STORY, AND AT THE SAME TIME, IT TAUGHT ME MANY THINGS. IT'S SOMETHING THAT I'LL BE PROUD OF FOR THE REST OF MY LIFE. I'LL TAKE EVERYTHING THAT I GOT FROM DENGEKI DAISY INTO MY NEXT ENDEAVOR. I HOPE THAT WE'LL MEET AGAIN IN MY NEXT WORK. I'LL KEEP DOING MY BEST.

THANK YOU SO MUCH. UNTIL NEXT TIME!!

KYOUSUKE MOTOMI

最富キョウスケ

PLEASE SEND YOUR CORRESPONDENCE TO:

DENGEKI DAISY
C/O VIZ MEDIA
P.O. BOX 77010
SAN FRANCISCO, CA
94107

ERR... THE FOLLOWING STORY IS MY DEBUT MANGA.

ACTUALLY, I NEVER EXPECTED THIS STORY TO BE PUBLISHED...SO FRANKLY, I'M FEELING REALLY, REALLY NERVOUS RIGHT NOW.

STILL, IT'S THANKS TO THIS STORY THAT I WAS ABLE TO WORK ON *DENGEKI DAISY*.

I'VE GROWN IN A FEW AREAS, BUT I THINK I'M STILL ME WHERE IT COUNTS. AND THAT'S WHY I WANT TO INCLUDE THIS STORY... SO THAT I'LL CONTINUE TO WORK WITH THE SAME INNOCENCE AND ZEAL.

I'D BE SO PLEASED IF YOU READ IT WITH AN INFINITELY OPEN MIND.

I still have lots of room for improvement...
But I'll keep doing my very best.

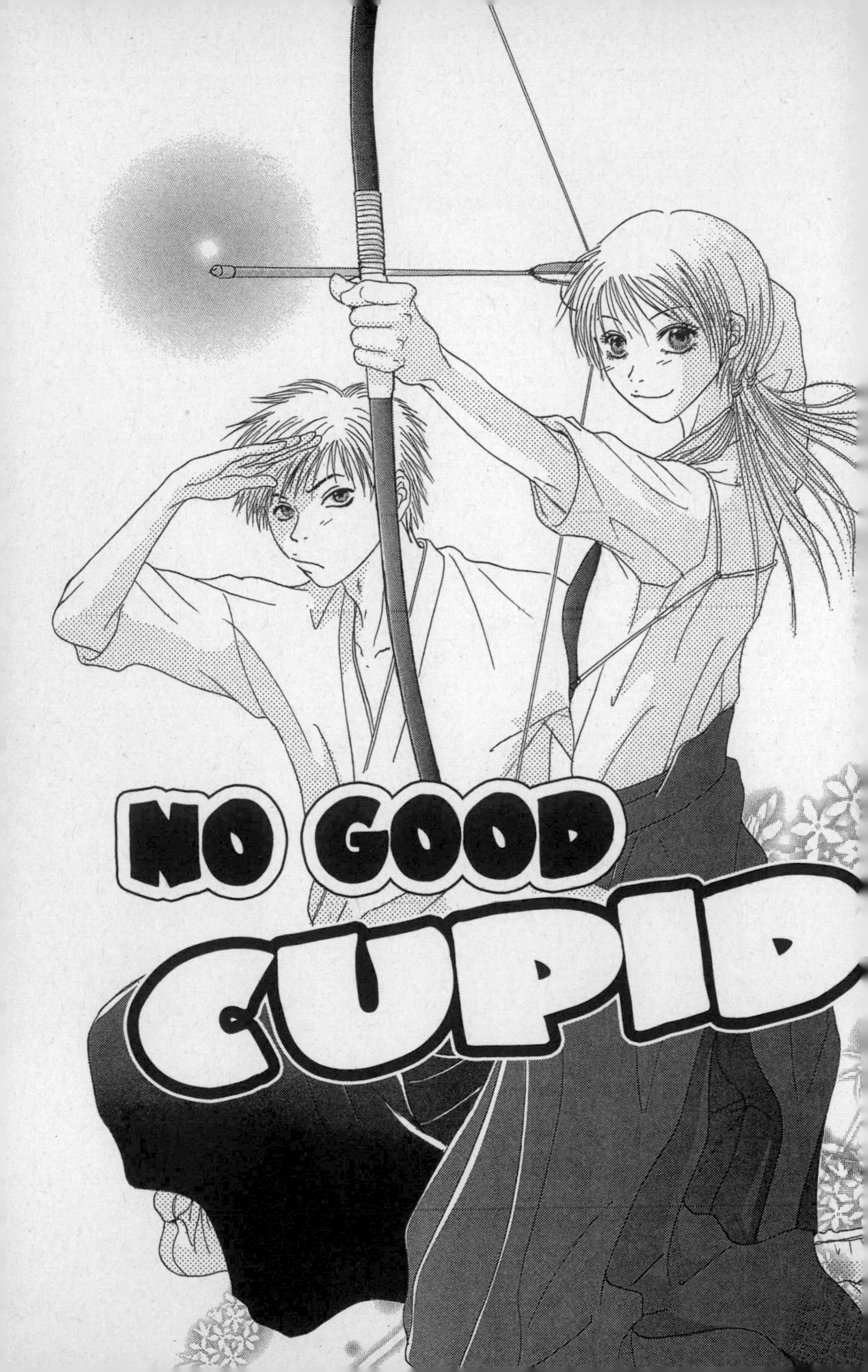
NO GOOD
CUPID

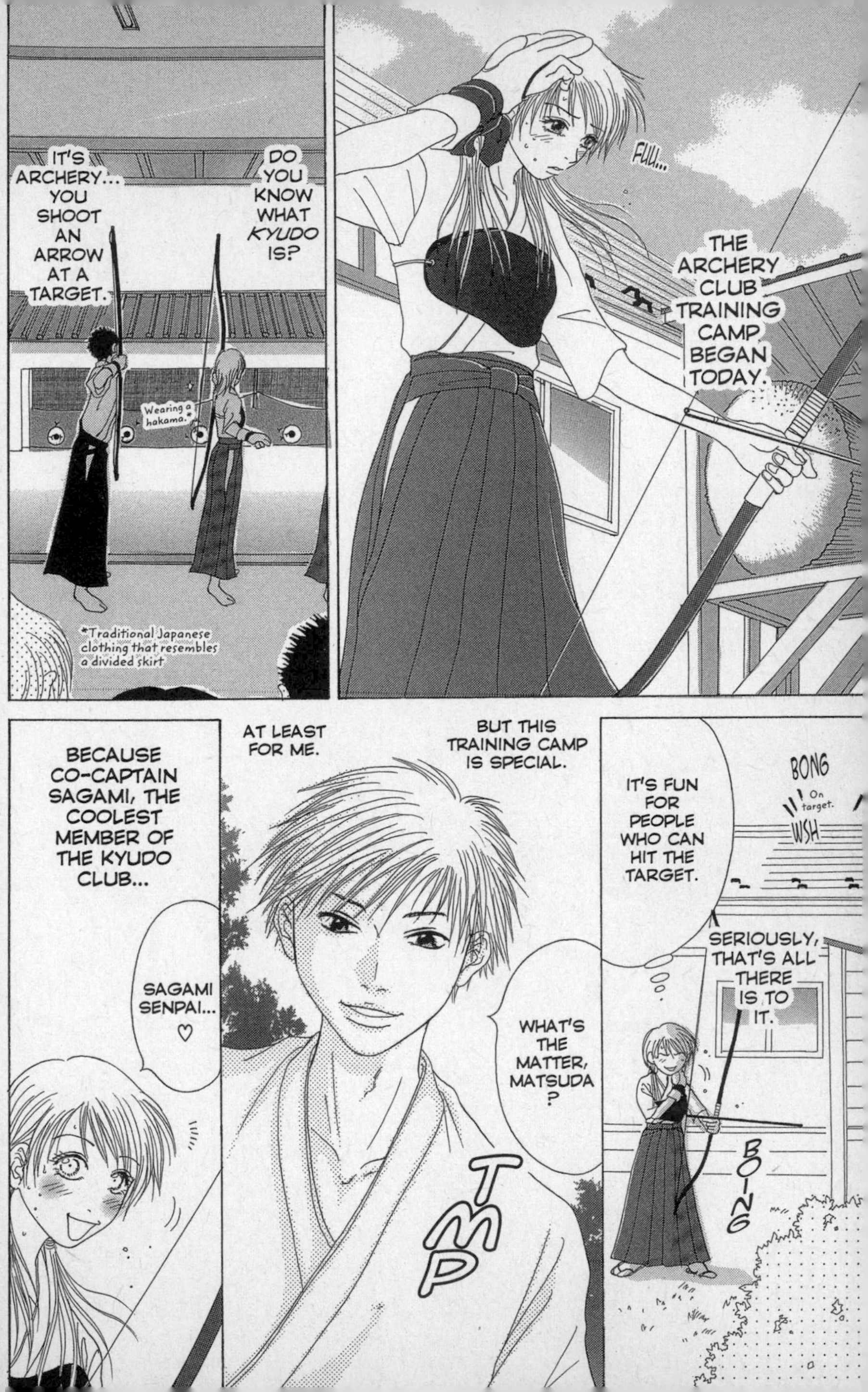
FUU...
THE ARCHERY CLUB TRAINING CAMP BEGAN TODAY.
DO YOU KNOW WHAT *KYUDO* IS?
IT'S ARCHERY... YOU SHOOT AN ARROW AT A TARGET.
Wearing a hakama.*
*Traditional Japanese clothing that resembles a divided skirt
BONG
On target.
WSH
IT'S FUN FOR PEOPLE WHO CAN HIT THE TARGET.
SERIOUSLY, THAT'S ALL THERE IS TO IT.
BOING
BUT THIS TRAINING CAMP IS SPECIAL.
AT LEAST FOR ME.
WHAT'S THE MATTER, MATSUDA?
TMP
BECAUSE CO-CAPTAIN SAGAMI, THE COOLEST MEMBER OF THE KYUDO CLUB...
SAGAMI SENPAI... ♡

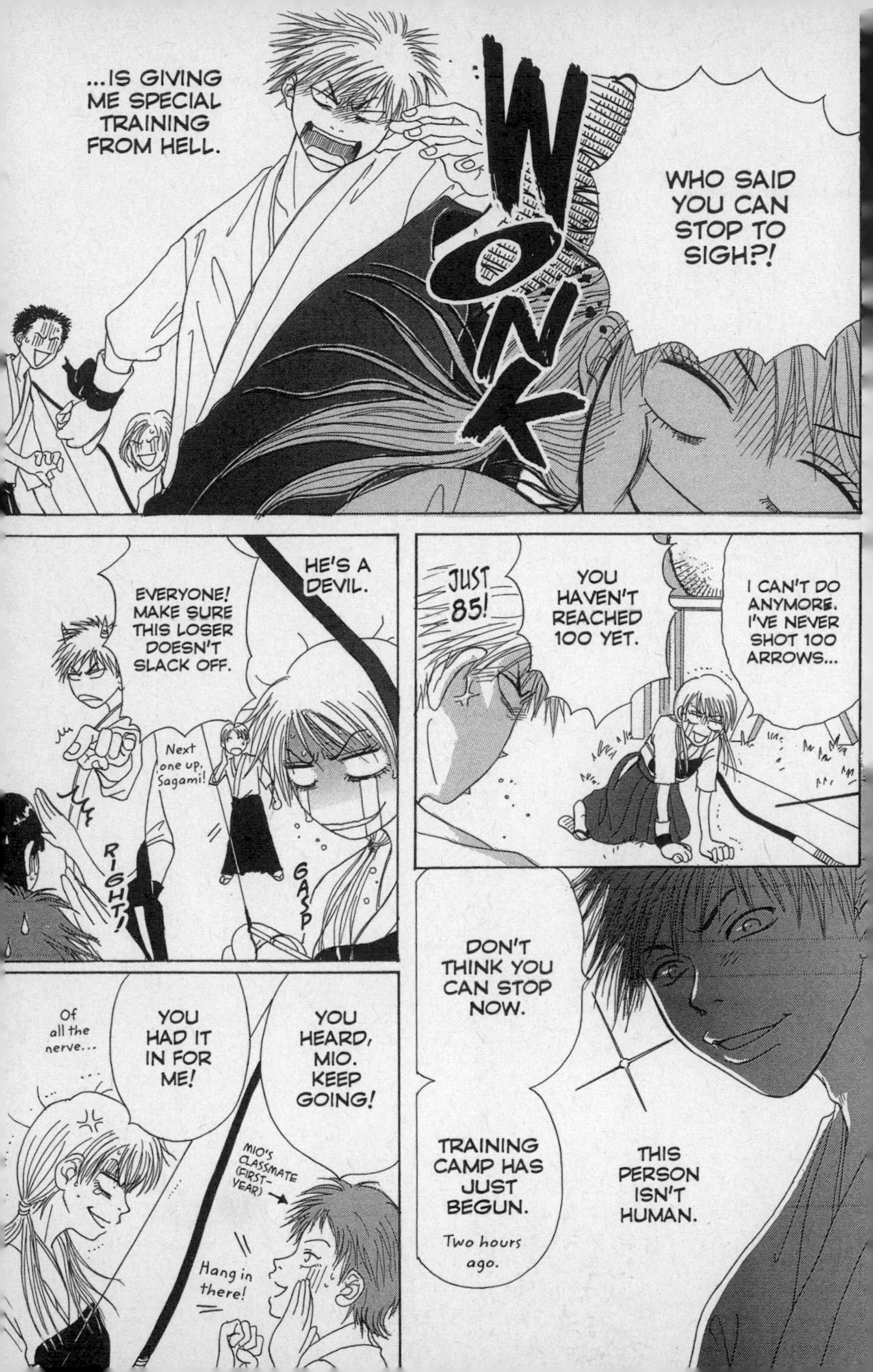
WHO SAID YOU CAN STOP TO SIGH?!
WONK
...IS GIVING ME SPECIAL TRAINING FROM HELL.
I CAN'T DO ANYMORE. I'VE NEVER SHOT 100 ARROWS...
YOU HAVEN'T REACHED 100 YET.
JUST 85!
HE'S A DEVIL.
EVERYONE! MAKE SURE THIS LOSER DOESN'T SLACK OFF.
Next one up, Sagami!
RIGHT!
GASP!
THIS PERSON ISN'T HUMAN.
DON'T THINK YOU CAN STOP NOW.
TRAINING CAMP HAS JUST BEGUN.
Two hours ago.
YOU HEARD, MIO. KEEP GOING!
YOU HAD IT IN FOR ME!
Of all the nerve...
MIO'S CLASSMATE (FIRST-YEAR)
Hang in there!

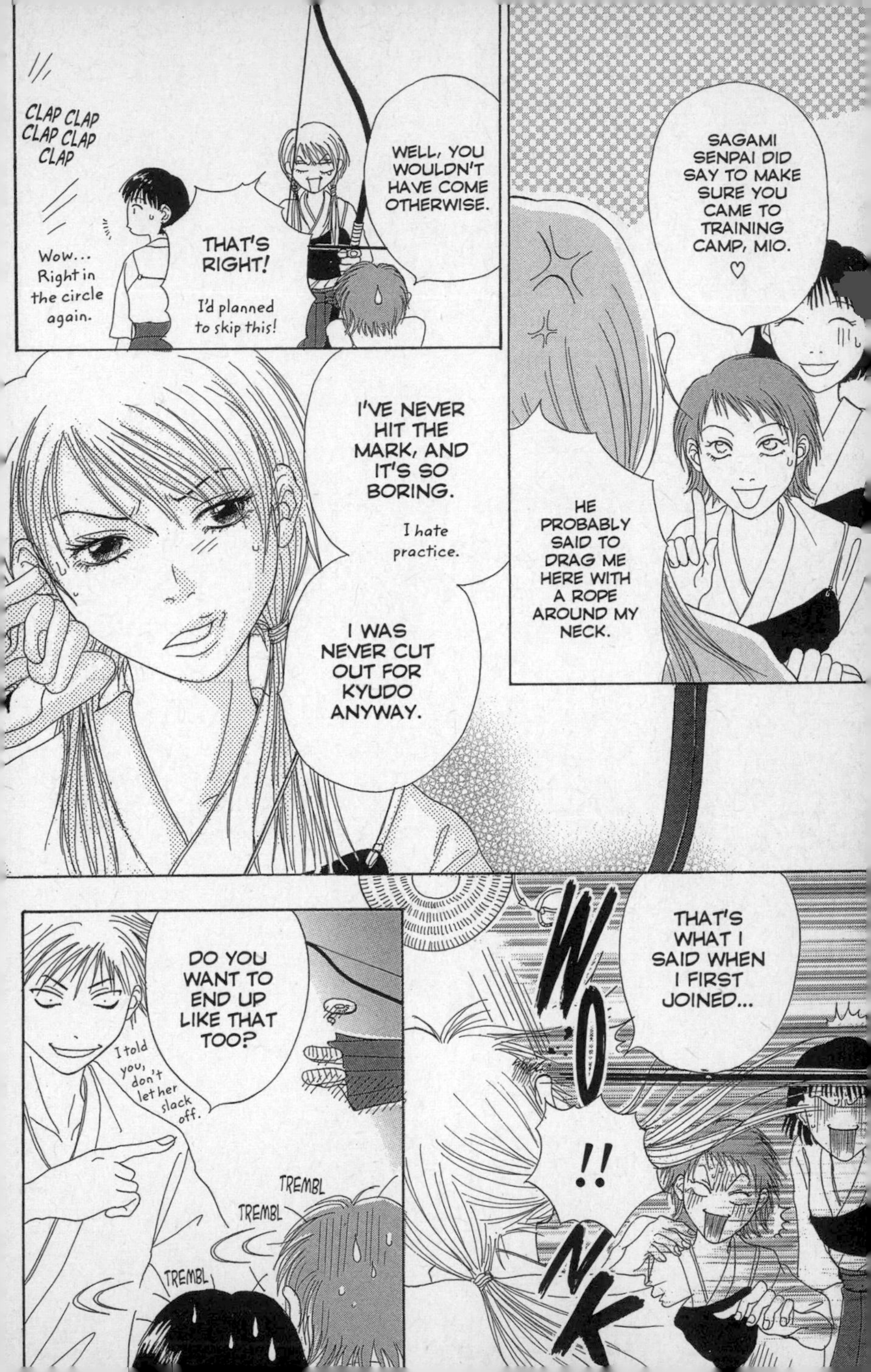
SAGAMI SENPAI DID SAY TO MAKE SURE YOU CAME TO TRAINING CAMP, MIO. ♡
HE PROBABLY SAID TO DRAG ME HERE WITH A ROPE AROUND MY NECK.
WELL, YOU WOULDN'T HAVE COME OTHERWISE.
THAT'S RIGHT!
I'd planned to skip this!
CLAP CLAP CLAP CLAP CLAP
Wow... Right in the circle again.
I'VE NEVER HIT THE MARK, AND IT'S SO BORING.
I hate practice.
I WAS NEVER CUT OUT FOR KYUDO ANYWAY.
THAT'S WHAT I SAID WHEN I FIRST JOINED...
WONK
!!
DO YOU WANT TO END UP LIKE THAT TOO?
I told you, don't let her slack off.
TREMBL
TREMBL
TREMBL

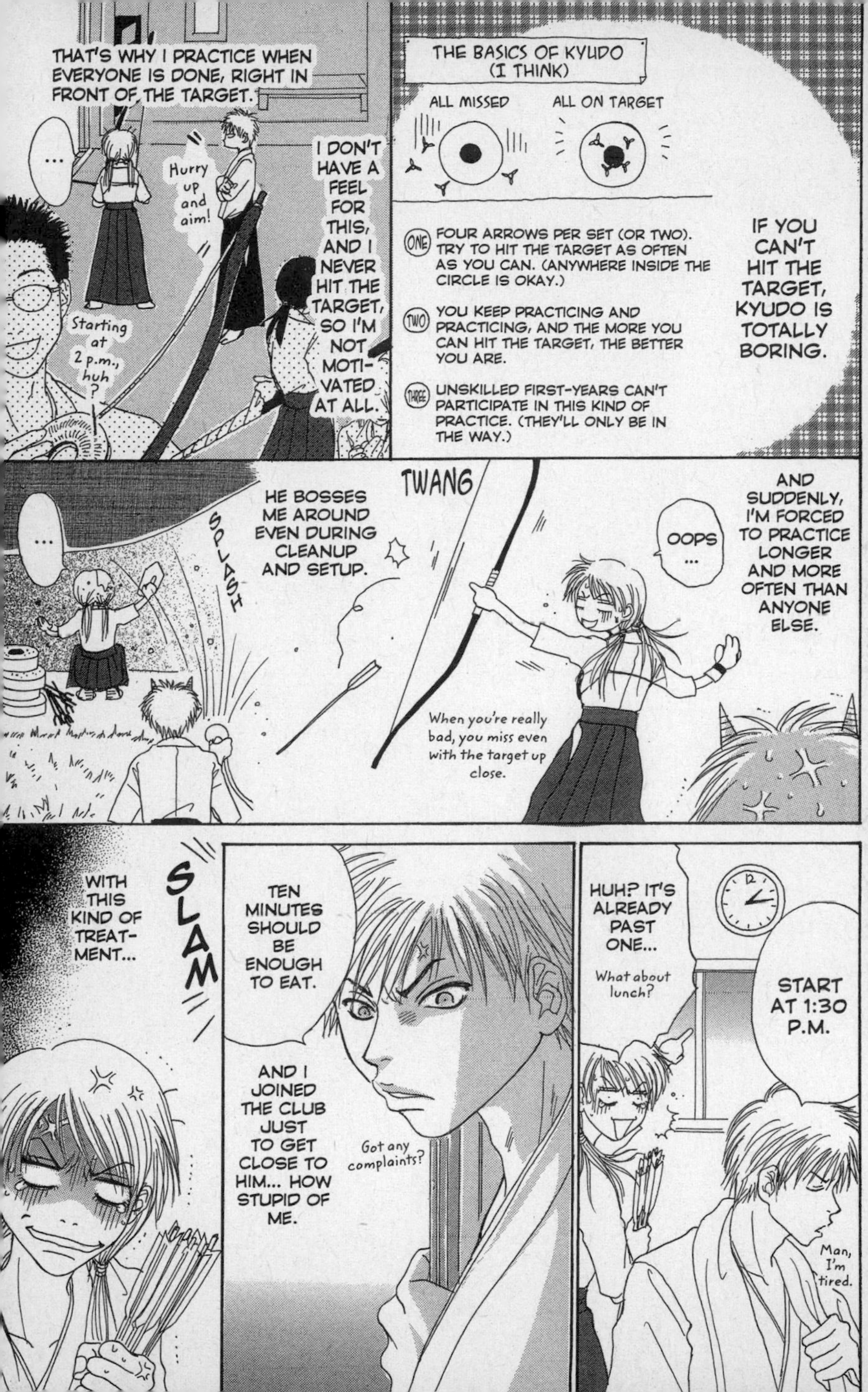
THE BASICS OF KYUDO (I THINK)
ALL MISSED
ALL ON TARGET
(ONE) FOUR ARROWS PER SET (OR TWO). TRY TO HIT THE TARGET AS OFTEN AS YOU CAN. (ANYWHERE INSIDE THE CIRCLE IS OKAY.)
(TWO) YOU KEEP PRACTICING AND PRACTICING, AND THE MORE YOU CAN HIT THE TARGET, THE BETTER YOU ARE.
(THREE) UNSKILLED FIRST-YEARS CAN'T PARTICIPATE IN THIS KIND OF PRACTICE. (THEY'LL ONLY BE IN THE WAY.)
IF YOU CAN'T HIT THE TARGET, KYUDO IS TOTALLY BORING.
I DON'T HAVE A FEEL FOR THIS, AND I NEVER HIT THE TARGET, SO I'M NOT MOTI-VATED AT ALL.
THAT'S WHY I PRACTICE WHEN EVERYONE IS DONE, RIGHT IN FRONT OF THE TARGET.
Hurry up and aim!
...
Starting at 2 p.m., huh?
AND SUDDENLY, I'M FORCED TO PRACTICE LONGER AND MORE OFTEN THAN ANYONE ELSE.
OOPS ...
TWANG
When you're really bad, you miss even with the target up close.
HE BOSSES ME AROUND EVEN DURING CLEANUP AND SETUP.
SPLASH
...
START AT 1:30 P.M.
HUH? IT'S ALREADY PAST ONE...
What about lunch?
Man, I'm tired.
TEN MINUTES SHOULD BE ENOUGH TO EAT.
AND I JOINED THE CLUB JUST TO GET CLOSE TO HIM... HOW STUPID OF ME.
Got any complaints?
SLAM
WITH THIS KIND OF TREAT-MENT...

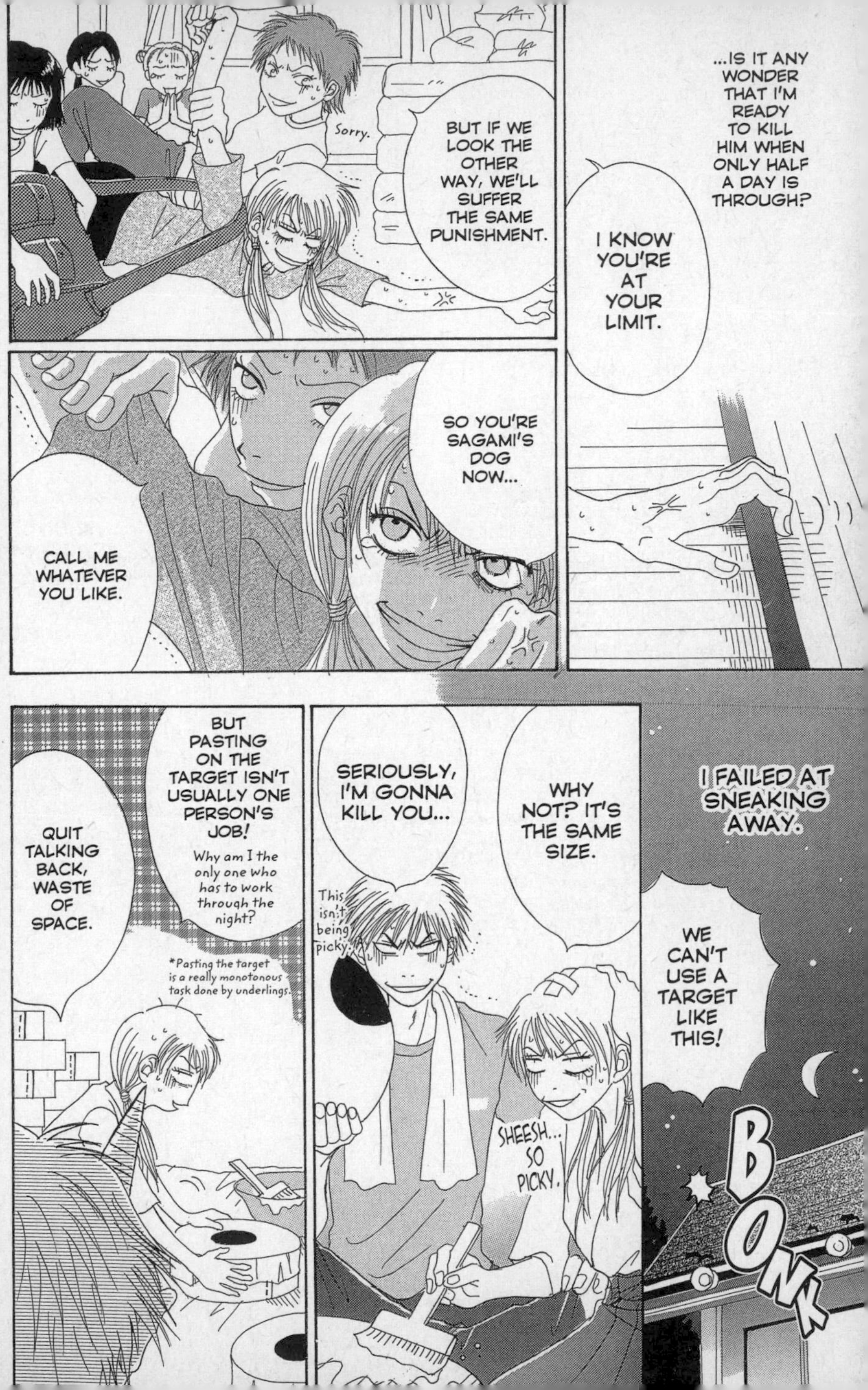
...IS IT ANY WONDER THAT I'M READY TO KILL HIM WHEN ONLY HALF A DAY IS THROUGH?
I KNOW YOU'RE AT YOUR LIMIT.
BUT IF WE LOOK THE OTHER WAY, WE'LL SUFFER THE SAME PUNISHMENT.
Sorry.
SO YOU'RE SAGAMI'S DOG NOW...
CALL ME WHATEVER YOU LIKE.
I FAILED AT SNEAKING AWAY.
WE CAN'T USE A TARGET LIKE THIS!
BONK
WHY NOT? IT'S THE SAME SIZE.
SERIOUSLY, I'M GONNA KILL YOU...
This isn't being picky.
SHEESH... SO PICKY.
BUT PASTING ON THE TARGET ISN'T USUALLY ONE PERSON'S JOB!
Why am I the only one who has to work through the night?
QUIT TALKING BACK, WASTE OF SPACE.
*Pasting the target is a really monotonous task done by underlings.

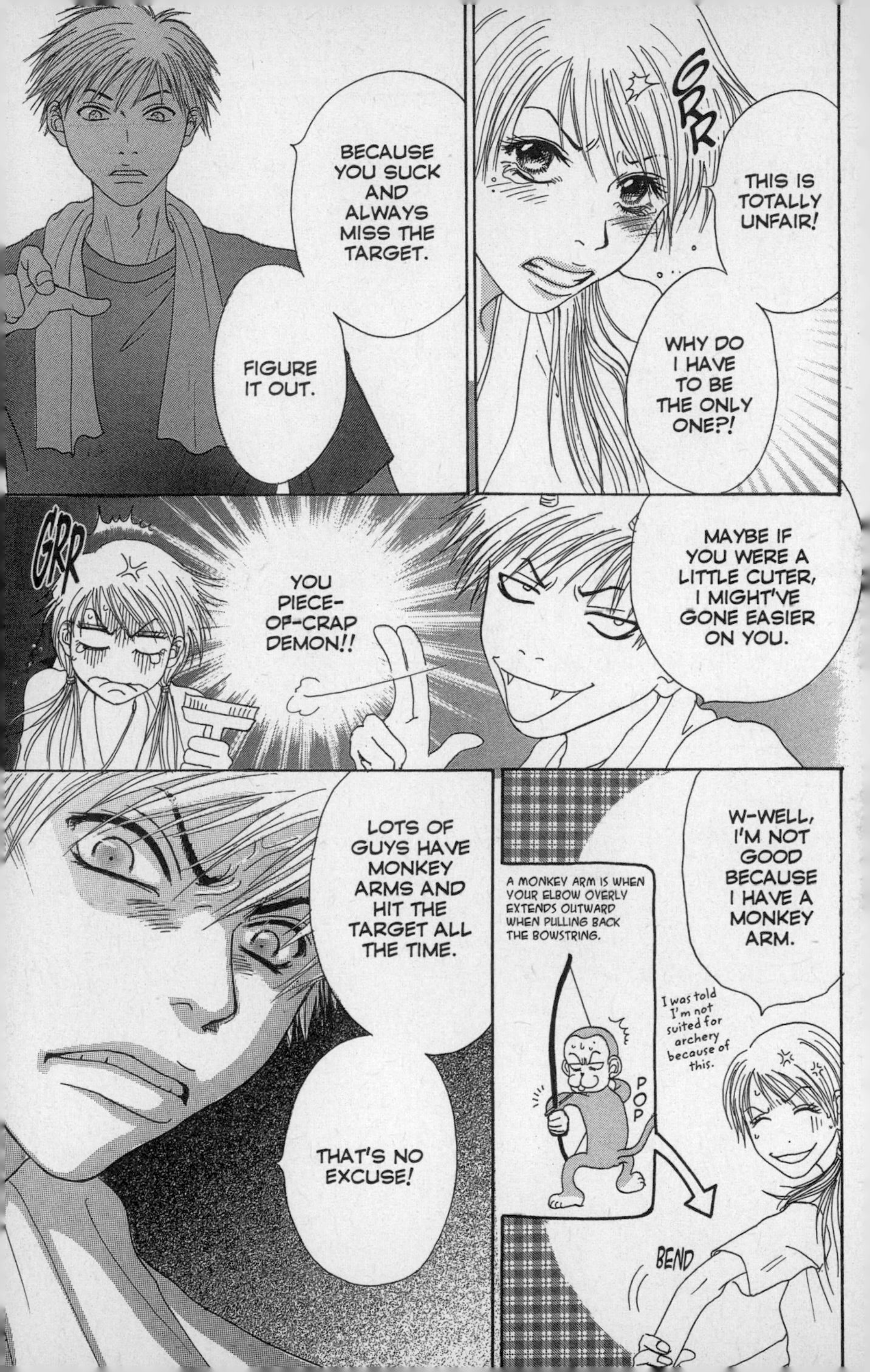
GRR
THIS IS TOTALLY UNFAIR!
WHY DO I HAVE TO BE THE ONLY ONE?!
BECAUSE YOU SUCK AND ALWAYS MISS THE TARGET.
FIGURE IT OUT.
MAYBE IF YOU WERE A LITTLE CUTER, I MIGHT'VE GONE EASIER ON YOU.
YOU PIECE-OF-CRAP DEMON!!
GRR
W-WELL, I'M NOT GOOD BECAUSE I HAVE A MONKEY ARM.
A MONKEY ARM IS WHEN YOUR ELBOW OVERLY EXTENDS OUTWARD WHEN PULLING BACK THE BOWSTRING.
I was told I'm not suited for archery because of this.
POP
BEND
LOTS OF GUYS HAVE MONKEY ARMS AND HIT THE TARGET ALL THE TIME.
THAT'S NO EXCUSE!

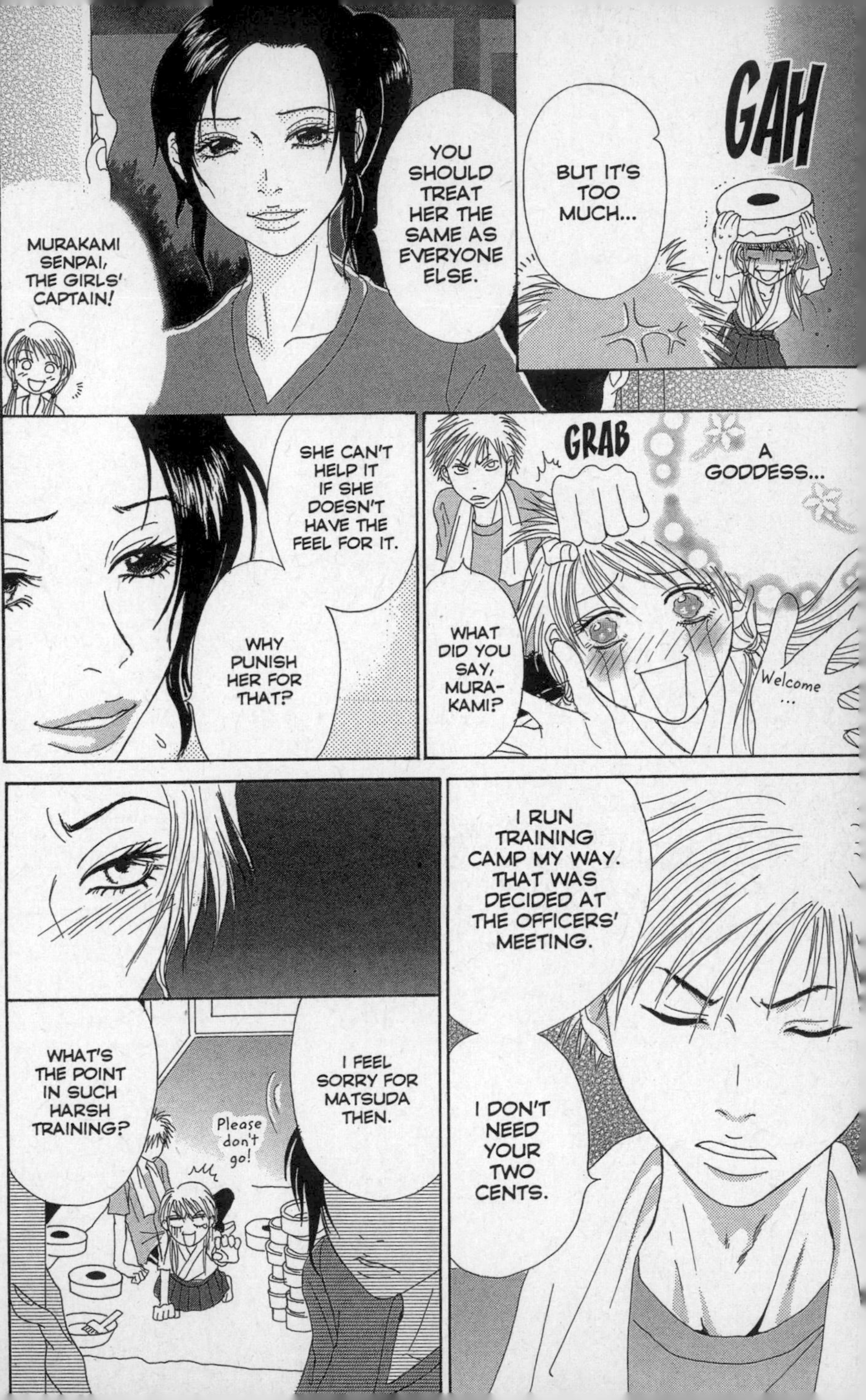
GAH
BUT IT'S TOO MUCH...
YOU SHOULD TREAT HER THE SAME AS EVERYONE ELSE.
MURAKAMI SENPAI, THE GIRLS' CAPTAIN!
GRAB
A GODDESS...
Welcome...
WHAT DID YOU SAY, MURA-KAMI?
SHE CAN'T HELP IT IF SHE DOESN'T HAVE THE FEEL FOR IT.
WHY PUNISH HER FOR THAT?
I RUN TRAINING CAMP MY WAY. THAT WAS DECIDED AT THE OFFICERS' MEETING.
I DON'T NEED YOUR TWO CENTS.
I FEEL SORRY FOR MATSUDA THEN.
WHAT'S THE POINT IN SUCH HARSH TRAINING?
Please don't go!

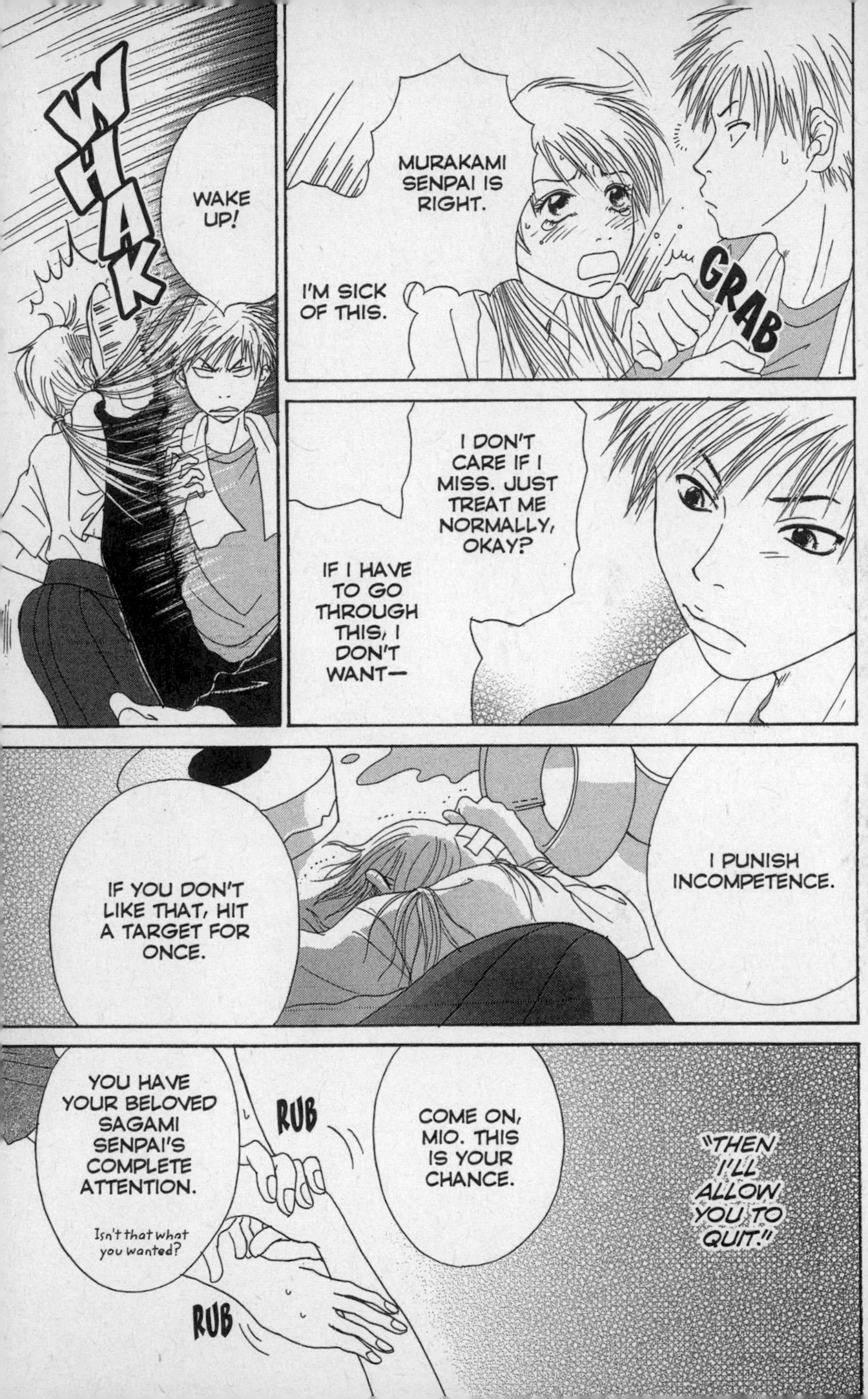
MURAKAMI SENPAI IS RIGHT.
I'M SICK OF THIS.
GRAB
I DON'T CARE IF I MISS. JUST TREAT ME NORMALLY, OKAY?
IF I HAVE TO GO THROUGH THIS, I DON'T WANT—
WAKE UP!
WHAK
I PUNISH INCOMPETENCE.
IF YOU DON'T LIKE THAT, HIT A TARGET FOR ONCE.
"THEN I'LL ALLOW YOU TO QUIT."
COME ON, MIO. THIS IS YOUR CHANCE.
RUB
YOU HAVE YOUR BELOVED SAGAMI SENPAI'S COMPLETE ATTENTION.
Isn't that what you wanted?
RUB

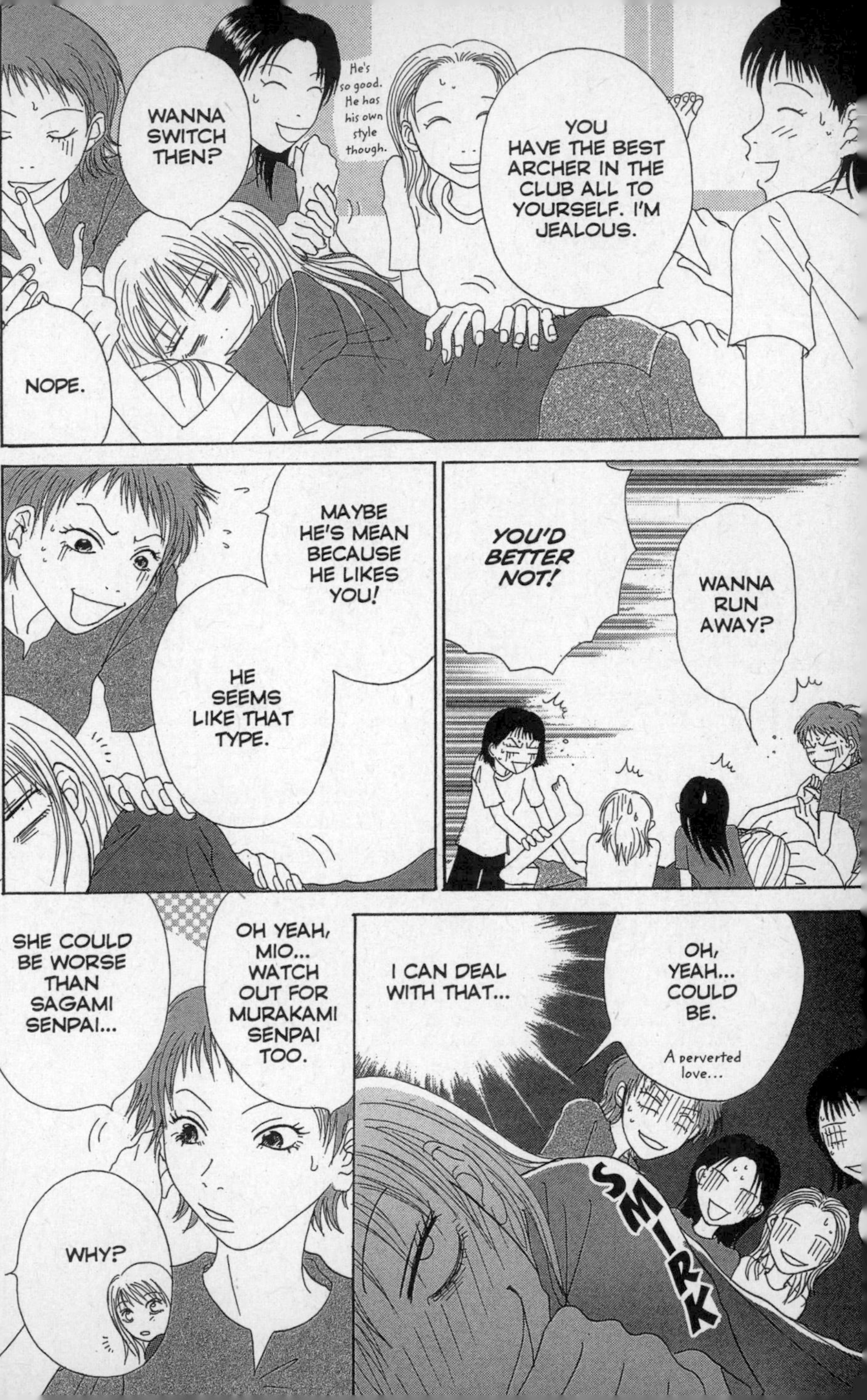
YOU HAVE THE BEST ARCHER IN THE CLUB ALL TO YOURSELF. I'M JEALOUS.
He's so good. He has his own style though.
WANNA SWITCH THEN?
NOPE.
MAYBE HE'S MEAN BECAUSE HE LIKES YOU!
HE SEEMS LIKE THAT TYPE.
WANNA RUN AWAY?
YOU'D BETTER NOT!
OH YEAH, MIO... WATCH OUT FOR MURAKAMI SENPAI TOO.
WHY?
SHE COULD BE WORSE THAN SAGAMI SENPAI...
OH, YEAH... COULD BE.
A perverted love...
I CAN DEAL WITH THAT...
SMIRK

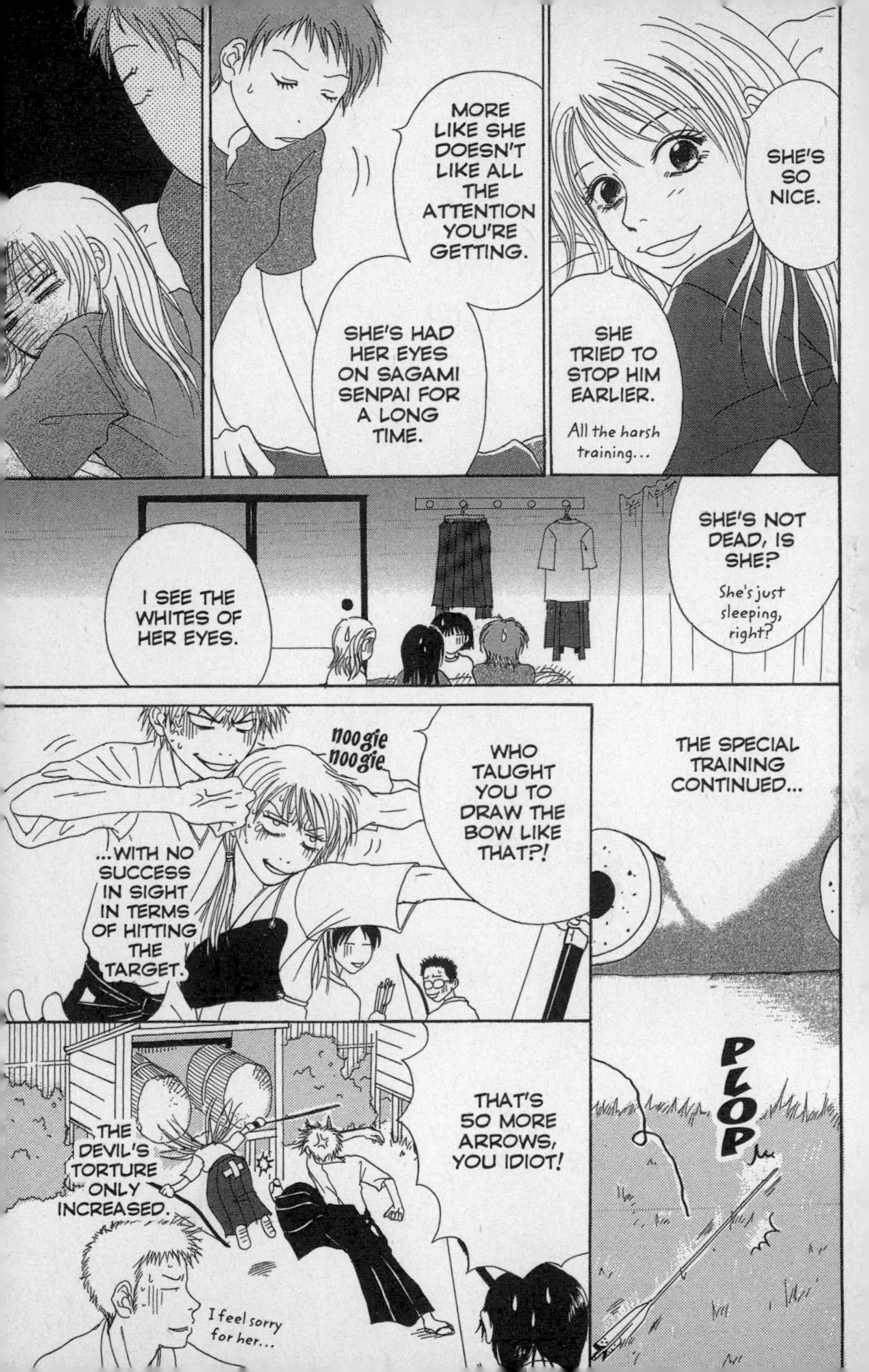
SHE'S SO NICE.
SHE TRIED TO STOP HIM EARLIER.
All the harsh training...
MORE LIKE SHE DOESN'T LIKE ALL THE ATTENTION YOU'RE GETTING.
SHE'S HAD HER EYES ON SAGAMI SENPAI FOR A LONG TIME.
SHE'S NOT DEAD, IS SHE?
She's just sleeping, right?
I SEE THE WHITES OF HER EYES.
THE SPECIAL TRAINING CONTINUED...
PLOP
WHO TAUGHT YOU TO DRAW THE BOW LIKE THAT?!
noogie noogie
...WITH NO SUCCESS IN SIGHT IN TERMS OF HITTING THE TARGET.
THAT'S 50 MORE ARROWS, YOU IDIOT!
THE DEVIL'S TORTURE ONLY INCREASED.
I feel sorry for her...

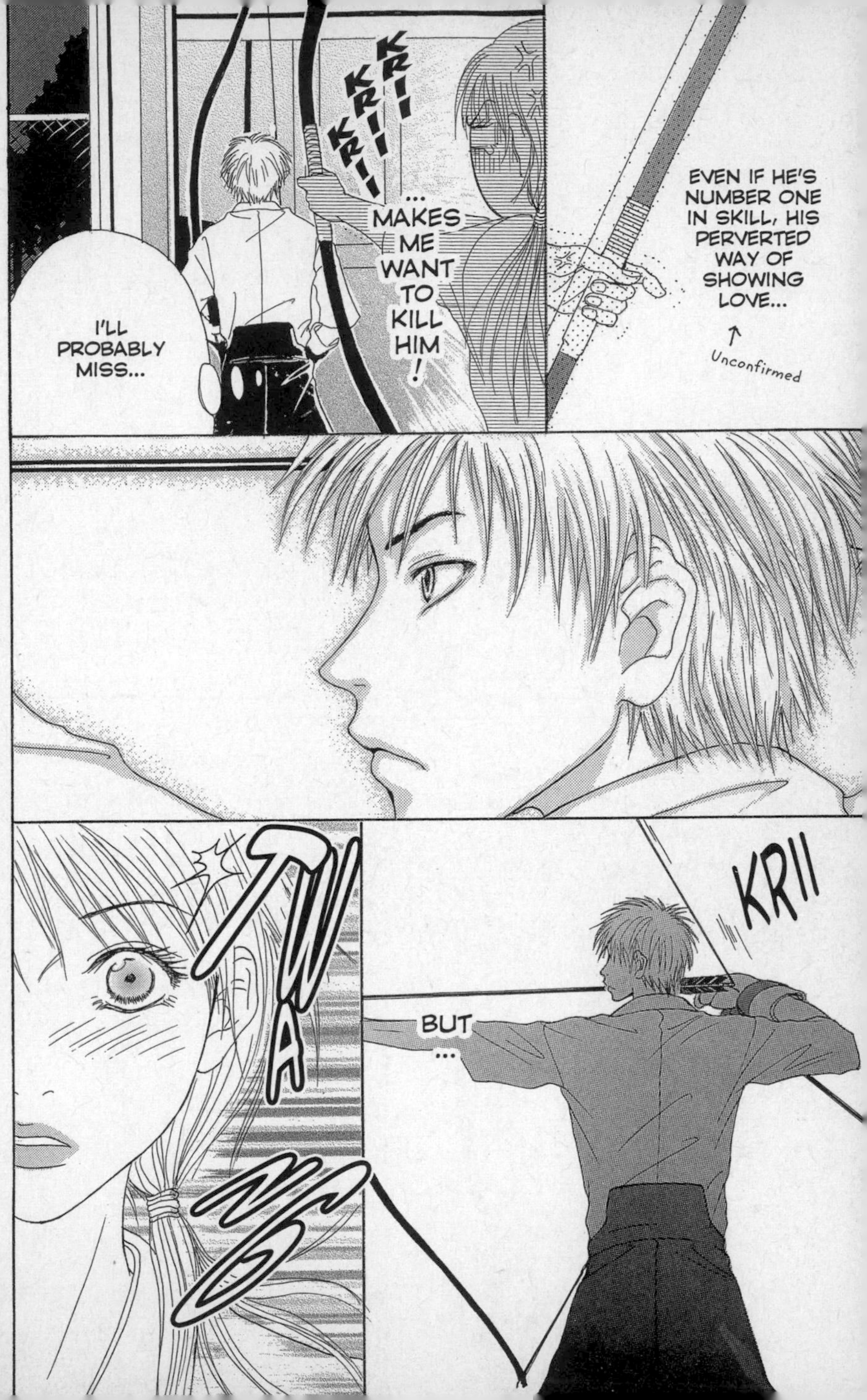
EVEN IF HE'S NUMBER ONE IN SKILL, HIS PERVERTED WAY OF SHOWING LOVE...
Unconfirmed
KRII KRII KRII
...MAKES ME WANT TO KILL HIM!
I'LL PROBABLY MISS...
KRII
BUT...
TWANG

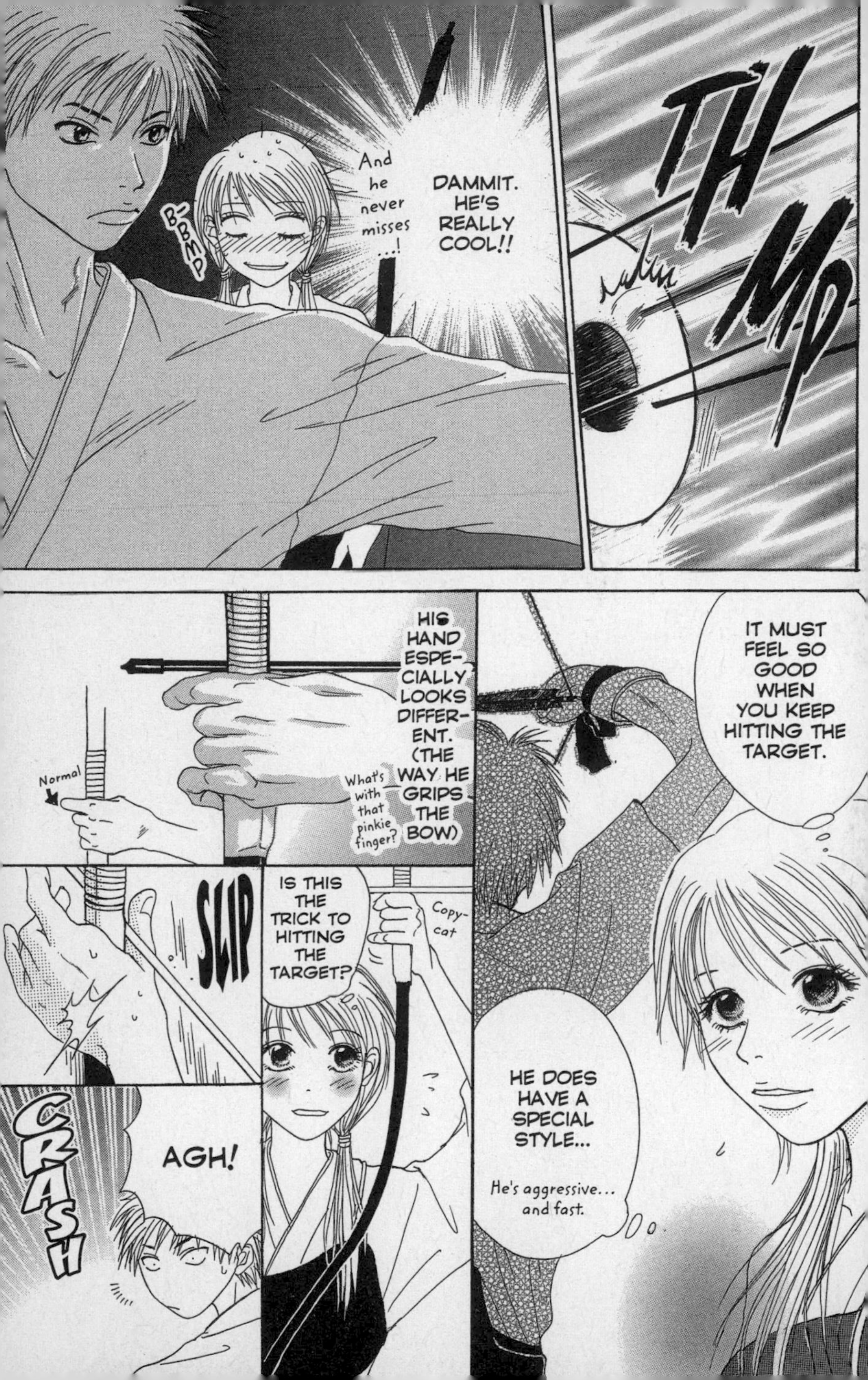
THMP
DAMMIT. HE'S REALLY COOL!!
And he never misses ...!
B-BMP
IT MUST FEEL SO GOOD WHEN YOU KEEP HITTING THE TARGET.
HE DOES HAVE A SPECIAL STYLE...
He's aggressive... and fast.
HIS HAND ESPECIALLY LOOKS DIFFERENT. (THE WAY HE GRIPS THE BOW)
What's with that pinkie finger?
Normal
IS THIS THE TRICK TO HITTING THE TARGET?
Copy-cat
SLIP
AGH!
CRASH

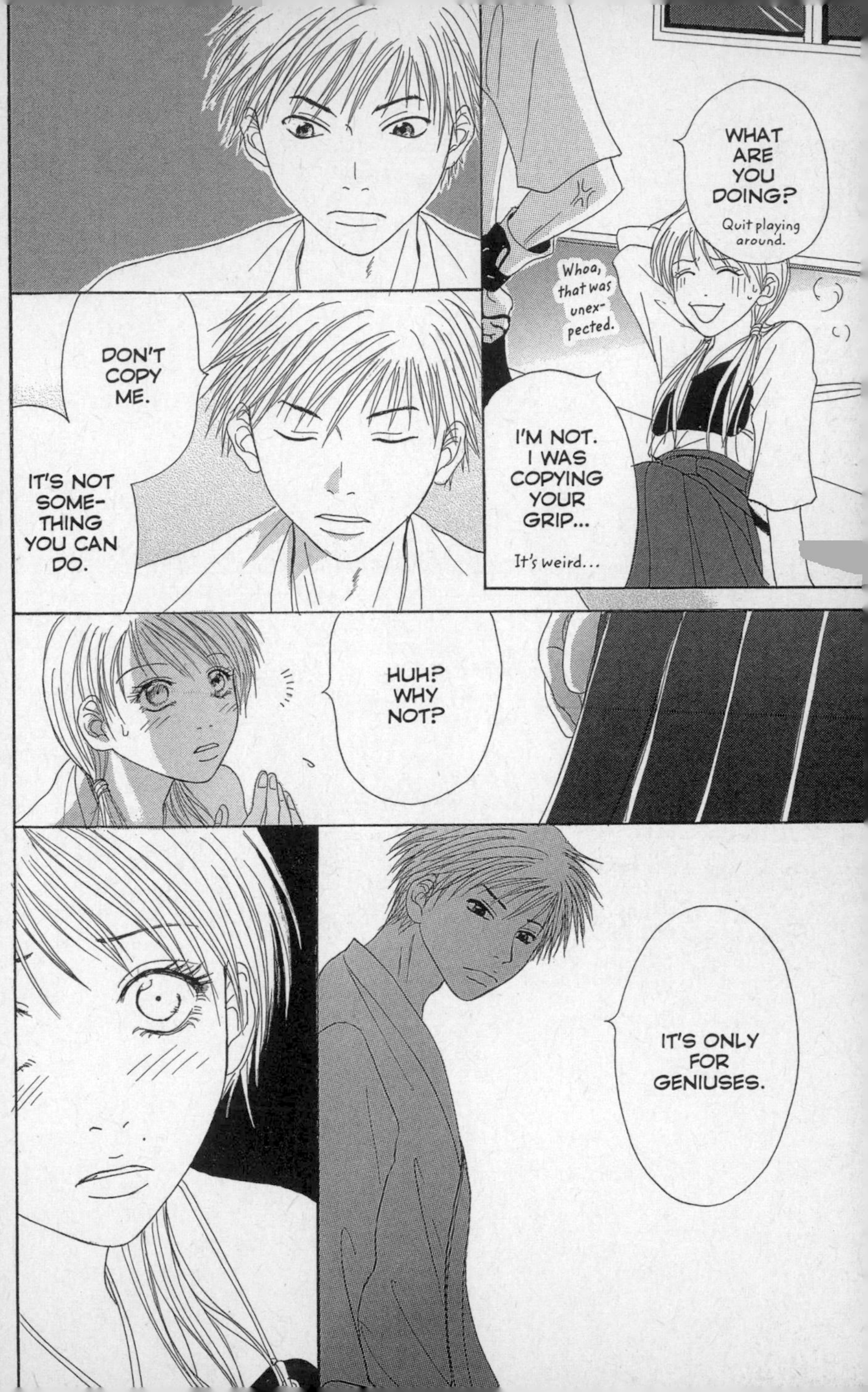
WHAT ARE YOU DOING?
Quit playing around.
Whoa, that was unexpected.
I'M NOT. I WAS COPYING YOUR GRIP...
It's weird...
DON'T COPY ME.
IT'S NOT SOMETHING YOU CAN DO.
HUH? WHY NOT?
IT'S ONLY FOR GENIUSES.

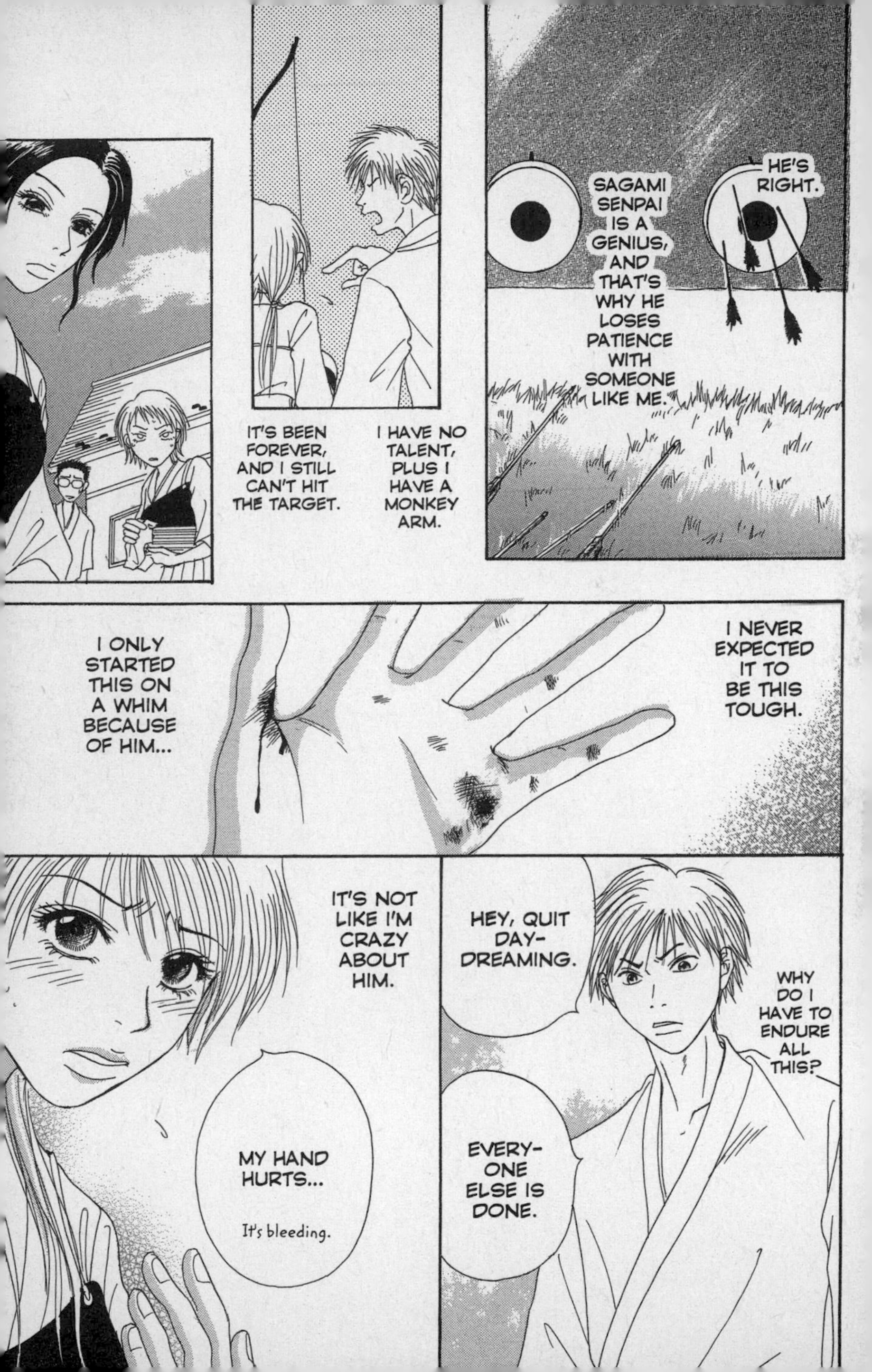
HE'S RIGHT.
SAGAMI SENPAI IS A GENIUS, AND THAT'S WHY HE LOSES PATIENCE WITH SOMEONE LIKE ME.
I HAVE NO TALENT, PLUS I HAVE A MONKEY ARM.
IT'S BEEN FOREVER, AND I STILL CAN'T HIT THE TARGET.
I NEVER EXPECTED IT TO BE THIS TOUGH.
I ONLY STARTED THIS ON A WHIM BECAUSE OF HIM...
WHY DO I HAVE TO ENDURE ALL THIS?
HEY, QUIT DAY-DREAMING.
EVERY-ONE ELSE IS DONE.
IT'S NOT LIKE I'M CRAZY ABOUT HIM.
MY HAND HURTS...
It's bleeding.

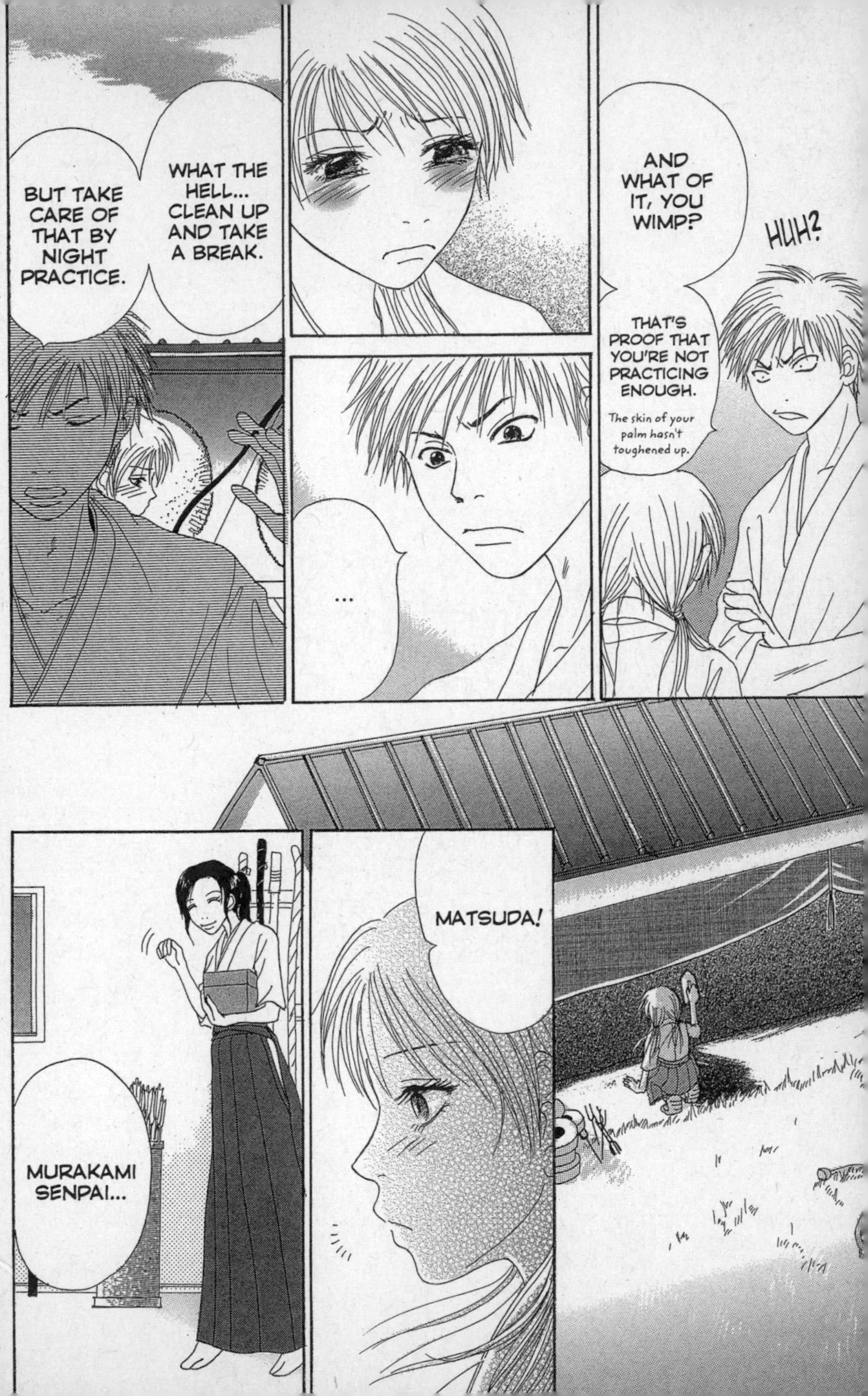
AND WHAT OF IT, YOU WIMP?
HUH?
THAT'S PROOF THAT YOU'RE NOT PRACTICING ENOUGH.
The skin of your palm hasn't toughened up.
...
WHAT THE HELL... CLEAN UP AND TAKE A BREAK.
BUT TAKE CARE OF THAT BY NIGHT PRACTICE.
MATSUDA!
MURAKAMI SENPAI...

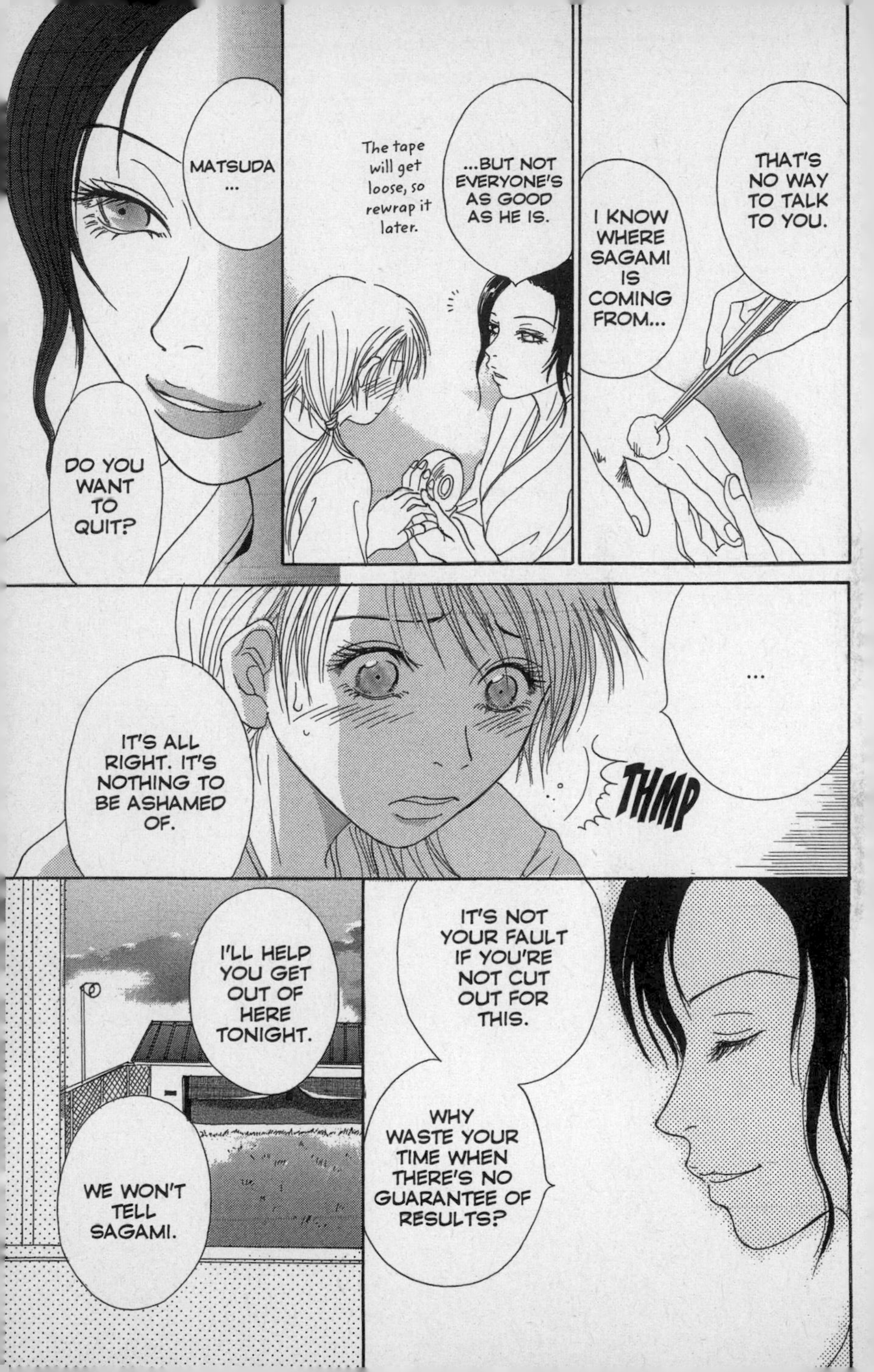
THAT'S NO WAY TO TALK TO YOU.
I KNOW WHERE SAGAMI IS COMING FROM...
...BUT NOT EVERYONE'S AS GOOD AS HE IS.
The tape will get loose, so rewrap it later.
MATSUDA ...
DO YOU WANT TO QUIT?
...
THMP
IT'S ALL RIGHT. IT'S NOTHING TO BE ASHAMED OF.
IT'S NOT YOUR FAULT IF YOU'RE NOT CUT OUT FOR THIS.
WHY WASTE YOUR TIME WHEN THERE'S NO GUARANTEE OF RESULTS?
I'LL HELP YOU GET OUT OF HERE TONIGHT.
WE WON'T TELL SAGAMI.

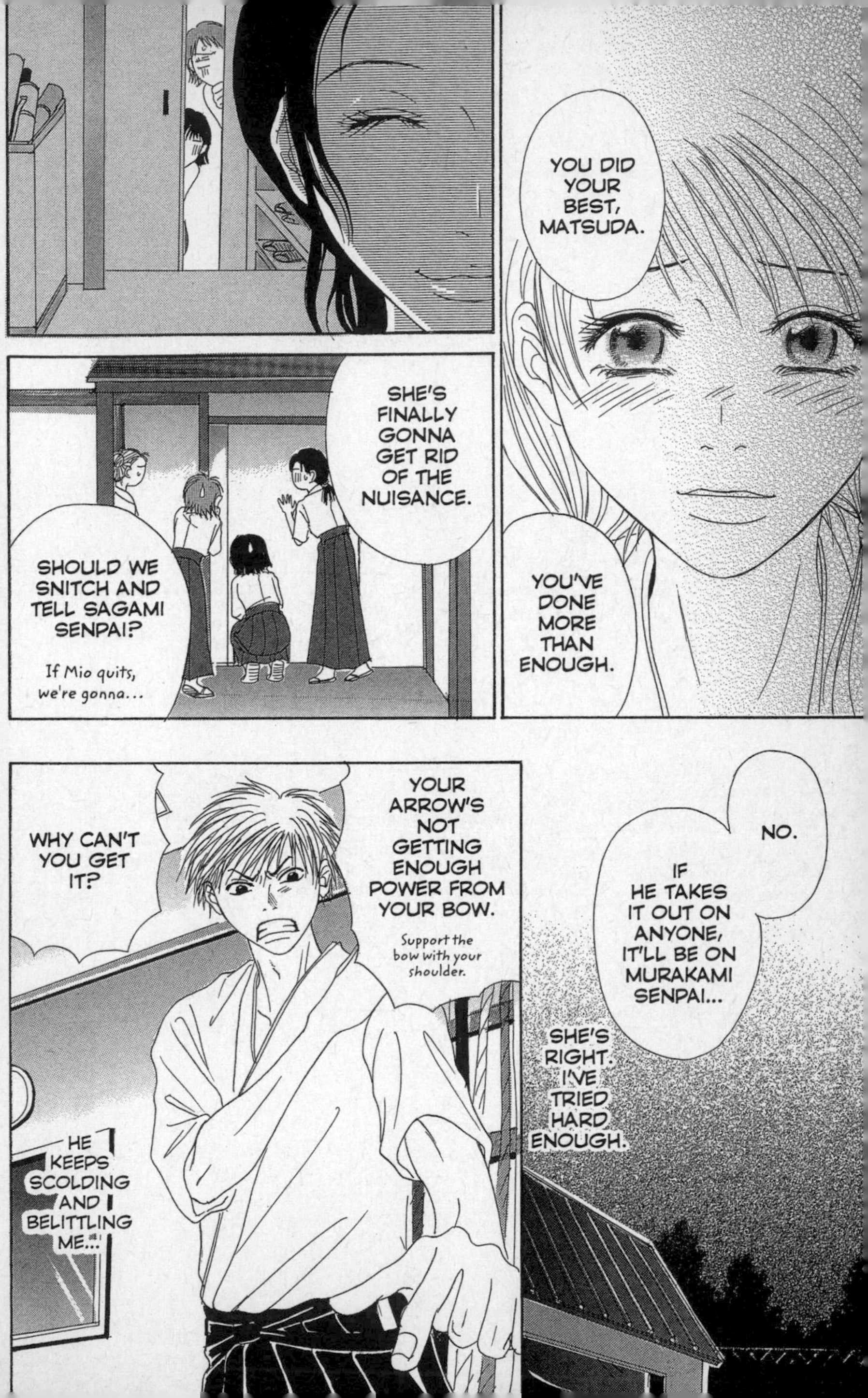
YOU DID YOUR BEST, MATSUDA.
YOU'VE DONE MORE THAN ENOUGH.
SHE'S FINALLY GONNA GET RID OF THE NUISANCE.
SHOULD WE SNITCH AND TELL SAGAMI SENPAI?
If Mio quits, we're gonna...
NO.
IF HE TAKES IT OUT ON ANYONE, IT'LL BE ON MURAKAMI SENPAI...
SHE'S RIGHT. I'VE TRIED HARD ENOUGH.
YOUR ARROW'S NOT GETTING ENOUGH POWER FROM YOUR BOW.
Support the bow with your shoulder.
WHY CAN'T YOU GET IT?
HE KEEPS SCOLDING AND BELITTLING ME...

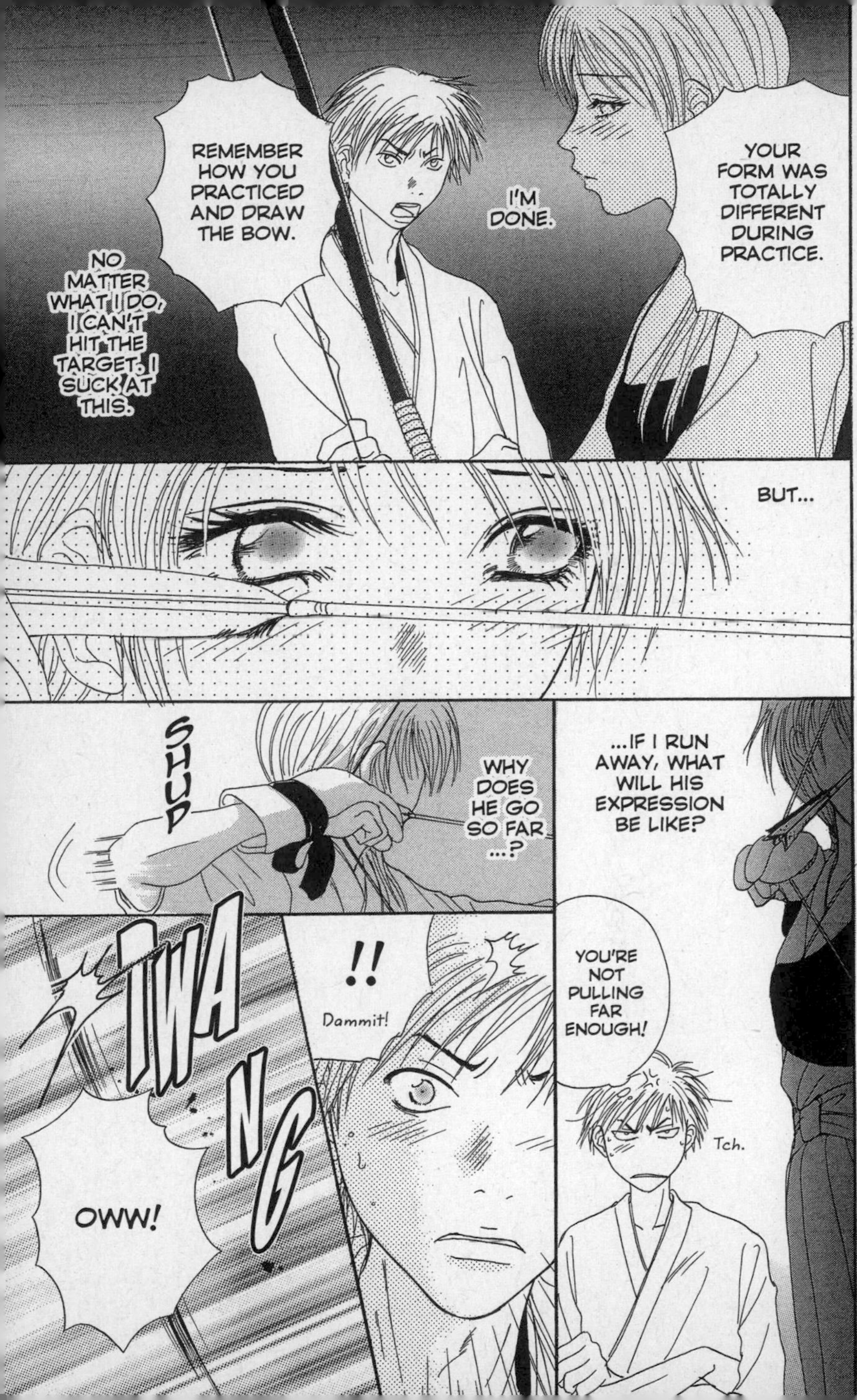
YOUR FORM WAS TOTALLY DIFFERENT DURING PRACTICE.
I'M DONE.
REMEMBER HOW YOU PRACTICED AND DRAW THE BOW.
NO MATTER WHAT I DO, I CAN'T HIT THE TARGET. I SUCK AT THIS.
BUT...
...IF I RUN AWAY, WHAT WILL HIS EXPRESSION BE LIKE?
WHY DOES HE GO SO FAR ...?
SHUP
YOU'RE NOT PULLING FAR ENOUGH!
Tch.
!!
Dammit!
TWANG
OWW!

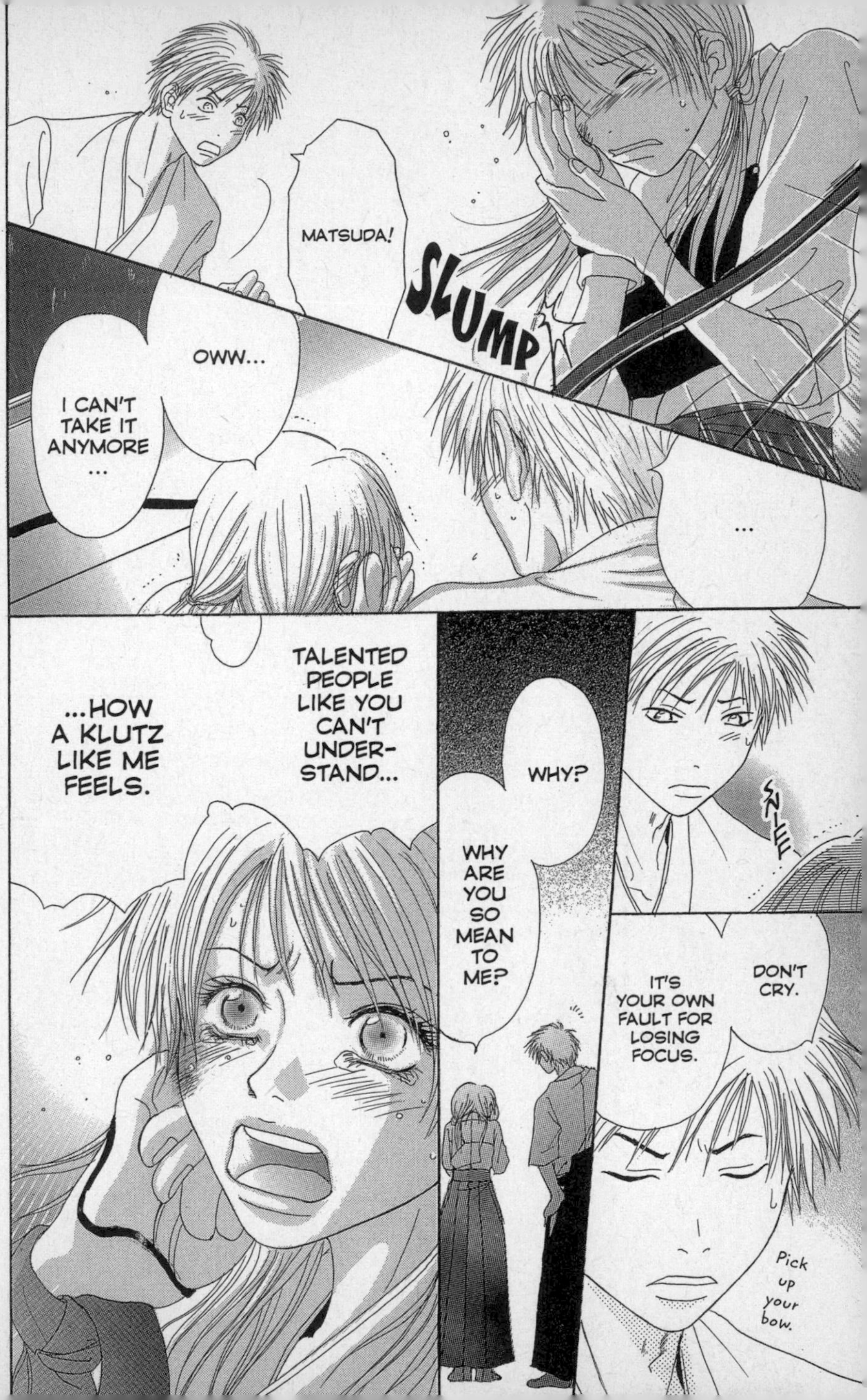
SLUMP
MATSUDA!
...
OWW...
I CAN'T TAKE IT ANYMORE...
SNIFF
DON'T CRY.
IT'S YOUR OWN FAULT FOR LOSING FOCUS.
Pick up your bow.
WHY?
WHY ARE YOU SO MEAN TO ME?
TALENTED PEOPLE LIKE YOU CAN'T UNDER-STAND...
...HOW A KLUTZ LIKE ME FEELS.

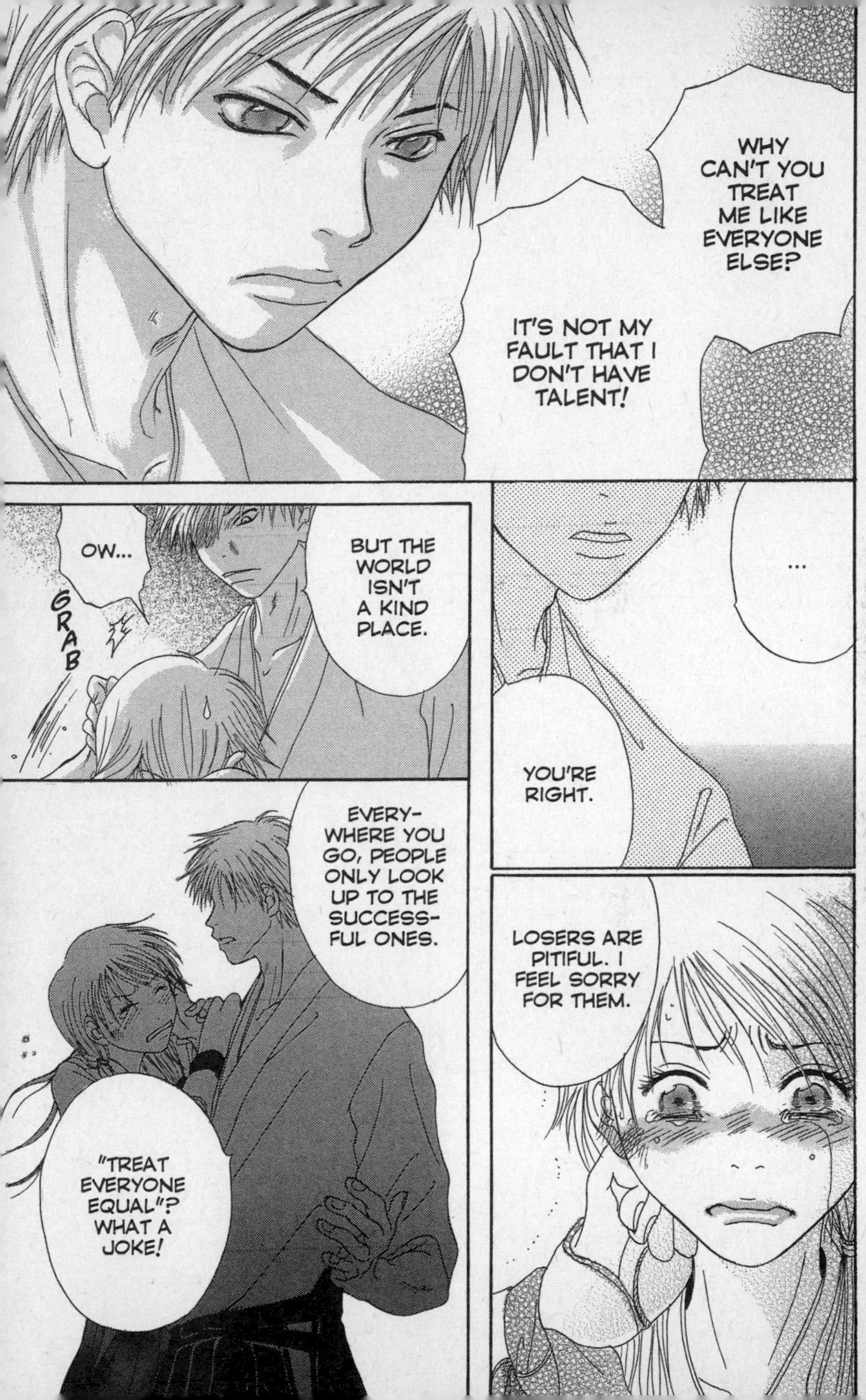
WHY CAN'T YOU TREAT ME LIKE EVERYONE ELSE?
IT'S NOT MY FAULT THAT I DON'T HAVE TALENT!
...
YOU'RE RIGHT.
BUT THE WORLD ISN'T A KIND PLACE.
OW...
GRAB
LOSERS ARE PITIFUL. I FEEL SORRY FOR THEM.
EVERY-WHERE YOU GO, PEOPLE ONLY LOOK UP TO THE SUCCESS-FUL ONES.
"TREAT EVERYONE EQUAL"? WHAT A JOKE!

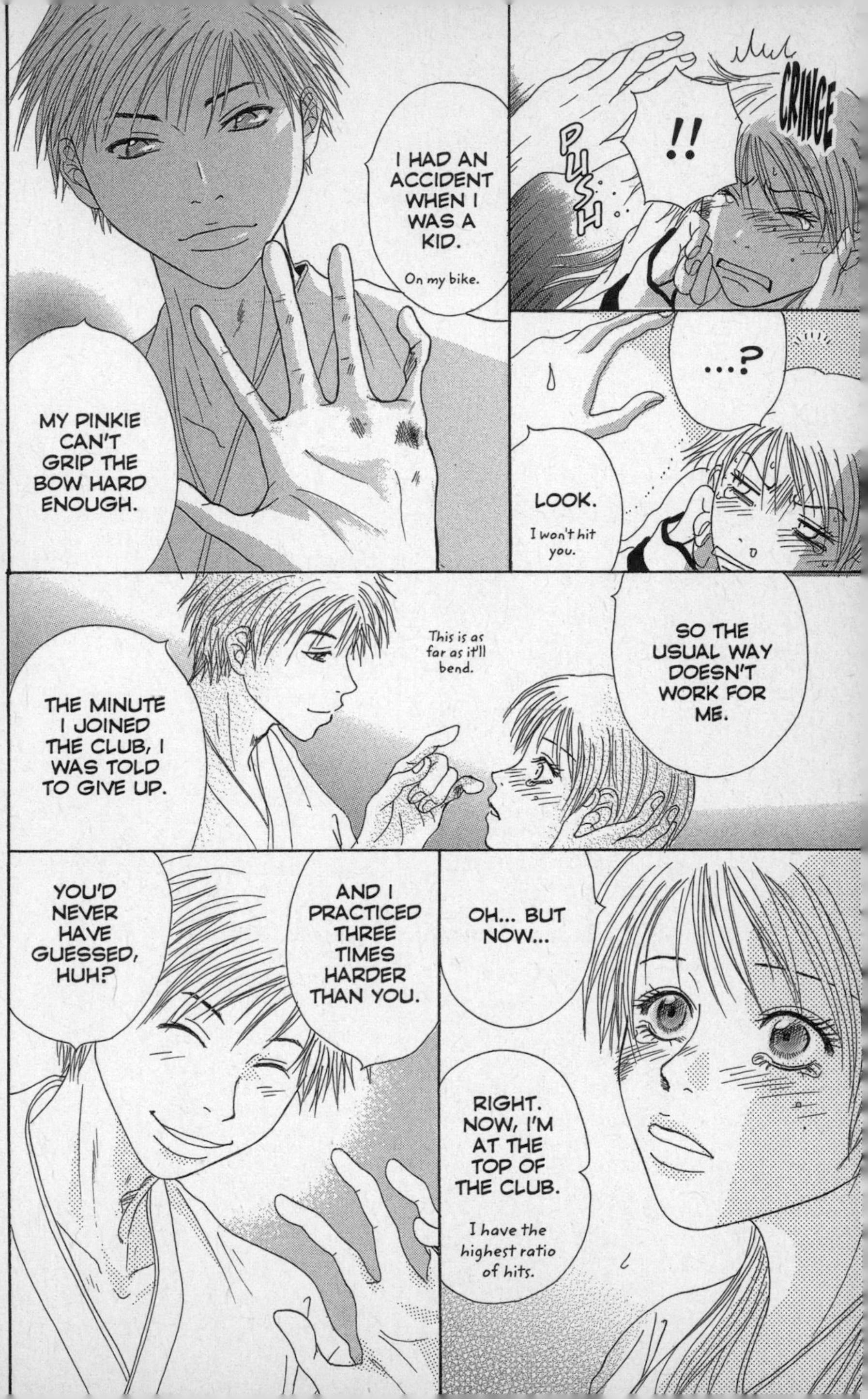
CRINGE
!!
PUSH
...?
LOOK.
I won't hit you.
I HAD AN ACCIDENT WHEN I WAS A KID.
On my bike.
MY PINKIE CAN'T GRIP THE BOW HARD ENOUGH.
SO THE USUAL WAY DOESN'T WORK FOR ME.
This is as far as it'll bend.
THE MINUTE I JOINED THE CLUB, I WAS TOLD TO GIVE UP.
OH... BUT NOW...
RIGHT. NOW, I'M AT THE TOP OF THE CLUB.
I have the highest ratio of hits.
AND I PRACTICED THREE TIMES HARDER THAN YOU.
YOU'D NEVER HAVE GUESSED, HUH?

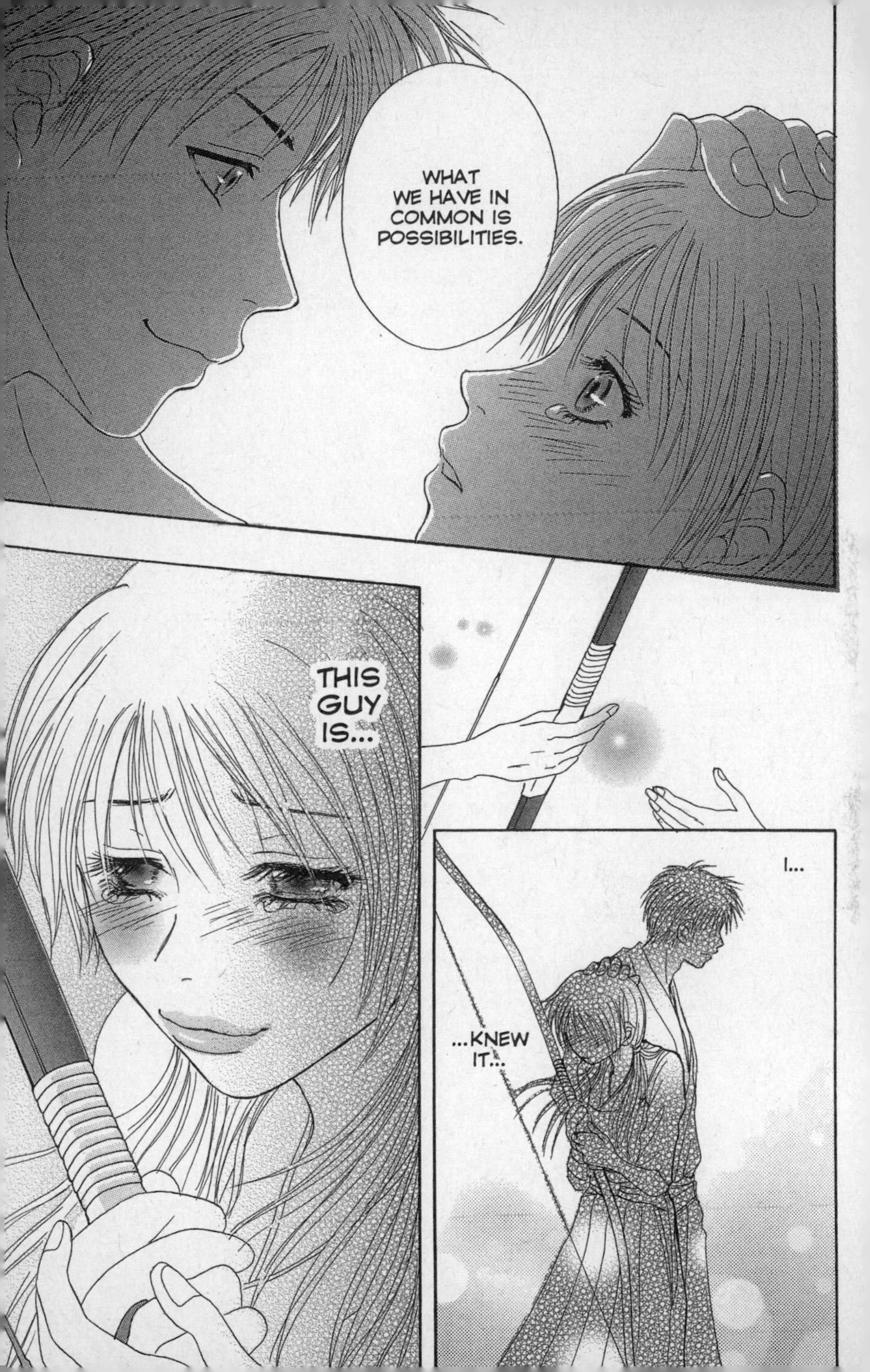
WHAT WE HAVE IN COMMON IS POSSIBILITIES.
THIS GUY IS...
I...
...KNEW IT...

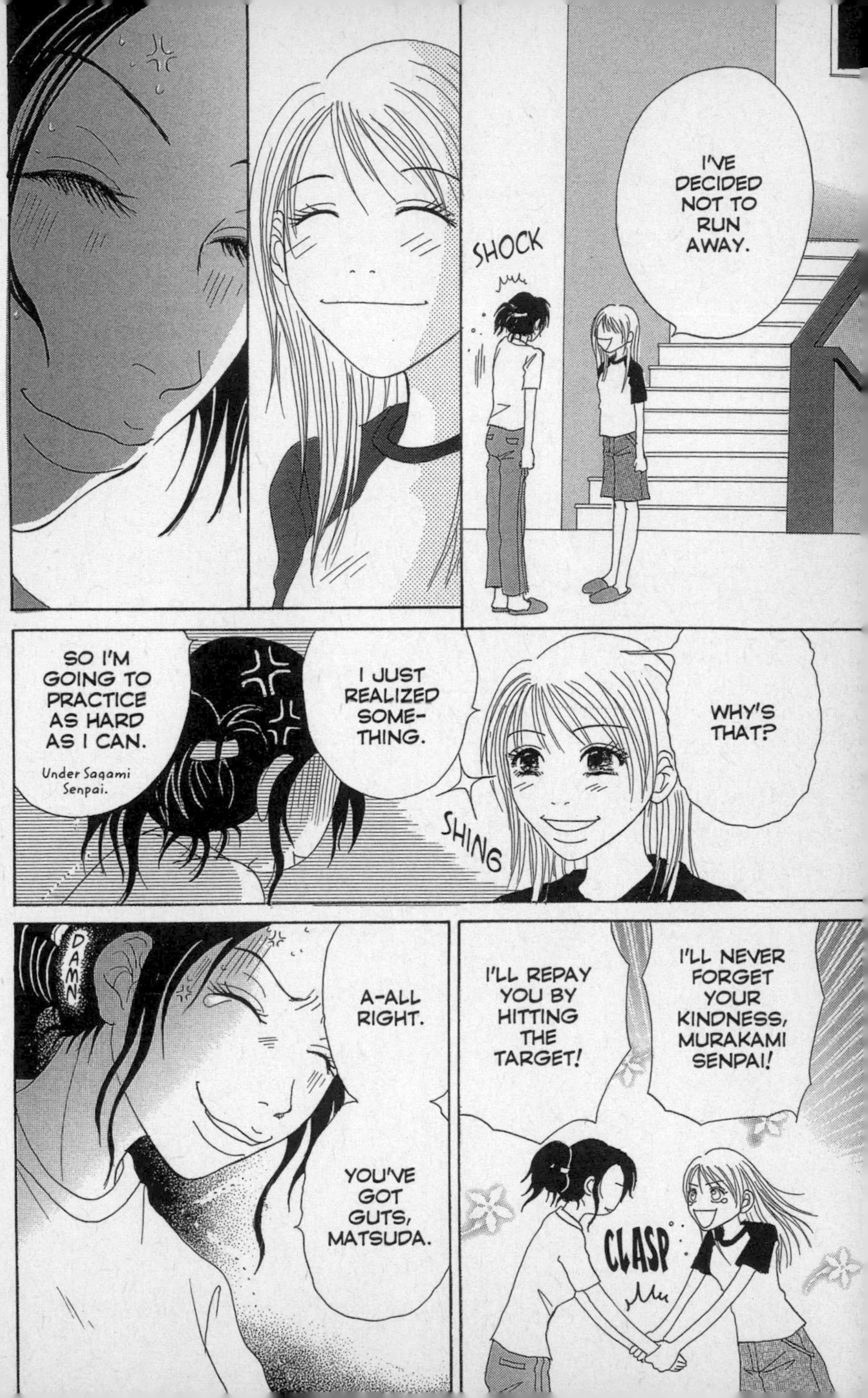
I'VE DECIDED NOT TO RUN AWAY.
SHOCK
WHY'S THAT?
I JUST REALIZED SOMETHING.
SHING
SO I'M GOING TO PRACTICE AS HARD AS I CAN.
Under Sagami Senpai.
I'LL NEVER FORGET YOUR KINDNESS, MURAKAMI SENPAI!
I'LL REPAY YOU BY HITTING THE TARGET!
CLASP
DAMN
A-ALL RIGHT.
YOU'VE GOT GUTS, MATSUDA.

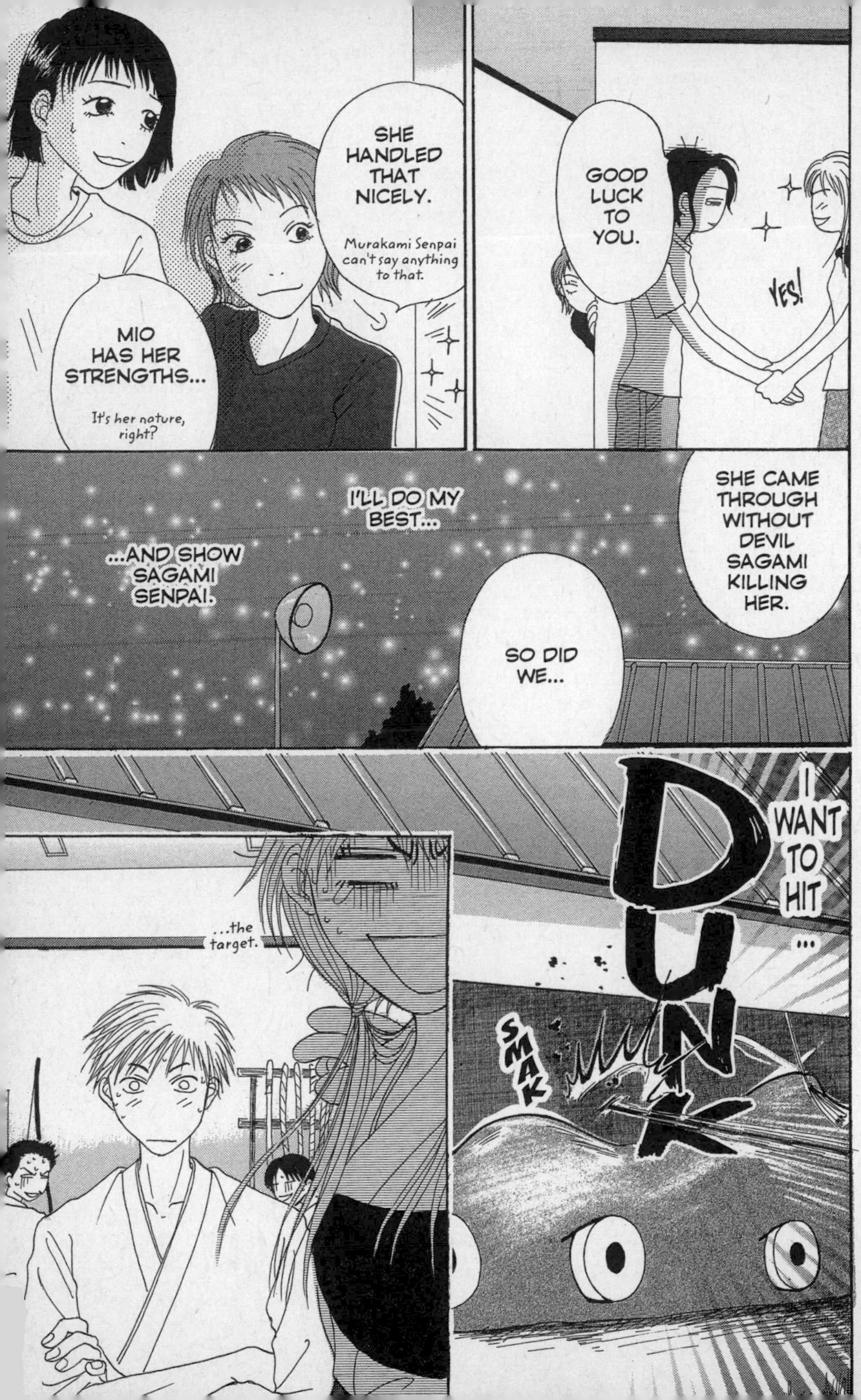
GOOD LUCK TO YOU.
YES!
SHE HANDLED THAT NICELY.
Murakami Senpai can't say anything to that.
MIO HAS HER STRENGTHS...
It's her nature, right?
SHE CAME THROUGH WITHOUT DEVIL SAGAMI KILLING HER.
SO DID WE...
I'LL DO MY BEST...
...AND SHOW SAGAMI SENPAI.
I WANT TO HIT...
DUNK
SMAK
...the target.

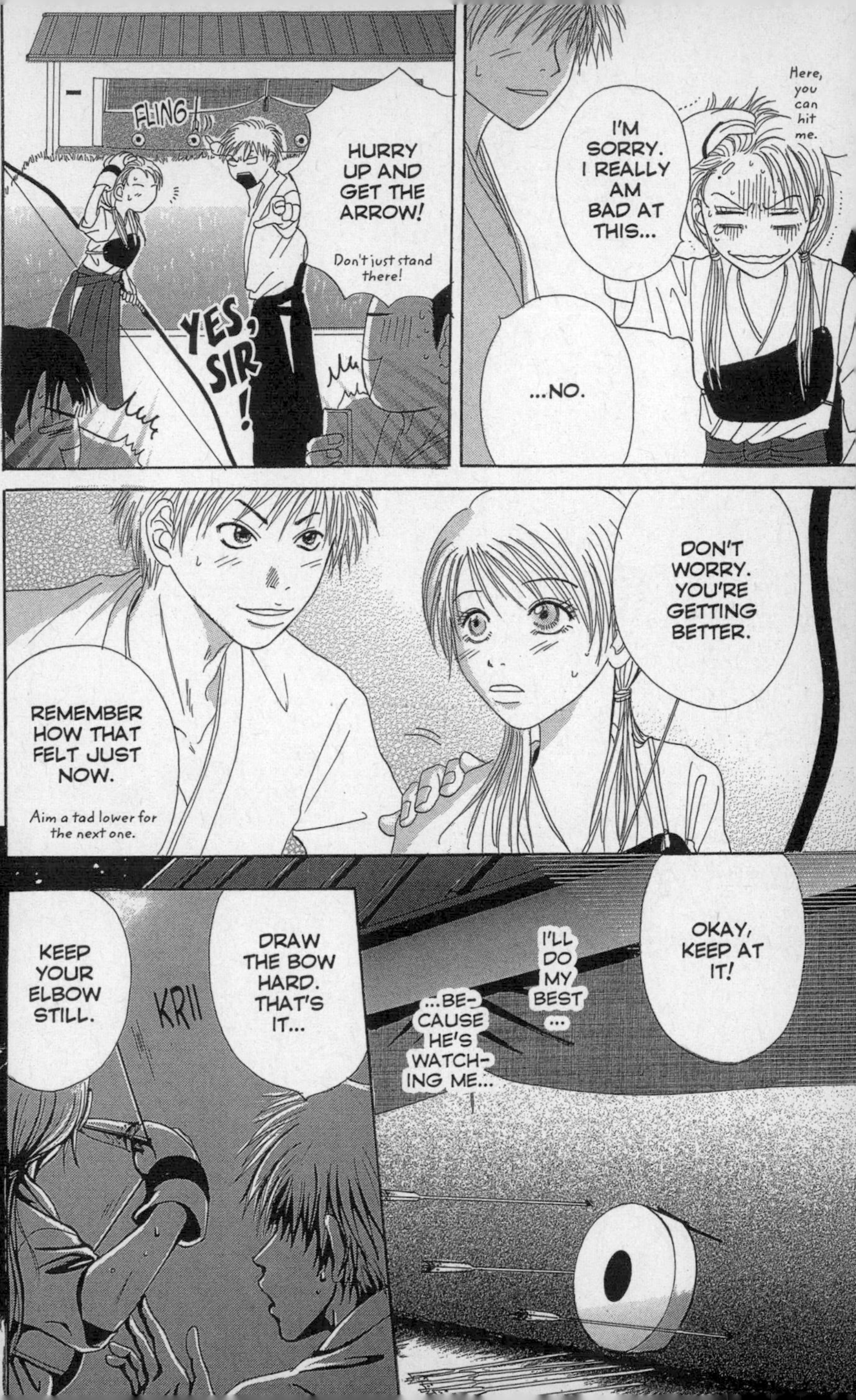
Here, you can hit me.
I'M SORRY. I REALLY AM BAD AT THIS...
...NO.
HURRY UP AND GET THE ARROW!
Don't just stand there!
FLING
YES, SIR!
DON'T WORRY. YOU'RE GETTING BETTER.
REMEMBER HOW THAT FELT JUST NOW.
Aim a tad lower for the next one.
OKAY, KEEP AT IT!
I'LL DO MY BEST...
...BECAUSE HE'S WATCHING ME...
DRAW THE BOW HARD. THAT'S IT...
KRII
KEEP YOUR ELBOW STILL.

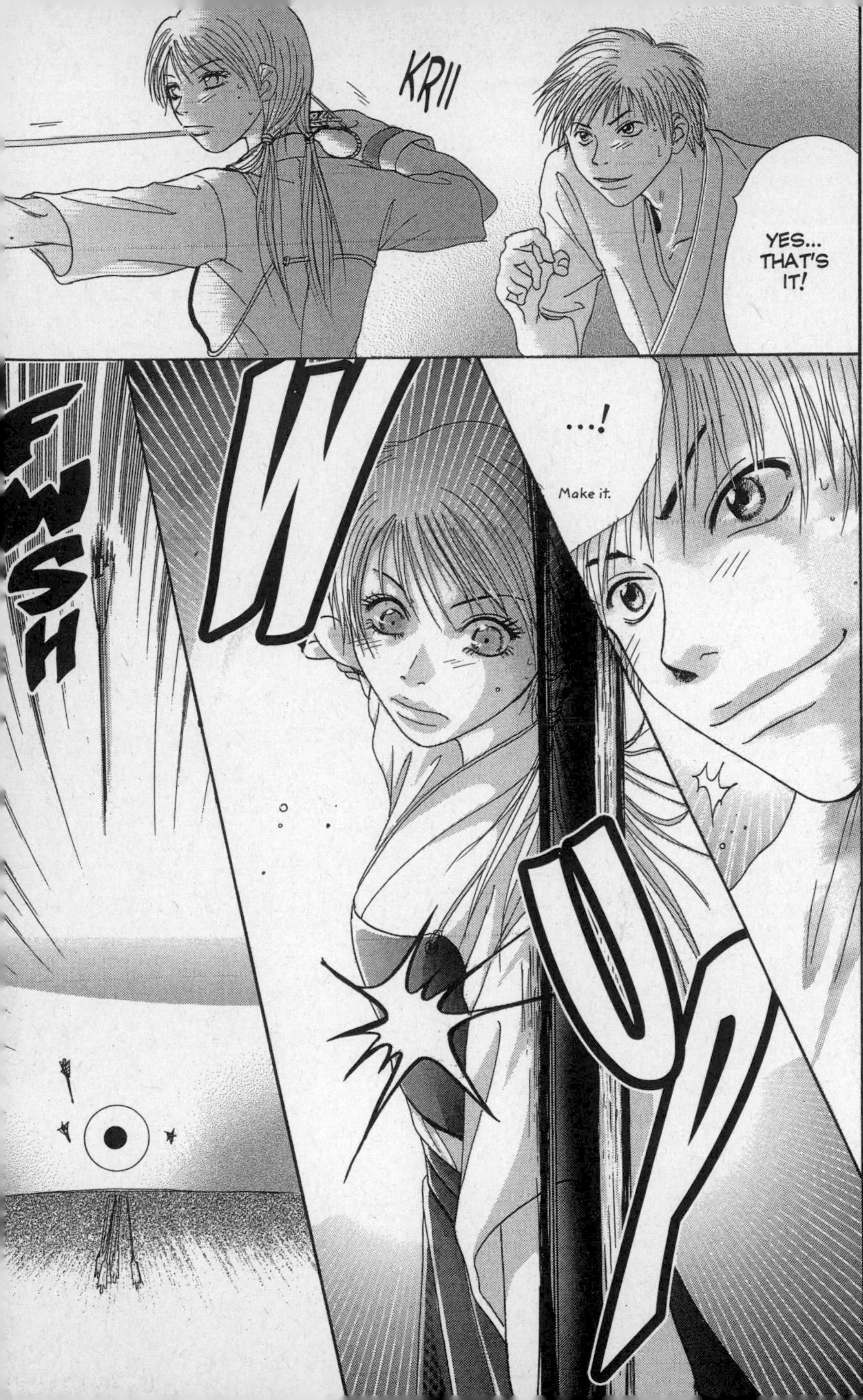
YES... THAT'S IT!
KRII
...!
Make it.
FWSH
WUSH

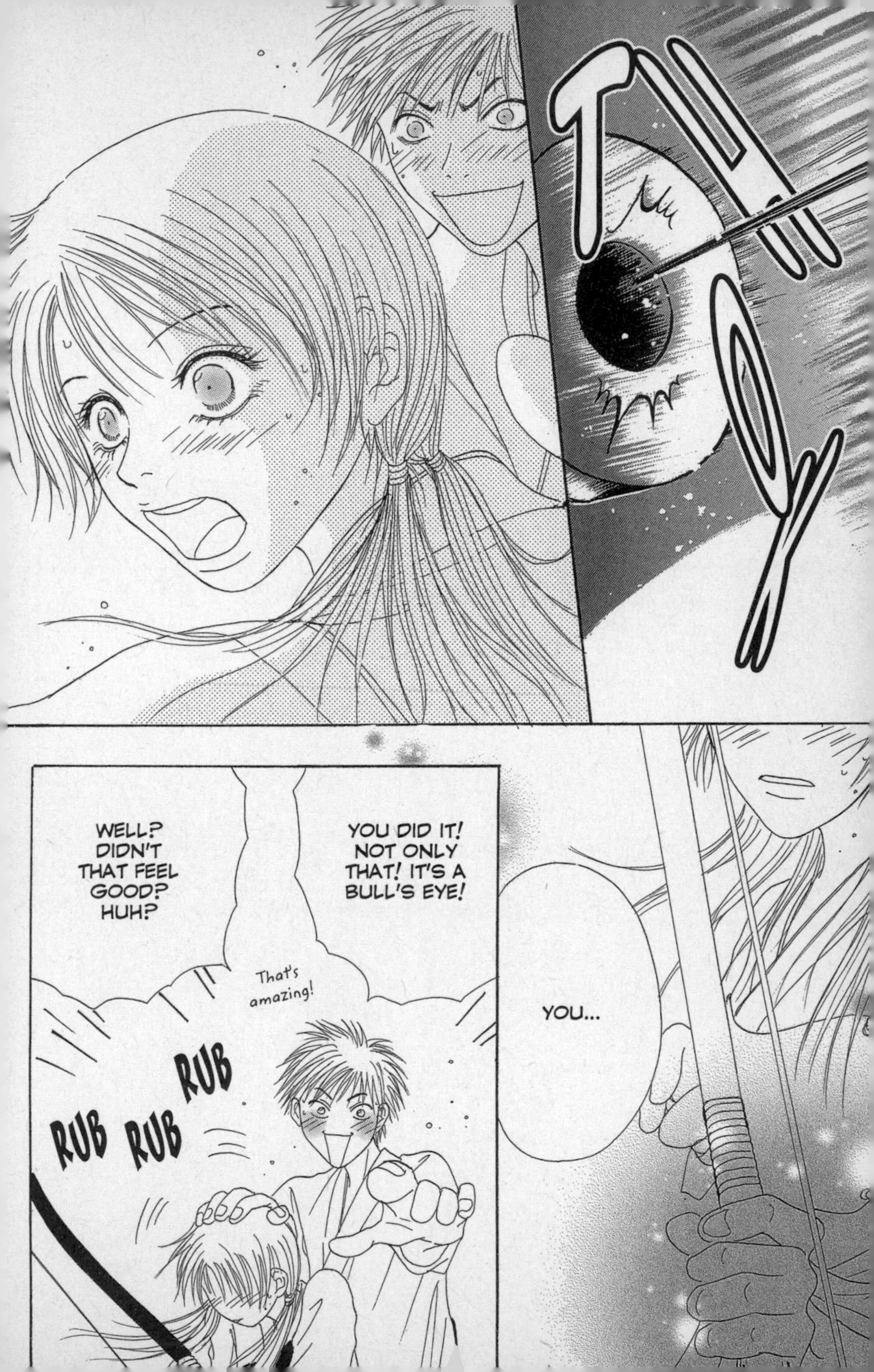
YOU...
YOU DID IT! NOT ONLY THAT! IT'S A BULL'S EYE!
WELL? DIDN'T THAT FEEL GOOD? HUH?
That's amazing!
RUB RUB RUB

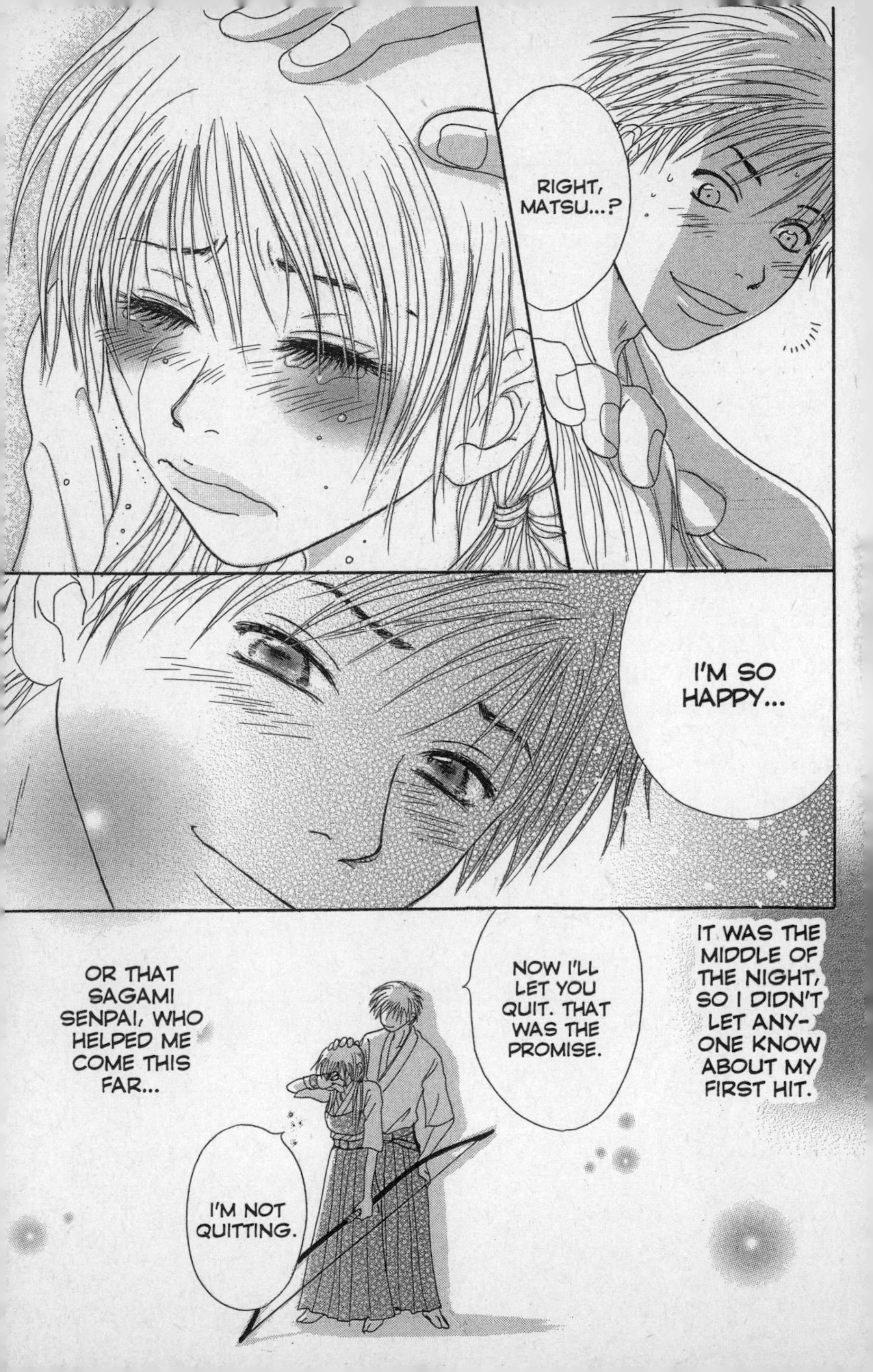
RIGHT, MATSU...?
I'M SO HAPPY...
IT WAS THE MIDDLE OF THE NIGHT, SO I DIDN'T LET ANY-ONE KNOW ABOUT MY FIRST HIT.
NOW I'LL LET YOU QUIT. THAT WAS THE PROMISE.
OR THAT SAGAMI SENPAI, WHO HELPED ME COME THIS FAR...
I'M NOT QUITTING.

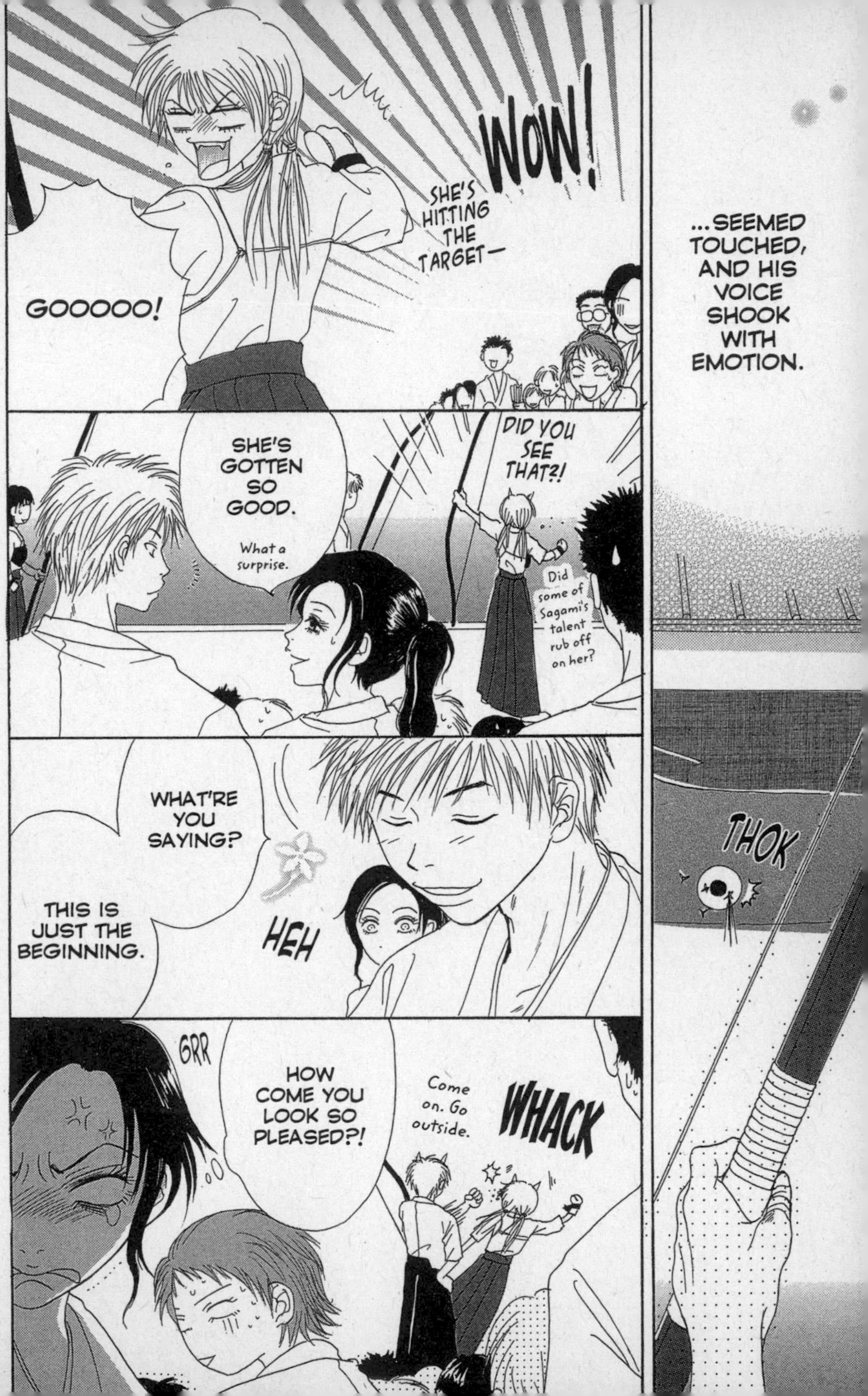
...SEEMED TOUCHED, AND HIS VOICE SHOOK WITH EMOTION.
THOK
WOW!
SHE'S HITTING THE TARGET—
GOOOOO!
DID YOU SEE THAT?!
Did some of Sagami's talent rub off on her?
SHE'S GOTTEN SO GOOD.
What a surprise.
WHAT'RE YOU SAYING?
THIS IS JUST THE BEGINNING.
HEH
WHACK
Come on. Go outside.
HOW COME YOU LOOK SO PLEASED?!
GRR

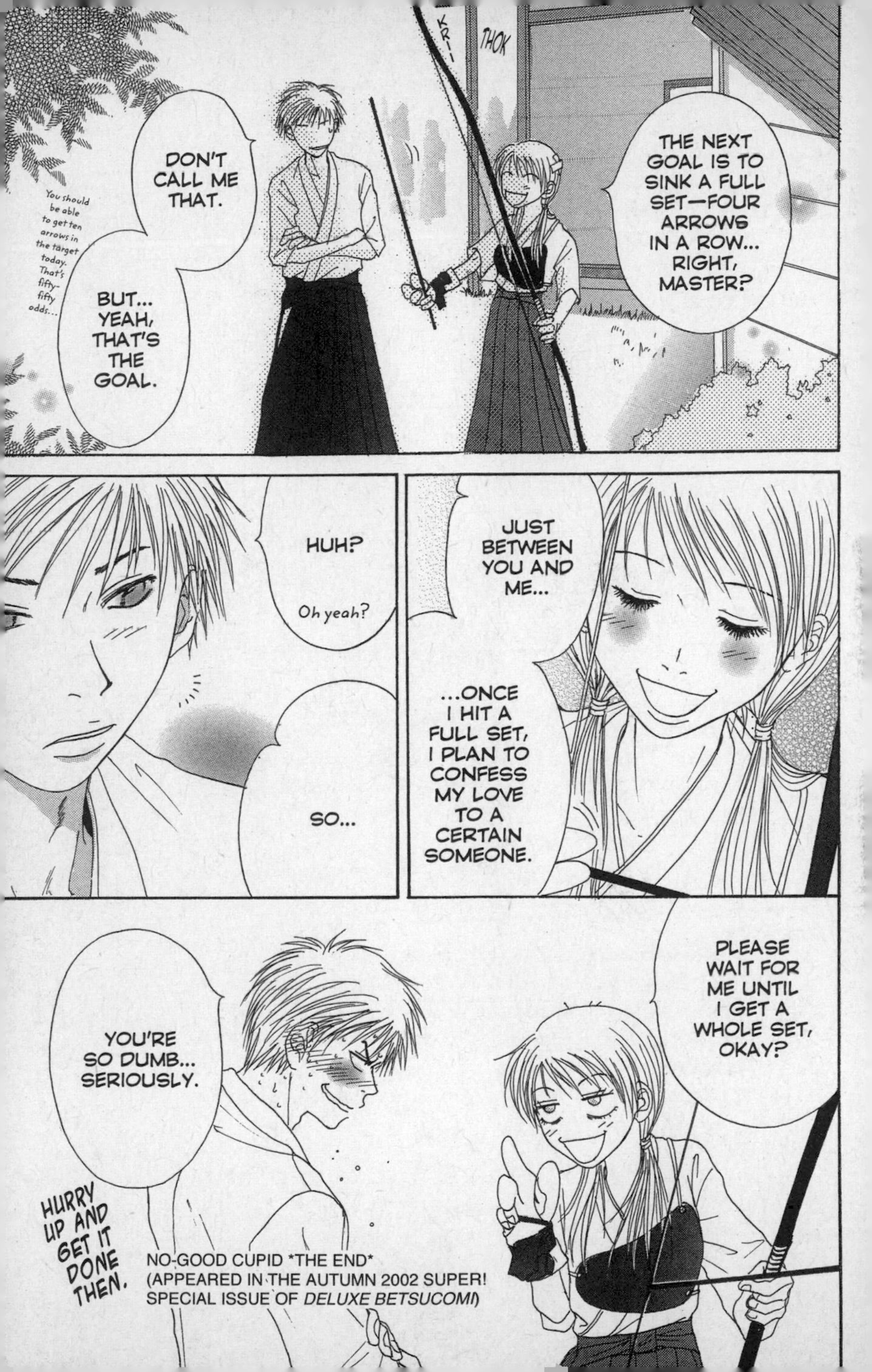
THOK
KRI
THE NEXT GOAL IS TO SINK A FULL SET—FOUR ARROWS IN A ROW... RIGHT, MASTER?
DON'T CALL ME THAT.
BUT... YEAH, THAT'S THE GOAL.
You should be able to get ten arrows in the target today. That's fifty-fifty odds...
JUST BETWEEN YOU AND ME...
...ONCE I HIT A FULL SET, I PLAN TO CONFESS MY LOVE TO A CERTAIN SOMEONE.
HUH?
Oh yeah?
SO...
PLEASE WAIT FOR ME UNTIL I GET A WHOLE SET, OKAY?
YOU'RE SO DUMB... SERIOUSLY.
HURRY UP AND GET IT DONE THEN.
NO-GOOD CUPID *THE END*
(APPEARED IN THE AUTUMN 2002 SUPER! SPECIAL ISSUE OF DELUXE BETSUCOMI)

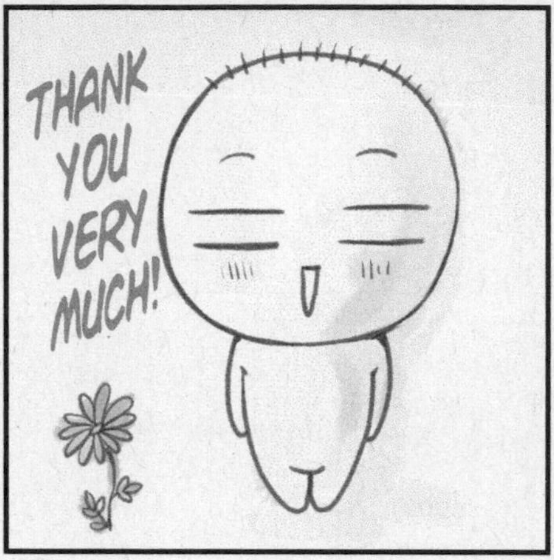
THANK YOU VERY MUCH!

Dengeki Daisy has finally come to an end! This manga was made possible because of your warm support. I hope that you enjoy it until the very last page.

-Kyousuke Motomi

Born on August 1, Kyousuke Motomi debuted in *Deluxe Betsucomi* with *Hetakuso Kyupiddo* (No-Good Cupid) in 2002. She is the creator of *Beast Master* and *Otokomae! Biizu Kurabu* (Handsome! Beads Club). Motomi enjoys sleeping, tea ceremonies and reading Haruki Murakami.

DENGEKI DAISY
VOL. 16
Shojo Beat Edition

STORY AND ART BY
KYOUSUKE MOTOMI

DENGEKI DAISY Vol.16
by Kyousuke MOTOMI
© 2007 Kyousuke MOTOMI
All rights reserved.
Original Japanese edition published by SHOGAKUKAN.
English translation rights in the United States of America
and Canada arranged with SHOGAKUKAN.

Translation & Adaptation/JN Productions
Touch-up Art & Lettering/Rina Mapa
Design/Stacie Yamaki
Editor/Amy Yu

The stories, characters and incidents mentioned in this
publication are entirely fictional.

Printed in the U.S.A.

Published by VIZ Media, LLC
P.O. Box 77010
San Francisco, CA 94107

10 9 8 7 6 5 4 3 2 1
First printing, April 2015

www.viz.com   www.shojobeat.com

This is the last page.

In keeping with the original Japanese comic format, this book reads from right to left—so action, sound effects, and word balloons are completely reversed. This preserves the orientation of the original artwork—plus, it's fun! Check out the diagram shown here to get the hang of things, and then turn to the other side of the book to get started!